Why Language Matters for Theory of Mind

Why Language Matters for Theory of Mind

EDITED BY

Janet Wilde Astington
Jodie A. Baird

UNIVERSITY PRESS
2005

OXFORD

UNIVERSITY PRESS

Oxford University Press, Inc., publishes works that further
Oxford University's objective of excellence
in research, scholarship, and education.

Oxford   New York
Auckland   Cape Town   Dar es Salaam   Delhi   Hong Kong   Karachi
Kuala Lumpur   Madrid   Melbourne   Mexico City   Nairobi
New Delhi   Shanghai   Taipei   Toronto

With offices in
Argentina   Austria   Brazil   Chile   Czech Republic   France   Greece
Guatemala   Hungary   Italy   Japan   Poland   Portugal   Singapore
South Korea   Switzerland   Thailand   Turkey   Ukraine   Vietnam

Copyright © 2005 by Oxford University Press, Inc.

Published by Oxford University Press, Inc.,
198 Madison Avenue, New York, New York 10016

www.oup.com

Oxford is a registered trademark of Oxford University Press

Library of Congress Cataloging-in-Publication Data
Why language matters for theory of mind / edited by Janet Wilde Astington and
Jodie A. Baird.
p.   cm.
Includes bibliographical references and index.
ISBN-13 978-0-19-515991-2
ISBN 0-19-515991-8
1. Philosophy of mind in children—Congresses.   2. Children—Language—
Congresses.   I. Astington, Janet W.   II. Baird, Jodie A. (Jodie Alison), 1973–
BF723.P48W59 2005
155.4'13—dc22   2004056810

9 8 7 6 5 4 3 2 1

Printed in the United States of America
on acid-free paper

Preface

This volume originated in a conference that was held at the University of Toronto in April 2002. The conference followed from two earlier ones organized at the University of Toronto: Developing Theories of Mind in 1986 and Developing Theories of Intention in 1997 (Astington, Harris, & Olson, 1988; Zelazo, Astington, & Olson, 1999). This third conference, Why Language Matters for Theory of Mind, took up an important issue that was left open following the earlier meetings. It concerns the developmental interdependence of theory of mind and language.

Recent work has shown strong relations between children's linguistic abilities and their understanding of mind. The conference provided a forum for an international group of scholars to explore these relations and to consider the role of language in children's developing theories of mind. Some researchers argue that an understanding of mind is innate but children cannot express their understanding until a certain level of cognitive and linguistic development is achieved. In contrast, many researchers argue that language actually contributes to the development of children's understanding of mind. However, because language simultaneously serves different functions—such as representation and communication—disagreement arises over the role that language plays. The papers presented at the conference considered the links between language and theory of mind from both representational and communicational perspectives, drawing on research from a variety of populations (e.g., typically developing children, children with autism, deaf children, nonhuman primates). They were supplemented by a poster session that presented work related to the general theme, enlarging and enriching the research base of the conference. The aim of the conference, and of this volume, is to reconcile and combine insights from various viewpoints, by treating different explanations of why language matters for theory of mind as complementary accounts rather than as competing hypotheses.

The conference could not have taken place, nor would the volume exist, without the contributions of many people, to all of whom we are extremely grateful. First and foremost, we thank the authors, whose presentations, discussions, and arguments at the conference got the project off to a fine start. We thank them, too, for staying the course as the volume was created. The poster presenters and members of the audience—too numerous to list here—added to the conference discussions and convinced us that the volume was a worthwhile venture. We also thank the many members of our department—the Department of Human Development and Applied Psychology, Ontario Institute for Studies in Education, University of Toronto (OISE/UT)—who helped in a great number of ways. Two graduate students, Eva Filippova and Mary Thelander, and an administrative assistant, Christine Davidson, formed the organizing committee for the conference, along with the two of us. Faculty members Jenny Jenkins, Jan Pelletier, Joan Peskin, and Keith Oatley chaired the conference sessions, and David Olson and Chris Moore were talented discussants at the conference close. Our business officers, Mary Macri and Toni Luke-Gervais, helped us to manage the conference budget. Our students—Terri Barriault, Ingrid Braun, Julie Comay, Karen Milligan, Kevin Runions, and Anita Zijdemans—provided conference hospitality and answered our technical questions. In addition, we are grateful for technical help that came from outside the Department: David Torre recorded the proceedings and Mark Sabbagh made sure the projection equipment worked as it should.

Funding support from various sources made it possible for us to host the conference and to invite a considerable number of international participants. We are very grateful to the Department of Human Development and Applied Psychology, OISE/UT; the Laidlaw Research Centre at the Institute of Child Study, OISE/UT; the Centre for Applied Cognitive Science, OISE/UT; the Connaught Committee of the University of Toronto; and the Social Sciences and Humanities Research Council of Canada. We also thank Paul Perron, Principal of University College, who provided a splendid location for the conference, and his assistant, Lynette Beron, who helped with the arrangements.

As work on the volume progressed we received further support for which we are extremely grateful. We thank all those who discussed the issues with us as we edited the chapters: Chris Moore, David Olson, Ana Perez Leroux, Jan Pelletier, Joan Peskin, and Phil Zelazo; as well as the students in our research group: Lisa Ain, Ingrid Braun, Thomas Chan, Julie Comay, Eva Filippova, Keelan Kane, Jonathan Leef, Belèn Pascual, Mary Thelander, and Rebecca Wells Jopling. We also thank the administrative staff who helped with technical matters, particularly Denese Coulbeck and Rosslyn Zulla. We are grateful to Catharine Carlin at Oxford University Press for enthusiastically embracing the project when it was first proposed, and for providing editorial support along the way, with her assistant, Jennifer Rappaport. Keith Faivre has been extremely helpful as production editor, expediting the appearance of the volume.

Finally, we dedicate this volume to the children whose developing theories of mind have inspired our work over the past few years: Jodie's son, Santiago, and Janet's grandchildren, Becky, Cameron, and Steven.

Janet Wilde Astington
Jodie A. Baird
Toronto, September 2004

References

Astington, J. W., Harris, P. L., & Olson, D. R. (Eds.). (1988). *Developing theories of mind*. New York: Cambridge University Press.

Zelazo, P. D., Astington, J. W., & Olson, D. R. (Eds.). (1999). *Developing theories of intention: Social understanding and self control*. Mahwah, NJ: Erlbaum.

Contents

Contributors

Janet Wilde Astington
University of Toronto

Jodie A. Baird
University of Toronto

Dare A. Baldwin
University of Oregon

Marcia Brophy
King's College London

Jill G. de Villiers
Smith College

Peter A. de Villiers
Smith College

Judy Dunn
King's College London

Paul L. Harris
Harvard University

Claire Hughes
University of Cambridge

Sophie Jacques
Dalhousie University

Robert M. Joseph
*Boston University School
of Medicine*

Heidemarie Lohmann
*Max Planck Institute for
Evolutionary Anthropology,
Leipzig*

Sonja Meyer
*Max Planck Institute for
Evolutionary Anthropology,
Leipzig*

Derek E. Montgomery
Bradley University

Katherine Nelson
*City University of New York
Graduate Center*

Daniela K. O'Neill
University of Waterloo

Josef Perner
University of Salzburg

Megan M. Saylor
Vanderbilt University

Manuel Sprung
University of Salzburg

Helen Tager-Flusberg
*Boston University School
of Medicine*

Michael Tomasello
*Max Planck Institute for Evolutionary
Anthropology, Leipzig*

Petra Zauner
University of Salzburg

Philip David Zelazo
University of Toronto

Why Language Matters for Theory of Mind

1   Introduction: Why Language Matters

Janet Wilde Astington and Jodie A. Baird

The present volume originated in a conference that was held at the University of Toronto in April 2002. Sixteen years earlier, a number of the authors included here had participated in the Oxford conference "Children's Early Concept of Mind" and/or the Toronto conference "Developing Theories of Mind" that together, along with the publication resulting from the two conferences (Astington, Harris, & Olson, 1988), helped to establish children's theory of mind as a new, lively, and important area of research in developmental psychology. "Theory of mind" became the way researchers referred to children's understanding of people as mental beings who have beliefs, desires, emotions, and intentions and whose actions and interactions can be interpreted and explained by taking account of these mental states. The gradual development of children's theory of mind, particularly during the early years, is by now well described in the literature, and we have some information regarding the antecedents, correlates, and sequelae of its development, in both typically developing and special populations, particularly deaf children and children with autism. What is still lacking, however, though not for want of debate on the topic, is a decisive explanation of how children acquire this understanding. Recent work in the area has shown strong relations between children's linguistic abilities and their theory of mind. The purpose of the present volume is to thoroughly explore the role of language in theory-of-mind development. Why does language matter for theory of mind?

The Multifaceted Nature of Theory of Mind

Despite our confident use of "theory of mind" in the previous paragraph, we should acknowledge that the term itself was controversial at the beginning and has only become more so as time has gone by, to the point where it is now something of a Humpty Dumpty word, in the Lewis Carroll sense (Astington, 1998): "'When *I* use a word,' Humpty Dumpty said in rather a scornful tone, 'it means just what I choose it to mean—neither more nor less'" (Carroll, 1872, p. 124). Perhaps we exaggerate—theory of mind cannot mean just anything—although it does have considerably broad scope.

The term "theory of mind" entered the developmental literature via at least two different routes. First, Wellman (1979, 1985), working in the area of meta-cognition, used it to refer to the child's conception of human cognition. Second, and probably better known, is Premack and Woodruff's (1978) use of the term in their investigation of primate cognition, when they defined it as a system of inferences that can be used to predict behavior by attributing mental states to individuals. This definition was quickly taken up and applied to children (Bretherton, McNew, & Beeghly-Smith, 1981; Wimmer & Perner, 1983) and even then it had broad scope—from Bretherton et al.'s study of infant communicative abilities to Wimmer and Perner's first description of the false-belief task and their discussion of the meta-representational ability that the task required. In the most precise use, theory of mind is a domain-specific, psychologically real structure, composed of an integrated set of mental-state concepts employed to explain and predict people's actions and interactions that is reorganized over time when faced with counterevidence to its predictions (Gopnik & Wellman, 1994). Researchers who hold this view have attempted to restrict its use to this sense, while other researchers who deny that children develop any theory about the mind have been careful to employ other terms, although sometimes acknowledging links to "theory of mind" hedged in scare quotes or footnotes (Astington, 1998). Despite all these efforts, however, theory of mind seems to be a term that refuses to be corralled.

Perhaps part of the problem is that "theory of mind" is used to refer to three different phenomena—a cognitive structure leading to certain abilities, an area of research investigating the development of these abilities, and a theoretical perspective explaining this development. There are other ways of referring to the research area and closely related areas, in which a wide variety of abilities are studied, and there are different ways in which the development of these abilities is explained (see table 1.1). While abilities, research areas, and theoretical explanations are different phenomena, they are obviously linked together, although we do not intend any one-to-one correspondence across rows in the three columns in table 1.1. At this point we merely want to indicate the broad range of phenomena that are included under the rubric "theory of mind" or are closely related to it.

A number of researchers (e.g., Hobson, 1991; Nelson, 1996) argue against any attribution of "theory of mind" to young children, viewing it as completely wrong as a description of, or even as a metaphor for, their attempts to make

Table 1.1 The Multifaceted Nature of Theory of Mind

Theory of Mind:
- cognitive structure leading to certain *abilities*
- *research area* investigating development of abilities
- *theoretical explanation* of development

Range of Abilities	Related Research Areas	Diverse Explanations
theory of mind	theory of mind	theory of mind
false-belief understanding	concept of mind	innate module
meta-representation	folk psychology	simulation
intentional stance	common-sense psychology	enculturation
belief-desire reasoning	understanding other minds	social construction, e.g.,
mental-state attribution	social understanding	community of minds
mentalizing	social cognition	domain general
mind-reading		developments, e.g.,
perspective-taking		executive functions
social intelligence		
social understanding		
social intuition		
social perception		
person perception		
intersubjectivity		

sense of the social world. However, on our view, Lillard (1998) is probably right in claiming that "theory of mind" is a useful term, and here to stay:

> the term is deeply entrenched and would not easily be abandoned, and in many ways serves us very well. It can be used to refer to simple infant interfacing of minds, or to complex adult understandings, or to anything in between . . . Because "theory of mind" is so versatile, arguing over its suitability will probably not be productive. (Lillard, 1998, p. 42)

Versatility may lead to ambiguity, however. "Theory of mind" is a broad term for a multifaceted system (see table 1.1). In considering the relation between theory of mind and language, we need to be clear which particular aspect(s) of theory of mind we are referring to, because different aspects of theory of mind may relate to language in different ways. It is fair to say that the authors of the various chapters in the present volume are not in complete agreement on how to apply the term "theory of mind" or on other issues. We regard this as part of the strength of the collection—there is sufficient agreement that we can focus on the core topic of why language matters, and sufficient disagreement that we can examine this issue from multiple points of view.

The Multifaceted Nature of Language

Like theory of mind, "language" too is a broad term—indeed, a broader term, although for our purposes in this volume, we do not need to consider all the details within its full range. However, there are some distinctions that we do need to make, at a number of levels, in order to consider language's relation to theory of mind. Perhaps the most fundamental distinction for our purpose is the functional one between representation and communication (see table 1.2). Many species represent and communicate, but only humans use one and the same system for both representing and communicating. Human language is used both as an intra-individual representational system, on the one hand, and as an inter-individual communication system, on the other. Representation, in this sense, is essentially equivalent to verbal thought (and when used in this way it includes only part of the full scope of the term "representation").

Communication, by definition, engages the child in dyadic interaction in discourse, which means that we must be careful to distinguish between children's own linguistic abilities and their linguistic environment (see table 1.2). First, children's linguistic abilities include their mastery of language structures (see next paragraph) and their competence in using these structures in communicative exchanges, that is, their pragmatic ability. Second, children's linguistic environment comprises the communicative exchanges in which they are involved as participants or bystanders, the stories and other books that are read to them, the songs that they hear, and so on. Obviously these two—individual competence and social context—are related to each other, but they may relate to theory of mind in different ways. The social context affects children's own linguistic abilities, and, indeed, their linguistic ability may affect their environment, in terms of the kinds of communications they receive. Nonetheless, one can consider the effects of the linguistic environment while controlling for individual differences in children's own linguistic competence.

Further distinctions can be made at a structural level. The basic distinction here is between form and meaning: phonology, morphology and syntax on the one hand and lexical and discourse semantics on the other. There is a great deal that could be said here, but we will not digress too far. In the present context of the relation between language and theory of mind, we first need to distinguish between language in general and mentalistic language in particular—that is, terms referring to the mind, to mental states and processes, for which verbs (e.g., *think, know, want*), rather than other parts of speech, are the most widely used (Astington & Pelletier, 1996; Astington & Peskin, 2004). Second, the structural distinction of importance with reference to mental verbs is the contrast between semantics and syntax (see table 1.2).

Some researchers argue that children's developing theory of mind is dependent on their acquisition of the semantics—that is, the meaning—of particular

Table 1.2 The Multifaceted Nature of Language

Language					
Functions			Structures		
Representation (*verbal thought*)	Communication (*discourse*)		Language in general	Mental terms, particularly verbs	
	Pragmatics	Linguistic environment		Semantics	Syntax
	(*individual ability*)	(*social context*)		(*lexical terms for mental states*)	(*sentential complements of mental verbs*)

lexical items that are used to refer to the mind—to mental states and mental activities (Bartsch & Wellman, 1995; Olson, 1988; Peterson & Siegal, 2000). Other researchers put more emphasis on the syntactic structures in which mental terms are used (de Villiers & de Villiers, 2000; Tager-Flusberg, 2000). Mental verbs frequently occur as the main verb in a complex sentence that has a subordinate clause (called a sentential complement) as its grammatical object; for example, "Maxi thinks that the chocolate is in the cupboard," "He wants to have some." Such constructions allow for a separation of the attitude and content of a person's mental state: the attitude denotes what kind of mental state it is (belief, desire, and so on), and the content describes what the mental state is about. Importantly, some mental verbs allow a false sentence to be embedded in a true one. In conversation, two people might say, for example: "The chocolate is in the cupboard"—"No, it's in the drawer." Obviously, if one of these sentences is true, then the other is false. However, when each sentence is embedded under a mental verb in a complex sentence, then both (complex) sentences can be true: "Maxi thinks *the chocolate is in the cupboard*" and "Mother knows *it's in the drawer*" (sentential complements italicized). Thus, this syntactic structure provides the format needed to represent beliefs as false.

Development of Theory of Mind: Why Language Matters

The previous two sections make it apparent that both theory of mind and language are broad, multifaceted systems. Each has many components, leading to the possibility of different relations among different components, and also the possibility of change in these relations over developmental time, as well as individual differences in the relations. The one point that is completely clear is that it is not at all a simple picture; indeed, to claim merely that there is a relation between language and theory of mind is so oversimplified as to be virtually use-less. Certainly, the rich collection of chapters in the present volume does not present a simple picture. Rather, it gives a kaleidoscopic view of the complexity of the relation between language and theory of mind. Further, and most important, it provides a variety of answers to the question of why language matters for theory of mind.

There is obviously an assumption embedded here—that is, that language does matter for theory-of-mind development. When we first decided to organize the conference that led to this volume, we thought of asking the question "Does language matter for theory of mind?," which is undoubtedly the prior question. However, probably no one would dispute the suggestion that language does matter, at least in some sense. In a trivial way, language matters because it is a fundamental human capacity that permeates almost everything that humans do. As Chris Moore (2002) said in the final discussion session of the conference, the critical question is whether there is anything special about theory of mind that requires language and, relatedly, whether there is anything special about language that allows theory of mind to develop. Language is involved in many aspects of conceptual development; the question is, what is special about its role in theory-of-mind development?

No Special Role for Language

From a number of different perspectives, language has no special role. First, nativist modularity theorists propose that theory of mind is innately specified but not evident until a certain level of linguistic and cognitive development is achieved (Fodor, 1992). A related argument, which does not necessarily assume innateness or modularity for theory of mind, is that language's role is only at a superficial level because many theory-of-mind tasks are verbal tasks, such that successful task performance requires a certain level of language ability (Chandler, Fritz, & Hala, 1989). Meanwhile, other researchers, also denying innateness or modularity, argue that theory-of-mind abilities rest on domain general cognitive operations that require language for their implementation (Frye, Zelazo, & Palfai, 1995). Finally, others see the role of language as no more than a natural way of providing children with the information they require for constructing a theory of mind (Gopnik & Wellman, 1994; Perner, 2000).

On the other hand, however, a large group of theorists ascribes a more fundamental, causal role to language in the development of theory of mind, particularly during the toddler and preschool period (18 months to 5 or 6 years of age), when both language and theory of mind are rapidly developing and intricately connected. We briefly summarize those positions here, without giving details of the evidence that supports each view—this follows in the rest of the volume.

A Role for Conversational Pragmatics

Some researchers argue that children's participation in conversation is critical to theory-of-mind development. Dunn and her colleagues, in an important early paper (Dunn, Brown, Slomkowski, Tesla, & Youngblade, 1991), showed that 2-year-olds' naturalistically observed conversational experiences are related to their understanding of other minds when they are 3 years old. Children whose mothers had talked to them about people's feelings and about causal relations and who themselves who had talked about feelings were more likely, seven months later, to give satisfactory explanations of behaviors premised on false beliefs. Harris (1999) points out that in conversational exchanges children are frequently exposed to the fact that different people know different things. They realize that they themselves know things that others don't know, and conversely, other people have information that is new to them. Harris argues that this experience of information exchange, of discovering that other people know something different, leads children to an understanding of people as epistemic subjects and an awareness that there are different points of view on the same material world.

A Role for Lexical Semantics

Other researchers emphasize that it is in conversation that children acquire concepts of mental states, such as belief, desire, intention, and so on (Bartsch & Wellman, 1995; Olson, 1988; Peterson & Siegal, 2000). Conversation provides a means of abstracting these underlying mental-state concepts from the conversation because the concepts are semantically encoded in the language of the culture. When they are 2 and 3 years old, children begin to acquire specific lexical terms that are used to refer to mental states: first perception, emotion, and desire terms (e.g., *see, look, happy, sad, like, love, want*) and then cognition terms (e.g., *know, think, remember*) (Bartsch & Wellman, 1995; Bretherton & Beeghly, 1982). Parents use these words in talking to their child about the child's own experiences. Importantly, parents also use the same terms to talk about other people's experiences, so that children are able to map other people's experiences onto their own and so come to attribute mental states to the self and others (Astington, 1996). In this way, children's phenomenal experience leads them to conceptual understanding because language allows for a level of abstraction that can support concepts about unobservable mental states.

Certainly, such conceptual understanding takes some time to develop. Nelson (1996) points out that young children's use of mental terms does not, at least at first, indicate that they understand the mental concepts to which those terms refer. Rather, she makes the Wittgenstein argument that children use these terms before they know the meaning of them and then they acquire meaning from use. That is, over time children's use of mental-state terms facilitates their ability to reflect upon and label their own mental states, as well as fosters their understanding of the mental states of others.

A Role for Complementation Syntax

Importantly, participation in conversation leads to an understanding of perspective and an awareness of mental states. But is this sufficient to allow for meta-representational interpretations of human behavior, as required, for example, in the false-belief task? Other researchers argue that it is not; they put less emphasis on the importance of semantics—the terms and concepts encountered in conversation—and more on the syntactic structures that are required to attribute different points of view using mental terms. As discussed earlier, mental verbs occur as the main verb in a complex sentence that has a subordinate clause—the sentential complement—as its grammatical object. Children use such complement constructions almost as soon as they start to produce mental verbs, that is, at 2 years of age (Bartsch & Wellman, 1995; Bloom, Rispoli, Gartner, & Hafitz, 1989). However, Diessel and Tomasello (2001) show that this early use is formulaic and argue that it does not provide evidence of mastery of complement syntax. In support of this argument, comprehension of complements is not mastered until a year or two later, when it predicts children's performance on false-belief tasks (de Villiers & Pyers, 2002). Thus, de Villiers and de Villiers (2000) argue that the acquisition of the syntactic ability to understand sentential complements underlies the development of false-belief understanding. In particular, the verb *say*, which provides overt evidence for the falsity of the complement in cases where what is said is known to be untrue, may bootstrap an understanding of complements for *think*, because *say* and *think* are used in the same discourse contexts. A training study (Lohmann & Tomasello, 2003) supports the general argument of the importance of complement syntax but gives no support to the particular role of *say*. However, naturalistic evidence does provide some support: at an early stage, while *think* complement use is only formulaic, *say* is flexibly used in more diverse complement forms (Diessel & Tomasello, 2001).

Roles Combined in Synergy

Something written more than ten years ago is no less true today: "When we attempt to separate the various theoretical positions in this way we always risk oversimplification. Many particular theorists' views combine different aspects of the accounts we have described here, and at the risk of sounding like wishy-washy liberals, there is some level at which they must all be true" (Astington & Gopnik, 1991, p. 25). Wishy-washy liberalism is a hard trait to throw off. We take the same position here—putting all of the preceding together, the whole is more than the sum of the parts. The explanations summarized earlier are not in competition but cohere to give a more complete explanation of why language matters for theory of mind. Pragmatic ability allows children to participate in communicative exchanges, where they hear mental terms used with sentential complements. From this experience, they acquire awareness of points of view, concepts of mental states, and mastery of the syntax for representing false beliefs. Both the social environment that provides this cultural input and the child's own cognitive resources that make use of it are needed for the child's theory of mind to develop. All this is true, though simplistic in its brevity. The remainder of the volume spells out these ideas in full detail.

Overview of the Volume

Part I: Communication and Social Understanding

Children acquire social understanding (or theory of mind) as participants in the social world, which is primarily a mental world—a community of minds (Nelson, Plesa, & Henseler, 1998; Nelson, Skwerer, Goldman, Henseler, Presler, & Walkenfeld, 2003). Participation in this world depends on communication, which is facilitated as children's linguistic abilities develop. Thus, through language, children gain access to the mental world and become part of the community of minds. They discover how minds interact—that beliefs can be changed, desires can be created, and emotions can be invoked in linguistic exchanges. The significance of communicative development emphasizes the importance of pragmatics to theory-of-mind development, and, reciprocally, early theory-of-mind abilities are important to the development of communicative competence.

The contributors to the first set of chapters take this social-cultural approach to theory-of-mind development and its relation to language. Katherine Nelson leads the endeavor in chapter 2, in which she reconceptualizes the acquisition of a "theory of mind" as entering into a "community of minds," where language plays a central role. This reconceptualization is necessary, Nelson argues, because theory of mind is too narrowly construed as a separate cognitive domain to the exclusion of domain general achievements (including language, memory, inference) and social experiences (such as attachment, play, and conversation). Moreover, Nelson argues that the developmental process some researchers claim to explain advances in children's theory of mind—namely theory construction and revision—is unwarranted. Thus, Nelson proposes to replace the theory metaphor with the notion of "community of minds," and she argues that entering into the community of minds is a developmental process made possible through language.

Language matters, Nelson argues, because to understand other minds is to participate in a communally shared belief system about human goals, motivations, and values. Nelson makes a special case for the emergence of the representational function of language that allows children to go beyond their own private thoughts and beliefs to consider the thoughts and beliefs of others. This is a Vygotskian view, in which children's experience with external verbal representations in social discourse supports the development of internal verbal representation. In particular, Nelson finds that children's receptive language ability—as exercised, for example, in listening to stories—is especially important for the development of the representational function of language and, thus, for children's entry into the community of minds.

In chapter 3, Judy Dunn and Marcia Brophy focus on the communicational aspect of language and its role in children's developing theory of mind. Like Nelson, they presume that participation in communicative exchanges underlies theory-of-mind development. However, and most important, they argue that the nature and efficacy of the communicative exchange is influenced by the quality of the relationship between the communicative participants. They propose that children's communicative experiences within close, familiar relationships play a central role in the development of understanding mind and emotion. According to Dunn and Brophy, it is through the experience of communication within close, dyadic relationships that children gain entry into the community of minds that Nelson describes. Dunn and Brophy find support for their argument in research on individual differences. For example, they report that children's participation in discourse about mental states predicts later differences in theory-of-mind understanding, over and above other contributing factors such as cooperative play.

Importantly, Dunn and Brophy argue that in order to understand relations between theory of mind and language, children's language experiences must be examined not solely in terms of a cognitive skill or individual characteristic but also in terms of children's dyadic experiences. To illustrate: Dunn and Brophy report that the relationship quality between child and communicative partner is systematically related to the frequency with which they interact in contexts that are rich in discourse about mental states. Thus, the aspects of conversation that are relevant to theory of mind depend on characteristics of both child and interlocutor, and on the relationship between them.

In chapter 4, Paul Harris also emphasizes the importance of communicative exchanges in fostering children's understanding of mind. With respect to mother-child conversation, Harris makes the important point that a simple count of mental-state terms may not be the most sensitive measure of effective maternal input, although it may be a useful correlate. Various aspects of maternal input are likely to co-vary, including the frequency of use of mental terms, the frequency of use of sentential complements, and the pragmatic intent to introduce varying points of view into the conversation. Harris argues that it is the mother's pragmatic intent that is the effective source of variation in promoting theory-of-mind development. In support of this suggestion, Harris cites two training studies (Hale & Tager-Flusberg, 2003; Lohmann & Tomasello, 2003), both of which indicate that conversation that emphasizes different points of view on one and the same object or event, without using mental terms or sentential complements, is sufficient to generate an improvement in children's performance on theory-of-mind tasks.

Harris also discusses the significance of pretend play in theory-of-mind development—in particular, the finding that role-taking abilities are related to children's performance on theory-of-mind tasks (e.g., Astington & Jenkins, 1995; Taylor & Carlson, 1997). He makes the intriguing suggestion that variation in conversational input to the child might interact with children's role-taking ability. Specifically, Harris suggests that certain types of conversation invite a subtle form of role-play by prompting children to imagine the world from another person's perspective. On this account, conversation and role-playing ability may unite to facilitate children's understanding of false belief and influence their social understanding more broadly.

Nelson, Dunn and Brophy, and Harris all explore ways in which children's participation in communicative exchanges mediates the development of a theory of mind. In chapter 5, Daniela O'Neill takes a different approach by exploring how children's theory of mind underlies their pragmatic competence in communicative exchanges. In particular, she summarizes a growing body of literature on children's ability to talk about new (as opposed to given, or known) information. O'Neill argues that in order to tailor their speech in an appropriate manner to include references to new information, children must take into account the mental states of the listener, for example, what he or she knows, does not know, or might want to know. Assessing information as new or given necessarily entails at least two communicative partners; thus, O'Neill finds a point of contact between her work and Nelson's idea of a "community of minds." In particular, O'Neill argues that children's ability to recognize topics that will be relevant to the listener is crucial for entering the community of minds.

Theory-of-mind abilities and pragmatic abilities are certainly closely related. Part of pragmatic competence is the ability to use and interpret language appropriately in social situations, by keeping track of listeners' and speakers' beliefs and intentions. Thus, it seems that pragmatics and theory of mind are related by definition. However, one could argue that understanding and awareness of belief and intention are part of theory of mind, and keeping track of them in language use is pragmatics—in which case one can then argue that theory-of-mind abilities underlie pragmatic abilities—which is the argument O'Neill makes.

Part II: Semantic Development and Mental-State Concepts

The chapters in the previous section focus, in varying ways, on how children's participation in communicative exchanges fosters their developing understanding of the mental world. A fundamental question is: what mechanism allows children to develop an understanding of the mental world through participating in it? The mental world is a world of unobservable abstract entities, such as beliefs, desires, intentions, and emotions, that are revealed in facial expressions, talk, and behavior. One complexity that arises when trying to understand how children acquire mental-state concepts is the great variety of ways in which each of these concepts may be expressed. That is, mentalistic notions such as belief, desire, and intention do not stand in one-to-one relations with specific behavioral patterns. It may well be language that provides children with a means of abstracting the underlying mental-state concepts, semantically encoded in the language of their culture, from the variety of behaviors in the ongoing stream of social interaction—but how? The first two chapters in this part tackle this fundamental problem.

In chapter 6, Derek Montgomery questions how children come to understand the meaning of mental terms such as *think*, *know*, *want*, and *gonna*. He sets up a contrast between two perspectives on word learning—what he calls the ostension paradigm and the contextual view. The first sees children working out word-referent relations, mapping mental terms onto mental concepts, whereas the second (his view) holds that children figure out the practical functions mental terms serve in social contexts. The central idea of ostension is that word meaning is based on the referential relation between mental states, which are experienced privately and internally, and the verbal labels of those states. That is, children themselves have mentalistic experiences that they categorize and then label (*thinking* versus *wanting*, for example). Montgomery challenges the ostension paradigm and suggests instead that children derive the meaning of mental terms from routine social interactions with their caregivers. On his view, mentalistic language and its meaning grow out of interactive, preverbal exchanges—language games, as he calls them. He suggests that everyday language games—in which children are exposed to mental-state terms across related but different scenarios—promote their understanding of mental terms and concepts. For example, infants engage in a language game of desire, in which they communicate <u>that</u> they want something and <u>what</u> it is that they want. These games begin with infants' gestures and nonverbal vocalizations, which elicit mentalistic language from their caregivers such as "what do you *want*?" or "is this what you *want*?" Then children start to say "*want* x" as they gesture toward what they want, and, at a later stage, even in the absence of the wanted item. Thus, Montgomery maintains that mental terms, and hence mental concepts, acquire their meaning from the pragmatic roles they play in these early language games. It is in these communicative exchanges, he argues, that mental terms and concepts are socially constructed.

Dare Baldwin and Megan Saylor (chapter 7) share Montgomery's view that mental-state concepts emerge in the context of social and linguistic interaction, but they take a somewhat different stance on the issue of how this understanding develops. They draw on Gentner's work (e.g., Gentner & Ratterman, 1991) in suggesting that language may facilitate children's acquisition of mentalistic concepts by serving as an aid to analogical reasoning and inductive inference. That is, language invites children to compare different behaviors that otherwise they would not attempt to align, thus promoting inferences about nonobvious commonalities across distinct expressions of mental states, such as belief, desire, attention, and intention. Baldwin and Saylor review a large body of research that suggests that, in the realm of physical objects, infants use information provided in language to draw inferences about nonobvious commonalities. For example, upon hearing the same label applied to two different objects, infants are more likely to use their knowledge of one object to guide their exploration of the other object than if the objects are given different or no labels. Baldwin and Saylor argue that, in the realm of mental states, language may function similarly to facilitate children's abstraction of mentalistic concepts.

They discuss two different aspects of this process. First, following Grice (1957; see also O'Neill, this volume, chapter 5), they argue that language in general, used in conversation, is intricately linked to mentalistic concerns as it embodies communicative intent and intentional focus, taking into account and attempting to influence the beliefs and desires of the conversational participant. They discuss in some detail how references to absent objects may give children clues for learning about referential intent (through structure mapping and alignment). Second, and more specifically, mental terms may act as labels that invite recognition across different behaviors and situations, leading to the development of mentalistic concepts by the abstraction of commonalities across behaviors. This view is closer to the ostension paradigm, although they do not call it that. From Montgomery's perspective, one problem with this argument is that it does not answer what is, for him, the fundamental question of how infants come to recognize distinct sensations related to different mental states.

Baldwin and Saylor's hypothesis about the effects of mental-state vocabulary as labels that lead to the acquisition of mental-state concepts links to the next chapter (chapter 8), in which Sophie Jacques and Philip D. Zelazo also investigate the labeling function of language, in this case as an aid to cognitive flexibility. They reinterpret the relation between language and theory of mind in terms of language-related effects on cognitive flexibility. Central to their argument is the claim that most of the variance on theory-of-mind tasks can be attributed to the development of flexible perspective taking. Indeed, Jacques and Zelazo recast theory of mind as cognitive flexibility, arguing that, although theory of mind undoubtedly involves the acquisition of mental-state concepts, the use of these concepts necessarily involves cognitive flexibility—the ability to consider multiple representations of a single object or event. Jacques and Zelazo then go on to review a number of studies that demonstrate that labeling relevant stimuli promotes children's cognitive flexibility, and they offer a number of suggestions for how labeling might similarly help theory-of-mind performance.

Despite clear evidence for the facilitative role of labeling in cognitive flexibility, Jacques and Zelazo are undecided regarding the precise mechanism by which labeling is effective. On the one hand, according to Zelazo's (1999) Levels of Consciousness model, labeling facilitates self-reflection, which in turn promotes flexible thought and action. On the other hand, Jacques argues that the arbitrary nature of labels is itself facilitative: because labels typically do not resemble their referents, they help create psychological distance between the symbol user and the external stimuli to which the symbols refer. Regardless of the mechanism, however, Jacques and Zelazo argue that labeling different perspectives in theory-of-mind tasks should benefit children's performance.

Jacques and Zelazo's hypothesis on the facilitative effects of labeling links directly to our chapter (Astington & Baird, chapter 9), in which we examine the influence of linguistic manipulations in the false-belief task on children's performance. Following Plaut and Karmiloff-Smith (1993), we hypothesize that the change-in-location false-belief task will be easier if children hear about but do not actually see the object transfer (because they will not be misled by the salience of reality) and that the task will be harder if children have to construct their own linguistic representation of the false belief, in conflict with the information presented in the visual display. To investigate this hypothesis, we compared children's performance on a standard version of the false-belief task (in which both verbal and visual representations were provided) with their performance on the verbal-only and visual-only versions described earlier. Across two studies, we found no evidence that these manipulations have any effect on children's false-belief task performance. The absence of condition differences surprised not only us but also Jacques and Zelazo (chapter 8), whose labeling hypothesis similarly would have predicted poorer performance on our visual-only version, which lacked a verbal narrative.

In an attempt to reconcile the absence of language-related condition differences in our studies, we go on to review other studies that manipulate verbal and visual information in the false-belief task. With respect to task versions that mask reality and thus should be easier for children, we find the evidence equivocal. Similarly, our review of nonverbal tasks does not indicate, as hypothesized, that these versions are more difficult. In the end, we conclude that children's false-belief task performance is not influenced by variations in the mode—visual, verbal, or both—in which the critical information is conveyed. Instead, we argue that language matters for false-belief understanding (and thus, theory of mind) because language supports the meta-representational model that underlies this understanding.

Part III: Syntactic Development and Mental-State Reasoning

The acquisition of mental-state concepts, discussed in the previous section, is fundamental to reasoning about mental states, which requires the representation of mental attitudes towards mental contents. As language develops, increased resources in syntactic structures provide the format required for such representation and thus, it is argued, syntactic development facilitates mental-state reasoning. A paradigm case of mental-state reasoning is that of reasoning about the behavioral consequences of holding a false belief. By investigating syntactic and other aspects of the linguistic input that are related to children's understanding of false belief, researchers have further explored the nature of the relation between language and theory of mind.

Jill de Villiers has been a central figure in this endeavor, proposing a theory of linguistic determinism (J. de Villiers, 1995) that has been refined and extended over the past decade (e.g., J. de Villiers & P. de Villiers, 2000, 2003). In chapter 10, she presents the most recent version of the theory, providing a summary of evidence in its favor and refuting some specific counterarguments. The theory posits that false-belief understanding crucially depends on mastery of the syntax of complementation. However, importantly, and perhaps more confusing to psychologists than to linguists, this syntactic development is not obvious at a surface level. First, it does not apply to all object complements, that is, it does not hold for desire [*want* + infinitive] in English. Second, nor does it apply to all tensed object complements [*that* + finite verb]; for example, it does not hold for [*want-that*] in German, and [*pretend-that*] in English, because these verbs take *irrealis* complements (i.e., about future or imaginary events). Rather, it applies only to belief and communication verbs, which take *realis* complements (i.e., about actual events). J. De Villiers posits that there is a Point-of-View (POV) marker on the complement clause, for belief and communication verbs, that is specified by the verb itself. That is, it is in some ways a semantic criterion, in so far as the POV feature is carried by the nature of the verb.

De Villiers argues that desire verbs (e.g., *want*) and belief verbs (e.g., *think*) develop along radically different trajectories. Early on, children come to understand that desire verbs take *irrealis* complements, because noun phrase complements of verbs of desire are recognized as intensional (e.g., "I want a candy" yet there is no candy present). She maintains that children extend their understanding that the object of the verb is *irrealis* to the understanding that all complements of desire verbs are *irrealis*. Furthermore, the verb "pretend" is treated in the same way.

However, complements of verbs of belief are never treated as *irrealis*; at an early stage, before children understand that belief verbs open up a new POV domain, belief complements are treated as true *realis* clauses. A crucial stage comes with the realization that complements embedded under the verb *think* can be false compared to the world. De Villiers claims that this comes about via analogy with the verb *say*. The two verbs are used in the same discourse contexts and are alike syntactically, and so they are placed in the same subclass. It is obvious that *say* takes false complements; that is, children have evidence that people's overt verbal expressions sometimes do not correspond to the way they themselves perceive the world to be. Children then extend this understanding to complements of the verb *think*. Thus, syntax provides a bootstrap from the overt evidence of falsity for complements of *say* to the possibility of false complements for *think*. The verb *want*, on the other hand, is not treated as analogous, because it clearly takes *irrealis* complements, whatever syntactic form they might have in different languages.

In chapter 11, Josef Perner, Petra Zauner, and Manuel Sprung present new data and review existing studies that they claim pose a challenge to J. de Villiers's theory. In particular, they take issue with de Villiers's emphasis on children's understanding of tensed *that*-complements as the key to understanding other minds and points of view.[1] Drawing on cross-linguistic data, Perner and his colleagues show that, regardless of whether a given language requires tensed *that*-complements to express beliefs and desires, children understand desires before beliefs. For example, German-speaking children understand and talk about desire substantially earlier than about belief, despite the fact that their language requires tensed *that*-complements to express both mental states. Chinese-speaking children similarly understand desire before belief, even though their language does not require tensed *that*-complements for either mental state. According to Perner et al., these findings challenge de Villiers's claims that the syntactic form of how we talk about the mind forms the basis for how we think about the mind.

Most important, Perner and his colleagues also point to a number of studies that show a correspondence between the age at which children understand differences in point of view in the context of conflicting desires and the age at which children understand differences in point of view in the context of false beliefs. The authors present these findings as an objection to de Villiers's argument that understanding point of view is derived from an understanding of the particular syntactic structure associated with belief verbs, which desire verbs do not share.

In some ways there is a close connection between J. de Villiers's (chapter 10) theory of POV markers and the theory of perspectival understanding that Perner and his colleagues put forward here. The question for us is how linguistic determinism and conceptual development are related. It depends in part on whether one assumes that the critical development is captured in the syntax or the semantics, and this depends on whether one takes syntax and semantics as an integrated whole, or separates syntax off and takes semantics and concepts as intertwined. De Villiers sees syntax and semantics as intricately entwined, whereas for Perner semantics is part of conceptual development. At best, there may be no fundamental disagreement, but rather a linguist's and a psychologist's different but consonant views on the same issue.

This is an ongoing debate for which further data are provided in the next three chapters. First, however, Heidemarie Lohmann, Michael Tomasello, and Sonja Meyer (chapter 12) consider the early stages of pragmatic language acquisition before taking up the issue of syntax and semantics. They suggest that the relation between language and theory of mind is different depending on which aspect of social understanding is at issue (as we emphasized earlier in the present chapter). In particular, they argue that an appreciation of other persons as intentional agents—the first level of social understanding—is prerequisite for language acquisition. On their view, language arises from infants' growing ability in the second year of life to tune into others' communicative intentions. Then, children's use of language in social exchanges leads to an understanding of other persons as mental agents, whose behavior is governed by desires and beliefs, including ones that are false. Thus, at this later stage in development, language gives rise to a new level of social understanding.

Lohmann and her colleagues substantiate this claim with a training study aimed at developing false-belief reasoning. In particular, they report that both conversation about deceptive objects and training on the syntax of complementation (in the absence of deceptive objects) promote 3-year-olds' false-belief understanding. Moreover, the largest training effect occurred in a condition that combined conversation and complements. Lohmann and her colleagues therefore suggest that perspective-switching discourse and the syntax of sentential complements make independent contributions to theory-of-mind development. Importantly, the fact that manipulating the deceptive objects without any conversation about them was ineffective, leads to the conclusion that language is a necessary condition for children to make progress in their understanding of false beliefs, lending support to the claim that language plays a causal role in the ontogeny of social understanding.

The next two chapters report findings that are similar to those of Lohmann et al. and provide further illumination on the role of language by investigating the relation between language and theory-of-mind development in atypical populations. Linguistic, cognitive, and social development are closely correlated in typically developing children. Insight into the nature of their relationship and their relative influence on theory-of-mind development can be acquired from investigations in populations where the typical correlations are not found, such as deaf children whose language acquisition is delayed and children with autism, whose development is impaired in a number of ways.

In chapter 13, Peter de Villiers examines deaf children as a window on the role of language in theory-of-mind development. Deaf children, he argues, provide a strong test for the causal role of language, because many of them have significantly delayed language acquisition but age-appropriate nonverbal intelligence and sociability. In his chapter, P. de Villiers compares the language and theory-of-mind abilities of two groups of deaf children: deaf children of hearing parents, whose language acquisition is delayed, and deaf children of deaf parents, whose language acquisition is not delayed. Across two studies, he finds that deaf children who acquire fluent sign language early are significantly better at reasoning about mental states than language-delayed deaf children. Indeed, the theory-of-mind development of deaf children with deaf parents is comparable to that of their typically developing hearing peers. In contrast, deaf children of hearing parents whose exposure to language (ASL or Oral) is delayed demonstrate significant delays in their mental-state reasoning. Importantly, P. de Villiers reports that both general verbal ability (vocabulary) and specific syntactic features of language (false complement structures) are independently predictive of false-belief reasoning in deaf children. Thus, P. de Villiers finds support for both the pragmatic theory of why language matters for theory of mind (e.g., Harris, this volume, chapter 4) and the theory that mastery of the syntax of complementation is what provides the representational mechanism for reasoning about false beliefs (e.g., J. de Villiers, this volume, chapter 10). P. de Villiers echoes our sentiment that these theories may be more complementary than exclusive.

The findings P. de Villiers reports in his chapter on deaf children bear a striking resemblance to the findings Helen Tager-Flusberg and Robert Joseph report in the next chapter (chapter 14) on individuals with autism. However, P. de Villiers notes an important difference between the theory-of-mind abilities of deaf children and those of individuals with autism. Although deaf children may rely on complex language for the mastery of false-belief understanding, other aspects of theory-of-mind reasoning are developed by deaf children much as they are in hearing children, despite language delays. For example, the ability to reason about desires and intentions and to engage in hide-and-seek deception games is spared in language-delayed deaf children. Individuals with autism, however, are severely impaired on tasks such as these.

Tager-Flusberg and Joseph examine autism as a window on the relation between language and theory of mind. It is well known that individuals with autism have deficits in both domains. However, despite these impairments, a small percentage of individuals with autism routinely pass theory-of-mind tasks, specifically, false-belief tasks. Tager-Flusberg and Joseph take a closer look at these individuals, focusing on the unique role language plays in facilitating their success on the false-belief task. Tager-Flusberg and Joseph argue that, for individuals with autism, language—in particular, knowledge of sentential complements—serves to bootstrap the meta-representational understanding of mental states necessary for success on false-belief tasks. In support of their view, Tager-Flusberg and Joseph present evidence from several cross-sectional studies and a longitudinal study that indicates that language is the single most predictive factor of false-belief task performance among individuals with autism. In particular, they find that general language ability and specific knowledge of sentential complements play independent roles in explaining how some individuals with autism come to pass false-belief tasks, echoing P. de Villiers's and our arguments. Moreover, they report that knowledge of complements for verbs of communication (e.g., *say*) is uniquely important for this group, suggesting that, in order to succeed on false-belief tasks, individuals with autism depend on linguistic structures for representing conflict between what someone says and what is true in reality. This finding, albeit with a special population, provides support for J. de Villiers's (chapter 10) model of development, in which recognition of the possibility of false complements for *say* leads to understanding false complements for *think*.

At the end of the chapter, Tager-Flusberg and Joseph take up the question of why language matters for theory of mind in autism. Tager-Flusberg (2001) suggests that there are two components to theory of mind: social-perceptual abilities and social-cognitive understanding (reminiscent of the two levels that Lohmann et al. propose in chapter 12). The social-perceptual component builds on infants' innate preferences for human faces and social stimuli, whereas the social-cognitive component involves making inferences about the mental states that underlie social stimuli. In typically developing children, the two components are related; that is, social-cognitive understanding grows out of children's social-perceptual abilities. However, children with autism fundamentally lack the social-perceptual abilities of typically developing children. Tager-Flusberg and Joseph suggest that, in autism, language becomes an artificial route to social-cognitive understanding. That is, instead of developing a conceptual understanding of mental states grounded in social-perceptual abilities, children with autism learn, via language, to reason logically through false-belief tasks. Whether individuals with autism are capable of developing a genuinely intuitive understanding of the mind remains an open question.

Part IV: Conclusion

The research with atypical populations reported in the previous two chapters highlights the fact that the development of theory of mind and of language is influenced by both genetic and environmental factors. An important question is whether these factors are shared by theory of mind and language or are unique to one or the other. Moreover, the answer to this question may depend in part on developmental and individual differences in relations between the two, as Claire Hughes makes clear in chapter 15. She reports data from two twin studies conducted at two different times in development—3;6 years and 5;0 years. Both studies showed a strong correlation between general verbal ability and theory of mind, in accord with many other studies in the literature. However, the twin study design provides a unique methodological perspective from which to investigate the nature of the relationship between language and theory of mind.

The first study, with a sample of 3-year-old twins, showed a large influence of genetic factors on theory of mind, with these having little overlap with genetic factors influencing verbal ability. This finding lends support to theories that propose genetic modularity for theory of mind. The second study, with a considerably larger sample of 5-year-old twins, provided a much greater possibility of detecting environmental effects because of the sample size. It did not replicate the first study's results regarding the importance of genetic factors (the genetic influence was small), but it did reveal a substantial environmental influence on theory of mind. Environmental factors accounted for a large proportion of the variance in theory of mind, and only genetic factors that were shared with verbal ability contributed to individual differences in theory of mind. The association between theory of mind and verbal ability was accounted for by common effects of shared genes, and the common effects of shared environment and socioeconomic status. Hughes concludes that there may be developmental change in the relative impact of genetic and environmental influences on individual differences in theory of mind. That is, genetic factors may play a limiting role in the earlier stages of theory-of-mind acquisition, with environmental factors becoming increasingly important as time goes by.

Hughes's idea that gene-environment effects may shift over developmental time fits nicely with the overall aim of this volume, which is to tell a developmental story about the relation of language and theory of mind. The overview of the chapters that we have given here provides only a snapshot of this relation and of why language matters. We invite you to turn to the chapters themselves for the whole big picture.

Acknowledgments We are grateful to Chris Moore, Ana Perez Leroux, and David Olson for their comments on an earlier version of this chapter. We also thank the Connaught Committee of the University of Toronto, the Natural Sciences and Engineering Research Council of Canada, and the Social Sciences and Humanities Research Council of Canada for financial support.

Note

1. It is important to note that the studies reported (Perner, Sprung, Zauner, & Haider, 2003) were conducted in response to an earlier version of J. de Villiers's theory (de Villiers & de Villiers, 2000) that did not posit POV markers specified by the verb but distinguished between desire and belief on the basis of the clause structure of the complement (i.e., infinitival *to*-complements for desire versus tensed *that*-complements for belief).

References

Astington, J. W. (1996). What is theoretical about the child's theory of mind? A Vygotskian view of its development. In P. Carruthers & P. K. Smith (Eds.), *Theories of theories of mind* (pp. 184–199). Cambridge: Cambridge University Press.

Astington, J. W. (1998). Theory of mind, Humpty Dumpty, and the icebox. *Human Development, 41,* 30–39.

Astington, J. W., & Gopnik, A. (1991). Theoretical explanations of children's understanding of the mind. *British Journal of Developmental Psychology, 9,* 7–31.

Astington, J. W., Harris, P. L., & Olson, D. R. (Eds.). (1988). *Developing theories of mind.* New York: Cambridge University Press.

Astington, J. W., & Jenkins, J. M. (1995). Theory of mind and social understanding. *Cognition and Emotion, 9,* 151–165.

Astington, J. W., & Pelletier, J. (1996). The language of mind: Its role in learning and teaching. In D. R. Olson & N. Torrance (Eds.), *The handbook of education and human development: New models of learning, teaching and schooling* (pp. 593–619). Oxford: Blackwell.

Astington, J. W., & Peskin, J. (2004). Meaning and use: Children's acquisition of the mental lexicon. In J. M. Lucariello, J. A. Hudson, R. Fivush, & P. J. Bauer (Eds.), *The development of the mediated mind: Sociocultural context and cognitive development* (pp. 59–78). Mahwah, NJ: Erlbaum.

Bartsch, K., & Wellman, H. M. (1995). *Children talk about the mind.* New York: Oxford University Press.

Bloom, L., Rispoli, M., Gartner, B., & Hafitz, J. (1989). Acquisition of complementation. *Journal of Child Language, 16,* 101–120.

Bretherton, I., & Beeghly, M. (1982). Talking about internal states: The acquisition of an explicit theory of mind. *Developmental Psychology, 18,* 906–921.

Bretherton, I., McNew, S., & Beeghly-Smith, M. (1981). Early person knowledge as expressed in gestural and verbal communication: When do infants acquire a "theory of mind"? In M. E. Lamb & L. R. Sherod (Eds.), *Infant social cognition* (pp. 333–373). Hillsdale, NJ: Erlbaum.

Carroll, L. (1872). *Through the looking-glass, and what Alice found there.* London: Macmillan.

Chandler, M. J., Fritz, A. S., & Hala, S. M. (1989). Small scale deceit: Deception as a marker of 2–, 3– and 4–year-olds' early theories of mind. *Child Development, 60,* 1263–1277.

de Villiers, J. G. (1995, March). Steps in the mastery of sentence complements. In J. W. Astington (Chair), *Language development and the acquisition of a theory of mind.* Symposium presented at the Biennial Meeting of the Society for Research in Child Development, Indianapolis, IN.

de Villiers, J. G., & de Villiers, P. A. (2000). Linguistic determinism and the understanding of false beliefs. In P. Mitchell & K. J. Riggs (Eds.), *Children's reasoning and the mind* (pp. 191–228). Hove, UK: Psychology Press.

de Villiers, J. G., & de Villiers, P. A. (2003). Language for thought: Coming to understand false beliefs. In D. Gentner & S. Goldin-Meadow (Eds.), *Language in mind: Advances in the study of language and thought* (pp. 335–384). Cambridge, MA: MIT Press.

de Villiers, J. G., & Pyers, J. E. (2002). Complements to cognition: A longitudinal study of the relationship between complex syntax and false-belief understanding. *Cognitive Development, 17,* 1037–1060.

Diessel, H., & Tomasello, M. (2001). The acquisition of finite complement clauses in English: A corpus-based analysis. *Cognitive Linguistics, 12,* 97–141

Dunn, J., Brown, J., Slomkowski, C., Tesla, C., & Youngblade, L. (1991). Young children's understanding of other people's feelings and beliefs: Individual differences and their antecedents. *Child Development, 62,* 1352–1366.

Fodor, J. A. (1992). A theory of the child's theory of mind. *Cognition, 44,* 283–296.

Frye, D., Zelazo, P. D., & Palfai, T. (1995). Theory of mind and rule-based reasoning. *Cognitive Development, 10,* 483–528.

Gentner, D., & Ratterman, M. J. (1991). Language and the career of similarity. In S. A. Gelman & J. P. Byrnes (Eds.), *Perspectives on language and thought: Interrelations in development* (pp. 225–277). Cambridge: Cambridge University Press.

Gopnik, A., & Wellman, H. M. (1994). The theory theory. In L. Hirschfeld & S. Gelman (Eds.), *Mapping the mind: Domain specificity in cognition and culture* (pp. 257–293). New York: Cambridge University Press.

Grice, H. P. (1957). Meaning. *Philosophical Review, 66,* 377–388.

Hale, C. M., & Tager-Flusberg, H. (2003). The influence of language on theory of mind: A training study. *Developmental Science, 6,* 346–359.

Harris, P. L. (1999). Acquiring the art of conversation. In M. Bennett (Ed.), *Developmental psychology: Achievements and prospects* (pp. 89–105). Philadelphia: Psychology Press/Taylor & Francis.

Hobson, R. P. (1991). Against the theory of "Theory of Mind." *British Journal of Developmental Psychology, 9,* 33–51.

Lillard, A. (1998). Theories behind theories of mind. *Human Development, 41,* 40–46.

Lohmann, H., & Tomasello, M. (2003). The role of language in the development of false-belief understanding: A training study. *Child Development, 74,* 1130–1144.

Moore, C. (2002, April). Discussant's comments. Presented at the International Conference on Why Language Matters for Theory of Mind, Toronto, Canada.

Moore, C., Pure, K., & Furrow, D. (1990). Children's understanding of the modal expressions of speaker certainty and uncertainty and its relation to the development of a representational theory of mind. *Child Development, 61,* 722–730.

Nelson, K. (1996). *Language in cognitive development: The emergence of the mediated mind.* New York: Cambridge University Press.

Nelson, K., Plesa, D., & Henseler, S. (1998). Children's theory of mind: An experiential interpretation. *Human Development, 41,* 7–29.

Nelson, K., Skwerer, D. P., Goldman, S., Henseler, S., Presler, N., & Walkenfeld, F. F. (2003). Entering a community of minds: An experiential approach to "theory of mind." *Human Development, 46,* 24–46.

Olson, D. R. (1988). On the origins of beliefs and other intentional states in children. In J. W. Astington, P. L. Harris, & D. R. Olson (Eds.), *Developing theories of mind* (pp. 414–426). New York: Cambridge University Press.

Perner, J. (2000). About + belief + counterfactual. In P. Mitchell & K. J. Riggs (Eds.), *Children's reasoning and the mind* (pp. 367–401). Hove, UK: Psychology Press.

Perner, J., Sprung, M., Zauner, P., & Haider, H. (2003). *Want that* is understood well before *say that, think that,* and false belief: A test of de Villiers' linguistic determinism on German-speaking children. *Child Development, 74,* 179–188.

Peterson, C. C., & Siegal, M. (2000). Insights into theory of mind from deafness and autism. *Mind & Language, 15,* 123–145.

Plaut, D. C., & Karmiloff-Smith, A. (1993). Representational development and theory-of-mind computations. *Behavioral and Brain Sciences, 16,* 70–71.

Premack, D., & Woodruff, G. (1978). Does the chimpanzee have a theory of mind? *Behavioral and Brain Sciences, 1,* 515–526.

Tager-Flusberg, H. (2000). Language and understanding minds: Connections in autism. In S. Baron-Cohen, H. Tager-Flusberg, & D. J. Cohen (Eds.), *Understanding other minds: Perspectives from developmental cognitive neuroscience* (pp. 124–149). Oxford: Oxford University Press.

Tager-Flusberg, H. (2001). A re-examination of the Theory of Mind hypothesis of autism. In J. Burack, T. Charman, N. Yirmiya, & P. Zelazo (Eds.), *The development of autism: Perspectives from theory and research* (pp. 173–194). Mahwah, NJ: Erlbaum.

Taylor, M., & Carlson, S. M. (1997). The relation between individual differences in fantasy and theory of mind. *Child Development, 68,* 436–455.

Wellman, H. M. (1979, November). A child's theory of mind. Paper presented at the conference The Growth of Insight in the Child, Madison, WI.

Wellman, H. M. (1985). The child's theory of mind: The development of conceptions of cognition. In S. R. Yussen (Ed.), *The growth of reflection in children* (pp. 169–206). San Diego, CA: Academic Press.

Wimmer, H., & Perner, J. (1983). Beliefs about beliefs: Representation and constraining function of wrong beliefs in young children's understanding of deception. *Cognition, 13,* 103–128.

Zelazo, P. D. (1999). Language, levels of consciousness, and the development of intentional action. In P. D. Zelazo, J. W. Astington, & D. R. Olson (Eds.), *Developing theories of intention: Social understanding and self control* (pp. 95–117). Mahwah, NJ: Erlbaum.

2 Language Pathways into the Community of Minds

Katherine Nelson

In this chapter I argue that adherence to the formulation "theory of mind" has narrowed the scope of attention to developments that contribute to children's ability to understand social and psychological phenomena. Developments in infancy and early childhood, such as shared attention and imitation, that are generally seen as precursors or predispositions to later theory of mind are, in the present view, better conceived as general characteristics of early development that have wide-ranging influences on all areas of psychological growth. At the same time, areas of competence, such as general reasoning, that are considered outside the "domain" of theory of mind can be shown to be crucial to its achievement, as it is usually evaluated in terms of the understanding of false belief. The resulting focus, I argue, has led theorists down a path that obscures the true importance of developments in early childhood, of which performance on theory-of-mind tasks is but one achievement. Further, and more germane to the questions raised in this volume, I argue that language is the most important general function that leads to higher-order cognitive processes, including the processes involved in theory of mind, and that these developments begin to have their effects during the preschool years.

In brief, theory of mind as usually considered is too narrowly construed, while those influences that lead to success on theory-of-mind measures are more general across development in different domains of social and general cognition. This argument has implications for domain theories in general, as well as for modularity and theory theories in the theory-of-mind area. Having construed theory of mind as a separate cognitive domain to begin with, researchers became vulnerable to claims of modules, and of domain-specific theories as explanations of its development. Meanwhile, aspects of development that are not domain-defined, including memory, language, inference, reasoning, concept formation, knowledge acquisition, and imagination, were considered ancillary "performance" factors. Most important, social experiences, including attachment, play, and conversation, have tended to be looked on as modulating factors that influence but do not determine the acquisition of theory of mind.

In addition, a novel developmental mechanism, implicit theory construction or theory revision, has been invented to explain development within this domain and has been extended to other areas of knowledge acquisition. Yet there has been no specification as to how an implicit theory could be constructed in infancy or early childhood or how it might relate to explicit theory construction or explicit knowledge in general. Some writers seem to take implicit theory construction to be essentially the same as general conceptual processes (and therefore a harmless usage), but others (Gopnik & Wellman, 1994; Wellman, 1988; Wellman & Gelman, 1992) make the larger claim that a theory, implicit or explicit, is coherent within a domain, is characterized by causal relations between its concepts, and is subject to revision in light of new data.

The theory approach has led to the description of a succeeding series of different theories that infants and young children are alleged to construct during the first 5 years of life, as illustrated in figure 2.1. Note that in this figure the data lie outside the theory, reflecting the presumption of an abstract epistemic structure separate from its experiential source. The guiding assumption seems to be that from birth (if not before), children have the same cognitive resources as ourselves (i.e., educated adults) for gathering and organizing data in the domain of psychological and social functioning and for forming and testing hypotheses—derived from causally connected theoretical structures—about these matters. I believe that this assumption is unwarranted and that it prevents researchers from entertaining both the breadth and the limitations of young children's knowledge sources in experience, as well as the breadth and limitations of their cognitive resources.

Theoretical approaches to this area other than the dominant "theory theory" propose various precursor abilities (e.g., attachment, pretense, executive function, meta-representation) as leading more or less directly, alone or in combination, to a successful achievement of theory of mind (Fonagy & Target, 1997; Frye, 1999; Leslie, 1987; Perner, 1991). Although this way of viewing the matter (illustrated in figure 2.2) has value in relating these earlier developments to the later understanding of false belief, the causal directions implied are theoreti-

$$\text{ToM}_1 \Longrightarrow \text{ToM}_2 \Longrightarrow \text{ToM}_3 \Longrightarrow \text{REAL ToM}$$
$$\quad\ \text{Data} \qquad\quad \text{Data} \qquad\quad \text{Data}$$

Figure 2.1. The theory view.

(Intersubjectivity) + (Self) + (Imagination) +

(Executive Function) + (Conversation)

 ToM

Figure 2.2. The generic development view.

cally and empirically vulnerable. It is not that any of these abilities are irrelevant to theory of mind; rather, it is the additivity assumption and the direct causal relation assumption that are in question here. All that has yet been shown is that some of these may be prerequisites to theory of mind; it has not been determined that they have a direct causal relation to its achievement. And, indeed, even the evidence that they are necessary if not sufficient is not really there.

The only ability that has clearly been shown to be directly related to theory-of-mind competence is language, in that children without language or with impoverished language do not achieve theory of mind, and neither do nonhuman primates that lack language. The present volume is devoted to uncovering why this is so.

In this chapter, I argue that the area under examination needs rethinking to bring it into its proper relation to the overall course of social and cognitive development during the crucial preschool years, and to the preceding as well as succeeding developments to which it has been related, theoretically or empirically. I believe that what is required is a developmental systems approach (Oyama, 1985) that indicates the interactions among the many and various social and cognitive processes as they develop. The most important development, the one with maximum impact on all social and cognitive functioning, is the acquisition of complex language—including semantics and syntax—and its use as a representational system in conveying and reflecting on knowledge, imaginative constructions, reminiscence, explanations, and other social and cultural, as well as cognitive, functions.

The metaphor that I propose to replace the theory metaphor ensconced in current terminology is the *Community of Minds*, and the developmental process I propose is that of *entering into the community of minds*, a process made possible through the use, comprehension, and production of language. In the first section I describe the construct of the community and its advantage over the theory construct. This conception was introduced in a paper by Nelson, Henseler, and Plesa (2000) and elaborated in Nelson et al. (2003). The second section of the chapter describes how the child proceeds, on the basis of general developmental processes but only with the aid of language, to begin to enter this community.

The Community of Minds

Assuming that during their first 10 years children are developing toward membership in a human community of minds broadens the concept of "theory of mind" from something that children invent for themselves (but that just happens to agree with everyone else's theory) to a cultural conception of what it is to be human within a human community. Importantly, the metaphor emphasizes two facets of this development: the concept of minds and the idea of community.

First, what is at stake is understanding—and thus basing predictions and explanations on—*minds* in the plural. Rather than putting the emphasis on the universal Mind, the emphasis is on minds that interact with and also differ from one another, as well as having certain similarities of structure and content. Ultimately, understanding differences among minds requires understanding the sources of differences among people—their backgrounds, personalities, relationships, and histories.

The main reason for "reading" minds is to interpret the difference between others' and one's own state of mind. Indeed, this is the first step toward entry into the community, and it begins as the child is exposed to what other people think in contrast to what the child thinks, which becomes possible through language in the early childhood years. At the beginning of life, a child has neither the concept of "mind" nor, therefore, any basis on which to believe that the contents of another's mind are any different from the child's own.

The second important emphasis in the metaphor is on the *community*. In work on theory of mind, typically the problem is posed as one of understanding the beliefs of other individuals on the basis of their actions or interpreting their actions on the basis of their beliefs. This is surely a useful component of social life, but the truly important understanding is far broader: it involves the myriad sources of beliefs, reasons for doubting beliefs, beliefs that are broadly held, beliefs that are held to be wrong, or that are held to be the truth, or that are held to be immoral. These are often matters of testimony (as Harris, 2000, 2001, has been investigating); they are the stuff of the knowledge and beliefs of the cultural community. These are where the minds interact and come to agreement and disagreement, and where matters of possibly great significance may result, for example, in the case of religious beliefs that bring one community into conflict with another.

As an example that has been used in theory-of-mind research, deception—lying—must be understood in its relation to cultural understandings and rules (Chandler, Fritz, & Hala, 1989; Polak & Harris, 1999; Sinclair, 1996). If it is just a question of my telling you that there are no more cookies so that I can sneak the last one into my room and eat it by myself, this may be seen as only a selfish way of achieving a personal goal. But in the context of the scarcity of food within a family or community, the lie takes on much greater significance. This is why parents, following the moral dictates of the community, place great stress on not telling lies; any lie in itself might be harmless, but the habit of lying is harmful to both the person and the community. Still, the 3-year-old who has just discovered the possibility of deception, the possibility that she may act one way and represent the opposite in language, has made a momentous discovery, one that is certainly related to achieving the conventional stage of theory of mind (Astington & Baird, this volume, chapter 1). Yet, in the Community of Minds this is held to be an unacceptable, even immoral, sometimes illegal, act, one that the child must learn to avoid. In the Community of Minds, that is, morality is not a domain separate from Mind, but it is foremost a domain of action and one that must be monitored. Morality itself, of course, is a matter of cultural, and linguistic, definitions, although there are clearly cultural universals, as well as cultural differences, in this area.

The Community of Minds depends inextricably on the capacity to talk about matters of interest to the members of the community, that is, to talk about things that are on members' minds. These may be matters of social relationships (gossip), political affairs, education, the natural world (weather, environmental disasters), economic affairs, literature and art, games and drama, reminiscences about the past, plans for the future, histories, myths, religious doctrine, moral principles, and other matters. In other words, the kinds of matters that are on people's minds in the community are as broad as life itself. In a literate world, some of the discussions of these matters are distributed through journals, newspapers, and books, as well as through electronic and audiovisual media.

Theory-of-mind theorists may protest that these are the various *contents* of belief, not the construct of belief itself (which it is alleged is what the child must attain). But it is precisely the fact that belief is always *about* something that is important; it is not a thing in itself. Children must come to understand the *contents* of belief, not primarily the concept of belief.[1] They acquire knowledge of procedures and actions that lead them to reason about whether someone could or does know about something that differs from one's own state of knowledge about that thing. It is this differentiation of another's states of knowledge from one's own that is the key to success on theory of mind, but the differentiation can be made only on the grounds of particular contents, not on the grounds of belief itself. Making these differentiations is a critical step in development, not only for discerning false belief in theory-of-mind tasks, and I return to discuss it later in the section on entering the Community of Minds.

Many theorists have attempted to place theory of mind in the context of specific human capacities evolved through natural evolutionary processes. For some, this involves a special brain module (e.g., Leslie, 1987), but others see it as a more general ability to deal with the demands of the social world, where social exchange requires vigilance against cheating, for example (Byrne & Whiten, 1988). These ideas are based in the widely accepted proposal that primates in general and humans in particular evolved large brains in response to the complexities of the relations involved in social groups. This is a reasonable assumption, based on the available evidence. However, it primarily accounts for one-to-one, face-to-face interactions and relations. What is specific to human life space is the proliferation of huge collections of individuals across space and time, and the cultural institutions and communicative systems, including language, devised to deal with these conditions. One-on-one relations may be typical of some family situations, but, in general, certainly in modern societies, social interactions involve collaborative and competitive groups of individuals, usually organized into institutions, such as religions, educational systems, economic systems, government systems, and so on within smaller and larger conglomerations.

The point here is that what has been studied in terms of theory of mind is a tiny step into generalizing one-on-one social understanding from the well-known intimate relations within the family to the same kind of relations among unfamiliar others (see Dunn & Brophy, this volume, chapter 3, for a discussion of the importance of intimate relations in theory-of-mind understanding). One might assume that once this kind of generalization is made, the way is open to begin to participate more competently in the concerns of the wider community. But it is possible that the particular one-to-one understanding involved in false belief is not a prerequisite but an outcome of understanding the concerns of the larger community. Conversations about the past between parents and children during the third and fourth years often concern issues of emotions and moral actions (Fivush, 1993, 1994). Parent-child conversations during book-reading also frequently include the interpretation of mental states of story characters (Harris, this volume, chapter 4). Such discussions may explicitly present the contrast between one character's beliefs and another's and may incorporate the norms of the community with respect to issues such as acting on one's desires and emotions.

These and other concerns of the community are displayed in communal narratives. Many theorists have suggested that language emerged during the prehistory of our species to support narratives, both gossip, talking about other people's stories (Dunbar, 1996), and myth, explaining matters of concern to the whole community (Donald, 1991). In both cases, such narratives incorporate the concerns with motivation, causation, and social distinctions that are embedded in theory of mind. In addition, they incorporate notions of temporality, the representation and manipulation of which is a unique aspect of human society. Complex, historically conscious societies construct elaborate structures for understanding time and its relation to the present. The young child has no access to these ways of thinking of time, but in the course of listening to the community's stories and conversing with its adults, the child finds that they come into focus in much the same way as constructs of mental states (Nelson, 1989, 1996). In the process, the child gains access to the concerns of the Community of Minds.

How to Enter the Community of Minds

The key to the door that opens into the Community of Minds lies in differentiating one's own private view of the world from that of others and joining in the common but variable mind-space there. The key question, then, is "How does that differentiation come about, in particular and in general?" Even as adults, we often assume that other people with whom we are communicating share our beliefs and background knowledge; we are often surprised to find that they do not. The very young child is different only in assuming that everyone has the same knowledge. Usually the way we discover that others' knowledge differs from ours is that they tell us. The core of the claim made here is that the young child learns the same way and thus gradually learns the general principle that people differ; the child also learns to track such differences when there are salient clues to be followed (as in theory-of-mind tasks).

In a complex, modern culture, children are bathed in verbal stuff from the beginning of life and begin to learn how to use pieces of the prevailing language between 1 and 2 years, but it is a few years more before they begin to tune into much of it or to begin to take part in its "mind exchange" system. Members of the community have special ways of talking about the activities of people in the community. They attribute thoughts to others ("he thinks it's a good idea to get out of the stock market now"), claim knowledge ("I know she's in town because I talked to her on the phone yesterday"), state beliefs ("I'm pretty sure it's going to be a long war"), and use mental-state language for many other purposes as well: "We're planning to go to the game on Saturday"; "I guess . . ."; "Remember when . . ."; "Imagine that. . . ."

To become a member of the community and enter into its "mind exchange system," children must learn the language of the mind. This is one of the prerequisites that language fulfills. But it is not the only one. Children must be able to understand not only that "think" and "know" and "remember" and so on refer to mental states but also that the propositions that follow these words represent the mental contents of the other (J. de Villiers, this volume, chapter 10; J. de Villiers & Pyers, 1997). They must become capable of turning someone else's statement about belief into their own mental representation of what the other believes. That is, they must be able to use language as a representational system. These are difficult accomplishments that require several years of experience with language in use.

Beginning Outside the Community

For the first several years of the child's life, all "knowledge" is strictly a private matter; that is, although it is acquired within a social world, its sources are those of individual perceptual mechanisms, primarily vision, supplemented by memory for individual experience, inference mechanisms, and constructive conceptual processes. It is not that the infant is a passive observer; infants actively explore as much as they are enabled to do by motor ability and parental restraints. But they are limited in their information-gathering to what their own perceptual and cognitive powers can glean. This proposition holds regardless of whether one assumes that infants have "built-in" knowledge of systems such as language, the physical world, or theory of mind and how that knowledge may be structured. Such "knowledge," to the extent that it exists and is available to all infants, is nonetheless private to each. It also holds despite the fact that the infant exists in a social world, is in intimate contact with others there, and has ways of communicating, sharing feelings through touch, facial and vocal expressions, and so on. The infant, however, has no way of either giving or receiving information about how she views the world, what she believes about its people, objects, and events, or other matters. Adults around the infant may attempt to read her mind and may even be successful in predicting what she wants and how she feels. But this is a chancy business on both sides.

During the second and third years, the child is able to use some active external mechanisms—imitation and play—to supplement those of observation and manipulation, but the interpretation of the meaning of what she experiences remains a private matter. We can think of the child as using observation to painstakingly construct a mental model of the world around her, but a model all from a single perspective, her own. The difference between this "baby model" and the parent's model is even greater than casual reflection might suggest. The world of the parents is an interpreted one; that is, it is a world of cultural scenes, situations, and artifacts, whose meaning is transparent to the adult, from the very structure and furnishing of the child's home and the appropriate clothing for an infant or child in the resident culture, to the significance of the toys that the child is given and the rituals, such as meals and bedtime, that the child is engaged in. The child's model of the world includes these things, but with only the personal, idiosyncratic meaning that personal babyish experience bestows upon them, in particular their relevance and function for the self.

As the child comes to learn words and receive verbal messages, the perspective of another may come into play. When Mother shouts NO! as the toddler reaches toward the electric socket, the child understands that the adult is opposing her own perspective on the activity. At first, as Fonagy and Target (1997) have argued, the way in which this perspective is perceived by the child may be emotionally disturbing, because, from the private mind view, there is only one reality, that of one's own experience. A mother's emotional reaction to one's actions may be especially frightening because it is merged with one's own disposition and action.

It is important, as Fonagy and Target emphasize, that the child can begin to distinguish the parent's desires and emotions from her own, and beginning language helps in achieving this distinction between the self and the significant other. In turn, this insight may be the beginning of seeing others as having goals different from one's own. Such a dual perspective does not require a two-mind view because the two goals or intentions are part of the representation of the single ongoing situation or scene. Perceiving another's goals does not imply conceiving of another's mind, nor does it imply imagining mother's beliefs as different from one's own. It does not, that is, require metarepresentation that is capable of tracking one representation in contrast to another. The conflicting goals are simply part of the same ongoing event. The child would have to get behind the goals to see why Mother is forbidding the child's intended actions in order to put the conflict on a mental rather than a behavioral plane.[2]

Becoming a Participant

In contrast to this view, the beginning of theory of mind is widely held to lie in the achievement of intersubjectivity in infancy, signaling the onset of a concept of intentionality of self and other (e.g., Tomasello, 1999). The milestones in infant development that provide the evidence for this attribution, in particular evidence of shared attention, and their significance for the ensuing phase of first language acquisition, are without doubt of real importance to the developments we are concerned with. However, I doubt that there is a direct route from such primitive intersubjectivity to a full-blown theory of mind. Rather, interaction in joint activities, involving the focus of other and self on the same object, for example, contributes directly to the successful achievements in motoric, communicative, and exploratory activities of the 10- to 12-month period of development. It allows sharing activities with another and taking different roles within the activity, as in feeding. It also allows the child to have a sense of sharing perception and action, while at the same time differentiating the self from the shared. It fosters the move toward associating the sounds of language with shared attention to objects and actions within those activities. It does not, however, require a concept of mind or minds. There is no evidence that children are cognitively tracking anything but the actions of self and other. The same can be said of the reciprocal imitation that is frequently observed (and studied) at this time (Meltzoff & Gopnik, 1993).

As for the somewhat later evidence of interpretation of another's *intention* in action, or in applying words to objects, as in Meltzoff's or Tomasello's work

(Meltzoff & Moore, 1999; Tomasello, 1999), the child's interpretation requires an implicit understanding of means-ends connections in others' as well as one's own actions but does not require attributing mental activity to another. It does not require that the child attribute to the other *thoughts* about a goal.

It is important to be clear here. These developments—shared attention, attributed intentionality, word learning—are important prerequisites for moving toward participation in the Community of Minds. But they are not yet evidence of participating in this community. The theoretical error arises, in my opinion, when they are treated as evidence of children's having some sort of theory of mind, although not yet a successful theory (Baron-Cohen, 2000; Gopnik, Capps, & Meltzoff, 2000). These theories, in different ways, project the same cognitive structures and functions in the infant as are assumed to exist in the older child or adult; thus, the descriptions of the child's accomplishments at 2 years are formulated in the favored cognitive science language of "theory of mind," although that theory lies in the distant future. I refer to this as the "analytic fallacy," whereby the characteristics of a completed structure are attributed to the system in development, for which the components may be quite different (Nelson, 1979, 1996). The general point is that disagreements here rest on interpretations from initial assumptions, not on any empirical evidence for intentional understanding.

In contrast, the claim here is that the understandings and practices of the infant and toddler period serve as background knowledge that enables the child to take part in the ongoing activities of that period, in particular, to learn basic language and thus to move on to the next point in the developmental sequence, when talk about causes and sequences with parents and others leads to encounters with the abstractions of mind talk. The teleology here of "moving on" is not in the child; the focus of the child is on the present, not on learning for the future. In sum, the existence of continuity in development does not justify the attribution of a nascent theory even before the alleged achievement of theory of mind.

Learning the Talk

Representing mental states and actions in language[3] requires abstraction from the real world of experience. This is not to say that mental states have no reality; but it is to say that they are abstract constructs designed to account for what we do mentally, to divide the domain of what we call cognition into convenient pieces for discussion. Like all bits of language, they take their meaning from the agreement within the community that they carve up and express a portion of reality in appropriate ways. For example, we can all commonly agree that we have memories and thus understand one another when a person says, "I remember X." But, going further, to divide up the domain of memory is far more controversial, even with scientific research to back up the divisions, as theoretical disagreements can attest (e.g., Schacter, 1992; Tulving, 1983). The point here is that to enter the Community of Minds, the child must learn the language of abstractions, where referents are matters of communal agreement on shared concepts, not material parts of the observable world (see also Montgomery, this volume, chapter 6). The language of the mind is of course only one aspect of the abstract and complex language of the community.

Considerable research is available on children's acquisition of the lexicon of mental states, especially words for beliefs (*think, know, guess*) but also words for perception (*see, hear*) and emotion (*happy, sad, angry*). Although the mental-state lexicon is far more extensive and dynamic than current studies generally reflect, the data available have indicated important conclusions about children's mastery of the focal terms (Bartsch & Wellman, 1995; Bretherton & Beeghly, 1982; Furrow, Moore, Davidge, & Chiasson, 1992; Johnson & Maratsos, 1977; Moore, Bryant, & Furrow, 1989; Shaw, 1999). First, children begin to use a variety of mental-state terms as early as 2 years, especially emotional and perceptual terms. Second, at 3 years, most children studied produce the focal cognitive terms *think* and *know* in the course of everyday conversations, at least occasionally. Third, it is not until about 4 years that children appear to use these terms to indicate specific mental states, distinguishing between the meanings of *think* and *know* on the basis of certainty. Fourth, it is not until the early school years that tests of comprehension show clear discrimination among the terms *think, know,* and *guess*. And even in the late elementary years, children do not demonstrate understanding of the full range of distinctive meanings of *know* (Booth & Hall, 1995).

This body of research has important implications for children's understanding of cultural concepts of mind that derive from our knowledge of semantics and the process of acquiring abstract word meanings. Many researchers assume that if the child responds appropriately to *think*, for example, in a test situation, that child understands the concept symbolized by the word. There are two problems with this assumption. First, the concepts behind these mental-state terms are invariably complex, with loosely associated meanings and uses, only some of which refer to mental states. They are used in conversation by adults in a variety of ways and contexts. Further, children begin to use the terms in restricted conversational contexts modeled on one or a few adult uses (Shaw, 1999). Second, the acquisition of meaning of abstract terms such as mental-state words is best conceptualized in terms of acquiring meaning from use (Montgomery, 2002; Montgomery, this volume, chapter 6; Nelson & Shaw, 2002). This is a gradual process that begins with appropriate uses in contexts where they have been used by adults, but the use by the child is "without meaning"—it is simply pragmatic. Subsequently, this use is extended to other contexts, and other uses by adults flag the attention of the child, who then gradually builds up an inferential understanding of what the term implies. Evidence for this process comes not only from recent research on the acquisition of mental-state terms but also research on other terms, such as temporal and causal relations, that do not have concrete referents (Levy & Nelson, 1994). (For recent evidence of the causal relation between mothers' use of mental-state terms, children's later uses, and their performance on theory-of-mind tasks, see Ruffman, Slade, & Crowe, 2002; also Harris, this volume, chapter 4).

We can conclude that children are attentive to the language of the mind from about 2 to 3 years but that its meanings are obscure at the outset and only gradually become clarified and distinctive. As Dunn (1988) has pointed out, children begin to be curious about people's intentions and emotions and to talk about them with family members from the age of 2 years or so. However, the fact that they talk about these matters, using the words of the mental, does not indicate that they have a concept of mind, much less a *theory* of mind, or even that they have concepts of thinking and knowing. These attributions are, I believe, overinterpretations of the data, based on the simplistic idea that children's language transparently expresses their thoughts and feelings.

The most plausible alternative interpretation is that children are eager to interact with others, others who talk about mental states, thus leading children to the topic. Woolfe, Want, and Siegel (2002) reported an important study of deaf children's delayed acquisition of theory of mind. They compared early sign language learners, who were children of deaf parents, with later sign learners, children of hearing and speaking parents, on pictorial theory-of-mind tasks. Early signers outperformed later signers, and the authors conclude that the critical explanatory factor was social understanding mediated by early experience in conversation (see P. de Villiers, this volume, chapter 13). This conclusion is highly consistent with the argument put forth here. That children are interested in talking about what lies behind actions, or why people attribute motives to others, and that they acquire some of the terminology for doing so, is an indication that they have entered a pathway that leads into the larger community of minds. However, it does not mean that they have arrived at that destination.

The following conversation between a 3½-year-old child and her mother, from Shaw's (1999) study of mental-state terms, provides insight into some of the gaps between words and concepts in the process of their acquisition.

Child K, 42 months, Meal Context, with Mother M

K: You know something?
M: What?
(Pause)
K: Let me think

(Pause)

K: What's her name again?

M: What?

K: What's her name again?

M: Who?

K: That girl

M: Who?

K: Don't you remember her?

K: You've seen her before

M: No

K: Yes

M: Where is she?

K: I don't know

M: Oh

K: I don't know her name

K: Somebody has a rocket

K: That can turn into a big rocket

M: Yeah?

K: (nods)

M: Who is this person?

K: I don't know her

M: Where'd you meet her?

K: At our house!

M: At our house?

M: Somebody with a rocket came to our house?

K: Uh huh

M: Was I home for this?

K: (shakes head)

M: No

M: So how would I know who this is?

M: How do you know she had a rocket?

K: Cause she told us

M: Oh, okay

M: Was this Katie?

K: (nods)

M: Oh, okay

Notice that this conversation is about something the child remembers but of which the mother has no knowledge. The child (K) opens the dialogue by asking, "You know something?" This is a purely pragmatic conversational device. She then continues, "let me think"; again, this is a familiar conversational device. She then asks her mother what the name of someone is, and the following turns are efforts to jog the mother's memory, including K's assumption that her mother should know the girl because she's seen her before, which is of course a good clue to knowledge. However, her mother has no clue as to which girl among many she's seen that K has in mind. Then follows the revelation that this person had a rocket "at our house." After four more turns, K acknowledges that mother wasn't home when the rocket episode occurred, and Mother asks, "so how would I know who this is?" In what follows after an irrelevant bit of talk, K acknowledges that she knew about the rocket because the girl told her, again relevant evidence of knowledge. On some basis obscure to us, Mother now "reads K's mind" and guesses the name of the child.

We know from this transcript that K has a reasonably extensive lexicon of cognitive mental-state terms: *know, remember,* and *think.* But it is also clear that she has not quite put together how shared knowledge comes into being. She knows that she cannot remember the name and that her mother knows the name, but, in trying to jog her mother's memory, she mentions an episode that the mother could not know about because she was not there. The bottom line here is that knowing about knowing is highly complex and that children who facilely use the language of the mind may have a very incomplete grasp of how real-world experience maps onto the abstract theoretical structure of the concepts they are invoking with their language.

The most important point revealed in this excerpt is that the conversation itself provides evidence for the child about the missing pieces of her concepts of knowing, as the mother feeds back her own ignorance of what the child is trying to uncover. The child is confused about the private and public status of experience-based knowledge, and her mother points this out quite clearly. Indeed, learning the meanings of words for talking about mind-stuff depends entirely on listening to the talk of others on these topics. For this reason, the practice of comprehension—listening, attending, and interpreting—is even more important for the child in this process than expressing one's own thoughts, although the latter is helpful in guiding adults in how to take advantage of the state of the child's knowledge. This point is considered further in the next section.

Representing in Language

Although learning the right words and how they are used in talking about mental processes is helpful in following mind talk, the most important achievement in language for entering the cultural community of minds is facility with language as a representational medium. This point seems to be where misconceptions of the significance of language to theory of mind are most pervasive, and it therefore requires elaboration. Several studies carried out at the City University of New York (CUNY) by my former students have contributed to our understanding of this development, which I will be drawing on in the discussion of representational language. I first want to clarify what we mean by representational language.

Most uses of language by the child up to about 2½ years, during the time when basic vocabulary and simple grammar are being acquired, are highly pragmatic, about the here and now, focused mostly on the interpersonal functions of speech, not on the mathetic, ideational, or cognitive functions. But despite the relative poverty of the 2-year-old's productive and receptive language, parents (at least middle-class Western parents) typically begin addressing fairly complex ideas, descriptions, and explanations in extended passages of speech to their children when they are as young as 18 months to 2 years. Such talk may include reference to sources of knowledge (such as seeing and hearing about), to the differentiation of one's own and other's knowledge and experience (as in the excerpt from K's dialogue), or the distinction between imagined action and real action, and other matters of testimony (Harris, 2001).

These practices have been studied especially in relation to parents' talk about the past in studies of children's emerging memory for experienced events (see Nelson & Fivush, 2004). Two-year-olds typically contribute one or a few words, perhaps a single observed fact, to these conversations, but they often listen attentively as mothers spin out a remembered episode through questions and elaborations (Reese, 2000). What is going on here? The listeners (and not all children are attentive listeners) are entering into the practice of listening, attending, and interpreting extended speech—episodes of the use of language as a representing medium. The words and sentences ideally evoke for both speaker and hearer an event from a different time and place. What is represented may be a remembered real occasion of an interesting experience, an imagined unreality in play, a fictional story, an explanation of a museum exhibit, or any other topic that the parent thinks the child is or should be interested in. In these extended passages, parents, of course, use complex grammatical constructions, abstract words, references to things, places, people, and events that the child has no other knowledge about, and so on. This is the language of the cultural world, the educational world, and the Community of Minds, where learning, knowing, and remembering are as important as, perhaps more important than, predictions and explanations about other people's actions. And, of course, pretense and stories are organized around the very matters that theory of mind measures—what people want, plan, think, and know in relation to what they do, and their emotional states in response to the outcomes of actions.

Bruner (1986) emphasized the distinction between two kinds of thought: paradigmatic and narrative, a distinction that has proved to be useful in analyzing how parents and children talk about events (Nelson, 1996; Tessler & Nelson, 1994). Bruner further pointed out that narrative is composed not only of a sequence of actions but also of intentions and goals, what he calls the landscape of consciousness, in contrast to the landscape of action. The landscape of consciousness is concerned with beliefs and thoughts, possibilities, temporality, motives (e.g., love, revenge, jealousy), emotions (e.g., surprise, outrage, happiness, disappointment), plans, goals, deception, and so on—in other words, the meanings behind the actions, meanings that might be in the minds of one actor but not another.

Over the past 20 years or so, the study of narrative thinking, understanding, and production by children as well as adults has become a focal topic among many developmental psychologists (e.g., Bamberg, 1997). Analyses of children's spontaneous narratives (Miller, Potts, Fung, Hoogstra, & Mintz, 1990; Nelson, 1989), elicited narratives (Fivush, 1994; Plesa, 2001) and story recall (Henseler, 2000) converge on the conclusion that prior to about 5 years of age, children include very little of the landscape of consciousness in their narrative productions, relying instead on the landscape of action, although they usually can report more of the motivations and emotions when prompted and when asked to recall a story that has been read to them. Despite extensive practice at story listening over the years from 3 to 5, most children seem to find the action in their own narratives of "what happened" to them, or in a made-up story, to be self-explanatory and to need little explanation in terms of mindfulness. Even 6-year-olds, when asked to recall the narrative after watching a video based on a version of the Maxi task story in which the motives for moving the desirable object were ambiguous, provided a simple action sequence and did not explain the action in terms of motivations, beliefs, desires, or emotions (Plesa, 2001).

At CUNY, we have become alerted to the possible significance of receptive language competence through finding that receptive language, as measured by standardized tests, related more highly than expressive language to verbal memory for an event, story understanding, narrative productions, and, according to some studies, theory-of-mind tasks. In a study of episodic memory in 3- and 4-year-olds, Walkenfeld (2000) used a clinical evaluation of language, the TELD, which includes measures of expressive and receptive components, to evaluate the relation between language and recall of a complex novel event after a 6-week delay. The study compared the effects of verbal reinstatement midway through the delay period with those of re-enactment of the event and of no interim re-experience. The difference between groups mildly favored the verbal reinstatement condition, but the main story was the influence of language ability on performance. Receptive language, entered as a control variable, was highly significant, overriding group differences. In regression analyses, age was not predictive of recall when entered with language, and receptive rather than expressive language was a significant predictor of both recall and narrative coherence. Episodic or autobiographical memory for a complex event demands connected and extended representations, involving temporal and causal connections, and attributions of personal involvement and actions. These are also the kinds of representations that are required in theory-of-mind studies, although the typical events used in such studies are shorter and less personally involving than events used in memory studies.

Listening to stories requires mastery of the representational language of narrative even more than does episodic memory in that psychological causal factors are usually involved and are either implicit or made explicit through descriptive and explanatory language. Listening to stories is therefore an important passage along the road to the Community of Minds. Indeed, in listening to stories, the child must become expert at hearing and retaining a passage of speech long enough to interpret its meaning as a whole and then to connect it to succeeding passages to understand a whole episode. In other words, story understanding requires the use of language as an *internal* personal representation, one derived from the external presentation. Further, the story is about something that is removed from the here and now, and from the child's own experience, possibly about something that is totally unreal, a product of the imagination of the author. This requires the child to represent in mind a reality that is at odds with the known and present reality.

Our assumption is that mental representations of this kind are not possible without the use of representational language and that therefore children's relative degree of language skill, as measured by standard tests, should be related to their understanding of story themes and characters. As expected, Fontaine's (2002) study of 4- and 5-year-olds' story understanding and representation with different story genres (fantasy and reality) found that receptive language was a significant predictor for both story understanding and understanding of the relation of fantasy and reality in stories. Henseler's (2000) study required 3- to 5-year-old children to produce a memory narrative of an experience of playing a game with another child. Children were also given a story recall task, a theory-of-mind task, and a standard language development test. Again, receptive language was found to significantly predict narrative productions, game recounting, and story recall. Total language scores, and not age, predicted theory-of-mind performance. Several additional findings bear on theory-of-mind issues. First, no child, even at 5 years, included references to mental states in recounting the game, although during the game the experimenter had used mental-state language extensively (e.g., what do you *think* is in the box?). This is consistent with previous findings that it is not until middle childhood that children usually include mental states in spontaneous narratives. Some children did include mental-state terms in their recall of the story, however, including variants of the terms used by the author; use of mental terms in this context was associated with age, rather than language scores.

In each of these studies, strong relations between receptive language and measures of story understanding and narrative productions were found, despite the fact that all of the data relied on the child's expressive language skills. This discrepancy implies that the variation in comprehension of linguistic representations among children of similar ages accounts for differences in their ability to remember, reason about, or understand complex relations between the matters presented in this form. Put this way, the conclusion appears obvious—language is necessary to perform on language-dependent tasks, such as theory of mind, that rely on verbally presented stories, recall, and answering questions as data. As suggested throughout this chapter, however, I am claiming that the relation is stronger than that and that higher-level cognitive skills require the ability to operate with linguistic representations.

Why might there be a particular relation between receptive language and the achievement of higher levels of the cognitive functions of language? On reflection, it is obvious that the basic requirement of engaging in those higher levels is the ability to represent alternative possibilities; two different states of the world (e.g., the past and the present); two different understandings or experiences, one's own and another's; two different beliefs; an imagined state and a real state. The suggestion here is that this duality of representations, enabling one to hold in mind two conflicting possibilities, becomes possible through the internalization of language as a cognitive representational tool. Initially, this move may come about through talk about the there and then, contrasting a language representation of the past with the present experience of reality, and discussions about past experience are common with children as young as 2 years (Fivush, 1994).

A further move is the contrast of two mental representations, as required in theory-of-mind tasks. In the theory-of-mind literature, these moves have been illustrated as "mind pictures" representing scenes where one person is thinking that another person is thinking (Perner, 1991; Wellman, 1990). Under the present analysis, such pictures are misleading; rather, internal linguistic representations enable the duality of beliefs to be entertained. The proposed sequence of development in brief is as follows: through relevant conversational experiences, the child is exposed to increasingly complex and extended uses of representational language and comes to master the skills, involving short-term memory and semantic interpretation—that are necessary for the comprehension of such linguistically formulated messages. Next, the child becomes capable of repeating to self or others what has been heard on the same or a later occasion. (This is reflected in tests of receptive language. It also appears in the repetition of stories or of other people's experiential reports.) Then the child may begin to use verbal representations both to compose stories or reminiscences (reflected in expressive language) and to serve as internal cognitive representations, enabling the duality of mental representations.

Children of 4 and 5 years have usually learned to "receive" information in story form and to remember it for future telling to a greater extent than they have learned to turn a memory of their own experience into a tale for the tell-ing, including the mental states of the characters involved. Such an asymmetry may help in understanding how children enter into the Community of Minds. What we don't know is what the relation is between the memory for the story and its use in further cognitive operations. Researchers often assume that young children are very good at story understanding and recall, to the extent that they use these modes in research on theory-of-mind and other complex tasks. Such studies should at least include a measure of language competence to determine to what extent children's performance on the task of interest is in fact a prod-uct of their skill in story understanding. Certainly, receptive language ability is a factor in story recall and story understanding, as the studies summarized here have shown.

At the very least, good performance on tests of receptive language, even of receptive vocabulary, such as the PPVT, is an indication of extensive experience with talking with adults about complex topics in extended discourse formats. Given the assumption that such discussions are a potent source of information about the relation of mental states to people's actions, as well as many other matters of interest to the Community of Minds, the relation between receptive language and various cognitive tasks becomes very understandable.

Finally, it should be noted that, to the extent that experience with narra-tives in stories or conversations is found to be critical to children's achievement of theory of mind, the case for beginning with an understanding of the relation of mental states to action among people in stories, that is, people symbolically represented, becomes plausible. It is within a narrative that differential under-standings and motivations are highlighted as crucial to understanding the goals and means to achieve them that constitute the plot of a story. This understand-ing then may in turn be generalized to singular examples that the child meets on a one-to-one basis in everyday experiential contexts.

Paths Leading into the Community of Minds

On the basis of the varying evidence and theoretical propositions presented here, I am proposing a different developmental scheme than those sketched earlier to illustrate the theory view (figure 2.1) and the generic developmen-tal view (figure 2.2). Here (figure 2.3), I envision the child moving along an experiential pathway, acquiring new skills, socializing with family members and others, and gradually developing insights into intentional action, reflect-ing on self, and then breaking through into language. What follows that break-through is not an immediate grasp of all that the Community of Minds has to offer, of course, but it significantly broadens experience, especially social ex-perience and experience of the symbolically organized world and of abstract concepts not accessible except through language, such as the concept of mind.

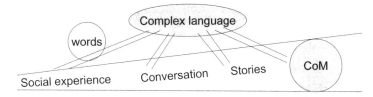

Figure 2.3. Pathways to the community of minds.

Equipped with complex, representational language, the child can participate in story listening, talk about her own experiences in the past and the future, and speculate with others about why things are the way they are, including why people do the things they do. This is the entry point into the Community of Minds, and the community enthusiastically welcomes all the children who enter there, ushering them forthwith into formal schooling, the acquisition of literacy, and complex cultural knowledge, including theories about the world.

Conclusion: Why Language Matters

Language matters because theory of mind is not an individual possession but part of a communally shared belief system about human goals, aspirations, motivations, knowledge systems, and value systems. The cognitive effects of linguistic communication are uniquely human and are set in place during the preschool years in normal development. Those who for one reason or another do not have these experiences (deaf children, autistic children) may linger on the outskirts of the community, able to participate only with difficulty. They may reason their way through certain tasks, but they do so using cognitive skills other than those of the normally developing 5-year-old.

Charles Taylor (1985, p. 263) said it very well: "there are three things that get done in language:

- making articulations, and hence bringing about explicit awareness;
- putting things in public space, thereby constituting public space;
- making the discriminations which are foundational to human concerns, and hence opening us to these concerns."

Although all of these are involved in the child's coming into the consciousness that language allows, it is the last, opening up to the concerns of the community, that I believe is most significant. It takes the child beyond his own private concerns and beliefs and opens up the possibility of understanding the concerns, and thereby the beliefs, of others in the Community of Minds.

Acknowledgments I would like to acknowledge with grateful appreciation the invaluable contributions of Sylvie Goldman, Sarah Henseler, Daniela Plesa Skwerer, Nechama Presler, Lea Kessler Shaw, and Faye Fried Walkenfeld for the projects and ideas reported in this essay.

Notes

1. ToM theorists may argue that it is not possible to understand the contents without the concept of belief. I believe this may be based on a conflation of the language of belief with the concept of belief. The child may learn to use the terms "think" or "know" in complement constructions indicating his or her own state of belief without having the requisite insight that this construction refers to a generalized concept of a kind of mental attitude toward the contents. Consider the following exchange: Mother: "Where are your shoes?" Child: "I know! They're in the closet." Here the child is accessing a belief (where the shoes are) and using the expression "I know." Next: Mother looks in the closet and does not find them, then says: "I think they're in the kitchen—I remember seeing them there." Child: "I'll get them," moving to the kitchen. What in this exchange requires us to assume that the child has a concept of belief, although she both expresses her own belief and interprets the expression (I think) by Mother? The position I take is that the concept of belief may be constructed on the basis of experience of many such exchanges but does not require at the outset the existence of such a concept in order to first compare one's own belief with the conflicting statement of another's belief state. Indeed, I find it hard to understand how a child could construct the concept of belief without the experience of using language that expresses such differences.

2. Again, ToM theorists may argue otherwise, but consideration of animal conflicts suggests that simple differences in goals and intentions do not necessarily lead to entertaining the possibility of conflicting mental states. (See Byrne & Whiten, 1988, for discussion of similar issues in regard to other primates.)

3. The assumption here is that there is no other way to represent them. The contrasting generally accepted assumption that concepts (representations) must be present prior to their appearance in language cannot be right for mental state and many other abstract concepts, as I implicitly argue in what follows.

References

Bamberg, M. (Ed.), (1997). *Narrative development: Six approaches*. Mahwah, NJ: Erlbaum.

Baron-Cohen, S. (2000). Theory of mind and autism: a fifteen-year review. In S. Baron-Cohen, H. Tager-Flusberg, & D. J. Cohen (Eds.), *Understanding other minds: Perspectives from developmental cognitive neuroscience* (pp. 3–20). Oxford: Oxford University Press.

Bartsch, K., & Wellman, H. M. (1995). *Children talk about the mind*. New York: Oxford University Press.

Booth, J. R., & Hall, W. S. (1995). Development of the understanding of the polysemous meanings of the mental state verb *know. Cognitive Development, 10,* 529–550.

Bretherton, I., & Beeghly, M. (1982). Talking about internal states: The acquisition of an explicit theory of mind. *Developmental Psychology, 18,* 906–921.

Bruner, J. S. (1986). *Actual minds, possible worlds.* Cambridge, MA: Harvard University Press.

Byrne, R., & Whiten, A. (Eds.). (1988). *Machiavellian intelligence.* Oxford: Oxford University Press.

Chandler, M., Fritz, A., & Hala, S. (1989). Deception as a marker of 2-year-olds', 3-year-olds', and 4-year-olds' early theories of mind. *Child Development, 60,* 1263–1277.

de Villiers, J. G., & Pyers, J. (1997). Complementing cognition: The relationship between language and theory of mind. In E. Hughes, M. Hughes, & A. Greenhill (Eds.), *Proceedings of the 21st Annual Boston University Conference on Language Development* (pp. 136–147). Somerville, MA: Cascadilla Press.

Donald, M. (1991). *Origins of the modern mind.* Cambridge, MA: Harvard University Press.

Dunbar, R. (1996). *Grooming, gossip and the evolution of language.* Boston: Faber & Faber.

Dunn, J. (1988). *The beginnings of social understanding.* Cambridge, MA: Harvard University Press.

Fivush, R. (1993). Emotional content of parent-child conversations about the past. In C. A. Nelson (Ed.), *Memory and affect in development* (Vol. 26, pp. 39–77). Hillsdale, NJ: Erlbaum.

Fivush, R. (1994). Constructing narrative, emotion, and self in parent-child conversations about the past. In U. F. Neisser, R. (Ed.), *The remembering self: Construction and accuracy in the self-narrative* (pp. 136–157). New York: Cambridge University Press.

Fonagy, P., & Target, M. (1997). Attachment and reflective function: Their role in self-organization. *Development and Psychopathology, 9,* 679–700.

Fontaine, R. G. (2002). Children's understanding of story: The influence of genre, affect and language. Unpublished Ph.D. dissertation, City University of New York Graduate School, New York.

Frye, D. (1999). Development of intention: The relation of executive function to theory of mind. In P. D. Zelazo, J. W. Astington, & D. R. Olson (Eds.). (1999), *Developing theories of intention: Social understanding and self-control* (pp. 119–131). Mahwah, NJ: Erlbaum.

Furrow, D., Moore, C., Davidge, I., & Chiasson, L. (1992). Mental terms in mothers' and children's speech: Similarities and relationships. *Journal of Child Language, 19,* 617–632.

Gopnik, A., Capps, L., & Meltzoff, A. N. (2000). Early theories of mind: What the theory theory can tell us about autism. In S. Baron-Cohen, H. Tager-Flusberg, & D. J. Cohen (Eds.), *Understanding other minds: Perspectives from developmental cognitive neuroscience* (pp. 50–72). Oxford: Oxford University Press.

Gopnik, A., & Wellman, H. (1994). The theory theory. In L. A. Hirschfeld & S. A. Gelman (Eds.), *Mapping the mind* (pp. 257–293). New York: Cambridge University Press.

Harris, P. L. (2000). *The work of the imagination.* Oxford: Blackwell.

Harris, P. L. (2001). Thinking about the unknown. *Trends in Cognitive Science, 5,* 494–498.

Henseler, S. (2000). Young children's developing theory of mind: Person reference, psychological understanding and narrative skill. Unpublished Ph.D. dissertation, City University of New York Graduate Center, New York.

Johnson, C. N., & Maratsos, M. P. (1977). Early comprehension of mental verbs: Think and know. *Child Development, 48,* 1743–1747.

Leslie, A. M. (1987). Pretense and representation: The origins of "theory of mind." *Psychological Review, 94,* 412–426.

Levy, E., & Nelson, K. (1994). Words in discourse: A dialectical approach to the acquisition of meaning and use. *Journal of Child Language, 21,* 367–390.

Meltzoff, A. N., & Gopnik, A. (1993). The role of imitation in understanding persons and developing theories of mind. In S. Baron-Cohen, H. Tager-Flusberg, & D. J. Cohen (Eds.), *Understanding other minds: Perspectives from autism* (pp. 335–366). Oxford: Oxford University Press.

Meltzoff, A. N., & Moore, M. K. (1999). A new foundation for cognitive development in infancy: The birth of the representational infant. In E. K. Scholnick, K. Nelson, S. A. Gelman, & P. H. Miller (Eds.), *Conceptual development: Piaget's legacy* (pp. 53–78). Mahwah, NJ: Erlbaum.

Miller, P. J., Potts, R., Fung, H., Hoogstra, L., & Mintz, J. (1990). Narrative practices and the social construction of self in childhood. *American Ethnologist, 17,* 292–311.

Montgomery, D. E. (2002). Mental verbs and semantic development. *Journal of Cognition and Development, 3,* 357–384.

Moore, C., Bryant, D., & Furrow, D. (1989). Mental terms and the development of certainty. *Child Development, 60,* 167–171.

Nelson, K. (1979). Explorations in the development of a functional semantic system. In W. Collins (Ed.), *Children's language and communication: Minnesota symposium on child psychology* (Vol. 12, pp. 47–81). Hillsdale, NJ: Erlbaum.

Nelson, K. (Ed.). (1989). *Narratives from the crib.* Cambridge, MA: Harvard University Press.

Nelson, K. (1996). *Language in cognitive development: The emergence of the mediated mind.* New York: Cambridge University Press.

Nelson, K., & Fivush, R. (2004). The emergence of autobiographical memory: A social cultural developmental theory. *Psychological Review, 111,* 486–511.

Nelson, K., Henseler, S., & Plesa, D. (2000). Entering a community of minds: A Feminist perspective on theory of mind development. In P. Miller & E. S. Scholnick (Eds.), *Toward a Feminist Developmental Psychology* (pp. 61–83). New York: Routledge.

Nelson, K., Plesa, D., Goldman, S., Henseler, S., Presler, N., & Walkenfeld, F. F. (2003). Entering a community of minds: An experiential approach to "theory of mind." *Human Development, 46,* 24–46.

Nelson, K., & Shaw, L. K. (2002). Developing a socially shared symbolic system. In E. Amsel & J. Byrnes (Eds.), *Language, literacy and cognitive development: The development and consequences of symbolic communication* (pp. 27–58). Mahwah, NJ: Erlbaum.

Oyama, S. (1985). *The ontogeny of information: Developmental systems and evolution.* New York: Cambridge University Press.

Perner, J. (1991). *Understanding the representational mind.* Cambridge, MA: MIT Press.

Plesa, D. (2001). Children's early construals of subjectivity: Understanding the interpretive mind. Unpublished Ph.D. dissertation, City University of New York Graduate School, New York.

Polak, A. & Harris, P. L. (1999). Deception by young children following non-compliance. *Developmental Psychology, 35*, 561–568.

Reese, E. (2000, March). A model of the origins of autobiographical memory. Memory Research Theme Symposium: Memory development: Biological, cognitive and social perspectives. University of Dunedin, New Zealand.

Ruffman, T., Slade, L., & Crowe, E. (2002). The relation between children's and mothers' mental state language and theory-of-mind understanding. *Child Development, 73*, 734–751.

Schacter, D. L. (1992). Understanding implicit memory. *American Psychologist, 47*, 559–569.

Shaw, L. K. (1999). The development of the meanings of "think" and "know" through conversation. Unpublished Ph.D. dissertation, City University of New York Graduate Center, New York.

Sinclair, A. (1996). Young children's practical deceptions and their understanding of false belief. *New Ideas in Psychology, 14*, 157–173.

Taylor, C. (1985). *Philosophy and the human sciences: Philosophical papers.* (Vol. 1). Cambridge: Cambridge University Press.

Tessler, M., & Nelson, K. (1994). Making memories: The influence of joint encoding on later recall. *Consciousness and Cognition, 3*, 307–326.

Tomasello, M. (1999). Having intentions, understanding intentions, and understanding communicative intentions. In P. D. Zelazo, J. W. Astington, & D. R. Olson (Eds.), *Developing theories of intention: Social understanding and self-control* (pp. 63–76). Mahwah, NJ: Erlbaum.

Tulving, E. (1983). *Elements of episodic memory.* New York: Oxford University Press.

Walkenfeld, F. F. (2000). Reminder and language effects on preschoolers' memory reports: Do words speak louder than actions? Unpublished Ph.D. dissertation, City University of New York Graduate School, New York.

Wellman, H. M. (1988). First steps in the child's theorizing about the mind. In J. W. Astington, P. L. Harris, & D. R. Olson (Eds.), *Developing theories of mind* (pp. 64–92). New York: Cambridge University Press.

Wellman, H. M. (1990). *The child's theory of mind.* Cambridge, MA: MIT Press.

Wellman, H. M., & Gelman, S. A. (1992). Cognitive development: Foundational theories of core domains. *Annual Review of Psychology, 43*, 337–375.

Woolfe, T., Want, S. C., & Siegal, M. (2002). Signposts to development: Theory of mind in deaf children. *Child Development, 73*, 768–778.

3 Communication, Relationships, and Individual Differences in Children's Understanding of Mind

Judy Dunn and Marcia Brophy

The issues that we discuss in this chapter center on the relations between children's talk and conversations and the development of their mind-reading abilities. Two particular interests frame the way we examine these connections. The first concerns the development of close relationships. The discoveries children make about others' inner states are central to the development of their relationships. No one who has been around children between 18 months and 3 years of age can fail to be impressed by the extraordinary blooming of children's sophistication in their relationships over this period. During their second and third years they become increasingly effective *teasers, deceivers, jokers, comforters, antagonists* in battles of will, *conspirators,* and (if you are lucky) *conciliators* in conflict and companions in *shared fantasy.* Centrally implicated in these developments are both their growing powers of communication and their increasingly mature understanding of emotion and, during their third year, of mind. Each feature of their close relationships—whether it is shared amusement, fantasy, intentional deceit or attempt to avoid blame or conflict, conversations about the state of the world, or narratives about shared experiences in past and future—illustrates how closely communicative skills and understanding of mind are linked.

So the normative developmental story of children's close relationships vividly shows us the intimate association between language and mind-reading and indeed sets up a framework for thinking about the nature of the links between the two. K. Nelson has emphasized that language provides a pathway into the community of minds (Nelson, this volume, chapter 2). We argue that a key entry into that community of minds may be through the experience of communication within close dyadic relationships—that communicative experiences within close, familiar relationships play an especially important role in the development of understanding of emotion and mind. We are concerned both with the concurrent relations among language, social understanding, and relationships and with the antecedent and consequent associations among these domains over time. Note that the focus here is upon the implications for theory of mind of the *communicational* aspects of language (the argument being that children become aware of people's mental states in part through conversations and stories), rather than the *representational* aspect of language (the argument that the development of prepositional language allows children to think about what is in people's minds when they [mis]represent the world).

The second interest that frames the chapter is a concern with individual differences in each of these domains. Why a focus on individual differences? Wellman, Cross, and Watson's (2001) meta-analysis has, after all, established that there is an impressive consistency across samples, studies, and countries in research on the normative course of the achievement of success on theory-of-mind tasks. If all children "pass" false-belief tasks by the age of 4 to 5 years, why study individual differences? Two reasons stand out, rather different in their implications. One is the developmental question of whether early abilities in social understanding are linked to later outcome differences—that is, whether being a "star" at reading minds and emotions as a preschooler sets a child off on a trajectory toward later skills—whether there are later sequelae of significance associated with early sophistication in mind-reading and what social processes might be implicated in such developmental patterns. The second is the more immediate issue of how children in fact "use" their theory-of-mind abilities in their real-life interactions. We know that children differ in their sensitivity to others' emotions, in their ability to comfort, in their insights into others' actions, in their close relationships. How are these real-life differences in social understanding related to performance on cognitive assessments, and what governs these associations? What contribution do individual differences in conversational and narrative skills, for instance, make to individual differences in mind-reading in real-life interactions?

Within the framework of this interest in individual differences, then, we consider here two issues. The first, the main issue with which this chapter is concerned, centers on the links between theory of mind and communication. Specifically, does conversation matter for the early development of theory of mind, and vice versa? If it does, then what aspects of conversational experiences are implicated? The second issue, which is discussed more briefly, concerns the developmental patterns and processes implicated beyond the early preschool years. What are the links between early theory of mind and later outcomes? Do the links among language, emotion, and mind-reading change as children grow up? Can a relationship approach illuminate the developmental patterns over these years?

A focus on individual differences in communication and understanding of other minds highlights some key lessons and questions about the social processes implicated in children's discovery of the mind. Central to these lessons is the notion that we need to look at children's language not solely as a cognitive skill or as an individual characteristic but also as a reflection of their participation in the social processes implicated in the development of understanding of mind. In what follows we raise a series of questions for discussion and highlight some cautions about inferences to be made from the evidence available on each of these issues.

Does Conversation Matter for Theory of Mind?

Are Individual Differences in Verbal Ability and in Theory-of-Mind Performance Correlated in Cross-Sectional Research?

As a starting point, it is evident that individual differences in children's grasp of theory of mind are marked in the third and fourth years of life, whether these abilities are assessed in terms of standard tasks such as false-belief tasks or in terms of how children use these abilities in real-life activities—for example, by deceit, in causal talk about why people behave the way they do, or in the sharing of imaginary worlds in joint fantasy (Dunn, Brown, Slomkowski, Tesla, & Youngblade, 1991; Dunn & Cutting, 1999). In a parallel fashion, individual differences in language development over this period are also marked (Hardy-Brown, 1983; Plomin & Dale, 2000; Shore, 1995). And repeated studies have reported correlations between theory-of-mind abilities and language scores, in both normal samples and in samples of children with various disabilities (for example, Happé, 1995; Jenkins & Astington, 1996). In a sample of children from widely differing family backgrounds, Cutting and Dunn (1999) found that language ability made a significant contribution to false-belief understanding and emotion understanding, independent of age and family background. The intractable questions of *how* precisely language may contribute to the understanding of mind and *vice versa* remain in need of clarification—cross-sectional correlational studies draw our attention to the intimate links between the two but can only take us so far. They cannot specify the causal links between them. It is evident that many standard assessments of emotion understanding and theory of mind are language-based. In focusing on these associations, are we simply picking up on differences in children's language abilities? Moreover, does it make sense to assume that there is some part of children's understanding of mind that can be assessed separately from their linguistic ability? The conventional approach of examining correlations between aspects of social cognition and partialing out the correlations of language with each may well be misleading in its implication that there is some portion of children's cognitive ability to be assessed separately from their linguistic experience that will give us a "pure" assessment of their understanding of mind. It is here that there may be some lessons to be learned from the longitudinal studies of individual differences.

Is Participation in Discourse about Inner States Linked to Later Success on Theory-of-Mind Tasks?

Does children's participation in discourse that explicitly refers to inner states have a significance for the development of understanding of mind, beyond the association between verbal ability and mind-reading? It is particularly clear in the work on emotion understanding and language that children start to ask questions about and comment on emotions as soon as they can talk. And the acquisition of language makes it possible for children to focus on and reflect on emotional experiences, through talk with others. They can share their experiences of emotions with others, and "be with" others in a new way. They can begin to appreciate others' feelings in a new way and to differentiate between their own and others' emotions. Being able to talk about feelings and thoughts leads children to participate in the shared cultural concepts of feelings in their particular culture and to talk about past inner states. We are language users, and talk about emotions and the mind is a major channel through which we come to understand our own inner states and those of others.

We know from a range of studies that children who grew up in families in which mental states and feelings were discussed, and who participated in such talk, over time performed more successfully on assessments of understanding mind and emotion. These studies draw on samples that include children growing up in rural and small-town America (Dunn, Brown, Slomkowski, et al., 1991), in very low income, chiefly African American families (Garner, Jones, Gaddy, & Rennie, 1997), families in deprived inner-city areas of London (Hughes & Dunn, 1997), urban samples that range in socioeconomic background (Cutting & Dunn, 1999), and middle- and working-class families in Cambridge, UK, and surrounding rural areas (Dunn, Brown, & Beardsall, 1991). Regression approaches have shown that the participation in such discourse about inner states plays a role in explaining later individual differences that is independent of other contributing factors (e.g., the interaction between other family members that is witnessed by the child or the child's experience of cooperative play with a sibling; see later discussion). A plausible, common-sense case can be made for why such talk that makes explicit the links between inner states and people's emotions or actions may be important in the growth of children's understanding of the mind.

But several notes of caution are in order here. First, we need to examine such conversations further, to gain precision about what *matters* in such discourse in terms of children's discovery of the mind—the chief topic of this chapter. Second, we know that there may be a host of other social processes beyond discourse about mind and emotion that are implicated in the development of individual differences in understanding of mind. The first study of individual differences in mind-reading and emotion understanding (Dunn, Brown, & Beardsall, 1991), for instance, showed clearly that a variety of aspects of family interaction were implicated, *independent* of the discourse measures. Two deserve emphasis: the interaction between other family members and the interaction between children and their siblings. Thus, aspects of the interaction between other family members—the frequency of control exchanges between mother and older sibling, for instance—were associated with later individual differences in the younger sibling's social understanding. Children are vigilant observers of what happens between other family members (Dunn, 1988), and these data indicated that such observations may be part of the story of the development of understanding others' minds and motivation. And—again independent of the parent-child discourse about mental states—children's experience of coopera-tive play with their siblings was associated with later understanding of mind— a point to which we will return.

More recent work has extended the range of aspects of family experiences and relationships that are implicated in the development of individual differ-ences in understanding of mind and emotion. Thus, Meins and her colleagues (Meins, 1997; Meins, Fernyhough, Russell, & Clarke-Carter, 1998) have shown that mothers' propensity to talk about the mind ("mind-mindedness") is associ-ated with other aspects of maternal sensitivity to their children and is also linked to the quality of attachment between children and their mothers, as well as to their performance on mind-reading tasks. And the evidence for important links among SES differences, parental educational background, and children's social understanding (in particular their grasp of false belief) *that are in addition to and independent of the contribution of language and age* (Cutting & Dunn, 1999) reinforces the need to investigate the mechanisms by which family background affects young children's understanding of themselves and other people. Is it via the conversations parents have with their children about the social world? Do different styles of parenting influence young children's grasp of why people behave the way they do?

These possibilities are, of course, not mutually exclusive. What about the intractable issue of the direction of effects? Do characteristics of children—such as differences in their curiosity about others, or their extraversion and persis-tence in pursuing what puzzles them—precipitate the discussions of inner states with their parents? Do initial differences in curiosity about other minds in fact *lead* to differences in conversations, rather than vice versa? The crucial role of children in initiating their conversations with their mothers was demonstrated in a classic study in the 1980s by Clarke-Stewart and Hevey (1981), which documented the developmental changes in this initiatory role, peaking at around 30 months.

Do Individual Differences in Mental-State Talk Explain Later Differences in Theory of Mind, Not Vice Versa?

Longitudinal research on language and theory of mind indicates that individual differences in language competence explain later differences in theory-of-mind skill, not vice versa (Astington & Jenkins, 1999). Early language abilities (independently assessed syntax and semantics, receptive and production skills) explained later theory-of-mind performance, not vice versa, when initial theory of mind was controlled. What about the links between mental-state discourse and success on theory-of-mind tasks?

Here we have relatively little evidence, but relevant are the findings of a study of children observed in dyadic play with a friend at three time points over a 13-month period between 3 years, 11 months and 5 years, with measures of theory of mind, emotional understanding, verbal ability, and mental-state talk (Hughes & Dunn, 1998). Children's early and later theory-of-mind scores were highly correlated over this period (with verbal ability contributing substantially to the correlations between the various ToM task scores), and individual differences in mental-state talk frequency were also correlated over time (though changing importantly in frequency and in use, developmentally). The children who engaged in frequent reference to mental states in conversations with their friends not only showed higher concurrent false-belief understanding but also were more likely than their peers to perform well on false-belief tasks 13 months later.

A key point is that this relation remained significant even when initial differences in theory-of-mind performance, age, verbal ability, and nonverbal ability were all taken into account. Regression analyses established the point that mental-state talk at Time 1 predicted theory-of-mind (ToM) scores at Time 3. Time 1 verbal ability and Time 1 ToM scores explained 32% of the Time 3 variance in ToM, but frequency of mental-state talk at Time 1 remained significantly associated with Time 3 ToM beyond the variance explained by these other variables. The reverse was not true: that is, initial theory-of-mind performance did not predict Time 3 mental-state talk.

A cautionary note here: this is just one study, relatively modest in scale, and replication is clearly needed. Also, we do not know how such longitudinal patterns might differ if we were to focus not only on false-belief task performance but also on evidence for understanding other minds-in-action, for instance, naturally occurring deceit, children's use of understanding others in their conflict management, or narratives. Moreover, there is recent challenging experimental evidence that suggests that understanding of mental states may emerge *earlier* in communication settings than in a standard change-of-location theory-of-mind task; Happé and Loth (2002) showed that children were significantly better at tracking a puppet's false belief in a word-learning situation than in the standard object-location task. The children in that study apparently had access to a representation of another's mistaken belief well before they were able to use such representation to predict a person's action. Happé and Loth argue that the difference in task difficulty "reflects the privileged status of language and communication in the young child's development of theory of mind" (p. 31).

We turn next to the question of what aspects of these discourse experiences, beyond the content (such as the particular context, the relationship of child and interlocutor, and the pragmatics of the discourse), may be key to fostering understanding of mind and emotion.

What Particular Social Contexts Foster Such Talk about Inner States?

We have learned that these conversations about inner states, which are rich in the discussion of how action and inner states are linked, are fostered in certain social contexts. One that appears to be particularly rich as a context for talking about inner states is discussion of the past. We know from experimental studies in which parent and child have been asked to talk about incidents from their shared past, from naturalistic observations (Brown, 1995), and, most recently, from the work of Lagattuta and Wellman (2002) that early parent-child talk that is about past experiences involving negative emotions produces talk that has a high concentration of key features for understanding inner states—explicit discussion of the causes of feelings and of mind-emotion connections. Lagattuta and Wellman conclude that conversations about negative emotions "encourage young children's more precocious ability to think constructively and causally about people's past experiences, their emotions, and their internal mental lives . . . conversations about negative emotions may comprise an essential cornerstone in the development of young children's emotional and psychological knowledge more broadly" (Lagattuta & Wellman, 2002, p. 577).

A second particularly good example of a social context that fosters talk about inner states is the context of joint pretend play between children and their friends or siblings, in which children are constructing a narrative together about imaginary characters. Several studies (again based on widely differing samples) have demonstrated that such shared imaginative play is especially fruitful as a setting for such discussions; in the course of working out the story of their make-believe narratives, discussion of what the characters (including the interlocutor) are thinking and feeling and why they act the way they do is frequent. And a high frequency of such play is also related to successful performance on assessments of theory of mind (Dunn, Brown, Slomkowski, et al., 1991; Howe, Petrakos, & Rinaldi, 1998), while assigning roles to self and others and making joint plans for shared pretense were related to false-belief task performance in another study (Astington & Jenkins, 1995). A cautionary note here is the question of whether what matters is the explicit discourse about inner states or whether successful joint pretense depends on a "meeting of minds" concerning the narrative, rather than explicit talk about inner states. A comparable point is made by Harris (this volume, chapter 4), with the argument that the crucial factor for theory-of-mind development in a mother's talk may not be her use of mental-state terms but her pragmatic intent to introduce different points of view, which may involve mental-state terms and object complements; distinguishing among the effects of semantics, syntax, and pragmatics is thus not easy.

The example of the construction of shared fantasy raises further issues about what matters for theory-of-mind development: do the contexts that foster discourse about inner states depend on the quality of the relationship between child and partner? Do the pragmatics or the connectedness of the talk matter? Or the characteristics of the interlocutor?

Do the Contexts That Foster Discourse about Inner States Depend on the Quality of the Relationship between Child and Partner?

Several studies report that shared fantasy between siblings occurs most frequently between siblings who like each other—who are affectionate and caring (Dunn, Brown, Slomkowski, et al., 1991; Dunn & Dale, 1984). It is not simply having a sibling that matters, but the kind of relationship that exists between them— notoriously this can range from close and affectionate to conflicted and hostile. Frequent shared fantasy plays a key part in relationships between siblings who are close, affectionate, and friendly. Such relationships occur in around a third of young sibling pairs.

The same qualification applies to friends. Friendships between young children differ notably in quality, and it is those pairs who are especially affectionate and close, who care for each other and are close emotionally, who engage in frequent shared pretense. As Gottman (1986) pointed out, shared fantasy forms the core of particularly close friendships for 3- and 4-year-olds. And, as Gottman reported for children in Urbana, Illinois, as too in our studies in London and in Pennsylvania, those friends who engaged in frequent shared pretense also were less likely to be in conflict and communicated smoothly, and *all these aspects of their interactions* were linked to their theory-of-mind abilities as formally assessed (Dunn & Cutting, 1999). As we will see in a moment, the quality of these early friendships carries profound implications for later development, including development of understanding of others.

The general point here is that the discourse shown to be linked to later theory-of-mind abilities flourishes within *certain sorts of relationship*. The question raised by this finding is whether there are relationship differences beyond the conversational experiences that are important for the development of understanding of mind and emotion. The same point is made by research on mothers' involvement in shared pretense. There are wide individual differences in mothers' involvement in their children's early fantasy play. Newson and Newson, in their Nottingham study (1968), pointed out that these differences were related to social class. For some of the working-class mothers in their study, such early imaginative play was a source of worry—it was seen as dangerously close to lying, as the following quotes illustrate. The quotes come from two miners' wives and a fitter's wife, talking about their 4-year-olds:

> "I've said to him, you know, 'That's never happened, you're imagining things!' I've told him, I've said, 'Now that's *wrong*—you've got a vivid imagination.'"

> "He'd make up stories . . . it got so bad that I tried to stop it, because I didn't want him to go from an imaginary story to a downright lie— because there's not much difference between the two."

> "He's got a . . . I'll tell you what it is—it worries me sometimes—he's got a vivid imagination; and it goes on and on and on till he *lives* it; and sometimes, these imaginary people, you have to *feed* them with him, do you see what I mean? It worries me."(Newson & Newson, 1968, pp. 198–199)

Consider the response of this mother of 2-year-old Nigel in one of our Cambridge studies. Nigel has slotted together two combs, and is pretending that this is a plane:

NIGEL   Look there. Plane coming.
MOTHER   You don't want to play with dirty combs. They want washing.
NIGEL   Plane wants washing.
MOTHER   Eh?
NIGEL   Plane wants washing.
MOTHER   Plane want washing? Them *combs* want washing.
NIGEL   Plane broken. Plane broken. Crash
MOTHER   Look. Come and throw out all them broken toys.

In contrast, another mother in this study for two and a half hours one morning engaged in a series of elaborate, if repetitive, adventures with her daughter, who for the moment (in fact, for about two weeks) was a particular railway engine. Such differences in engagement in shared pretense are associated with a broad range of other differences in the relationship between children and mothers.

The quality of the relationship between child and partner, then, is systematically related to the frequency with which they interact in contexts that are rich in discourse about inner states. Three related issues extend the point that beyond the *content* of conversations, there are features of the discourse that may be related to later mind-reading and emotion understanding abilities: we consider next the evidence on whether the pragmatics of the discourse, the connectedness of the talk, and the characteristics of the child's interlocutor are linked to individual differences in mind-reading and emotion understanding.

Does the Pragmatics of the Discourse Matter, Not Solely the Content in Terms of Reference to Inner States?

First, one line of evidence has highlighted the importance of considering not only the content of discourse between children and their family and friends but also what the interlocutors are trying to achieve in terms of pragmatics in a particular exchange (recall Bruner's [1983] emphasis on the significance of "contexts of practice" in language acquisition; see also O'Neill, this volume, chapter 5, for an emphasis on how theory of mind matters for pragmatic development). Thus, in a longitudinal study of children in Pennsylvania, we investigated the conversations between the children and their mothers that involved discussion of cause and included an examination of the pragmatics of the particular exchanges referring to causal relations (Dunn & Brown, 1993). The results showed that it was not simply the amount of "causal talk" between mothers and children that was associated with later differences in children's social understanding but what was being done pragmatically in these conversations. Thus, children whose mothers' causal talk was chiefly in the context of controlling them did *poorly* on assessments of emotion understanding later, while those whose mothers' causal talk was in the context of shared play, comforting, or joking were more successful on the later cognitive assessment. A measure of total "causal talk" would have masked these differences. The general lesson from these analyses of individual differences is that, in considering the developmental significance of children's experience in discourse, we need to look not just at the total exposure of children to talk about a particular content area but also at what this talk is used for. What people are *trying to do* in an interaction may influence the ways that things are learned.

Does the "Connectedness" of the Talk between Interlocutors Matter?

Here we are concerned with the extent to which each speaker is tuned in to what the other is talking about—the semantic relatedness of one speaker's turn to that of the other speaker. This is an aspect of conversation which differs markedly between dyads. For example, some mothers and their 3-year-olds hold extensive connected conversations. For others, there is much less close tuning of one speaker with the other. In such pairs, it is relatively common for a child's comment or a bid for attention to be ignored, and similarly for mothers' comments or questions to be ignored by their children. Similarly, some friends engage in connected conversation with relative frequency, while others rarely do so.

There is now evidence from three separate studies to suggest important links between children's experience of engagement in connected conversation and their understanding of mind. First, children in our Pennsylvania sample who performed more successfully on theory-of-mind tasks at 40 months engaged in more frequent and extensive "connected" conversation with their friends at 47 months (Slomkowski & Dunn, 1996). Second, similar—but concurrent—correlations were found in our sample of friends in South London (Dunn & Cutting, 1999). And findings from a third study of a very different sample—"hard-to-manage" preschool children in inner-city London who were at risk for problems in theory of mind, emotion understanding, and executive function (Brophy & Dunn, 2002; Hughes, Dunn, & White, 1998)—tell a similar story. Among these children, from a notably deprived background, the extent to which they had engaged in connected conversation with their mothers during our home visits was related to their performance on the cognitive assessments. Those who had experienced more frequent connected conversations with their mothers were significantly more successful in an aggregate score of performance on eight theory-of-mind tasks (r (76) = .23 for mothers' connected conversational turns, and r (76) = .23 for children's connected conversational turns). This "connectedness" reflects a tuning in to the other person's interests and intentions—perhaps, then, it is not so surprising that it should link to assessments of children's social understanding. However, the evidence brings us squarely to the point that conversations involve two people and to the importance of taking account of the characteristics of the interlocutor.

Are the Characteristics of the Child's Interlocutor Important?

By definition, the features of discourse that have been highlighted—the connectedness of conversation, the frequency of shared imaginative play, the engagement in conversation about causes of people's actions or feelings—all are emergent properties of discourse between two individuals. Most of the research that has focused on the relation of children's abilities in language and in theory of mind has treated each of these domains as individual characteristics of children and attempted to describe their association within the individual. But these aspects of conversation, and children's experiences in such discourse, depend on the characteristics of both the child and her interlocutor—they are dyadic experiences that reflect the characteristics of both child and partner. If we are to clarify the relation of language and theory of mind, we have to grapple with this issue—that it is children's experiences as members of dyads that play a key role.

Two lines of investigation are relevant here. First, we can study the current contribution to joint discourse of each speaker, either in terms of his explicit verbal contribution to the talk or in terms of his broad sociocognitive or linguistic characteristics, and explore the significance of speaker A's characteristics on speaker B's later social understanding. Second, we can examine the developmental significance of certain dyadic experiences for individual development. Our recent studies of young friends in London have provided some challenging findings from such analyses.

We studied the children initially as 3- and 4-year-olds, with observations and assessments made at nursery and at home. Pairs of friends were selected on the basis of observations and children's, parents', and teachers' nominations (following Howes & Phillipsen's, 1992, criteria). Both children in the friendship dyad were studied as individuals in terms of their sociocognitive abilities, and their conversations and dyadic interactions were also investigated (Dunn, Cutting, & Fisher, 2002). The findings established three key points concerning the dyad. The first was that during the preschool period, *the characteristics of the friend* as well as of the child (specifically the friend's language and theory-of-mind abilities) were associated with the quality of discourse, joint pretense, and connectedness of communication established by the dyad. Thus, the smoothness of children's communication with their friends was related to both the child's and the friend's theory-of-mind abilities; the friend's theory-of-mind skills contributed an additional 7% of variance in failed communication beyond that explained by the child's own social understanding. (Note that failures in communication were more closely related to the theory-of-mind scores than were vocabulary scores.)

The second finding, most strikingly, was that *these friend characteristics from the preschool period were also important predictors of children's later social understanding*—their insight into and expression of liking of their friends as 5-year-olds in kindergarten. Third, *the interaction of the preschool dyad, specifically the extent of connected conversation and cooperative pretend play*, also independently predicted the school-age children's insight into and liking for their friends. In cases where the friendship had remained stable, this is perhaps not surprising, and the pattern could well reflect continuity in individual characteristics of child and friend. But, for one-third of our sample, the children had formed new friendships after the transition to school, because they were separated by circumstances from their "old" friends, who were sent to different schools. The analyses showed that the preschool experiences of smooth, successful, connected communication and cooperative pretend play with the *preschool friend* contributed to the quality of their later, new friendships formed after the transition to school. This contribution was independent of their covarying social understanding and language abilities at school. The pattern of findings lends further weight to the argument that the experiences of sharing and negotiating an imaginary world in pretend play provides a potent context for talking and learning about why other people behave the way they do and about the links between inner states and human action. The correlations with early language skills also remind us of how important children's conversational exchanges are in the social processes implicated in the development of their relationships—their ability to cooperate, to resolve conflicts, and to explore feelings and shared experience.

Perhaps most important of all, the links among children's preschool interaction experiences with their friends, the sociocognitive characteristics of both children in preschool, and the children's later insights into and liking of their friends are compatible with Howes's important argument that children may form internal representations of friendship relationships in the preschool period upon which they draw in subsequent friendships at school (Howes, 1996).

As a final example of the importance of a relationship perspective on the links between language and the development of mind-reading, a comparison of the same children interacting with their siblings and with their friends showed that the relative significance of language for social understanding differed in the two relationships. As part of the friendship study described earlier (Dunn et al., 2002), observations of the children playing alone with a friend and playing alone with an older sibling were conducted. From these observations, we investigated children's shared pretend play with the partner and the smoothness of communication between child and partner and asked how the children's theory-of-mind skills, and language ability (in terms of vocabulary) were related to these aspects of interaction. Theory-of-mind ability was significantly related to shared pretend play with both sibling and friend; however, language ability was significantly related to shared pretend play only with the friend (r (45) = .41, p <.01), not with the sibling (r (45) = .12, n.s.). Shared pretend play with the friend was related to the quality of the friendship (assessed by the teacher, r (42) = .41, p <.01) but not to the quality of the sibling relationship, while shared pretend play with the sibling was related to the positivity shown by the sibling to the child (r (43) = .37, p <.01) but not to the quality of the friendship. Language skills, it seems, are particularly important for the establishment of a shared imaginative narrative with a friend; they are not important for the establishment of such shared imaginative play with an older sibling (who presumably can "carry" the development of the narrative even if the child has relatively poor language). Conclusions about the significance of language for social understanding-in-action depend, then, on the particular dyadic relationship that is being considered.

Summary

In summary, these claims concerning what matters in conversational experiences for theory-of-mind development and the evidence supporting them indicate that to understand the relations between theory-of-mind development and the communicative aspects of language, we need to look at children's language ability not solely in terms of a cognitive skill or individual characteristic but also in terms of their dyadic experiences. The aspects of conversation that have been discussed depend on characteristics of both child and interlocutor and on the quality of the relationship between them. This point is highlighted by a summary of the developmental associations as children grow beyond the preschool years.

Developmental Patterns: What Are the Links between Early Social Understanding and Later Outcomes—and What Do We Need to Know Now?

Are There Links between Individual Differences in Early Theory-of-Mind Abilities and Later Outcomes?

Evidence from studies in both the United States and the United Kingdom, summarized in table 3.1, shows that a range of developmental outcomes are associated with individual differences in early emotion understanding and mind-reading, including the quality of relationships with friends during the school years (Dunn et al., 2002), children's moral sensibility (Dunn, Cutting, & Demetriou, 2000; Hughes & Dunn, 2000), and children's sensitivity to criticism and adjustment to school (Cutting & Dunn, 2002; Dunn, 1995).

These data suggest that early abilities in mind-reading and emotion understanding are linked to particular developmental trajectories—in which conversational experiences are clearly implicated. However, it should be noted that these sequelae include the "costs" of early sophistication in reading others' minds and feelings. Children who performed particularly well on aggregate tests of understanding other minds as preschoolers were, a year later, as school children, especially sensitive to teacher criticism and to failure (Cutting & Dunn, 2002). Individual differences in preschool social cognition explained unique variance in later sensitivity to criticism and failure, beyond the variance explained by concurrent social understanding. It appears there may be costs as well as benefits to understanding other people well early in life.

What deserves special emphasis is the similarity of these findings across two very different samples of children—one in rural and small town Pennsylvania, one in inner-city London. Such replication of findings reinforces the claim that

Table 3.1 Sequelae of Early Social Understanding: Correlations between
Preschool and School Measures

| | School Years | | | | | |
| | Friendship Quality | | | | Child View School | Child Response Criticism |
	Child-Sibling	Child-Friend	Friend-Child	Moral Understanding		
Preschool						
PA Study[1]						
ToM[3]	*	*	*	*	*	*
APT[4]	*	*	*	*	—	—
London II[2]						
ToM[3]	—	*	*	*	*	*
APT[4]	—	*	*	*	*	*
EU[5]	—	*	*	*	*	*

* = significant correlation.
[1]Pennsylvania Study of Social Understanding (Dunn, Brown, Slomkowski, et al. 1991).
[2]Friendship Study (London) (Dunn, Cutting, & Fisher 2002).
[3]Theory of mind: False-belief tasks.
[4]Affective Perspective taking (Denham, 1986).
[5]Emotion Understanding (Cutting & Dunn, 1999).

early theory of mind and emotion understanding have significance for a broad
range of social outcomes. Of course, it must be acknowledged that, while it is
very plausible that language abilities are part of the continuing pattern of individual differences, the underlying mechanisms remain to be clarified.

Do Emotional Experiences and Emotion Understanding
Have a Role in the Developmental Story?

In the early stages of the development of social understanding, emotional experiences have a role as precipitators of the discourse about inner states. Mothers'
talk about feelings is much more frequent when children are expressing negative
affect (Dunn & Brown, 1994). Moreover, a powerful case has been made for the
understanding of emotion as key to the later development of understanding mental states—the evidence that understanding of mind grows from a foundation of
understanding of emotions (Bartsch & Wellman, 1995). From their analyses of
children's talk about the mind from the CHILDES archive, Bartsch and Wellman
make a compelling argument that very young children explain people's actions
first in terms of emotions and desires, then through their social experiences come

to incorporate the notion of belief into their understanding of why people behave the way they do. An important implication of this argument is that an understanding of cognitive states arises through an earlier understanding of emotions. As Bartsch and Estes (1996) have pointed out, this has wide implications for our understanding of development—that accounts of metacognition will have to be anchored in a much broader understanding of development.

A cautionary note here is that we do not know about the developmental significance of talk about emotional experiences when children are older than the 2- to 5-year-olds who have chiefly been the focus of research. We also do not know how emotion understanding and theory of mind are linked, after the early years. We do not know whether the "powerful triad" than Lagattuta and Wellman (2002) have described—conversations about negative emotions having a high concentration of talk about the past, about causes of emotions, and about mind-emotion connections—also characterizes later child-adult or child-child conversations.

How Important Are Language Abilities in the Later Developments in Social Understanding?

It seems that language abilities are key to the early stages of mind-reading. What happens after the preschool years? Is there some process such as "bootstrapping" between the domains of language and mind-reading? Close connections between individual differences in communicative abilities and mind-reading during middle childhood are suggested by Fisher's (2002) follow-up study at 8 years of the "hard-to-manage" children we studied in London. It was language and communicative problems that chiefly accounted for the children's failures on "advanced theory-of-mind" tasks.

How Important Are Cultural and Community Differences in the Role of Talk about Inner States as Children Develop?

Finally, it must be noted that we remain very ignorant about the significance of cultural and linguistic differences in how inner states are discussed, explained, emphasized, and reflected on in different cultures (for exceptions see the work of Lillard, 1998; Tardif & Wellman, 2000; Vinden, 1996, 1997). We do not yet know whether developmental pathways differ in different cultural and social class groups. Some information is available on discussion of emotions in different cultural worlds (Saarni, 1998; Wierzbicka, 1995), but it could be that talk about other mental states is more invariant (Wellman, 1998). The comparison of Mandarin- and Cantonese-speaking children conducted by Tardif and Wellman (2000) is particularly illuminating here. Their findings demonstrate important consistency in the overall sequence of development of mental-state language across English-speaking and Chinese-speaking children, in spite of variation in the use of desire terms and of terms for thinking in the two cultures. There were, however, variations in the timing of the beginning and end of this developmental sequence, which were attributable to various linguistic and cultural differences in the children's language environments. Tardif and Wellman conclude that the overall sequence of the development of a theory of mind was consistent in the two cultural worlds compared, and they highlight how cross-linguistic research can be informative for understanding children's discovery of the mind.

A Relationship Approach to Understanding the Links between Language and Theory of Mind

A recurrent theme in the evidence on the links between children's communicative experiences and their understanding of mind and emotion has been the need to look at children's language not solely in terms of their cognitive skills or as individual characteristics but also in terms of their relationship experiences—their participation in the social processes that are key to the discovery of the mind. A relationship perspective on the development of social understanding and the role of language has much to offer us.

First, in children's early essays into behavior that reflects understanding of feelings and intentions, it is the push to get things done in relationships that is so striking: teasing, getting attention, cooperating in exciting pretend play, anticipating when rivals are going to get precious parental attention and subverting that attention.

Second, the variety and complexity of social processes implicated in the development of understanding minds is striking, and these are the processes that operate in close relationships: it is not solely talk about minds and feelings that matters; it is who you talk with, and why you do so that matters—and this has to do with the quality of close relationships. Talk may be the most powerful mediator influencing understanding of mind within the relationship, but the quality of relationships influences talk.

Third, emotion is central to close relationships and to children's curiosity about others, and a cornerstone of their growing understanding of mind in the early years.

Fourth, relationships go on through time (a defining criterion), and putting together thoughts, actions, and feelings over time in explaining people's behavior is key developmentally. As adults, we understand that people's actions and thoughts are shaped by events and experiences in the past; as Lagattuta and Wellman (2001, 2002) have argued, for children to be able to construct coherent explanations of their own and others' lives, they need to grasp how emotions, thoughts, and actions are linked over time.

Finally, in terms of the issue of possible cultural diversity in patterns of emotion knowledge and mind-reading, we should recognize that it is through close relationships that children develop their awareness and understanding of such cultural matters (Hinde, 1987).

Acknowledgments The research on which we based this chapter was supported by the MRC and by grants from NICHD (HD 23158).

References

Astington, J. W., & Jenkins, J. M. (1995). Theory of mind development and social understanding. *Cognition and Emotion, 9,* 151–65.

Astington, J. W., & Jenkins, J. M. (1999). A longitudinal study of the relation between language and theory-of-mind development. *Developmental Psychology, 35,* 1311–20.

Bartsch, K., & Estes, D. (1996). Individual differences in children's developing theory of mind and implications for metacognition. *Learning and Individual Differences, 8,* 281–304.

Bartsch, K., & Wellman, H. M. (1995). *Children talk about the mind.* New York: Oxford University Press.

Brophy, M., & Dunn, J. (2002). What did Mummy say? Dyadic interactions between young "hard-to-manage" children and their mothers. *Journal of Abnormal Child Psychology, 30,* 103–112.

Brown, J. R. (1995). What happened?: Emotional experience and children's talk about the past. Unpublished manuscript.

Bruner, J. (1983). *Child's talk.* Oxford: Oxford University Press.

Clarke-Stewart, K. A., & Hevey, C. M. (1981). Longitudinal relations in repeated observations of mother-child interactions from 1 to 2 and a half years. *Developmental Psychology, 17,* 127–145.

Cutting, A. L., & Dunn, J. (1999). Theory of mind, emotion understanding, language and family background: Individual differences and inter-relations. *Child Development, 70,* 853–865.

Cutting, A. L., & Dunn, J. (2002). The costs of understanding other people: social cognition predicts young children's sensitivity to criticism. *Journal of Child Psychology and Psychiatry, 43,* 849–860.

Denham, S. (1986). Social cognition, prosocial behavior, and emotion in preschoolers: Contextual validation. *Child Development, 57,* 194–201.

Dunn, J. (1988). Relations among relationships. In S. Duck (Ed.), *Handbook of personal relationships* (pp. 193–210). Chichester: Wiley.

Dunn, J. (1995). Children as psychologists: The later correlates of individual differences in understanding of emotions and other minds. *Cognition and Emotion, 9,* 187–201.

Dunn, J., & Brown, J. R. (1993). Early conversations about causality: Content, pragmatics and developmental change. *British Journal of Developmental Psychology, 11,* 107–123.

Dunn, J., & Brown, J. (1994). Affect expression in the family, children's understanding of emotions, and their interactions with others. *Merrill-Palmer Quarterly, 40,* 120–137.

Dunn, J., Brown, J., & Beardsall, L. (1991). Family talk about feeling states and children's later understanding of others' emotions. *Developmental Psychology, 27,* 448–455.

Dunn, J., Brown, J., Slomkowski, C., Tesla, C., & Youngblade, L. (1991). Young children's understanding of other people's feelings and beliefs: Individual differences and their antecedents. *Child Development, 62,* 1352–1366.

Dunn, J., & Cutting, A. (1999). Understanding others, and individual differences in friendship interactions in young children. *Social Development, 8,* 201–219.

Dunn, J., Cutting, A., & Demetriou, H. (2000). Moral sensibility, understanding others, and children's friendship interactions in the preschool period. *British Journal of Developmental Psychology, 18,* 159–178.

Dunn, J., Cutting, A., & Fisher, N. (2002). Old friends, new friends: Predictors of children's perspectives on their friends at school. *Child Development, 73,* 621–635.

Dunn, J., & Dale, N. (1984). I a Daddy: 2-year-olds' collaboration in joint pretend with sibling and with mother. In I. Bretherton (Ed.), *Symbolic play: The development of social understanding* (pp. 131–158). San Diego, CA: Academic Press.

Fisher, N. (2002, April). *Language and theory of mind in children with autism and learning difficulties.* Poster presented at the International Conference on Why Language Matters for Theory of Mind, Toronto, Canada.

Garner, P. W., Jones, D. C., Gaddy, G., & Rennie, K. M. (1997). Low-income mothers' conversations about emotions and their children's emotional competence. *Social Development, 6,* 37–52.

Gottman, J. M. (1986). The world of coordinated play: Same- and cross-sex friendship in young children. In J. M. Gottman & J. G. Parker (Eds.), *Conversations among friends* (pp. 139–191). Cambridge: Cambridge University Press.

Happé, F. G. E. (1995). The role of age and verbal ability in the theory of mind task performance of subjects with autism. *Child Development, 66,* 843–855.

Happé, F., & Loth, E. (2002). "Theory of mind" and tracking speakers' intentions. *Mind & Language, 17,* 24–36.

Hardy-Brown, K. (1983). Universals and individual differences: Disentangling two approaches to the study of language acquisition. *Developmental Psychology, 19,* 610–624.

Hinde, R. A. (1987). *Individuals, relationships, cultures.* Cambridge: Cambridge University Press.

Howe, N., Petrakos, H., & Rinaldi, C. (1998). "All the sheeps are dead. He murdered them": Sibling pretense, negotiation, internal state language and relationship quality. *Child Development, 69,* 182–191.

Howes, C. (1996). The earliest friendships. In W. M. Bukowski, A. F. Newcomb & W. W. Hartup (Eds.), *The company they keep: Friendship in childhood and adolescence* (pp. 66–86). New York: Cambridge University Press.

Howes, C., & Phillipsen, L. C. (1992). Gender and friendship: Relationships within peer groups of young children. *Social Development, 1,* 231–242.

Hughes, C., & Dunn, J. (1997). "Pretend you didn't know": Preschoolers' talk about mental states in pretend play. *Cognitive Development, 12,* 477–499.

Hughes, C., & Dunn, J. (1998). Understanding mind and emotion: Longitudinal associations with mental-state talk between young friends. *Developmental Psychology, 34,* 1026–1037.

Hughes, C., & Dunn, J. (2000). Hedonism or empathy?: Hard-to-manage children's moral awareness, and links with cognitive and maternal characteristics. *British Journal of Developmental Psychology, 18,* 227–245.

Hughes, C., Dunn, J., & White, A. (1998). Trick or treat?: Uneven understanding of mind and emotion and executive function among "hard to manage" preschoolers. *Journal of Child Psychology and Psychiatry, 39,* 981–994.

Jenkins, J. M., & Astington, J. W. (1996). Cognitive factors and family structure associated with theory of mind development in young children. *Developmental Psychology, 32,* 70–78.

Lagattuta, K. H., & Wellman, H. M. (2001). Thinking about the past: Early knowledge about links between prior experience, thinking, and emotion. *Child Development, 72,* 82–102.

Lagattuta, K. H., & Wellman, H. M. (2002). Differences in early parent-child conversations about negative versus positive emotions: Implications for the development of emotion understanding. *Developmental Psychology, 38,* 564–580.

Lillard, A. (1998). Ethnopsychologies: Cultural variations in theories of mind. *Psychological Bulletin, 123,* 3–32.

Meins, E. (1997). *Security of attachment and the social development of cognition.* Hove, UK: Psychology Press.

Meins, E., Fernyhough, C., Russell, J. T. & Clarke-Carter D. (1998). Security of attachment as a predictor of symbolic and mentalising abilities: A longitudinal study. *Social Development, 7,* 1–24.

Newson, J., & Newson, E. (1968). *Four years old in an urban community.* Harmondsworth: Penguin.

Plomin, R., & Dale, P. S. (2000). Genetics and early language development: A U.K. study of twins. In D. V. M. Bishop & B. E. Leonard (Eds.), *Speech and language impairments in children: Causes, characteristics, intervention and outcome* (pp. 35–51). Hove, UK: Psychology Press.

Saarni, C. (1998). Issues of cultural meaningfulness in emotional development. *Developmental Psychology, 34,* 647–652.

Shore, C. (1995). *Individual differences in language development.* Newbury, CA: Sage.

Slomkowski, C., & Dunn, J. (1996). Young children's understanding of other people's beliefs and feelings and their connected communication with friends. *Developmental Psychology, 32,* 442–447.

Tardif, T, & Wellman, H. M. (2000). Acquisition of mental state language in Mandarin- and Cantonese-speaking children. *Developmental Psychology, 36,* 25–43.

Vinden, P. G. (1996). Junin Quecha children's understanding of mind. *Child Development, 67,* 1707–1716.

Vinden, P. G. (1997, April). Parenting and theory of mind. Paper presented at the Biennial Meeting of the Society for Research in Child Development, Washington, DC.

Wellman, H. M. (1998). Culture, variation, and levels of analysis in folk psychologies: Comment on Lillard. *Psychological Bulletin, 123,* 33–36.

Wellman, H. M., Cross, D., & Watson, J. (2001). Meta-analysis of theory of mind development: The truth about false-belief. *Child Development, 72,* 655–684.

Wierzbicka, A. (1995). Everyday conceptions of emotion: A semantic perspective. In J. A. Russell, J. Fernandez-Dols, A. Manstead, & J. C. Wellenkamp (Eds.), *Everyday conceptions of emotion: An introduction to the psychology, anthropology, and linguistics of emotion* (pp.17–48). Boston: Kluwer Academic.

4   Conversation, Pretense, and Theory of Mind

Paul L. Harris

In this chapter, I discuss two different activities that appear to facilitate children's understanding of mind: conversation and pretend play. I first review the evidence suggesting that each has an influence. I then go on to discuss the relationship between these two factors. I speculate that variation in conversational input to the child might interact with children's role-taking ability. Under optimal conditions, children will often be invited in the course of conversation to consider the world from another person's point-of-view, and they will have the capacity to respond to those invitations.

Studying the Effect of Conversational Input on the Child's Theory of Mind

As Bradley and Bryant (1983) pointed out in analyzing variation in reading ability, it is helpful to combine training studies with correlational studies of relationships that exist over time in the ordinary world of the child. This combination is powerful because the particular strengths of each type of study compensate for the particular weaknesses of the other type. Correlational studies using longitudinal data are helpful because they can identify relationships that exist in the real world, for example, a relationship between early phonological awareness and subsequent reading ability. At the same time, correlational studies cannot establish whether the observed link is a causal one. Training studies are helpful because they can establish genuine causal relationships. For example they can establish whether or not training in phonological awareness improves subsequent reading. At the same time, such training studies—when conducted in the absence of appropriate correlational analyses of real-world relationships—may identify a potentially effective cause, but not one that ordinarily plays a role outside of the laboratory or training study.

Applying these lessons to the study of language and theory of mind, we would do well to seek a convergence between correlational studies of naturally occurring relationships between language and theory of mind and training studies that seek to put such relationships on a sound causal footing. More specifically, we can ask (1) what type of variation in conversational input to the child is associated with variation in theory-of-mind performance; and (2) whether deliberate variation in conversational input to the child brings about a change in theory-of-mind performance. In this chapter, I take up each of these questions in turn. Note that I concentrate on correlational studies that have examined conversational input to the child, rather than on studies that have measured the language competence of the child. I do so because, when we examine training studies, it is easy to identify studies that have manipulated the conversational input to the child; manipulating the child's language competence is more difficult, albeit not impossible.

Correlational Studies of Conversational Input and Theory of Mind

A pioneering study of possible links between conversational input to the child and the child's theory of mind was carried out by Dunn, Brown, Slomkowski, Tesla, and Youngblade (1991). They noted a correlation between aspects of family conversation and the child's performance on a measure of false-belief understanding. The authors appropriately cautioned, however, that the correlation could be interpreted in various ways (for a related caution, see Dunn & Brophy, this volume, chapter 3). One possibility is that conversational input to the child promotes the child's understanding of mental states, notably false belief. A second possibility is that a child with an advanced understanding of mental states might be particularly likely to elicit and sustain a conversation about thoughts and feelings. On this second interpretation, then, the type of conversational input a child receives might be a consequence rather than a cause of the child's mental-state understanding.

Ruffman, Slade, and Crowe (2002) designed a longitudinal study to remove this ambiguity. They obtained three different measures: (1) children's language competence, as indexed by the linguistics concepts subtest of the CELF-Preschool[1] (Clinical Evaluation of Language Fundamentals-Preschool, Wiig, Secord, & Semel, 1992); (2) their theory-of-mind skills, as indexed by a battery of standard tasks; and (3) the mother's tendency to engage in discussion of mental states, as indexed during her discussion with the child of characters in a picture book. Each of these three measures was taken at three different time points (t_1, t_2, and t_3) over the course of approximately 1½ years.

Mothers' mental-state language during the picture task (at t_1 and t_2) predicted children's later theory-of-mind performance (at t_2 and t_3) beyond any contribution made by children's prior language ability or theory-of-mind performance (at t_1 or t_2). The reciprocal relationship did not hold. Thus, children's theory-of-mind performance was a poor predictor of mothers' later mental-state talk. By implication, the characteristics of the child alone cannot account for the correlation between children's early involvement in conversation about mental states and their later performance on theory-of-mind tasks. Rather, conversational input from the mother appears to be causing a change in the child's mental-state understanding. Indeed, in the analyses reported by Ruffman et al. (2002), mothers' mental-state talk proved to be a more consistent predictor of children's subsequent theory-of-mind performance than was children's prior language competence.

Despite these encouraging findings concerning the role of conversational input, there are at least two points for discussion. First, if we think more carefully about the way in which mothers talk to their children, the following chain of speculation is not implausible. First, mothers vary in their emotional and psychological insight. That variation might lead mothers to discuss the thoughts and feelings of story characters to varying degrees, but it might also lead them to display differential sensitivity and understanding toward their child's own mental states. Arguably, it is the mother's psychological sensitivity toward her child that is the main engine of the child's mental-state understanding. The mother's tendency to discuss thoughts and feelings, especially those of storybook characters, might be an ineffective by-product of that sensitivity. Attachment theorists who have looked for continuities between a mother's psychological sensitivity and children's later mental-state understanding have proposed more or less exactly such a causal chain (e.g., Fonagy & Target, 1997; Steele, Steele, Croft, & Fonagy, 1999). Their proposal—in line with the biological and ethological roots of attachment theory—has been that the mother's emotional and nonverbal sensitivity to her child promotes a secure attachment that in turn promotes the child's mental-state understanding (Harris, 2000a). In short, looking at the findings of Ruffman et al. (2002), we cannot tell whether it is the mother's conversational input that promotes her child's mental-state understanding or some "deeper," nonverbal sensitivity that simply happens to be correlated with the extent to which she refers to mental states. This concern is particularly acute if we keep in mind the claims of attachment theory, namely that a mother's nonverbal sensitivity is likely to affect the course of a child's development even during the first year of life, before the child can enter into any kind of verbal dialogue (De Wolff & van IJzendoorn, 1997; Van IJzendoorn, Juffer, & Duyvesteyn, 1995).

A second consideration is that Ruffman et al. (2002) assessed mothers' mental-state language when they were in conversation with their child. Arguably, mothers are alert to the fact that preschoolers differ in their interests: some want to talk about trucks and airplanes; others want to talk about tigers and lions and ponies; still others want to talk about what Spot thinks and feels. Mothers might cater to such variation by adjusting their conversational input. Arguably, children with an interest in what Spot thinks and feels might thereby proceed more rapidly to an understanding of mental states, and they might do so irrespective of whether their interest is met by their mother's conversational input. Admittedly, Ruffman et al. (2002) found no indication that the level of children's earlier theory-of-mind performance was linked to the frequency of their mother's later references to mental states. However, it is conceivable that mothers do monitor the focus of their children's interests, even if they are not particularly sensitive to the sophistication, from a developmental point of view, that is shown by the child with regard to that interest.

With these caveats in mind, therefore, it is worth asking whether the frequency with which mothers refer to mental states is a good predictor of children's mental-state understanding when two key precautions are taken. First, we may make an independent assessment of maternal nonverbal sensitivity. For example, there is considerable evidence that maternal sensitivity is a predictor of a secure mother-child attachment. Accordingly, we may ask whether the frequency with which mothers refer to mental states is a good predictor of their children's theory-of-mind performance even when the child's early attachment status is taken into account. Second, in assessing the frequency with which mothers talk about mental states, we may seek to eliminate or minimize any impact of the child's conversational interests upon the mother. More specifically, we can ask the mother to talk about the child to the experimenter, rather than to engage in a conversation with her child. For example, we can ask the mother to provide a description of her child and to comment on a short film of the child. De Rosnay (2003) conducted a longitudinal study with these precautions in mind. He studied 75 children (aged 4½ to 6 years) whose attachment to their mother had been assessed 4 to 5 years earlier, when the children ranged from 12 to 15 months. Children were assessed for (1) their understanding of belief-based emotion (using variants of the so-called nasty surprise task devised by Harris, Johnson, Hutton, Andrews & Cooke, 1989) and (2) their performance on the TEC (Test of Emotion Comprehension, Pons & Harris, 2000), a more wide-ranging assessment of children's emotion understanding (for details see Pons, Lawson, Harris, & de Rosnay, 2003). Mothers' talk was sampled in two different contexts: (1) mothers watched the previously recorded video of their child in the Strange Situation and described his or her reactions during the sequence of separations and reunions; (2) mothers provided a description of their child in the context of an open-ended interview with the experimenter. In each of these two contexts, mothers' references to mental states were coded. The results showed that mothers who made a higher proportion of mentalistic comments about their child in either context had children who performed better on both the narrower test of emotion understanding and the more wide-ranging test of emotion mentioned earlier, namely the TEC. These effects remained when sex, verbal mental age, number of older siblings, socioeconomic status, and prior attachment status were accounted for.

The implication of these findings is that the connection between maternal input and children's mental-state understanding is not the result of either a deep or long-standing emotional characteristic of the mother-child relationship, as indexed by attachment status, or a conversational style on the part of the child (e.g., the child's interest in story book characters), because the two assessments of maternal references to mental states were not made when mothers were engaged in conversation with their children. More generally, the findings from Ruffman et al. (2002) and from de Rosnay (2003) indicate that the frequency with which mothers refer to mental states predicts their child's later performance on theory-of-mind tasks, over and above any contribution made by child's earlier language or of theory-of-mind competence. The critical variation among mothers appears to be linguistic (rather than emotional or nonverbal), and it is measurable in the child's absence.

What Aspect of Maternal Input Is Critical?

The correlational evidence indicating a real-world relationship between maternal conversation and theory-of-mind performance by the child is encouraging. We may now examine various training studies with two questions in mind. First, can we confirm, with the help of training studies, that conversational input is a cause and not just a correlate of theory-of-mind performance? Second, what aspect of conversational input is important? In the observational studies described in the preceding section, the frequency with which mothers referred to mental states was measured, but it would be wrong to jump to the conclusion that it is indeed the frequency or diversity of such lexical items that plays a critical role in promoting the child's understanding of mental states.

Consider the following comment taken from the transcripts collected by de Rosnay (2003). The mother is describing her daughter's response to her absence in the course of the Strange Situation: "And then [she] was really quite inconsolable. . . . Um possibly thought I was gone for good." This comment includes two mental-state references—*inconsolable* and *thought*. A mother who is prone to use such lexical items in talking to her child might thereby promote the child's mental-state understanding. However, it is worth underlining two other aspects of the mother's comment. First, she acknowledges that the child might have a mistaken perspective on what is happening: "possibly thought I was gone for good." Second, she uses a particular type of verb—the verb *thought*, which takes a tensed complement. Arguably, either of these aspects of maternal input might be just as important as the sheer frequency of mental-state references. Indeed, explicit claims have been made for each of these aspects.

I have argued that conversational discourse can be a vehicle for conveying the fact that people differ in their point of view and in the information that they have available to them, irrespective of whether a particular party to the conversation makes any explicit lexical reference to any given mental state (Harris, 1996, 1999). This emphasis on the pragmatics of conversational discourse contrasts with the emphasis on the role of syntax that is advocated by de Villiers and de Villiers (2000; see also J. de Villiers, this volume, chapter 10). These authors have proposed that children's mastery of verbs that take tensed complement (verbs such as *think* and *say* in English) is a key condition for children's more general appreciation of the way that people can entertain propositions that may or may not be true.

These two accounts make different predictions about what type of conversation-based intervention would improve children's understanding of mental states. The discourse-based model predicts that if individual expectations or interpretations are articulated even in the absence of complement-taking mental verbs—or even in the absence of references to mental states in general—an improvement in the child's theory of mind should still occur. Moreover, that improvement need not be associated with an improvement in children's mastery of the use of complement-taking verbs. The syntax-based model, by contrast, implies that discourse that simply highlights differences in point of view should be ineffective. More specifically, it predicts that little improvement in false-belief understanding should occur unless there is a significant gain in the mastery of complement-taking verbs. With these opposing predictions in mind, we can review two recent intervention studies. (My description is selective because these studies are described in more detail in other chapters.)

Lohmann and Tomasello (2003; see Lohmann, Tomasello, & Meyer, this volume, chapter 12) gave children a series of misleading objects (e.g., a candle shaped like an apple). One particular intervention—the "discourse only" training—included no complement-taking verbs. It simply drew children's attention to the apparent and also the actual identity of the objects. This discourse-only training led to an improvement in children's subsequent performance on a set of standard theory-of-mind tasks. The improvement occurred even though there was only a small change in the children's performance on complement structures (suggesting that complement performance was not critical for theory-of-mind performance).

Hale and Tager-Flusberg (2003) obtained similar results. They trained children by talking them through a series of false-belief stories. This "discourse-only" training was akin to that of Lohmann and Tomasello insofar as it included no complement-taking verbs. Rather, the conversation focused on where the child expected the story protagonist to search and where the story protagonist would actually search. The training boosted theory-of-mind performance. Moreover, in this study there was no detectable change in performance on complement structures. Thus, both of these studies indicate that discourse that emphasizes different points of view with regard to the same event or object is sufficient to lead to an improvement in children's performance on standard theory-of-mind tasks. The findings obtained by Hale and Tager-Flusberg provide especially convincing support for the discourse model because the improvement in theory-of-mind performance could not be attributed to increased mastery of complement structures.

Both of these studies also included a group of children who were trained on sentential complements alone. In the study by Lohmann and Tomasello (2003), the deceptive aspect of the objects was not highlighted. Instead, children were asked to clarify what the story protagonist had done or said. For example, the story protagonist, Ernie, said: "This chair belongs to my grandfather. I know that!" Children were then asked: "What does Ernie know?" Children in the study by Hale and Tager-Flusberg (2003) received a similar form of training. They heard a story character make a claim and were asked to report on the claim (e.g., "What did he say?"). These interventions also proved effective in boosting children's performance on theory-of-mind tasks. Unfortunately, the reason for the training effect remain ambiguous. It is true that children were trained on complement structures, but they were also confronted by a story character who asserted a piece of knowledge that they themselves did not share. Thus, these results do not undermine the conclusion that children learn from conversational input that exposes them to different points of view.

The questionable role of complement structures is further underlined by Perner, Zauner, and Sprung (this volume, chapter 11). German children handle *wollen + dass* ('*want that*') + complement quite well, despite poor performance on *think + that* + complement and on false-belief tasks. In addition, Van der Lely, Hennessey, and Battell (2002) found that children with specific language impairment could do well on false-belief tasks despite poor performance on complements. Taken together, these various studies suggest that mastery of complement structures is neither sufficient nor necessary for performing well on false-belief tasks.

Combining the Correlational and Training Studies

What can we conclude when we combine the evidence from correlational studies on the one hand and from training studies on the other? First, we have strong evidence from both types of study that language does matter for the child's developing understanding of mental states. The correlational evidence shows that mothers vary in the conversational input that they offer to their children, and the training studies show that conversational input can promote children's understanding of mental states. Less clear is the exact way in which conversational input promotes children's understanding of mental states. There is a certain amount of slippage as we move from studies of naturally occurring dialogue to training studies in order to ask exactly what aspect of conversational input is effective.

Investigators who have examined naturally occurring dialogue have focused primarily on the semantic level: they have assessed the proportion of maternal utterances that include particular lexical items, notably mental-state terms. The training studies, by contrast, have not focused on the semantic level of mental-state terms. They have moved either to the pragmatic level by examining the impact of conversational discourse that introduces different points of view or to the syntactic level by training children on embedded complements.

However, this does not necessarily mean that the observational studies and the training studies are in direct conflict with one another. The semantic index that is used in the observational studies almost certainly correlates with both syntactic and pragmatic aspects of maternal discourse. For example, a subset of mental-state terms are complement-taking verbs such as *think, know, hope*, and so forth. In addition, that same semantic index probably correlates with more wide-ranging, pragmatic aspects of maternal discourse. For example, the use of mental-state verbs is likely to be just one manifestation of a larger disposition to articulate and compare different points of view on a given topic. Thus, whatever conclusion we draw from the training studies, they underline the possibility that a simple count of mental-state terms may not be the most sensitive measure of effective maternal input even if it is a useful correlate. More generally, we should keep in mind the likelihood that many aspects of maternal input are likely to covary. The mother's pragmatic intent in holding a dialogue with her child, the frequency with which she deploys mental-state terms, and the frequency with which she uses particular syntactic frames, notably embedded complements, are all likely to covary. My own working conclusion, which is based on the training studies to date and set out in the preceding section, is that it is the mother's pragmatic intent, notably her efforts to introduce varying points of view into a given conversation, that is the underlying and effective source of variation. Nevertheless, given the semantic and syntactic factors that typically covary with that intent, it may take some time before we can reach any firm consensus about just how conversational input has its effect on children's understanding of mental states.

The Role of Pretense

In searching for possible correlates of theory-of-mind competence, investigators have not confined their attention to the role of language. Several recent studies have shown that children's pretend play is correlated with their performance on theory-of-mind tasks. For example, the frequency of joint proposals (e.g., "you have to stay in my arms" or "let's make cookies") and of role assignments in the course of pretend play (e.g., "you be mommy") are correlated with children's performance on theory-of-mind tasks (Astington & Jenkins, 1995; Jenkins & Astington, 2000). Similar findings have emerged from studies by Youngblade and Dunn (1995), Taylor and Carlson (1997) and Schwebel, Rosen, and Singer (1999).

In these various studies, measures of joint pretend play or role-play correlated with measures of performance on theory-of-mind tasks (typically false-belief and/or appearance-reality tasks). By contrast, other measures of pretense (e.g., amount of pretense; diversity of themes; impersonation of a machine; solitary pretend play) did not correlate with measures of performance on theory-of-mind tasks. Thus, the results do not support the claim that pretend play in general is associated with the understanding of mental representation. Instead, they suggest that children's ability to set aside their own identity and to act out the part of another person is linked to children's performance on standard theory-of-mind tasks. As I have argued elsewhere, this pattern of results can be interpreted as support for simulation theory, which assumes that the solution to classic theory-of-mind tasks can be reached via a form of role play in which one's own current situation and knowledge are temporarily set to one side (Harris, 2000b). Still, it must be acknowledged that the link between role-play and theory-of-mind performance rests for the moment on correlational data only, although in one recent correlational study, there was some indication that earlier false-belief understanding predicts later role assignment and joint proposals, rather than the reverse (Jenkins & Astington, 2000). However, there have been no intervention studies to assess whether training in role-play leads to better performance on standard theory-of-mind tasks. Nonetheless, we do have the suggestive findings of an earlier research tradition that provided convincing evidence that educational programs in dramatic play have beneficial effects on children's social cognition in general (Smilansky, 1968).

Irrespective of the validity of the simulation interpretation, we may ask in more detail about the relationship between language and pretense as predictors of theory-of-mind performance. We may ask, first, whether the relationship between pretense and theory-of-mind understanding disappears once we take into account the possible contribution of children's language ability. After all, we have seen in the previous section that conversational input to the child accounts for a good deal of variation in children's theory-of-mind performance. We also know that children's language ability is a good predictor of their performance on standard false-belief tasks (Happé, 1995). Finally, we know that deaf children with language delays perform poorly on false-belief tasks (Peterson & Siegal, 1999; P. de Villiers, this volume, chapter 13). Accordingly, there is a definite possibility that the link between pretense and theory of mind will disappear once due allowance is made for the contribution of language ability. In fact, this issue was examined in all the studies cited. In each case, they report that the relationship between pretense and theory of mind held up even when language ability was controlled for (with language ability variously measured in terms of vocabulary, MLU, or syntax). Moreover, and somewhat surprisingly, only one of the studies reported a relationship between children's pretend skills and their language ability (Taylor & Carlson, 1997), and even in that study, the relationship was very modest. Thus, children with superior pretend skills scored higher on a vocabulary measure than children with standard pretend skills (PPVT-R, mean = 109 versus mean = 105, respectively).

Overall, therefore, these studies suggest that we may identify two distinct contributions to children's theory-of-mind skills. On the one hand, children benefit from having superior language ability and, as we have seen in the preceding sections, from conversational input that includes frequent references to mental states and calls their attention to different points of view regarding the same object or event. On the other hand, children may also benefit from having superior pretend skills, especially with respect to the type of play that involves pretending to be another person. In the next section, I speculate in more detail on how to interpret this pattern of results.

Conversation and Pretense

One way to interpret the preceding results is to suppose that children learn in two relatively separate and distinct contexts: when engaged in conversation and when engaged in pretend play, especially role-play. However, the assumption that children are either engaged in conversation or engaged in role-play is unnecessary and probably misleading. Children use language to good effect in the course of their play both when they step out of role to make suggestions and when they step into role and give voice to the person whose part they are playing (Miller & Garvey, 1984). Probably even more widespread and important, however, is the fact that a form of role-play is frequently called for in following a conversation.

Certain types of conversation explicitly invite children to engage in role taking. For example, in the course of disciplinary encounters with their children, caretakers may ask their children to imagine another person's perspective (e.g., "How would you feel if . . . ?"). Indeed, caretakers vary in the frequency with which they claim to resort to such invitations, and that variation is correlated with children's performance on standard theory-of-mind tasks (Ruffman, Perner, & Parkin, 1999). Other types of conversation do not issue an explicit invitation but elicit a form of role-play, nevertheless. For example, when children are introduced to a story protagonist in a given setting (e.g., "Cinderella was sitting on the chair by the fireplace, dreaming about the ball"), they appear to mentally displace themselves and to imagine subsequent narrative events from Cinderella's perspective seated at the fireplace inside her cottage. For example, when Cinderella's fairy godmother arrives at her cottage, children tend to think of the fairy godmother as *coming* rather than *going* into the cottage (Rall & Harris, 2000). Thus, whether explicitly or implicitly, children will be prompted in the course of conversation to set their own current perspective aside and to imagine what another person might feel or perceive.

Arguably, because of variation in role-taking ability, children vary in the ease with which they can respond to such prompts and invitations and imagine the world from that alternative perspective. So, children might benefit differentially from conversational input depending on their role-taking abilities. This proposal can be tested by studying the effects of discourse training on children with different levels of role-taking skill. One plausible outcome is that the two factors are simply additive: the greater children's role-taking skill and the more they are alerted to alternative points of view in the context of discourse, the better children will perform on theory-of-mind tasks. However, it is also possible that the two factors interact. For example, to achieve the same increment in mental-state understanding, greater conversational input may be needed for children with limited role-taking ability.

Conclusions

The study of why language matters for children's theory of mind has made rapid progress. Research in the mid-1990s indicated that language competence was an important correlate of false-belief performance. However, the effective role of language had not been systematically studied or analyzed. As argued in this chapter, we now have converging evidence from both observational and training studies that the conversation to which children are exposed does indeed matter for their theory of mind.

Less clear, at present, is exactly why conversational input matters. My own conclusion is that, to varying degrees, conversation highlights different points of view—and the understanding of alternative points of view is critical for tackling standard theory-of-mind tasks. Still, it must be acknowledged that this conclusion rests on a particular reading of both the observational and the training studies—a reading that draws those two forms of evidence together but rides rough-shod fashion over the gaps between them, particularly with respect to measurement techniques.

One theoretical advantage of an emphasis on the pragmatic functions of conversation is that it points to a possible bridge to recent findings concerning pretend play, and more specifically pretend role-play. Children who engage in such play appear to perform better on standard theory-of-mind tasks. Certain types of conversation also invite a subtle form of role-play. In the course of conversation, children may not be led to act out a role in an overt fashion, but they are often prompted to imagine the world from another person's perspective. On this account, then, conversation and role-playing ability may form a virtuous circle, one that is manifest in children's understanding of false belief but likely goes beyond to influence their social understanding in other contexts— when considering other people's feelings, when thinking about historical characters, and when enjoying the world of fiction.

Note

1. Items on this test require children to listen to a test sentence and to then point appropriately to a picture in reply. For example, children might be asked: "Point to a dog but not the one that is eating" (having been shown a picture of three dogs, only one of whom is eating).

References

Astington, J. W., & Jenkins, J. M. (1995). Theory-of-mind development and social understanding. *Cognition and Emotion*, 9, 151–165.

Bradley, L., & Bryant, P. E. (1983). Categorizing sounds and learning to read—A causal connection. *Nature*, 301, 419–421.

De Rosnay, M. (2003). Children's understanding of emotion: The roles of attachment and maternal discourse. Unpublished doctoral thesis, Department of Experimental Psychology, University of Oxford.

de Villiers, J. G., & de Villiers, P. A. (2000). Linguistic determinism and the understanding of false beliefs. In P. Mitchell and K. J. Riggs (Eds.), *Children's reasoning and the mind* (pp. 191–228). Hove, UK: Psychology Press.

De Wolff, M., & van IJzendoorn, M. H. (1997). Sensitivity and attachment: A meta-analysis on parental antecedents of infant attachment. *Child Development*, 68, 571–591.

Dunn, J., Brown, J., Slomkowski, C., Tesla, C., & Youngblade, L. (1991). Young children's understanding of other people's feelings and beliefs: Individual differences and their antecedents. *Child Development*, 62, 1352–1366.

Fonagy, P., & Target, M. (1997). Attachment and reflective function: Their role in self-organization. *Development and Psychopathology*, 9, 679–700.

Hale, C. M., & Tager-Flusberg, H. (2003). The influence of language on theory of mind: A training study. *Developmental Science*, 6, 346–359.

Happé, F. G. E. (1995). The role of age and verbal ability in the theory of mind task performance of subjects with autism. *Child Development, 66,* 843–855.

Harris, P. L. (1996). Desires, beliefs, and language. In P. Carruthers & P.K. Smith (Eds.), *Theories of theories of mind.* (pp. 200–220). Cambridge: Cambridge University Press.

Harris, P. L. (1999). Acquiring the art of conversation: Children's developing conception of their conversation partner. In M. Bennett (Ed.), *Developmental psychology: Achievements and prospects* (pp. 89–105). London: Psychology Press.

Harris, P. L. (2000a). Individual differences in understanding emotion: The role of attachment status and psychological discourse. *Attachment and Human Development, 1,* 307–324.

Harris, P. L. (2000b). *The work of the imagination.* Oxford: Blackwell.

Harris, P. L., Johnson, C., Hutton, D., Andrews, G., & Cooke, T. (1989). Young children's theory of mind and emotion. *Cognition and Emotion, 3,* 379–400.

Jenkins, J. M., & Astington, J. W. (2000). Theory of mind and social behavior: Causal models tested in a longitudinal study. *Merrill-Palmer Quarterly, 46,* 203–220.

Lohmann, H., & Tomasello, M. (2003). The role of language in the development of false belief understanding: A training study. *Child Development, 74,* 1130–1144.

Miller, P., & Garvey, G. (1984). Mother-baby role play: Its origins in social support. In I. Bretherton (Ed.), *Symbolic play: The development of social understanding* (pp. 101–130). Orlando, FL: Academic Press.

Peterson, C., & Siegal, M. (1999). Representing inner worlds: Theory of mind in autistic, deaf and normal hearing children. *Psychological Science, 10,* 126–129.

Pons, F. L., & Harris, P. L. (2000). *Test of Emotion Comprehension—TEC.* Oxford: University of Oxford.

Pons, F. L., Lawson, J., Harris, P. L., & de Rosnay, M. (2003). Individual differences in children's emotion understanding: Effects of age and language. *Scandinavian Journal of Psychology, 44,* 347–353.

Rall, J., & Harris, P. L. (2000). In Cinderella's slippers? Story comprehension from the protagonist's point-of-view. *Developmental Psychology, 36,* 202–208.

Ruffman, T., Perner, J., & Parkin, L. (1999). How parenting style affects false-belief understanding. *Social Development, 8,* 395–411.

Ruffman, T., Slade, L., & Crowe, E. (2002). The relationship between children's and mothers' mental state language and theory-of-mind understanding. *Child Development, 73,* 734–751.

Schwebel, D. C., Rosen, C. S., & Singer, J. L. (1999). Preschoolers' pretend play and theory of mind: The role of jointly constructed pretence. *British Journal of Developmental Psychology, 17,* 333–348.

Smilansky, S. (1968). *The effects of sociodramatic play on disadvantaged preschool children.* New York: Wiley.

Steele, H., Steele, M., Croft, C., & Fonagy, P. (1999). Infant-mother attachment at one year predicts children's understanding of mixed emotions at six-years. *Social Development, 8,* 161–178.

Taylor, M., & Carlson, S. M. (1997). The relation between individual differences in fantasy and theory of mind. *Child Development, 68,* 436–455.

Van der Lely, H. K. J., Hennessey, S., & Battell, J. (2002) *Linguistic determinism and false belief: Insight from children with Specific Language Impairment.* Unpublished manuscript, Department of Human Communication Science, University College, London.

Van IJzendoorn, M. H., Juffer, F., & Duyvesteyn, M. G. C. (1995). Breaking the intergenerational cycle of insecure attachment: A review of the effects of attachment-based interventions on maternal sensitivity and infant security. *Journal of Child Psychology and Child Psychiatry, 36*, 225–248.

Wiig, E. H., Secord, W., & Semel, E. (1992). *Clinical Evaluation of Language Fundamentals-Preschool (CELF-Preschool)*. San Antonio, TX: Psychological Corporation, Harcourt Brace Jovanovich.

Youngblade, L. M., & Dunn, J. (1995). Individual differences in young children's pretend play with mother and sibling: Links to relationships and understanding of other people's feelings and beliefs. *Child Development, 66*, 1472–1492.

5 Talking about "New" Information: The Given/New Distinction and Children's Developing Theory of Mind

Daniela K. O'Neill

Successful communication is the result not only of knowing what the words of a language mean and how to put the words together in grammatically appropriate ways but also of knowing how to use the language with others—the domain of pragmatics (O'Neill & Happé, 2000). For example, the ability to communicate utterances that are informative, relevant, polite, ironic, or sarcastic relies on more than simply knowing how to put the words of a language together into a sentence.

The focus of this chapter is the pragmatic ability to provide a listener with information that is *new* rather than information that is already known by the listener and that would be *old* (or, as it is usually referred to by linguists, *given*) and presumably of little interest. The distinction between new and given information has been a recurring theme in my work over the past ten years, during which time it has become apparent to me that the notion of new information can be very slippery. That is, in different contexts it appears to mean very different things. In this chapter, I do not attempt to provide a complete description of what it means to communicate new information. What I do is describe a diverse set of studies—involving children making requests, commenting on events, and learning new words—that, taken together, emphasize different ways of conceptualizing new information and that pose an interesting challenge with respect to describing what kind of an understanding of mind might underlie a child's ability to assess new and given information in these different situations. Toward the end of the chapter, I also provide an overview of how new/given information is defined within the context of adult communication, in order to appraise the young child's competence. I end this chapter by situating this discussion of what is "new" within the larger domain of pragmatics and theory of mind, with particular reference to a few of the other chapters in this volume.

My interest in the ability of children to provide new information began with the writings of Grice (1975) and his seminal idea that it is reasonable to assume that speakers and listeners, in conversing with each other, try to meet certain general standards:

> Our talk exchanges . . . are characteristically, to some degree at least, cooperative efforts; and each participant recognizes in them, to some extent, a common purpose or set of purposes, or at least a mutually accepted direction . . . at each stage, some possible conversational moves would be excluded as conversationally unsuitable. We might then formulate a rough general principle which participants will be expected (ceteris paribus) to observe, namely, Make your conversational contribution such as is required, at the stage at which it occurs, by the accepted purpose or direction of the talk exchange in which you are engaged. (Grice, 1975, p. 45)

Grice referred to this as the cooperative principle and developed it into four maxims of conversation—namely, four assumptions that participants in a conversation are aware of that guide their conduct (1975):

Maxim of quantity

Make your contribution as informative as is required, but not more informative than is required.

Maxim of quality

Try to make your contribution one that is true. That is, do not say anything you believe to be false or have inadequate evidence for.

Maxim of relation

Make your contribution relevant to the aims of the ongoing conversation.

Maxim of manner

Be clear. Try to avoid obscurity, ambiguity, wordiness, or disorderliness in your use of language.

The maxim of quantity caught my attention initially for its clear reliance on a theory of mind and, in particular, its assessments of another person's knowledge. That is, if a speaker is to provide only that information that a listener needs and not more, then a speaker must be able to assess what knowledge the listener can be assumed to share in common and adjust his/her speech accordingly.

A discussion of Grice's maxims is not frequently encountered in the literature pertaining to child language development (but see Surian, Baron-Cohen, & Van der Lely, 1996; Waters, Siegal, & Slaughter, 2000), although one does find much discussion of a related notion, that is, the distinction between new and given information (Clark & Clark, 1977; Greenfield & Smith, 1976; Halliday, 1967). Those who discuss this distinction argue, for example, that an important aspect of using language is the distinction between given information, which the speaker believes the listener already knows and accepts as true, and new information, which the speaker believes the listener does not yet know (Clark & Haviland, 1977).

But how is it that speakers achieve what is captured in Grice's maxim of quantity or the given/new distinction? It's one thing to say that speakers should strive for a certain level of informativeness or "newness," but it is an altogether different question to ask how speakers are able to determine the level at which to pitch a contribution to a conversation.

What Is "New" Information?

New Information Is Information Obtained While a Listener Is Physically Absent

In my first study examining children's ability to communicate new information (O'Neill, 1996), I began by asking myself what might be one of the first factors children take into account when assessing whether some information might be new or given for a communicative partner. That is, if a child was going to adapt her communication to include only new and not given information, what information about another person (i.e., the listener) might be relevant? My intuition was that one of the first circumstances under which children might note that they and a listener have different knowledge is when they and the listener are not *physically copresent* for an event. Indeed, Clark and Marshall (1981) have argued that physical copresence is one important factor that communicative interactants take into account when assessing common ground and mutual knowledge. This intuition was borne out.

In Study 1 of O'Neill (1996), older 2-year-old children (mean age 2;7) were faced with the task of having to ask their parent (generally their mother) to retrieve a toy that I had hidden in one of two containers—a box or a cup—located on the far-right or far-left side of a high shelf out of the children's own reach. On two *parent-present* trials, the parent was present in the room when I first showed children the toy and hid it in one of the two locations. On two other *parent-absent* trials, the parent did not view the introduction and hiding of the toy because she had either left the room or closed her eyes during this time. The parent then reentered the room or opened her eyes following the hiding. The children were instructed at this point to tell their parent what they wanted her to do. (It should be noted that when the parent entered the room, she was surreptitiously told the location of the toy so as to be able to respond to the child's first request and not to need to ask for feedback, which would present a confound on later trials. On closed-eye trials, the parents peeked.) The question of interest was whether children would adjust their requests for the toy according to whether their parent was absent or not for the introduction of the toy and its hiding. Of particular interest were three types of new information that children might include more often in their requests on parent-absent trials: (1) a point to the container in which the toy was hidden, (2) the name of this container, and (3) the identity of the toy (e.g., duck, pig).

The results clearly showed that 2-year-old children adjusted their requests for the toy depending on whether their parent had been present during the introduction and hiding of the toy. When their parent had been in the room, children's requests were of a very general nature, simply asking for help (e.g., "Gimme help . . . er, helper, helper"). However, when their parent had been absent or had closed her eyes for the introduction and hiding of the toy, the children significantly more often pointed to the location of the toy, named the location of the toy, and named the toy (e.g., "Get that. Get that duck in the box," accompanied by a point to right side of shelf). Overall, 73% of the 2-year-old children provided more new information in their requests on parent-absent trials than on parent-present trials.

In Study 2, these results were replicated with young 2-year-olds (mean age 2;3) using a simplified design in which children had to ask for a sticker placed in one of two identical-looking containers located, out of reach, in the far corners of the table at which the children sat. Because these younger children would not tolerate their parent leaving the room, an open-eye/closed-eye procedure was used. On two *closed-eye* trials, the parent closed her eyes during the hiding of the sticker and, on the other two *open-eye* trials, the parent kept her eyes open. The identity of the sticker was not revealed to children, and thus the question of interest in this study was whether children would gesture to the container in which the sticker was hidden more often when the parent had not witnessed its placement than when the parent had. As in Study 1, I found that children gestured to the location of the sticker significantly more often on closed-eye trials than on open-eye trials.

Thus, in this set of first studies, new information was viewed as information that a listener had not shared with a speaker as a result of being physically absent at the time the information was made available. It should be noted that the notion of physical absence in this study included actually being out of the room when the new information was conveyed and being "absent" due to having visual access obstructed. In this sense, the definition of physical absence/copresence may be broader than that implied in the work of Clark and Marshall (1981) mentioned earlier. Despite this broader interpretation, children as young as 2 years of age were found to adapt their requests for help in getting a desired object, depending on whether their parent had witnessed the object's introduction and hiding location.

What type of an understanding of mind might mediate this observed tailoring of children's requests? I addressed this question in detail in O'Neill (1996) and present only a summary of my argument here. Even 3- and 4-year-old children have difficulty recognizing the particular knowledge possessed as a result of particular perceptual and sensory experiences and have difficulty answering questions such as "Who knows x?" (cf. source of knowledge studies such as O'Neill, Astington, & Flavell, 1992; O'Neill & Gopnik, 1991). Hence, I argue that 2-year-old children do not tailor their communication on the basis of such a sophisticated conception of knowing as *"seeing = knowing."* Rather, I propose a *"disengagement + updating"* explanation whereby the 2-year-old children adapted their communication, first by taking into account their parent's disengagement from the events taking place and, second, by wanting to update the parent about the significant and relevant events that had happened while the parent was disengaged (i.e., because the parent had left the room or had kept her eyes closed). In using the phrase "taking into account a parent's disengagement," I mean to imply only that a child has realized in some global sense that the parent had become disengaged from an ongoing event—much in the same way that even a 9-month-old will react if a parent suddenly adopts a "still-face" (e.g., Trevarthen, 1977; Weinberg & Tronick, 1996) or discontinues her involvement in a game (e.g., Ross & Lollis, 1987). A child's assessment that the parent has become disengaged from an interaction can take into account a whole host of factors, such as whether the parent is absent from the room, has her eyes closed, is talking about unrelated matters, or appears distracted. Such a notion of disengagement does not necessarily imply that the child recognizes that one or more of the parent's specific sensory capabilities has been negatively affected, such as the ability to hear, see, and so forth. This type of understanding is implied, however, in an explanation that relies on *"seeing = knowing."*

The second part of my explanation involves the notion of updating. I suggest that, after a parent's disengagement from the game, children were motivated to update the parent regarding the significant events that had occurred during the period of disengagement. In the context of these studies, these "significant events" are taken to be the identity of the toy and its location, as opposed to other aspects of the situation, such as the fact that the experimenter hid the toy, about which the children are not predicted to want to update their parent. That is, children's adaptations may have relied on a simple understanding of the form "Tell other people about significant happenings they did not take part in (or witness) with me." It is also possible that such significant events do not include other possible new information not relevant to the goal of finding the toy, such as the experimenter accidentally dropping the toy on the way to the shelf. Because this study did not manipulate such factors, this cannot be known for sure. Nevertheless, if children are assessing new/given information not only according to physical absence or visual occlusion but also according to the relevance of the new information to the task at hand, then it appears that this distinction encompasses not only the maxim of quantity but also the maxim of relation: make your contribution relevant to the aims of the ongoing conversation. As the reader will see, this notion of relevance and its relation to the new/given distinction arises again in connection with the next two studies to be discussed.

New Information Is "the Relevant Thing to Say"

In the study just described (O'Neill, 1996), the communicative situation was an imperative one for children—they were making requests. I began to wonder, however, about communicative interactions of a more *declarative* nature—situations, for example, in which children are simply commenting on events around them. What underlies their ability to provide new information in such settings, and how is new information even to be defined? Consider, for example, two children looking at a flower. One child says, "It's got a bug on it." Some could argue that the very term *new* is inappropriate here, given that both listener and speaker are looking at the same thing and the information to be communicated is not likely to be new to either as both are perceptually aware of it. As we shall see, such situations force an expansion of the definition of new information beyond that of information not available to a listener due to physical absence or disengagement.

Indeed, in the literature and research concerning children's early communicative utterances, new information has been defined in a more lenient manner as information that has been noticed and is new for the speaker alone, rather than according to the more sophisticated definition of new information as information not known by a communicative partner. In what they refer to as the "principle of informativeness," Greenfield and Smith (1976) and Greenfield and Zukow (1978) have argued that, in the one-word stage, "what is taken for granted [i.e., perceived as certain] goes unstated by the child, while uncertain, informative, or changing elements are given verbal expression in the single word utterance" (Greenfield & Zukow, 1978, p. 290). Beyond the one-word stage, a number of studies have suggested that children make explicit the information that is situationally the least redundant (e.g., Hornby, Hass, & Feldman, 1970;

MacWhinney & Bates, 1978; Weisenberger, 1976) or that reflects changing, as opposed to unchanging, elements (e.g., Rowan, Leonard, Chapman, & Weiss, 1983; Snyder, 1978. See also O'Neill & Happé, 2000, for a full review of this early-language literature.)

One question this previous research cannot answer, however, and that my study with Francesca Happé (O'Neill & Happé, 2000) sought to answer, is whether one might see, even at the one- or two-word stage, *consistency* in the types of *topics initiated* by children. That is, how early might children demonstrate, by the timing and topic of their utterances, that they share an adult intuition of what aspects in a situation could be topics of conversation? In other words, when do children recognize those aspects in the environment that are *salient*, in the sense of being potentially of shared interest to others, and worth communicating about (O'Neill & Happé, 2000)? The question is not a trivial one. For example, it has been well documented that individuals with autism display pragmatic impairments that include great difficulty initiating topics, choosing an appropriate topic, staying on topic, and knowing when a topic should be changed (e.g., Baron-Cohen, 1988; Eales, 1993; Fay & Schuler, 1980; Tager-Flusberg, 1981). Thus, these individuals lack the pragmatic ability to determine what is an appropriate or good topic of conversation. For typically developing children, on the other hand, an early, significant step in their pragmatic development is the recognition of those aspects in the environment that have the potential to be of shared interest to the self and a communicative partner and thus worth communicating about.

In O'Neill & Happé (2000), children were presented with eight sets of four objects in the following kind of scenario. A child was seated at a small table with the experimenter on her right and her mother on their left. The experimenter handed the child a small, yellow, plastic duck (Trial 1). The child was free to explore the toy for as long as she wanted, and when she was finished with it she could "give it to Big Bird" by sending it down a chute. Once she had gotten rid of the toy, the experimenter handed her another, identical-looking small duck (Trial 2). Once she had gotten rid of that toy, another identical-looking small duck was produced (Trial 3). And finally, the fourth time (Trial 4), the experimenter handed her a yellow, plastic duck that was about three times larger than the previous three ducks.

In this type of scenario, we might assume that children might name the duck or say something about it (e.g., yellow) on the first trial, say less on the second and third trials when they are given ducks identical to the first, and then, on the fourth trial, comment on the change in the size of the duck (e.g., "big duck"). That is, the new information to be communicated would be related to the attentional system being captured by the perceptually salient or changing aspects of the situation, namely the introduction of the toy on Trial 1 and the change in the property on Trial 4 (cf. Bates, 1976; Greenfield & Zukow, 1978). In this sense, saying "big duck" on the fourth trial would be the "relevant thing to say."

We (O'Neill & Happé, 2000) presented children with eight such series of four objects, which included changes in the identity of the object (e.g., three dogs followed by a ball) and property changes (e.g., three intact teddy bears followed by one teddy bear with an ear missing). Three groups of children participated: 20 typically developing children (mean age = 22 months), a group of 11 children with Down syndrome (mean age = 45 months), and a group of 10 children with autism (mean age = 55 months). The three groups of children did not differ significantly with respect to the size of their productive vocabularies as measured by the MacArthur Communicative Development Inventories (Fenson, Dale, Reznick, et al., 1993). Indeed, all the children were at about a one- or two-word linguistic level. For the purposes of this discussion of new and given information, I highlight only two main findings from the study.

One behavior we measured was children's naming of the toys throughout the four trials and/or their talk about the change on the fourth trial. Interestingly, and somewhat surprisingly, there were no differences overall among the groups in the total number of such utterances observed. However, the *timing* of these utterances among the four trials did differ. Among the typically developing children, significantly more such talk occurred on the first and fourth trials than on the second and third trials, producing a pronounced U-shaped pattern of responding. In contrast, among the children with autism, no prominent U-shaped pattern of responding was observed. In addition, and unlike among the typically developing children, their utterances were also very rarely directed to the mother or the experimenter and occurred largely while the child was looking at the toy. The pattern of responding among children with Down syndrome fell in between that of the other two groups of children.

In addition to these differences at the level of children's vocalizations, differences were also seen at the overall level of children's behavioral actions with the toys. For example, we observed the pattern of certain target behaviors occurring on each of the four trials for a given toy—behaviors such as manually or visually exploring a toy, producing any play behavior with a toy, or producing any verbal or communicative behavior to mother or the experimenter. If any such behaviors were observed on a trial, a score of 1 was given; if none, a score of 0. We were interested in seeing, across all the toys, whether the pattern of responding over the four trials would differ among the three groups. And it did. Among the typically developing children, the two most common patterns of responding were either to produce the target behaviors on the first and fourth trials but not on the intervening trials (i.e., a U-shaped pattern of responding: 1001) or to produce the target behaviors on the first two trials only, followed by a recovery on the fourth trial (i.e., 1101). Among the children with Down syndrome, the most common pattern was to produce the target behaviors on all four trials (i.e., 1111). Among the children with autism, the most common pattern seen was one we referred to as "other," in which the occurrence or absence of the target behaviors was more randomly distributed across the four trials and not timed with the changes in identity or property of the toys on the first and fourth trials (e.g., patterns such as 0111, 0011, or 0100). That is, the children with autism often behaved as though they were oblivious to the changes on the first and fourth trials, or as suddenly interested in the toys on the second and third trials.

These findings are the first to suggest that, even at the one- and two-word stage, typically developing children direct their attention in a remarkably similar way to certain aspects of the environment around them—at least with respect to the toys we showed them. That is, their vocalizations occurred at very similar times during the game, and their content was remarkably similar. These results also suggest that the difficulty children with autism face in initiating what others consider appropriate or relevant topics of conversation may be in part a result of the fact that they do not, even at an attentional level, appear to find the salient, changing aspects of the toys of interest in the same way the typically developing children and children with Down syndrome do.

With respect to the typically developing children, furthermore, the results of this study raise the question of how children as young as 22 months have come to understand that the first appearance of a toy, or a change in its property, is something worth talking about. It could be argued that children's utterances simply reflected their own interests. But I argue that they reflected more than this. If children were just commenting on their own subjective interests, how does one explain the fact that the timing and content of their utterances were so similar? Presumably their own subjective interests were changing moment by moment, and so, if their comments reflected these changing interests, they would not have shown consistency with respect to timing and content. An example that comes to mind is the child with autism who commented "pig" rather inexplicably on a trial that did not involve any pigs, although the child had encountered pigs on an earlier series of four trials. In contrast, the typically developing children seemed to be selectively attuning their comments to certain salient, more objective changes in the situation, resulting in similarities with respect to the timing and content of their utterances. The findings of this study may indeed rest, in part, on the ability of these children, by 22 months, to assess what other people around them pay attention to and communicate about. Such assessments, leading to a general sense of "what people talk about," could be based on a number of cues, such as observation of another person's line of regard, use of referential gestures, or actions with an object. These behaviors could serve as a means whereby children could note regularities in what interests another person and other people in general. And research has amply demonstrated that children are sensitive to such nonverbal behaviors from as early as 9 months of age (e.g., Baldwin, 1991; Butterworth, 1991; Butterworth & Grover, 1990; Corkum & Moore, 1995; Leung & Rheingold, 1981; Murphy & Messer, 1977; Scaife &

Bruner, 1975). In addition, the ability to initiate the kinds of topics observed in this study seem, in some cases, to rely on an appreciation of what is the canonical or typical situation (e.g., an intact teddy bear). There is certainly developmental evidence to suggest that the noting of discrepancies from the norm may be of growing (and even particular) importance to children during the second to third year of life (e.g., Kagan, 1991).

New Information Is an Unshared Perspective on an Event

In this final study that I will discuss (O'Neill, Topolovec, & Stern-Cavalcante, 2002), the situation remained a declarative one, but the roles for the child and the adult were reversed. It was now the child's task to determine the intended new information being conveyed by an adult and the particular perspective in the communicative situation being highlighted by the speaker.

In this study, children were presented with a situation in which they had to assume some aspects of a particular situation (jointly viewed by the adult and the child) to be given or irrelevant and one particular aspect to be the new or nonshared information to which the speaker was intending to refer. The use of adjective terms is a case in point. Suppose a child witnesses an adult holding a teddy bear and saying "fuzzy." What is the child to make of this label? The possible meanings of the term "fuzzy" are almost limitless—brown, fat, furry, two-eyed, round, big, heavy, and so on. Indeed, adjectives are often used to capture aspects of an object that relate to how our senses are impacted by the object—its taste, smell, appearance, sound, and feel. Given this, it makes sense that many aspects could be salient and competing for attention. A simple account based on some notion of perceptual salience, in which the relevant salient dimension simply "pops out" to the child (or a listener of any age), is not likely to offer a full explanation of how the relevant dimension is determined.

So, in such a situation, how is a "meeting of minds" achieved? How does a child zero in on the intended perspective of the speaker? In this study, precisely because adjectives often relate sensory information, it made sense to me that children would zero in by attending, in addition to the label, to the actions performed by the speaker that might specify more clearly the intended "sensory perspective." The intended "sensory perspective" of interest in our study was touch—that is, the novel adjective term used by the adult referred to a tactile property of an object. The prediction was that gestures used by a speaker that accompanied the novel adjective term and illustrated the tactile property in question would be noticed by children and used in determining the intended meaning of the term.

Two- and 3-year-old children participated in the study. For each novel adjective term to be learned, children were first given a teaching trial on which they were presented with a target object (that they all knew the identity of) to explore manually and that had an interesting tactile property—the "target" property. For example, they were given a mouse that was filled with rubber, grapelike balls. During this exploration time, half of the children, those randomly assigned to the *descriptive gesture* group, heard the experimenter label the object as *globby* five times according to a preset script (e.g., "Wow, it's a globby mouse. Look, it's a globby mouse."). Each time the label was used, it was accompanied by a descriptive gesture that highlighted the insides of the object (e.g., rolled balls between thumb and forefinger). The other half of the children, assigned to the *point gesture* condition, also heard *globby* used in the same preset script, but instead of the label being accompanied by a descriptive gesture, it was accompanied by a point gesture to the object as a whole. Immediately following this teaching phase for each novel adjective term, children were presented with two identical-looking test objects, for example, two fish, that differed only with respect to their insides. In the case of the fish, one fish "matched" the target object during teaching and was also filled with grapelike balls. The other "nonmatching" fish was filled with cotton wool. Children were asked to find the globby fish.

Did presenting the novel adjective term with a descriptive or point gesture make a difference? The answer was clearly yes. Children given a descriptive gesture chose the correct test object significantly more often than children provided with only a point gesture. When choosing the test object, these children were also significantly more likely to reproduce the descriptive gesture with the test toys. Children given the point gesture also indicated more uncertainty at the time they needed to choose the matching object, asking such questions as "This one?" significantly more often.

In addition to this effect of the gesture types on children's test choices, when children's comments during the teaching phase were transcribed, a further difference was found with respect to the number of properties of the toys mentioned by children at the time of teaching the target term. Among the children given the descriptive gestures, repetitions of the adjective term were most commonly observed. Among children provided only with point gestures, repetitions were also observed, but another type of comment was also observed that was rarely observed among the descriptive gesture group—comments about other *nontarget* properties and parts of the toys, as in the following examples:

> His tail is grey.
> It walks. It has a mouth. It has a nose and it has a chin. And it has a
>   butt. This thing on it.
> He looks like a big squirrel. But, he looks like a round circle.
> Look it. The spongy cow is pretty good. He has funny little spots.

Such comments, we argued, reflect the fact that, given only a point gesture, the speaker's intended referent was not clear, and therefore children were more likely to name properties and parts of the object that were salient and that caught their attention in their effort to discern the meaning of the novel adjective term. That is, we believe these comments reflect the greater number of properties children in the point gesture were entertaining with respect to the possible meaning intended by the adult when using the novel adjective term.

So, overall, in this study of adjective learning, children were presented with situations in which the sensory information being highlighted (i.e., tactile information, in most cases) was not visually salient and could not be ascertained through visual inspection. This study demonstrates that, in such situations, children as young as 2 years of age approach the task of word learning very actively and utilize relevant pragmatic gestural cues provided by the speaker to decipher the meaning of the new information (i.e., the novel adjective term) uttered by the speaker.

The situation children encountered in our study may sound similar to that encountered in other studies that examine word learning and the role of nonverbal information provided by a speaker. For example, Baldwin (e.g., 1991, 1993) has shown that children as young as 16 months of age will check a speaker's line of visual regard to determine which of two possible referents the speaker is referring to when uttering a novel label. The situation children encountered in our study was quite different, however, in that only *one* referent was ever present at the time of teaching, and the child needed to determine the *particular aspect* of the object the speaker was referring to. This, I argue, is a more difficult task for children than determining which of two referents is intended by a speaker.

It is interesting to contemplate how the situation presented to children in this study of adjective learning actually made things quite a bit easier than may be often the case when people use adjective terms. In this study, the adjective terms all referred to sensory properties of the objects. This makes it possible for a speaker to use some sort of accompanying sensory action to help the listener zero in on the intended aspect of the object. However, many adjective terms are much more subjective and abstract—lovely, terrible, ugly, pretty—and cannot be so easily accompanied by a physical action that helps to clarify their intended referent. Indeed, in many such cases it may be difficult even for the speaker to define exactly what aspect of the object leads her to use the adjective in question (e.g., what aspect of a painting is a speaker referring to when she calls it "lovely" or "horrible" or "interesting"?)

Taxonomies of New and Given Information

Up to this point in the chapter, I have presented a relatively informal discussion of some of the different types of new information that I have observed children to provide or to utilize in their early communicative interactions with others across a number of different studies of mine. One reason I chose this focus is that the topic of new and given information is one that has not been studied very much among children. With respect to adult communication, in contrast, a fairly vast literature exists on the topic of new and given information. I do not attempt to review this literature in full here but highlight some work where the focus has also been to distinguish different types of new or given information or to consider what information about others might be taken into account when making assessments about new and given information. It is of interest to note that, in many of these discussions, different means by which information may be considered to be new, or assumed to be given, are contrasted. However, a detailed account of *how* a speaker or hearer might decide what information is new or given to a conversational partner is left unspecified.

In a review of the adult literature, Prince (1981) identified three main ways in which various authors have defined givenness:

1. Givenness defined in terms of *predictability* or *recoverability* (e.g., Geluykens, 1989; Gundel, Hedberg, & Zacharski, 1989; Halliday, 1967; Halliday & Hasan, 1976; Kuno, 1972, 1978; Ostman and Virtanen, 1997):

   Givenness$_p$: *The speaker assumes that the hearer* can predict or could have predicted *that a* particular linguistic item *will or would occur in a particular position* within a sentence *(Prince, 1981, p. 226).*

2. Givenness in the sense of *saliency* (e.g., Chafe, 1976):

   Givenness$_s$: *The speaker assumes that the hearer has or could appropriately have some particular thing/entity/ . . . in his/her consciousness at the time of hearing the utterance (Prince, 1981, p. 228).*

3. Givenness in the sense of referring to *shared knowledge* (e.g., Clark & Haviland, 1977; Kuno, 1972), which may be most dependent on extralinguistic information and perhaps a prerequisite for the other types of givenness:

   Givenness$_k$: *The speaker assumes that the hearer "knows," assumes, or can infer a particular thing (but is not necessarily thinking about it) (Prince, 1981, p. 230).*

Another approach to the issue of what constitutes "shared knowledge" has been to outline, as Clark and Marshall (1981) have done, the types of mutual knowledge that may be taken into account by speakers and listeners.[1] Clark and Marshall proposed that the following four kinds of mutual knowledge may be taken into account:

1. *Community membership*: things that everyone in a community knows and assumes everyone else in the community knows.

2. *Physical copresence*: things that we assume another person knows by virtue of the fact that the person was physically copresent in a situation.
3. *Linguistic copresence*: things that people assume others know as a result of what was previously communicated to them.
4. *Indirect copresence*: things that people assume a communicative interactant knows indirectly as a result of being physically or linguistically copresent.

In terms of the studies discussed in this chapter, givenness$_k$, and, more specifically, *physical copresence*, was a primary consideration in the design of O'Neill (1996), in which it was presumed that the presence or absence of the parent might represent a salient and noticeable event to children and result in their taking this into account when addressing the parent, as children as young as 2 years of age were able to do.

Givenness$_s$, in contrast, is closer to the notion of new and given information explored in the study of children's exploratory behavior and commenting while observing new and old toys (O'Neill & Happé, 2000). It is also explored in the study of children's sensitivity to gestural information provided by the speaker indicating the "new" property to be discovered (O'Neill et al., 2002). In these two communicative settings, a certain piece of information or a certain perspective became salient as a result of extralinguistic factors, such as the sequence of toys encountered or the gestures used by the speaker.

When discussing the O'Neill and Happé (2000) study earlier in this chapter, the notion of relevance was brought up, in the sense that typically developing children seem to possess, as early as 22 months of age, a sense of what the "relevant" thing to say is. In the adult communication literature, Sperber and Wilson (1986, 1987; also Wilson, 1994) have proposed a *theory of relevance*, at the heart of which it is assumed that "human cognition is relevance-oriented: we pay attention to information that seems relevant to us" (Wilson, 1994, p. 44). Relevance theory abandons the notion of mutual knowledge in favor of a notion of "cognitive environment" that includes a set of facts "manifest" to an individual, where "manifest" is defined as being perceptible or inferable (Sperber & Wilson, 1986, 1987). For example, one way in which information can be made more manifest to a hearer is through acts of ostension, as in the study of adjective learning discussed earlier (O'Neill et al., 2002), in which descriptive gestures were used to highlight the tactile properties of the objects. Any such act of ostension, according to relevance theory, conveys a presumption of relevance and does so "because attention goes only to what is presumed relevant" (Sperber & Wilson, 1987, p. 700).

Overall, relevance theory has as its focus the explanation of interpretations made by *hearers* and the main inferential abilities involved in verbal comprehension. Distinctions between given and new information (or similar distinctions of topic and comment; presupposition and assertion) are argued to be better explained in terms of "foreground implications" and "background implications" (Sperber & Wilson, 1986, 1987). Moreover, such implicatures are viewed not as resulting from conscious effort but rather as arising as automatic effects of the hearer's tendency to maximize relevance and the speaker's exploitation of that tendency. Many aspects of relevance theory have received vigorous debate (the reader is directed to the open peer commentary in Sperber & Wilson, 1987).

With respect to children's communicative competence in particular, I would point out that it is quite likely the case that at times what would be "presumed relevant" by adult standards may not be so for children, calling into question the automaticity of this process as described by Sperber and Wilson (1986, 1987). That is, children may overassess or underassess the aspects of a scene or object presumed to be relevant by adults. Indeed, Sperber and Wilson (1987) may be implying this when they state that "humans have a number of heuristics, some of them innate, others developed through experience, aimed at picking out relevant phenomena" (p. 703). We have gained very little knowledge from research to date, however, as to what might be the nature of such heuristics developed through experience.

Pragmatics, Theory of Mind, and Language

In this last section of the chapter, I attempt to place the evidence and ideas discussed so far within the realm of pragmatics and the overall theme of this volume, namely the interdependent relation between language and theory of mind.

Pragmatics is a notoriously difficult area of inquiry to define, although a general description is that it refers to the study of ways in which speakers and listeners *use* language in social interaction (Levinson, 1983). In most conceptualizations, a boundary is drawn between pragmatics and the phonological, morphosyntactic, and semantic components of language. At the heart of pragmatics is the use of language in an appropriate manner. For example, the ability to give a listener just the right amount of information in reply to a question so as not to sound rude (too little information) or pedantic (too much information). Or, for example, knowing that while "kitty" may be an appropriate term for the cat with a 2-year-old, it is not generally the appropriate term to use with adults. Studies of mine, such as the ones described in this chapter, have been concerned with the question of how speakers come to adapt their speech in an appropriate manner, particularly in contexts where what determines the most appropriate utterance requires an assessment of newness or givenness. In such contexts, the mental states of the listener and the speaker (i.e., attentive state, knowledge state, etc.) must be taken into account at some level in order to designate certain information as new or given. This is not to say that the child's understanding of mind always plays a role in the production of pragmatically appropriate utterances. For example, observed frequency alone may explain the use of "kitty" with children and "cat" with adults. Nevertheless, particular areas of pragmatic development, such as the assessment of new versus given information, are certain to rely on a child's developing understanding of their own mind and other people's minds.

For example, in several other chapters in this volume, authors discuss how pragmatic factors may play a role with respect to (a) developments in a child's understanding of mind achieved through communication, and (b) developments in communication achieved as a result of the child's developing understanding of the mind. But it is not the case that in all of these situations the effect of the pragmatic factors will depend on a child's current level of understanding of the mind.

Consider two events of type (a) discussed separately by Dunn and Brophy (this volume, chapter 3) and Harris (this volume, chapter 4). Dunn and Brophy discuss the findings of Dunn and Brown (1993) in which the pragmatic intent of the speaker when engaged in talk about causes (i.e., the intent to control the child or to share in play) was later found to influence children's understanding of emotion and their performance on cognitive assessments. Relatedly, following a review of several training studies, Harris concludes that the variation in children's performance on theory-of-mind tasks may be attributable to a greater degree to a mother's pragmatic intent to introduce varying points of view in a conversation or narrative, rather than simply to the total number of explicit references to mental states that she makes. In both of these cases, the pragmatic factor can be viewed as part of the situational context of children's learning, brought about as a result of the goal of the speaker. That is, the pragmatic stance of the speakers in these cases can operate independently of any need on the part of the listener (i.e., the child) to assess this stance. The pragmatic intent of the adult, so to speak, is simply a feature of the context in which the information is learned by the child. The effect of this pragmatic intent operates independently of the child's level of understanding of mind.

Such situations stand in contrast to those in which the pragmatic factors involved do require a certain level of understanding of the mind in order for the goal of the communication to be achieved. These are the types of situations encountered by children in the three studies of mine described in this chapter and provided as examples of how children's own understanding of the mind may contribute to their communicative competence. Other examples can be found in this volume. For example, Slomkowski and Dunn (1996, cited by Dunn & Brophy, this volume, chapter 3) found that better performance on theory-of-mind tasks by children at 40 months of age was associated with more frequent and extended "connected" conversation with their friends at 47 months of age. Similarly, Dunn, Cutting, and Fisher (2002) found that the characteristics of the child's friend, including his/her theory-of-mind ability, was related to the quality of discourse, joint pretend, and connectedness of communication of the dyad as preschoolers. "Connectedness" is viewed by Dunn and her colleagues as reflecting "the extent to which each speaker is tuned in to what the other is talking about..." (Dunn & Brophy, this volume, chapter 3, p. 59) and could, as such, be argued to represent not just a pragmatic feature of talk but rather the pragmatic ability to produce connected talk that relies on an understanding and sharing or meeting of minds.

The assessment of information as new or given also always implies at least two communicative interactants—underscoring the nature of such situations as representing a "meeting of *minds*." Consider that by the age of 22 months, the typically developing children in the O'Neill and Happé (2000) study already demonstrated a common understanding of what is relevant to talk about in the context of the series of toys shown to them. This ability is similar to the notion of "community of minds" discussed by Nelson (this volume, chapter 2). She states that, "the Community of Minds depends inextricably on the capacity to talk about matters of interest to the members of the community, that is, to talk about things that are on members' minds" (p. 30). I would agree with Nelson that the ability to recognize topics that will engage and be relevant to other minds is crucial to entering the community of minds. A question for further research is how children actually come to recognize certain topics as such.

The three studies described in this chapter do raise questions, however, about the level of understanding of mind that a child needs in order to enter the community of minds. For example, if, as Nelson (this volume, chapter 2) argues, entering the cultural community of minds requires a full-fledged understanding of how shared knowledge comes into being, then the consequence is that none of the children in my studies would be granted entry. They would be instead, as Nelson would most likely agree, on "a pathway that leads into the larger community of minds" (p. 37). However, the 2-year-old children in the O'Neill (1996) study clearly demonstrated an ability to track the difference in their parent's shared/nonshared information based on the salient cues to the parent's presence or absence that were provided. Thus it would appear that they have certainly, even in Nelson's view, acquired "the key to the door that opens into the Community of Minds" (this volume, chapter 2, p. 32) at a much earlier age than would be suggested by their performance on traditional theory-of-mind tasks, such as false-belief tasks.

Finally, as Dunn and Brophy (this volume, chapter 3) wisely remind us, our understanding of communication and of minds is played out in a dyadic context (at minimum!). When considering relations between an understanding of the mind and communicative competence, one must therefore not forget that two minds are interacting. As Dunn and Brophy state, "the aspects of conversation that have been discussed depend on characteristics of both child and interlocuter, and on the quality of the relationship between them" (p. 63). In many discussions of the relation of language to theory-of-mind understanding, it is the interlocuter's language that is at focus and its effect on the child's theory of mind. However, the results of Brophy and Dunn (2002), Hughes, Dunn, and White (1998), and Dunn et al. (2002), described in Dunn and Brophy's chapter, clearly suggest that the influence of the interlocuter's language on the child's theory of mind may be mediated by the theory of mind held by the interlocuter— for example, the child's mother or the child's friend in the studies cited. The same issue is raised by Harris (this volume, chapter 4), who argues that it is very possible that mothers will vary in their emotional and psychological insight, and in their disposition to articulate and compare different points of view. Indeed, it is hard not to wonder about the consequences of a child's mother's theory of mind when reading the transcripts provided by Dunn and Brophy (this volume, chapter 3) and recognizing that, for one mother at least, the line between lying and imaginary stories is so fragile that the solution is to try to stop the imaginary stories.

Summary

I have shown through this brief overview of several studies of mine that the notion of given and new (or shared and nonshared) information in communicative settings is a multifaceted concept. Different levels of theory-of-mind understanding will be needed to explain how speakers and listeners comprehend or decide to treat information as new or given. The simplest account may be based on a definition that takes into account only the physical copresence or absence of speaker and listener. But it may be even more often that we encounter situations in which speaker and listener are privy to the same event, but a speaker or listener adopts a certain perspective on the event. Hence, the definition of new information needs to broadened to include: (a) cases in which the new information almost seems to "jump out" of the scene, in a manner that suggests something more to do with visual or perceptual salience than cognitive or informational salience (e.g., the situation encountered by children in O'Neill & Happé, 2000) and (b) cases in which the new information may comprise a particular sensory perspective that needs to be ascertained using paralinguistic pragmatic cues, such as gestures, to determine which of many possible (perhaps nonvisible) salient features is being highlighted by the speaker and referred to by the novel adjective term (e.g., the situation encountered by children in O'Neill et al., 2002). Impressively, even the latter is within the grasp of children as young as 2 years of age.

In addition, in this chapter I have conveyed that understanding the inter-dependent relation between language and an understanding of the mind will require further refinement of key components within each domain and an approach that highlights the fact that minds are interacting. For example, with respect to the key components in the domain of language and pragmatics, it is important to distinguish the contribution of nonverbal means of communication (often referred to as pragmatic factors); the varying contexts of communication (the pragmatics of a situation); the varying intents of speakers and listeners (pragmatic intents); and the ability to use language appropriately (the domain of pragmatics and the correct pragmatic use of language). Although some of these features may have implications with respect to the level of theory-of-mind understanding required, others may speak more to the theory-of-mind understanding achieved as a result (rather than required to produce such talk). With respect to understanding the mind, this chapter and several others in this volume discussed in this chapter, have identified what appear to be key components when considering the relation between these two domains and two minds interacting: namely, an understanding of a community of minds, an appreciation of different points of view, an understanding of relevance, and an appreciation of different sources of knowledge.

Note

1. Inferences regarding shared knowledge, and the potential importance of other factors such as group and category membership (e.g., gender, nationality, age, place of residence), are also discussed in a large body of work examining the general question of how people form models of what other people know and whether one's own knowledge is used as the primary basis from which the knowledge potentially possessed by another is imputed (see review by Nickerson, 1999).

References

Baldwin, D. A. (1991). Infants' contribution to the achievement of joint reference. *Child Development, 62,* 875–890.

Baldwin, D. A. (1993). Infants' ability to consult the speaker for clues to word reference. *Journal of Child Language, 20,* 395–418.

Baron-Cohen, S. (1988). Social and pragmatic deficits in autism: Cognitive or affective? *Journal of Autism and Developmental Disorders, 18,* 379–402.

Bates, E. (1976). *Language and context: The acquisition of pragmatics.* New York: Academic Press.

Brophy, M., & Dunn, J. (2002). What did Mummy say? Dyadic interactions between young "hard-to-manage" children and their mothers. *Journal of Abnormal Child Psychology, 30,* 103–112.

Butterworth, G. E. (1991). The ontogeny and phylogeny of joint visual attention. In A. Whiten (Ed.), *Natural theories of mind: Evolution, development and simulation of everyday mindreading* (pp. 223–232). Oxford: Basil Blackwell.

Butterworth, G., & Grover, L. (1990). Joint visual attention, manual pointing, and preverbal communication in human infancy. In M. Jeannerod (Ed.), *Attention and performance XIII* (pp. 605–624). Hillsdale, NJ: Erlbaum.

Chafe, W. L. (1976). Givenness, contrastiveness, definiteness, subjects, topics, and point of view. In C. Li (Ed.), *Subject and topic* (pp. 25–55). New York: Academic Press.

Clark, H. H., & Clark, E. V. (1977). *Psychology and language.* New York: Harcourt Brace.

Clark, H., & Haviland, S. (1977). Comprehension and the given-new contract. In R. Freedle (Ed.), *Discourse production and comprehension* (pp. 1–40). Hillsdale, NJ: Erlbaum.

Clark, H. H., & Marshall, C. R. (1981). Definite reference and mutual knowledge. In A. K. Joshi, B. L. Webber, & I. A. Sag (Eds.), *Elements of discourse understanding* (pp. 10–63). Cambridge: Cambridge University Press.

Corkum, V., & Moore, C. (1995). Development of joint visual attention in infants. In C. Moore & P. J. Dunham (Eds.), *Joint attention: Its origins and role in development* (pp. 61–83). Hillsdale, NJ: Erlbaum.

Dunn, J., & Brown, J. R. (1993). Early conversations about causality: Content, pragmatics and developmental change. *British Journal of Developmental Psychology, 11,* 107–23.

Dunn, J., Cutting, A., & Fisher, N. (2002). Old friends, new friends: Predictors of children's perspectives on their friends at school. *Child Development, 73,* 621–635.

Eales, M. J. (1993). Pragmatic impairments in adults with childhood diagnoses of autism or developmental receptive language disorder. *Journal of Autism and Developmental Disorders, 23,* 593–617.

Fay, W. H., & Schuler, A. L. (1980). *Emerging language in autistic children.* London: Edward Arnold.

Fenson, L., Dale, P. S., Reznick, J. S., Thal, D., Bates, E., Hartung, J. P., Pethick, S., & Reilly, J. S. (1993). *MacArthur Communicative Development Inventories: User's guide and technical manual.* San Diego: Singular.

Geluykens, R. (1989). Information structure in English conversation: The given-new distinction revisited. *Occasional Papers in Systemic Linguistics, 3,* 129–147.

Greenfield, P. M., & Smith, J. (1976). *The structure of communication in early language development.* New York: Academic Press.

Greenfield, P. M., & Zukow, P. G. (1978). Why do children say what they say when they say it?: An experimental approach to the psychogenesis of presupposition. In K. Nelson (Ed.), *Children's language,* Vol. 1 (pp. 287–336). New York: Gardner Press.

Grice, H. P. (1975). Logic and conversation. In P. Cole & J. L. Morgan (Eds.), *Syntax and semantics,* Vol. 3: *Speech acts* (pp. 225–242). New York: Academic Press.

Gundel, J., Hedberg, N., & Zacharski, R. (1989). Givenness, implicature, and demonstrative expressions in English discourse. *Papers from the regional meetings, Chicago Linguistics Society, 25,* 89–103.

Halliday, M. A. K. (1967). Notes on transitivity and theme in English. Part 2. *Journal of Linguistics, 3,* 199–244.

Halliday, M. A. K., & Hasan, R. (1976). *Cohesion in English*. London: Longman.

Hornby, P., Hass, W., & Feldman, C. (1970). A developmental analysis of the psychological subject and predicate of the sentence. *Language and Speech, 13*, 182–193.

Hughes, C., Dunn, J., & White, A. (1998). Trick or treat? Uneven understanding of mind and emotion and executive function among "hard to manage" preschoolers. *Journal of Child Psychology and Psychiatry, 39*, 981–94.

Kagan, J. (1991). The theoretical utility of constructs for the self. *Developmental Review Special Issue: The development of the self: The first three years, 11*, 244–250.

Kuno, S. (1972). Functional sentence perspective. *Linguistic Inquiry, 3*, 269–320.

Kuno, S. (1978). Generative discourse analysis in America. In W. Dressler (Ed.), *Current trends in textlinguistics* (pp. 275–294). New York: De Gruyter.

Leung, E. H. L., & Rheingold, H. L. (1981). Development of pointing as a social gesture. *Developmental Psychology, 17*, 215–220.

Levinson, S. C. (1983). *Pragmatics*. Cambridge: Cambridge University Press.

MacWhinney, B., & Bates, E. (1978). Sentential devices for conveying givenness and newness: a cross–cultural developmental study. *Journal of Verbal Learning and Verbal Behavior, 17*, 539–558.

Murphy, C. M., & Messer, D. J. (1977). Mothers, infants, and pointing: A study of a gesture. In H. R. Schaffer (Ed.), *Studies in mother/infant interaction* (pp. 325–354). London: Academic Press.

Nickerson, R. S. (1999). How we know—and sometimes misjudge—what others know: Imputing one's own knowledge in others. *Psychological Bulletin, 125*, 737–759.

O'Neill, D. K. (1996). Two-year-old children's sensitivity to a parent's knowledge state when making requests. *Child Development, 67*, 659–677.

O'Neill, D. K., Astington, J. W., & Flavell, J. H. (1992). Young children's understanding of the role that sensory experiences play in knowledge acquisition. *Child Development, 63*, 474–490.

O'Neill, D. K., & Gopnik, A. (1991). Young children's ability to identify the sources of their beliefs. *Developmental Psychology, 27*, 390–397.

O'Neill, D. K., & Happé, F. (2000). Noticing and commenting on what's new: differences and similarities among 22-month-old typically developing children, children with Down syndrome, and children with autism. *Developmental Science, 3*, 457–478.

O'Neill, D. K., Topolovec, J. C., & Stern-Cavalcante, W. (2002). Feeling sponginess: The importance of gesture in two-year-old children's acquisition of adjectives. *Journal of Cognition and Development, 3*, 243–277.

Ostman, J. O., & Virtanen, T. (1997). Theme, comment, and newness as figures in information structuring. In K. Kibrik, A. A. Noordman, & G. M. Leonard (Eds.), *Discourse studies in cognitive linguistics: Selected papers from the 5th International Cognitive Linguistics Conference* (pp. 91–110). Amsterdam: John Benjamins.

Prince, E. (1981). Toward a taxonomy of given-new information. In P. Cole (Ed.), *Radical Pragmatics* (pp. 223–255). New York: Academic Press.

Ross, H. S., & Lollis, S. P. (1987). Communication within infant social games. *Developmental Psychology, 23*, 241–248.

Rowan, L. E., Leonard, L. B., Chapman, K., & Weiss, A. L. (1983). Performative and presuppositional skills in language-disordered and normal children. *Journal of Speech and Hearing Research, 26*, 97–106.

Scaife, M., & Bruner, J. S. (1975). The capacity for joint visual attention in the human infant. *Nature, 253*, 265.

Slomkowski, C., & Dunn, J. (1996). Young children's understanding of other people's beliefs and feeling and their connected communication with friends. *Developmental Psychology, 32*, 442–447.

Snyder, L. S. (1978). Communicative and cognitive abilities and disabilities in the sensorimotor period. *Merrill-Palmer Quarterly, 24*, 161–180.

Sperber, D., & Wilson, D. (1986). *Relevance.* Cambridge, MA: Harvard University Press.

Sperber, D., & Wilson, D. (1987). Précis of relevance: Communication and cognition. *Behavioral and Brain Sciences, 10*, 697–754.

Surian, L., Baron-Cohen, S., & Van der Lely, H. (1996). Are children with autism deaf to Gricean maxims? *Cognitive Neuropsychiatry, 1*, 55–71.

Tager-Flusberg, H. (1981). On the nature of linguistic functioning in early infantile autism. *Journal of Autism and Developmental Disorders, 11*, 45–56.

Trevarthen, C. (1977). Descriptive analyses of infant communicative behavior. In H. R. Schaffer (Ed.), *Studies in mother-infant interaction* (pp. 227–270). London: Academic Press.

Waters, L. J., Siegal, M., & Slaughter, V. (2000). Development of reasoning and the tension between scientific and conversational inference. *Social Development, 9*, 383–396.

Weinberg, M. K., & Tronick, E. Z. (1996). Infant affective reaction to the resumption of maternal interaction after the still-face. *Child Development, 67*, 905–914.

Weisenberger, J. L. (1976). A choice of words: Two-year-old speech from a situational point of view. *Journal of Child Language, 3*, 275–281.

Wilson, D. (1994). Relevance and understanding. In G. Brown, K. Malmkjaer, A. Pollitt, & J. Williams (Eds.), *Language and understanding* (pp. 37–58). Oxford: Oxford University Press.

6   The Developmental Origins of Meaning for Mental Terms

Derek E. Montgomery

Between 18 and 36 months, a variety of new mental terms begin to appear in children's lexicon (Bartsch & Wellman, 1995). This chapter asks what children mean when they begin using these words. Answering this question involves first posing an even more fundamental question: what is the meaning of "meaning"? The nature of meaning is a longstanding concern of philosophers, and their analyses and clarifications shed light on developmental investigations of the semantic development of mental terms. The questions researchers ask, the type of data they collect, and the interpretations they make are all directly influenced by their assumptions about the nature of word meaning. Consequently, the chapter begins by describing two contrasting ways to conceptualize meaning. One characterization (the ostension paradigm) is commonly held in theory-of-mind research but is, I contend, misguided. A second conception of meaning, which I have termed the contextual view, is offered as a corrective to the ostension paradigm. Like a fork in the road, the conclusion one draws about the nature of linguistic meaning subsequently influences how one studies and understands the developmental relations between language and theory of mind. This influence is highlighted throughout the chapter as meta-linguistic concerns are interwoven with data and theory from the theory-of-mind literature.

The Meaning of Mental Terms

"Mental terms" are those words commonly understood by researchers to refer to mental states. Words referring to desire ("want," "wish"), intention ("gonna," "on purpose," "trying"), and belief ("think," "know") are prototypical in theory-of-mind research. At first glance, the acquisition of meaning for these terms can seem fairly straightforward. If mental terms refer to corresponding internal experiences, then word learning encompasses three essential steps: a person *has* mentalistic experiences, *categorizes* those experiences, and then *labels* each category. The relation between the first two steps, having mentalistic experiences and categorizing them, is variously explained depending upon the extent first-person experiences are viewed as mediated by interpretive processes (see Bartsch & Wellman, 1995, ch. 9). Despite this variability, the fundamental components of the picture, which I term the ostension paradigm, remain the same: (a) meaning is tied to the nature of the referent of the word, (b) the referent is a mental state of some type, and (c) mental states are internal and private experiences.

The ostension paradigm is the predominant conceptualization of language in theory-of-mind research (Montgomery, 2002) and, consequently, warrants close scrutiny. If words and sentences can be ordered along a continuum from purely descriptive to purely performative (Austin, 1962), the referential picture belongs on the descriptive end, with mental terms denoting, or pointing toward, inner states and experiences. An illustration of this picture is the claim that children use the verb "want" to "refer to a person's internal state of wanting or longing to obtain an object, engage in action, or experience a state of affairs" (Wellman & Phillips, 2001, p. 130). I attempt in this chapter to provide reasons why mental words are more appropriately placed on the performative side of the continuum than on the descriptive side. That is, meaning emerges from the pragmatic ends for which mental terms are used rather than from word-referent relations. To foreshadow this discussion, two characterizations of the genesis of the meaning of mental terms can be distinguished. One is that the foundation of meaning is the referential relation between mental states and the verbal labels of those states. A second possibility is that the meaning of mental terms is directly related to routine social activities between the young child and caregiver, with language and its meaning growing out of preverbal exchanges. The emphasis in this case is on *interactive* experiences rather than *introspective* experiences.

Introspection and the Ostension Paradigm

One immediate problem for the ostension paradigm is the internal and private nature of mental states. If nobody can see or experience another person's mental state, then how can mental verbs be meaningfully used in the second or third person? An apparent solution to this problem, the argument from analogy, concludes that the nature of others' experiences can be understood on analogy to the nature of one's own experiences (see Meltzoff, Gopnik, & Repacholi, 1999; Tomasello, 1999). The meaning of mental verbs, therefore, is essentially the same in the first and third person since the referent is assumed to be the same (analogous) for self and for other. Meltzoff et al. (1999, p. 35) elaborate by claiming that infants consider three factors when inferring the mentalistic experiences of others:

> (a) When I perform that bodily act I have such and such a phenomenal experience, (b) I recognize that others perform the same type of bodily acts as me, (c) the other is sharing my behavioral state; ergo, perhaps the other is having the same phenomenal experience.

There are various critiques of the argument from analogy focusing on the legitimacy of drawing third-person inferences from first-person experiences (steps "b" and "c") (see Mueller & Runions, 2003). I wish to draw attention, however, to the initial assumption that the infant or child can delineate his or her own internal experiences and categorically mark them. To appreciate the problematic nature of this assumption, it is necessary to first clarify the claim underlying it. Consider Meltzoff's (2002, pp. 22–23) characterization of the infant's introspective capacities: "the infant knows that when it wants something it reaches out and grasps it. The infant experiences her own internal desires and the concomitant bodily movements (hand extension, finger movements, etc.)." Meltzoff goes on to write that infants impute the experience of desire to others when the outward behavioral cues warrant such an inference. To say that the infant has propositional knowledge about her own mind (that wanting leads to grasping) assumes that she has already at least roughly categorized the experiences of wanting so that they are differentiated from other internal experiences. In other words, the child has formed a sort of private language in which internal sensations are identified and meaningfully differentiated from outward behaviors and from other types of internal sensations. This is an important first step if these experiences are eventually labeled with mental terms.

Categorizing one's own internal sensations so that they can be labeled or imputed to others involves second-order knowledge about the mind. Second-order knowledge, when it is self-knowledge, involves the belief that one has (or can have) a particular mental state or experience. In contrast, the occurrence of a belief or desire, or any other mental state, is a first-order state. Presumably, infants and children can express these first-order states without a reflective awareness that such states exist (as, for instance, when young infants express an emotion without, presumably, a concomitant concept of the emotion). A second-order belief about one's own mind, where the person possesses some form of propositional knowledge about his or her own mental activities, is presupposed in any account of a private language. Labeling or imputing a mental experience involves thinking about the experience as some type of distinctive entity (e.g., a category that encompasses all such experiences).

The assumption that linguistic meaning can be determined individually through a process of (1) forming second-order concepts from first-order experiences and then (2) labeling those concepts is problematic for at least the three reasons given in the following sections.

Indeterminacy

First, identifying and labeling internal sensations entails the ability to form categories (e.g., "this is a desire; this is not a desire"), but the sensations have many properties that are not categorically distinct. The sensation of a desire, or any mental experience, is multifaceted, and so aspects of particular internal sensations that are tangential must be dissociated from those core features that help define the category. For instance, mental states are probably nearly always conflated with content. One does not experience an "empty attitude" devoid of content, and so the variety of things (content) a child wants, knows, or intends cannot be mistaken by the word learner as the mental state being referred to. In short, a well-known question in the word-learning literature asks how children limit the indeterminate possibilities for what any one word might be referring to. In the case of mental verbs, where the referent is internal and private, the challenge is particularly acute. Somehow the child must distinguish private sensation A from private sensation B, despite their overlapping commonalties, while also categorizing $A1$ with $A2$, $A3$, and so on, despite their differences. One possibility, the formation of analogies of the sort A is analogous to $A1$ (see Baldwin & Saylor, this volume, chapter 7, for a discussion of the formation of abstract categories), leaves unanswered the crucial question of how the infant comes to recognize sensation A, and its distinctiveness, in the first place.

Empirical Considerations

Empirical evidence suggests the capacity for reflective awareness of one's own mental states and experiences is tenuous for preschoolers. Flavell and colleagues have concluded that preschoolers are relatively impervious to their own very recent processes of attention, thought, and self-talk (Flavell, Green, & Flavell, 1995; Flavell, Green, & Flavell, 2000; Flavell, Green, Flavell, & Grossman, 1997). For instance, when prompted to think about an object or problem, few preschoolers report having had such thoughts when queried moments later (Flavell et al., 1995).

A recent study investigating preschoolers' ability to correctly apply the verb "try" to their own self-directed movement further suggests that even when self-awareness is present, its relation to verbal labels can be unclear to young children (Montgomery & Lightner, 2004). From the perspective of the ostension paradigm, the meaning of "try" inheres in the experience of volition to which it refers. So, for instance, when a child says "I'm trying to do this," he or she is, in effect, describing an expected outcome (expressed by the infinitive phrase) and is also saying that the attempt to attain the expected outcome is volitional. This volitional experience, Searle (1983, p. 90) writes, is the "obvious phenomenal difference between the case where one moves one's hand and the case where one observes it move independently of one's intentions." It is reasonable to expect that if "try" is referring to the feeling of volition, then children should readily use the verb to describe their activity when it is self-directed and deny its application when their movement is passive.

In our study (Montgomery & Lightner, 2004), 3- and 4-year olds' movements were self-guided in one condition as they drew an item independently. Their movements were passive in a second condition as the experimenter placed a marker in the child's hand and moved the child's arm. The child's eyes were closed during the passive movement to prevent him or her from knowing the identity of the drawing as it was created by the experimenter. Children were aware of the difference between self-guided and passive movement in these two conditions. When asked, "Who drew (that picture), me or you?" preschoolers typically said "me" in the self-guided condition and "you" in the passive movement condition.

We did not find evidence, however, for a belief that the verb "try" is directly connected to the experience of agency. In other trials, preschoolers were asked following passive movement whether they tried to draw the item and they nearly always said yes. Even when given a forced-choice between two drawings, one the product of passive movement and the other the result of self-directed movement, 3- and 4-year-olds were indiscriminate in indicating which one they tried to draw ["Did you try to draw (A) or (B)?"]. As long as children were somehow physically connected with an outcome, whether by self-guided movement or by passive movement, they judged that the verb "try" applied to themselves. This finding is consistent with others showing that preschoolers tend to mistakenly describe reflexive movement as intentional (e.g., Lang & Perner, 2002). Their self-awareness of the difference between agency and passivity is not, apparently, accompanied by a belief that the verb "trying" characterizes self-guided movement rather than passive movement.

Private Language Argument

Wittgenstein's private language argument presents a third reason why the meaning of mental terms does not inhere in a referential relation between mental term and state (Wittgenstein, 1958). A full examination of Wittgenstein's private language argument as it applies to the acquisition of mental words is beyond the scope of this chapter (see Montgomery, 1997, 2002), and for present purposes it suffices to focus on the argument as it pertains to the relation between meaning and use. Rules that guide word use are necessary for the establishment of word meaning. The semantic confusion that would result from an absence of rules-of-use is obvious; for instance, a person who arbitrarily used the word "red" when labeling colors would essentially render the term meaningless. In the same way, mental terms cannot be meaningful if used indiscriminately; instead, they also must have rules that constrain their application so that one can say the words have been used correctly or incorrectly.

The ostension paradigm implies that a mental term has been used correctly when it is labeling the appropriate referent and incorrectly when it is attached to the wrong referent. For instance, one can imagine a rule stating "label Y applies to sensation X" that would guide word learning. If the utterance is in the first person, the speaker simply identifies and labels, with the mental predicate, his internal sensation. Wittgenstein's (1958) private language argument questions how one could follow such a rule when the referents for mental terms are internal and private. Essentially, correct and incorrect application of terms to a private referent cannot be properly differentiated because *following* a rule and *thinking* one is following a rule are necessarily conflated. The inability to privately distinguish correct and erroneous identifications and classifications of internal sensations makes any notions of private rule-following incoherent (Wittgenstein, 1958).

Rules that guide word use must be public and shared to make possible the differentiation between following a rule and seeming to follow one. In Wittgenstein's terms, these shared rules are found within "language games." A language game is a social activity in which words play customary roles. Words, Wittgenstein said, are analogous to chess pieces in that both have specified roles within the context of a game. Meaning is bound up in the roles, or purposes, a word serves, and these roles are fixed, in a loose sense, by the customs (or rules) of the game. Within the "Community of Minds" (see Nelson, this volume, chapter 2), children use language to obtain things, to give orders, to seek permission, to differentiate themselves from others, to express similarities and agreements, and so forth. Children, like everyone, use language for pragmatic ends and describing how mental terms are used to accomplish particular ends provides key insight into what these words mean.

Thus, the corrective to the ostension paradigm begins by placing the nature of meaning in the pragmatic roles words play in interpersonal communicative exchanges. Tying semantic development to the contexts in which words are used is common to other theories of word learning (see Budwig, 2002; Carpendale & Lewis, 2004; Nelson, 1996), and I have labeled this perspective the *contextual view* (Montgomery, 2002). One of the foremost challenges for the contextual view in addressing the semantic development of mental terms is to describe the purposes for which the words are used within the contexts where they are most commonly found. Since first-person utterances predominate in children's early use of mental terms (e.g., Bartsch & Wellman, 1995), the next section of the chapter focuses primarily on those types of utterances, although the general thesis, that meaning is tied to the way a word is used in familiar settings, also applies to second- and third-person utterances.

Language Games and Semantic Development

Language games begin with social interactions between infants and others. Canfield (1993) describes naturally occurring patterns of interaction from which language games emerge (e.g., feeding, comforting, and dressing) as "proto language games." Deliberate gestures from the child, as well as one- and two-word utterances, subsequently build upon these natural foundations; for example, the proto language game of feeding is expanded when the child begins gesturing by pointing to a bottle in an apparent request to be fed. These gestures are eventually accompanied or replaced by vocalizations and utterances like "bottle." Syntactic and lexical developments bring about the emergence of mental terms (e.g., "I want a bottle") and expand the number and complexity of language games the child can play. This process of replacing gestures and vocatives with linguistic forms is not a reflexive or unthinking one; instead, it requires sensitivity to social expectations, as well as an understanding of how to accomplish tasks and goals with language within a particular context (Bruner, 1983). In other words, young children's primary cognitive task with respect to the semantic development of mental terms is to figure out the practical functions these words serve within the appropriate cultural context, rather than inferring their own (or someone else's) mental state and then learning to label it.

In fact, it is quite possible that children's knowledge of the mind can be limited even if their use of mental terms is meaningful and appropriate. As noted earlier, explicit and reflective beliefs about mental states are distinct from experiences of them. This means, in principle at least, that mental terms can *express* internal experiences without also implying that the speaker is using mental terms with the second-order purpose of referring to a concept encompassing the internal experience. This is Wittgenstein's point in the following example:

> A child has hurt himself and he cries: and then adults talk to him and teach him exclamations and later sentences. They teach the child new pain-behavior. "So you are saying that the word 'pain' really means crying?"—On the contrary, the verbal expression of pain replaces crying and does not describe it. (Wittgenstein, 1958, para. 244)

In the expressivist account that Wittgenstein appears to endorse (Jacobsen, 1996), the mentalistic experience of pain is expressed with gestures, cries, and with words. Each act is "pain-behavior," and each act is potentially meaningful. The verbal expression "this hurts" is meaningful even if the child lacks a second-order concept of pain. In the same way, requesting, smiling, and using the verb "want" are instances of desire-behavior that are meaningful even if the child does not possess a reflective, abstract concept of wanting. My point, at this juncture, is to simply say that children can meaningfully use mental terms, as expressions of internal experiences, even if they do not have accompanying beliefs about the mind. Rather than viewing these early uses as preceding meaning, the Wittgensteinian dictum "meaning is use" suggests that, to an extent, meaning is already established by the role mental terms play in interpersonal exchanges.

Children can express their ideas and feelings without having a theory of how the mind works and without having theoretical beliefs about which mental state they (or others) are experiencing. Nelson (this volume, chapter 2) similarly points out that talking about beliefs does not necessarily entail having an explicit concept of beliefs (see also Ninio & Snow, 1996, ch. 3). The communicative end of saying "I know (that X)," Nelson points out, is to express the content of the belief rather than to describe the experience or nature of believing. Hacker (1999) similarly points out that the purpose of such utterances is not to describe or draw attention to the act of believing but rather to impart information about the true state of affairs: "If one is asked, 'Where is N.N.?' and one replies, 'I believe he is in London,' the response 'what an interesting piece of autobiography; now tell me where N.N. is' would be a joke" (Hacker, 1999, p. 33).

Returning to Wittgenstein's example, the word "pain" functions the way nonverbal expressions of pain function when both are interpreted by the listener as demanding some sort of assistance or attention to a malady of some type. The meaning (or role) of the child's expression, whether verbal or nonverbal, is dependent upon the way listeners routinely respond to it within a particular setting. Meaning emerges within the conventionalized interplay between expression and response. Thus, semantic connections exist between nonverbal expressions and later verbal expressions when similar roles are played by both communicative forms (Malcolm, 1986).

At the outset, children's early utterances and nonverbal expressions are highly context-specific in that they are dependent on the interpretive skills of a recipient who is highly familiar with the child, the setting, and the routines (see Nelson, 1996). In this way the quality of the parent-child relationship relates to theory-of-mind development (see Dunn & Brophy, this volume, chapter 3, for a discussion of the importance of relationships for language and theory of mind). Language games develop when parents are connected and responsive conversational partners encouraging the child's self-expression and also sensitive to the speaker's interests and goals. In short, the development of early language games is highly dependent on the establishment of familiar routines and on the skills of attentive adults who read their children's nonverbal signals.

The following section illustrates how vocalizations, one- and two-word utterances, and nonverbal gestures can each express an infant's or toddler's internal experience. It further illustrates how the semantic development of mental terms is rooted in the role these early expressions play. The focus in the next section is upon the early semantic development of terms of volition (desire and intention) (for related discussions of verbs of belief, see Montgomery, 2002; Nelson & Kessler-Shaw, 2002). How children understand the motivations of behavior is a core concern for theory-of-mind researchers, and thus the semantic development of these verbs is particularly relevant to current research and theory.

Language Game of Intention

Drawing from his own naturalistic observations, Canfield (1993) described how intentions are expressed in the very early stages of language acquisition. The focus of the nascent language game of intention is upon "anticipating another's actions and . . . conveying what one is up to—of signaling or indicating or stating what we are up to" (Canfield, 1993, p. 179). In essence, this early language game revolves around the child conveying a goal either in anticipation of attaining it or while the attainment of the goal is still in progress. The focus is on futurity as the child informs another about the aim of an action and the outcome that is expected. Observations of the early expressions of intention were recorded in diary observations (Canfield, 1993, pp. 180–181):

> a. While stacking toys with the adult the child (21 months) says "off" as she starts to remove the stack. The utterance is apparently aimed at conveying her goal, or reason, for acting.
> b. The child (23 months) says "climbing chair" before beginning to climb it in an apparent attempt to express her goal.
> c. Prior to taking her duck and frog toys downstairs the child (24 months) says "Duck, frog downstairs."

In each of these examples, the speaker's communicative aim is to relate the present to the immediate future by sharing her goals with the listener. This shared expectation can be especially important if obstacles arise and the child must request help for attaining the goal. In these instances, *requests for supportive action* can be nonverbal, such as when a child hands an object to an adult and points to the location where it needs to be repaired (Bruner, 1983). In general, Bruner observed an increase in such requests around 18 months as infants enlisted adults' assistance in attaining goals such as getting a toy assembled or freeing a wedged object.

How do these early expressions of intent connect to the explicit lexicalization of intent? The earliest linguistic expressions of intent appear to be statements of futurity as auxiliaries "will" and "gonna" generally appear well before children's third birthday (see Astington, 1999, for a discussion of the relevant literature). The verb "try," which children associate with action by age 3 (Astington, 1999), can also be useful for expressions of futurity. For instance, when used in transitive sentence structures in the present progressive tense (e.g., "I'm trying to get it"), the speaker is describing the expected outcome of the activity. Canfield's (1993) description of the nascent language game of intention, and its focus on futurity, fits particularly well with these first intention terms and their focus on futurity.

The larger point is that the semantic foundation for intention terms is set before these words appear in the lexicon. The semantic similarity between a child's preverbal request for supportive action as she attempts to retrieve a toy and a full-fledged utterance, such as "I'm trying to get this toy," is evident. So, too, the semantic connection between "Duck, frog downstairs" and "I will/am gonna take my duck and frog downstairs" is also clear. The roles intention terms such as "try" and "will" serve, to express futurity or to inform what one is up to, are already familiar to children.

This brief overview of the early language game of intention illustrates how children's expressions of intent can be nonverbal (e.g., handovers to adults of broken objects), verbalizations where intention terms are absent (e.g., "off" or "Duck, frog downstairs"), and explicit ("I'm trying . . . "). These various forms of expression are semantically related to the extent they serve similar purposes in communicative exchanges. The next section illustrates how this semantic continuity is also evident in the emergence of the verb "want" in children's early lexicon.

Language Game of Desire

One of the most prominent communicative goals of infants is to convey that they are in want and, more specifically, what they want. Their success in doing so is aptly described by Bruner (1983, p. 93) in his observations of two mother-child dyads:

> The point at which our two mothers began successfully to interpret referential intent in their sons' signaling . . . (had) entirely to do with the child's first "requestive referential" maneuver: arm extension *toward* a desired object, occurring at about eight months in both children. At first, this reach is as if "real": it is effortful, the body is inclined with the reach, and the child makes "effortful" noises while opening and closing his extended hand. In a few months, this reach has become stylized and conventional. The reach is now open-handed, noneffortful, and its accompanying vocalization . . . becomes distinctive. It is, in effect, an "ostensive reach" that seems to be intended to indicate an object of desire.

Although requests were initially directed at objects that were visible and close to the child, by 14 months requests were extended to objects that were visible but remote and also to objects that were completely out of view of the child (Bruner, 1983). This is consistent with recent evidence that by 15 months (if not slightly earlier), infants understand the possibility of absent reference in communication (see Baldwin & Saylor, this volume, chapter 7). The challenge for the child of nonverbally communicating a request for an absent object evoked uses of the verb "want" from mothers (e.g., "What do you want?") (Bruner, 1983), thereby providing exposure to the verb within this specific context. By age 2, children's requests to obtain something have increased in sophistication to the point where the detail in the requests can be adjusted to account for whether the listener possesses, or lacks, pertinent information (see O'Neill, this volume, chapter 5).

If the verb "want" emerges as an extension of preverbal requests to obtain something, then it should appear in transitive sentence structures very early. The informativeness of saying "I wanna," absent an object phrase describing the target of the request, would be limited, and, not surprisingly, such utterances are rare among young children (Bartsch & Wellman, 1995). Instead, children very quickly link "want" with an object phrase. In fact, in one observational study, "want" was often the first verb children learned to combine with a direct object (Ninio, 1999).

In her analysis of the pragmatic uses of "want," Budwig (2002) reported that children younger than age 2 primarily used the verb to request to obtain something: the straightforward utterance "I want some" (child at 20 months) was typical (Budwig, 2002). As children recognized the convention of seeking permission before doing something, she found the verb "want" was increasingly used for requests to act (e.g., "I wanna talk in it [microphone]" by a child at 33 months) (Budwig, 2002). Budwig's results, like those of Bartsch and Wellman (1995), also indicate that the vast majority of the earliest uses of "want" were in the first person. The lag between first- and third-person utterances is sometimes interpreted as reflecting the predominance self-awareness plays in mental concept formation (e.g., Bretherton, 1991). From the contextual view, however, the pragmatic importance to the speaker of using "want" to obtain something is more directly responsible for the preponderance of first-person uses.

In sum, as the verb "want" emerges in the lexicon, it is typically found in first-person utterances requesting an object. Its semantic foundation in this context (and related others) is rooted within the familiar language game of request and obtainment. Viewed this way, "want" is one member of a family of verbs and nonverbal expressions in which the communicative end is expressing a desire to obtain an end of some type.

Alternatively, however, semantic discontinuity between "want" and other expressions can be said to exist if the mental predicate is meaningfully tied to a referent (an internal state of desire) in ways that other expressions are not. In particular, within the theory-of-mind literature, "want" is cordoned off, so to speak, as directly referring to the psychological experience of desire and, therefore, uniquely reflective of the child's concept of desire. In their extensive and influential study of mental term use in natural language samples, Bartsch and Wellman (1995) attempted to provide criteria to set apart those uses of "want" that refer to the psychological experience of desire from other uses that lack that particular referential relation. This approach raises the question of how closely these categories actually reflect semantic differences. If an utterance containing the verb "want" is judged to refer to a mental state, does this referential use give the utterance a meaning substantially different from that of expressions where the psychological reference is deemed to be absent?

One set of referential uses, requests for unavailable objects, were termed *contrastive* uses because the desire referred to by the speaker contrasted with an overt outcome (i.e., the unfulfilled request) (Bartsch & Wellman, 1995). The following exchanges are examples of contrastive uses (Bartsch & Wellman, 1995, pgs. 33; 78):

   a. Eve (1;11): "I don't want some soup. I want some cheese sandwich."
   b. Peter (2;3): "I want my paper: be right back."
   c. Adam (2;10): "More milk."
      Adult: "You don't need more milk."
      Adam: "Why not? Want some milk in it."

Bartsch and Wellman (1995, p. 79) claim that when children distinguish desires from outcomes, as in these examples, "they demonstrate an understanding of desires as something like a personal disposition or experiential state."

In contrast, those utterances where the requested object was visible to the speaker were generally not regarded as contrasting internal and external states and were coded instead as behavioral references. A "behavioral reference" was defined as the:

> simple, unadorned request for a concrete object, such as saying "I want the ball" when a ball was in plain view. Such a statement could too easily, in the absence of additional context or evidence, be a mere request for an object as in "Give me the ball" or even a polite form of "Hand me the ball." (Bartsch & Wellman, 1995, p. 67)

Although a behavioral reference is equated with a "mere request for an object," the contrastive uses in these examples, and presumably in many other instances, are also expressing a request to obtain an object. This was also the aim of the nonverbal requests for absent objects described earlier (see Bruner, 1983). Requests are not categorically distinct, in terms of their meaning, on the basis of whether or not the requested objects are present. From a pragmatic standpoint, the meaning of an expression of desire is similar whether it is coded as a "behavioral reference" or as a "psychological reference" or whether it is expressed with nonverbal gestures, when its purpose is to request the obtainment of some end (or, often in the past tense, to describe failed requests).

Consider also whether semantic distinctions rest upon inclusion of the verb "want" in descriptions of goal-related activity. Bartsch and Wellman (1995) write:

> Expressions of a desire connected to the child's own action, for example, "I want to move this block" said while the child is pushing a block across the room, were included as references to desire when the child seemed to be *commenting on an attitude toward the act* in addition to describing his own action (i.e., not just announcing "I'm moving this block," but in addition expressing his experience of wanting). (Bartsch & Wellman, 1995, p. 70, italics added)

The rationale appears to be that adding "want" to the utterance changes the meaning of the sentence "I'm moving this block" because the speaker is calling attention to his or her mental attitude about the activity. However, the purpose for either utterance ("I'm moving this block" or "I want to move this block") would seem to involve informing the listener about the goal the speaker is attempting to accomplish. The larger point is, again, to question not only whether children are referring to mental states but also how the occurrence of such a reference would categorically alter the meaning of the utterance containing the mental verb.

Another way to view this issue is to consider how *obtaining verbs* (e.g., give, get, bring, find, take) (see Ninio, 1999) can serve as expressions of desire. In particular, to the extent that obtaining verbs serve the same purpose as "want," they possess a similar meaning to the mental predicate. Table 6.1 provides examples taken from the CHILDES database (MacWhinney, 2000) of Adam (Brown, 1973) that use the obtaining verbs "give" and "get." Rephrasing these utterances so that they feature the predicate "want" does not alter their meaning because the communicative role is the same in each case: expressing a request to obtain something (see table 6.1). The point, once again, is this: if meaning depends on the pragmatic role the word serves rather than its referent, then categories based on supposed differences in referential relations may not reflect semantic differences at all.

Conclusions: Why Language Matters for Theory of Mind

Discussions of semantic development are invariably discussions of conceptual development. Minimally, one might say that language matters for theory of mind because a mental term manifests the child's underlying mental concept. More

Table 6.1 Examples of Obtaining Verbs Used to Express Desire

Obtaining Verb (actual utterance)		Mental Verb (restated)
Adam (3;0): "I want some more water." Mother: "Please." Adam: "Please *give* me some more water."	→	"I *want* some more water."
Adam (2;3): *Give* me tractor . . . OK?	→	"I *want* the tractor.
Adam *(2;5)*: "*Get* cranberry. Adam: "Cranberry." Mother "Adam, your juice is out here."	→	"I *want* cranberry juice."
Adam (2;8): "I *get* more. Let me have more coffee." (said during pretend play) Mother: "More coffee?"	→	"I *want* more coffee."

substantially, language matters because learning to use mental terms across a variety of social contexts shapes the meaning and nature of the corresponding concepts. The second view is the one advanced in this chapter. In short, from the perspective of the contextual view, children learn the pragmatic roles mental terms play, and these roles are integral to the conceptual meaning of the words. Children express themselves (e.g., their desires, intents, beliefs), and the meanings of these expressions are formed by the responses of the community. In essence, the roles mental terms play are fashioned by the characteristic responses of others; thus, communicative interplay is the crucible in which meaning is socially constructed. There are at least three implications of this view for understanding theory-of-mind development.

First, viewing mental concepts as inextricably social diverges from the perspective that the concepts are essentially abstract theoretical entities. I have suggested in this chapter that using mental terms meaningfully in discourse, for ends such as self-expression and describing or influencing the behavior of others, can occur without attendant *realist* beliefs about the mind. Young children's emerging mentalistic expressions are only very loosely, if at all, concerned with describing, or corresponding to, facts (second-order beliefs) they hold about the mind. Thus, it is misguided to view the acquisition of meaning for mental terms as a process of inductively inferring relations between mental verbs and corresponding referents.

Second, mentalistic expressions come in many forms (including nonverbal gestures), and accurately assessing conceptual knowledge of the mind involves broadening the range of words and visual and situational cues employed in assessment tasks. Task modifications along these lines are not designed necessarily to uncover nascent competencies but to instead expose the full range of the child's conceptual knowledge. From a methodological standpoint, the gap between traditional theory-of-mind tasks designed to index propositional knowledge and the familiar contexts and discourse settings where mental terms are typically used by young children is problematic (see Nelson, Skerer, Goldman, Henseler, Presler, & Walkenfield, 2003). Closing this gap through task modification requires first of all a consideration of the familiarity children have with various mental terms and the contexts and purposes for which young children typically use those terms.

For instance, the false-belief task is generally regarded as the unparalleled assessment of whether the child has a declarative store of propositional knowledge about the mind (e.g., propositions such as "beliefs are formed from perception" or "beliefs mediate the desire-action causal relation"). And yet, as Hughes (this volume, chapter 15) points out, the social competencies of 3-year-olds suggest that they possess a cache of social knowledge discrepant with their failure on false-belief tasks. In fact, it may be that one of the factors making the false-belief task difficult is young children's pragmatic awareness that expressions of belief (e.g., "know," "say," and "think") are presumed by the speaker and the listener to convey something about the true state of affairs. As Bartsch and Wellman (1995) note in their analyses, most of children's uses of "know" were aimed at describing correct statements or successful actions. Returning to an earlier example, for a listener the most informative part of the statement "I know he is in London" is the complement "he is in London." Its veridicality is simply assumed in most circumstances. Children have to override this conventional assumption by inhibiting it and considering that someone could "know" or "think" something that is false in false-belief tasks. In other words, children are generally interested in learning and reporting what is true, and this "reality bias" is difficult to inhibit when considering how to respond to a query about what someone thinks (see Carlson & Moses, 2001, for a discussion of inhibitory control and theory-of-mind development). When the reality bias is removed, as in those situations where the true state of affairs is unknown, 3-year-olds respond more sensibly to questions containing belief terms. For instance, 3-year-olds consistently predicted that a protagonist would look for a puppy where he thought it was located when they were unaware of its actual location (Wellman & Bartsch, 1988).

Finally, the arguments in this chapter implicate a much smaller role for introspective knowledge in mental concept formation than is sometimes claimed. Having internal experiences and meaningfully expressing them is distinct from reflecting upon those internal experiences and forming beliefs (of the sort "this mental state corresponds to this verbal label"). Second-order beliefs about the mind (thinking about thinking) are not necessary for children to meaningfully use mental terms. Children's use is meaningful so long as the expression is used appropriately within the conventional setting. The disconnect between intro-spection and the semantic development of mental terms further illustrates the impoverishment of any notion that knowledge about the mind is an individual-istic process. A person experiences internal sensations privately but joins with others to imbue those experiences with meaning.

Acknowledgments Sarah Cruce and Nicole Misemer assisted with the CHILDES data searches.

References

Astington, J. W. (1999). The language of intention: Three ways of doing it. In P. D. Zelazo, J. W. Astington, & D. R. Olson (Eds.), *Developing theories of intention: Social understanding and self-control* (pp. 295–315). Mahwah, NJ: Erlbaum.

Austin, J. L. (1962). *How to do things with words.* Cambridge, MA: Harvard University Press.

Bartsch, K., & Wellman, H. M. (1995). *Children talk about the mind.* New York: Oxford University Press.

Bretherton, I. (1991). Intentional communication and the development of an understanding of mind. In D. Frye & C. Moore (Eds.), *Children's theories of mind: Mental states and social understanding* (pp. 49–75). Hillsdale, NJ: Erlbaum.

Brown, R. (1973). *A first language: The early stages.* Cambridge, MA: Harvard University Press.

Bruner, J. S. (1983). *Child's talk.* New York: W. W. Norton.

Budwig, N. (2002). A developmental-functionalist approach to mental state talk. In E. Amsel & J. P. Byrnes (Eds.)., *Language, literacy, and cognitive development: The development and consequences of symbolic communication* (pp. 59–86). Mahwah, NJ: Erlbaum.

Canfield, J. V. (1993). The living language: Wittgenstein and the empirical study of communication. *Language Sciences, 15,* 165–193.

Carlson, S., & Moses, L. J. (2001). Individual differences in inhibitory control and children's theory of mind. *Child Development, 72,* 1032–1053.

Carpendale, J. I. & Lewis, C. (2004). Constructing an understanding of mind: The development of children's social understanding within social interaction. *Behavioral and Brain Sciences, 27,* 79–96.

Flavell, J. H., Green, F. L., & Flavell, E. R. (1995). Young children's knowledge about thinking. *Monographs of the Society for Research in Child Development, 60*(1, Serial No. 243).

Flavell, J. H., Green, F. L., & Flavell, E. R. (2000). Development of children's awareness of their own thoughts. *Journal of Cognition and Development, 1,* 97–112.

Flavell, J. H. Green, F. L., Flavell, E. R., & Grossman, J. B. (1997). The development of children's knowledge about inner speech. *Child Development, 68,* 39–47.

Hacker, P. M. S. (1999). *Wittgenstein.* New York: Routledge.

Jacobsen, R. (1996). Wittgenstein on self-knowledge and self-expression. *The Philosophical Quarterly, 46,* 12–30.

Lang, B. & Perner, J. (2002). Understanding of intention and false belief and the development of self-control. *British Journal of Developmental Psychology, 20,* 67–76.

MacWhinney, B. (2000). *The CHILDES project: Tools for analyzing talk* (3rd ed.). Vol. 2: *The database.* Mahwah, NJ: Erlbaum.

Malcolm, N. (1986). *Nothing is hidden: Wittgenstein's criticism of his early thought.* Oxford: Blackwell.

Meltzoff, A. (2002). Imitation as a mechanism of social cognition: Origins of empathy, theory of mind, and the representation of action. In U. Goswami (Ed.), *Blackwell handbook of childhood cognitive development* (pp. 6–25). Malden, MA: Blackwell.

Meltzoff, A., Gopnik, A., & Repacholi, B. (1999). Toddlers' understanding of intentions, desires, and emotions: Explorations of the dark ages. In P. D. Zelazo, J. W. Astington, & D. R. Olson (Eds.), *Developing theories of intention: Social understanding and self–control* (pp. 17–41). Mahwah, NJ: Erlbaum.

Montgomery, D. E. (1997). Wittgenstein's private language argument and children's understanding of the mind. *Developmental Review, 17,* 291–320.

Montgomery, D. E. (2002). Mental verbs and semantic development. *Journal of Cognition and Development, 3,* 357–384.

Montgomery, D. E., & Lightner, M. (2004). Children's developing understanding of differences between their own intentional action and passive movement. *British Journal of Developmental Psychology, 22,* 417–438.

Mueller, U., & Runions, K. (2003). The origins of understanding self and other: James Mark Baldwin's theory. *Developmental Review, 23,* 29–54.

Nelson, K. (1996). *Language in cognitive development: Emergence of the mediated mind.* New York: Cambridge University Press.

Nelson, K., & Kessler Shaw, L. (2002). Developing a socially shared symbolic system. In E. Amsel & J. P. Byrnes (Eds.), *Language, literacy, and cognitive development: The development and consequences of symbolic communication* (pp. 27–57). Mahwah, NJ: Erlbaum.

Nelson, K., Skwere, D. P., Goldman, S., Henseler, S., Presler, N., & Walkenfeld, F. F. (2003). Entering a community of minds: An experiential approach to "theory of mind." *Human Development, 46,* 24–46.

Ninio, A. (1999). Pathbreaking verbs in syntactic development and the question of prototypical transitivity. *Journal of Child Language, 26,* 619–653.

Ninio, A., & Snow, C. E. (1996). *Pragmatic development.* Boulder, CO: Westview Press.

Searle, J. (1983). *Intentionality: An essay in the philosophy of mind.* Cambridge: Cambridge University Press.

Tomasello, M. (1999). Having intentions, understanding intentions, and understanding communicative intentions. In P. D. Zelazo, J. W. Astington, & D. R. Olson (Eds.), *Developing theories of intention: Social understanding and self-control* (pp. 63–75). Mahwah, NJ: Erlbaum.

Wellman, H. M., & Bartsch, K. (1988). Young children's reasoning about beliefs. *Cognition, 30,* 239–277.

Wellman, H. M., & Phillips, A. T. (2001). Developing intentional understandings. In B. F. Malle, L. J. Moses., & D. Baldwin (Eds.), *Intentions and intentionality: Foundations of social cognition* (pp. 125–148). Cambridge, MA: MIT Press.

Wittgenstein, L. (1958). *Philosophical investigations.* (G. E. M. Anscombe, Trans.). New York: Macmillan.

7 Language Promotes Structural Alignment in the Acquisition of Mentalistic Concepts

Dare A. Baldwin and Megan M. Saylor

A colleague recently remarked on what he took to be high spirits in one of us, wondering what was behind such joie de vivre. In fact, the relevant emotion was nothing more than sheer relief from having just escaped—oh so temporarily—from the intricacies of attempting to mediate a truce in the ongoing hostilities of front-office politics. Smiles and laughter were certainly in evidence—but genuine happiness or pleasure was not the source. The basic phenomenon here won't be new to anyone; we all have recognized from childhood that facial expressions and emotional states—or behavior and internal states, put more generally—do not stand in one-to-one relation. Internal states have correlates in others' facial expressions, language, and movements, but the correlations are far from perfect. The upshot is that internal states can't be gleaned whole-hog from others' surface appearance or behavior—they are drastically underdetermined.

The under-determination of internal states raises a range of interesting questions, many of which have been remarked on previously by philosophers (e.g., Davidson, 1980; Gordon, 1987; Quine, 1960) and behavioral scientists (e.g., Ekman & Davidson, 1994; Harris & Saarni, 1989; Schweder, 1994). One of the obvious implications of such under-determination is the obstacle it presents to us understanding one another. Drawing inferences about others' internal states is actually a challenging inductive task, and research on empathic reasoning indicates that our inferences are all too often off base (e.g., Klein & Hodges, 2001; Marangoni, Garcia, Ickes, & Teng, 1995). Another implication is the challenge to acquisition. Given the underdetermination of internal states, how do youngsters ever manage in the first place to acquire an understanding of distinct kinds of internal states—emotions, desires, beliefs, and intentions—and how such states interact?

Consider the notion of "belief," for instance. There really is no particular behavioral pattern that seems strongly indicative that an individual is in the grip of a belief. Even Rodin seems to have confronted this. Having given us "The Thinker" (a seriously questionable rendition, upon consideration), he appears not even to have attempted to sculpt "The Believer." In fact, it is entirely unclear what one could do to capture the general notion of belief within a single behavioral stance.

There is likewise typically no particular behavioral pattern strongly indicative that an individual is in the grip of a *specific* belief. To illustrate, I always believe that doughnuts taste great, but this continuing belief bears a surprisingly tenuous link to my actual behavior. I am frequently confronted with doughnuts but rarely choose to buy or eat them. Occasionally, I do succumb, but I also occasionally buy and eat brussels sprouts, even though my corresponding belief about brussels sprouts is altogether different. Of course, it is obvious to all of us with an intact folk psychology that these inconsistencies occur because behavior seldom arises from a lone belief but instead results from the complex interplay of a variety of factors—including whole sets of interacting beliefs, desires, and intentions, as well as external factors such as the setting, the timing, the presence of others, and one's beliefs about their beliefs, desires, intentions, and the like. The complexity of the relation between beliefs and behavior raises the serious question of how children, presumably initially naïve to the whole notion of belief, could ever construct the notion on the basis of behavioral evidence alone. What do children take to be evidence for the existence of beliefs, or for the presence of a particular, specific belief?

These same questions must be asked about any and all internal and mental states. Given the abstract nature of such states, how is it that children within a given culture—and perhaps, to some degree, universally—manage to converge on roughly the same folk psychological notions? What forces assist children in constructing folk notions of the mind on the basis of experience? Surely, language is one such force. Language ought to facilitate the acquisition of folk psychological concepts on a number of fronts. Other contributors to this volume have explored a variety of ideas along these lines. Like Montgomery (this volume, chapter 6) in particular, we advocate viewing mental-state concepts as emerging in the context of social and linguistic interaction. We are especially interested in discovering how "publicly available evidence" (Quine, 1960), such as language use, may encourage infants and young children to construct ideas about the mentalistic realm. Our tack in this chapter is to pursue this issue as a specific case of Gentner and colleagues' (e.g., Gentner & Medina, 1998) general proposal that language is a catalyst for abstraction in part because it serves as an aid to analogical reasoning and inductive inference. Our specific hypothesis is that language invites one to compare people's behavior across distinct action scenarios, thereby helping to highlight commonalities, foster attention to relevant differences, and promote inferences about non-obvious sources of commonality and difference.

Abstraction: How Does It Happen?

We began with the commonsensical and noncontroversial point that mentalistic notions such as belief, desire, and intention cannot be equated with specific behavioral patterns and thus are highly abstract. This claim gives rise to the puzzle of how children come to converge on roughly the same mentalistic abstractions. As a starting point, it is worth considering what is known about abstraction of any sort and the role language might play in processes of abstraction more generally. In post-Piagetian times, analogical reasoning, or, more broadly speaking, relational mapping, has figured centrally in accounting for how abstraction happens (e.g., Case, 1985; Gentner, 1983; Goswami, 1992, 1996; Halford, 1987, 1993; Holyoak & Thagard, 1995; Pascual-Leone, 1987). For example, Gentner (1999, p. 1) remarked, "One of the key issues in psychology is how human knowledge develops. I suggest that analogy is a key learning mechanism by which abstract knowledge can arise from experience." Approaches to characterizing analogical reasoning differ in their details (e.g., Gentner, Holyoak, & Kokinov, 2001), but these differences are fairly immaterial for the issues we aim to address in this chapter. Thus, for exposition's sake, we will rely particularly heavily on the work of Gentner and colleagues, in large part because they have specifically traced links between language and analogical reasoning in children's conceptual development. We will provide a far-from-comprehensive sketch of their conceptualization of analogical reasoning, followed by brief coverage of findings indicating that language facilitates analogical reasoning. With this background established, we will turn to applying these ideas to the case of present interest: construction of mentalistic concepts.

What Is Analogizing?

According to Gentner and colleagues, analogy arises through comparison, which is a structure-mapping process. Structure mapping is directed toward discovery of alignment across elements within an object, event, or structure; across objects, events, or structures; and across relations among those elements or entities. Once alignments have been discovered, they can be encoded as relations in their own right, meaning that a higher or more abstract level of representation is achieved. Iterative application of structure mapping (i.e., comparison) can lead to discovery of new mappings across already encoded alignments, enabling progressively higher levels of abstraction. Upon identification, alignment relations promote inferences about other relations, in part because of a default preference for parallel sets of relations across entities, as well as coherence among those relational sets. That is, in some cases, direct one-to-one mappings aren't possible for all relations; when inconsistencies are encountered, inferences at a more abstract level are triggered that might generate parallel connectivity and coherence.

In many cases of analogizing, one possesses some understanding of an object or event, and then encounters another object or event that is less well understood. Examples of this are rife in the history of scientific thinking, such as Darwin's attempts to map what was known about breeding practices with domesticated animals into mechanisms of natural selection to account for evolution more generally. One's understanding of the first thing (the "source domain") is brought to bear in an attempt to make sense of the second thing (the "target domain"). Relations that are already encoded in the source domain are mapped into the target domain. Where inferences are needed to generate successful structural alignment, these inferences often feed back onto one's understanding of the source domain. That is, the structural alignment process not only can elucidate the target domain but can also reshape encoding of the structure of the source domain.

Conceptualized in this very general way, comparison processes have the potential to generate analogies of diverse kinds that vary enormously in their complexity and their degree of abstraction. To illustrate, structure mapping can foster recognition of seemingly simple, everyday object categories such as cat and canary (e.g., the concept of "cat" is a higher level encoding of structural alignments across a group of cats actually encountered that differ in their surface details), as well as highly abstract analogies such as Dennett's (1991) humorous statement likening tenured professors to a sea-squirt species that, on reaching maturity, eats its brain.

Comparison-driven structure mapping is thought to be fundamental to human cognition and knowledge acquisition. Extensive research has confirmed the basic structure-mapping phenomena we have just described in adults (e.g., Gentner et al., 2001, provide a relatively up-to-date compendium of such findings) and, to some degree, in children (see, for example, Gentner & Medina, 1998). Computational models that embody structural alignment principles also confirm that structure mapping can achieve analogical retrieval, mapping, inference, and learning (see Forbus, 2001, for a review). Gentner's developmental account of analogizing predicts that infants also are structure-mappers, and Goswami (2001) presents some initial evidence to this effect.

Triggering Abstraction and the Role of Language

One central question regarding the structure-mapping account concerns what factors trigger or otherwise facilitate the comparison that yields initial recognition of alignable structures. Gentner suggests that a range of factors may promote the initiation or success of comparison processes that lead to such recognition, and the literature provides evidence for at least three such factors. First, simple juxtaposition of two disparate things in one's experience increases the likelihood that comparison will take place (e.g., Genter, 1999). Juxtaposition is likely to put diverse things at the forefront of mental activity in close succession, easing comparison. On this view, for example, infants should more readily note mappable elements across tigers and kitty cats if they are encountered side by side than if they are encountered at opposite ends of the house. And, for analogies like Dennett's, learning about sea-squirt behavioral patterns just at a time when thoughts of tenure are salient in one's mind will greatly increase the likelihood that mappable elements will be discovered.

Second, an explicit invitation to compare seemingly distinct things further facilitates discovery and/or encoding of alignable structures. In the now classic "tumor problem" studies, for example, Gick and Holyoak (1983) found that college students were more likely to make use of an analogy in problem-solving if they had been explicitly instructed to compare two different problem-solving scenarios with potentially alignable solutions. Language is, of course, a primary vehicle by which such explicit invitations can be made, and this is then one respect in which language promotes structure mapping and, hence, abstraction. The role of language in facilitating structure mapping seems to go well beyond this, however. In a variety of ways language seems to *implicitly* invite the comparison that yields structure mapping. We offer two examples here, both from the developmental literature.

Ratterman, Gentner, and colleagues (Gentner & Medina, 1998; Gentner & Ratterman, 1991; Ratterman, Gentner, & DeLoache, 1987, 1989) noted a particular structure-mapping task that poses difficulty for 3-year-olds—the so-called cross-mapping task in which relational similarity is pitted against object identity. In this task, children and an experimenter each had a set of objects decreasing continuously in size (e.g., flowerpots each progressively smaller; small object replicas decreasing in size; see Gentner & Medina, figure 3, p. 279). Children watched as an experimenter placed a sticker on the bottom of one of the objects in her set; their task was to locate a comparable sticker on the bottom of one of the objects in their own set. The correct location was always the object in the child's set that shared *relative size* with the comparable object in the experimenter's set. Children had the opportunity to see the correct answer and were able to keep the sticker if they had selected the correct object. What made the task challenging for children was the need to resist choosing the object in their set that was identical to the object on which the experimenter placed the sticker in her set; to be correct, they needed to ignore the identity match and instead base their selection on a relational match (e.g., choosing the largest object in their set, even though this was an object different in actual size from the largest object in the experimenter's set).

At age 3, children were highly error prone, especially with the richly detailed object replicas in which the similarity of identity matches was especially compelling: they selected the correct object (the relational match) 54% of the time with the "sparse" flowerpots but only 32% of the time with the object replicas. A small—but highly relevant—change to the language that accompanied the task, however, made for startling improvements in children's performance. When 3-year-olds were given relational language that implicitly captured the relevant seriation relation—such as "Daddy, Mama, Baby"—in the task instructions, their ability to respond in terms of the mappable seriation relationship skyrocketed: they showed 89% and 79% correct relational responding for "sparse" flowerpots and "rich" object replicas, respectively.

Clearly, the added language provided powerful assistance to children, enabling them to discover or sustain attention to abstract relational mappings even in the face of distracting physical similarities that otherwise would have monopolized their attention. In fact, the presence of relevant relational language (strikingly, just three words) enabled 3-year-olds to achieve the equivalent of two years' worth of development on the cross-mapping task! Also noteworthy is that the benefit relational language conferred was neither transient nor dependent on the continuing presence of relational language (Gentner & Medina, 1998). When children returned to the lab four weeks after their original participation, those who had heard relational language performed significantly better (65% correct) at cross-mapping than those who had not heard such language (31% correct).

Abstraction and a Role for Language in Infancy?

Recent infancy research also reveals a facilitative role for language in promoting mapping and abstraction. To develop this claim, a first step is to make the case that infants are in fact capable of abstraction. On the one hand, much of the recent, very large volume of research on infant cognition seems to provide such evidence. For example, a number of studies indicate that infants interpret object motion in terms of abstract principles, such as solidity, continuity, and cohesion (e.g., Spelke, 1994), causality and agency (Cohen & Oakes, 1993; Leslie, 1984; Oakes & Cohen, 1990), and goal-directedness (e.g., Woodward, 1998). However, perhaps one could argue that some, or possibly even all, of these abstract principles that guide motion processing arise via human evolutionary preparedness. This argument has, of course, been made with respect to all these cases (e.g., Baron-Cohen, 1995; Johnson, 2000; Leslie, 1986; Premack & Premack, 1995; Spelke, 1994). If this is the correct way to view these examples of early sophisticated functioning, then the examples do not speak to the issues at hand because they do not bear on the processes by which new abstract ideas emerge in the course of development via experience in the world. On the other hand, largely constructivist accounts have been offered for each of the principles mentioned (e.g., Baldwin, 2002; Bullock, Gelman, & Baillargeon, 1982; Cohen & Oakes, 1993; Oakes & Cohen, 1990; Tomasello, 1999; Woodward, Sommerville, & Guajardo, 2001). If the constructivist perspective holds weight, then the group of skills at issue are indeed relevant to the present focus on abstraction. The debate is far from settled, however, and for present purposes it makes sense to find a less controversial source of evidence concerning infants' skill at constructing new abstract forms of under-standing. A small body of research concerning infants' ability to draw inductive inferences about hidden, nonobvious object properties seems to serve the pur-pose. Interestingly, this same body of research provides clear evidence that lan-guage facilitates infants' inductive inferences, pointing to an early role for language as an abstraction promoter.

Baldwin, Markman, and Melartin (1993) showed infants (ranging between 9 and 16 months of age) a series of novel objects that possessed unexpected, yet highly salient, functional properties. After infants gained just 30 seconds of experience with a given object—during which they invariably discovered the hidden, nonobvious property—the object was retrieved, and infants were shown a second object similar, but not identical, in appearance to the first object. The second object happened to have been altered (without any surface indication to this effect) such that it was rendered incapable of producing the hidden prop-erty of interest. In question was whether infants would (a) produce actions on the second object that previously had elicited the hidden property for the first object, and (b) persist in such attempts when the actions failed to have the expected (and desired) effect. Such persistence would clearly indicate that in-fants had inferred that the second object likely possessed the nonobvious prop-erty they had encountered in the first object. As it turned out, infants across the 9- to 16-month age range displayed this pattern. They immediately at-tempted to elicit the hidden property with the second object and persevered upon initial failure. As well, a baseline control condition confirmed that the appearance of the second object did not, in and of itself, suggest or "afford" the nonobvious property. A range of other, more involved, controls were also in-corporated, and infants' patterns of exploratory play across conditions served to rule out all the alternative accounts probed.

All in all, this study provides convincing evidence that infants as young as 9 months of age can draw inferences about highly idiosyncratic, nonobvious properties of novel objects. These findings cannot plausibly be explained in terms of the triggering of evolutionarily prepared abstractions but instead point to a powerful mechanism for constructing ideas about the nonobvious on the fly with relatively little input. Clearly, infants can readily "go beyond the obvious" to infer hidden sources of similarity, providing convincing evidence that infants from at least 9 months of age are already fluent at positing hidden, hypothetical, abstract commonalities.

Infants' sensitivity to language as a source of information about nonobvious commonalities has also been investigated (e.g., Desjardins & Baldwin, 1992; Graham, Kilbreath, & Welder, 2002; Welder & Graham, 2001). For example, Desjardins and Baldwin (1992) showed infants of 20 to 22 months a novel object that possessed an interesting hidden property (e.g., opera glasses that spring open when squeezed). In some cases, this object was given a novel label (e.g., "I'm going to show you a *toma!*"), and in other cases no label was provided (just generally enthusiastic speech, such as "I'm going to show you a new one!"). Then infants had the opportunity to play with a second object that was only moderately similar to the first object.

On being shown the second object, infants who had previously heard the first object labeled heard either the same label for the second object (same label condition) or a different label (different label condition). Infants who had been introduced to the first object with generally enthusiastic speech were introduced to the second object with the same kind of speech. Infants' play with the second object showed a striking pattern of differences across conditions. First, when infants heard only generally enthusiastic speech in conjunction with toys, their play showed few signs that they had inferred a common, nonobvious property across the two objects. These findings indicate that moderate perceptual similarity alone was not enough to trigger infants to structurally align two objects, at least when they viewed them in immediate succession as occurred in this study.

Of specific interest, however, were the findings regarding the role of language. In particular, the provision of a *common label* to two objects of only moderate similarity provoked infants to infer that these objects shared the same nonobvious property. For example, infants who heard a first toy that sprung open when squeezed called a "toma" and encountered a second toy only moderately similar but also called a "toma" immediately showed in their play with that second toy that they expected it to likewise spring open when squeezed. Importantly, infants for whom the two moderately similar objects were given *different* labels did not expect the second toy to possess the nonobvious property evinced by the first toy (see figure 7.1).

These findings provided new evidence that, even for infants, language facilitates abstraction. In these studies, infants regarded a shared label as licensing inferences of hidden commonality. Put in Gentner's terms, hearing that a second object shared the same label as a first object triggered infants to align the two objects. Mere juxtaposition in time coupled with a moderate degree of perceptual similarity was not sufficient to trigger such alignment. Welder and Graham (2001), as well as Desjardins and Baldwin (1992), first documented this understanding in infants as young as 16 to 22 months, and more recently Graham and colleagues (Graham et al., 2002) have documented the same skills in infants only 12 months old. Such an early appearance of the understanding

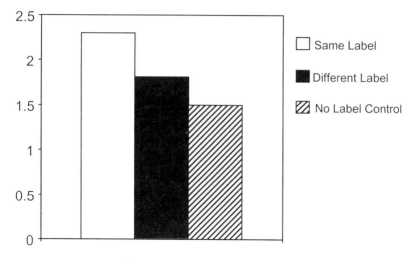

Figure 7.1. Frequency of target actions on disabled second toy.

that labels license inferences about the nonobvious is especially striking given that 12-month-olds are at the earliest phases of language learning. At this age it is typical for normally developing infants to be just beginning to build comprehension vocabularies, and many are not yet producing any words. Thus infants who are very much linguistic novices seem already to possess tacit appreciation that language offers insights about the physical world that penetrate deeper than the surface.

Abstracting Mental States

It seems only a small stretch to consider the possibility that young children who can exploit language for discovering nonobvious commonalities among objects might likewise capitalize on language to guide insights about human action. The Gentnerian essence of the idea is this: language invites children to compare people's behavior across diverse scenarios that they otherwise would not attempt to align. By triggering comparisons, language could help to promote inferences about nonobvious commonalities across distinct actions, such as intention, desire, and belief.

If this hypothesis is at all correct, a first prediction is that parents' use of mental-state terms should be a nontrivial aid in assisting children to construct mentalistic concepts. Parents who frequently use mental-state terms are potentially providing children with a wealth of alignment-relevant data. Imagine the quantity of everyday contexts in which a parent who is inclined to talk about desires, intentions, and beliefs will actually use these terms. Everyday terms such as "want" (desire), "gonna" (intention), and "know" (knowledge/belief) get said frequently by the "mind-minded" parent (e.g., Meins & Fernyhough, 1999) across a variety of contexts. For example, "want" might be heard by a child when she is crying (e.g., "Oh, you *want* that? Here you go."), just before snack (e.g., "What do you *want* to eat? Banana or cracker?"), and when asking the child to cease and desist (e.g., "I *want* to read my book right now. Here's your train to play with."). Given basic talents for alignment and inference, children might readily take up the challenge to comparison that such language offers. Some existing evidence offers initial confirmation for this prediction. That is, children of mind-minded parents—those who frequently produce reference to mentalistic notions—progress faster in their acquisition of mentalistic reasoning (e.g., Dunn, Brown, Slomkowski, Tesla, & Youngblade, 1991; Meins & Fernyhough, 1999; Meins, Fernyhough, Wainwright, et al., 2002; Ruffman, Slade, & Crowe, 2002; Sabbagh & Callanan, 1998). These findings help to bear out the overall plausibility of the hypothesis that language facilitates the abstraction processes necessary to constructing a theory of mind.

At the same time, we suspect that the implications of language for the acquisition of mentalistic concepts are considerably more pervasive than just the availability of explicit talk about mental states as marked by use of mental-state vocabulary. Our suspicion is grounded in Grice's (1957) idea that language really is all about mental states and influencing one another's mental states. For Grice, to mean something with language or any other conventionalized communication system (what he termed "nonnatural" meaning or "meaning-nn") is to intend to cause an effect in the addressee, which can be achieved simply by the addressee recognizing that intention (see Levinson, 1983, for discussion of this account). Levinson's (1983, p. 16) gloss for Grice's definition is that "communication consists of the 'sender' intending to cause the 'receiver' to think or do something, just by getting the 'receiver' to recognize that the 'sender' is trying to cause that thought or action. So language is a complex kind of intention that is achieved or satisfied just by being recognized."

Framed in this way, linguistic interaction is steeped in the mentalistic, and likely it is riddled with clues to that effect. Put another way, language use and mentalistic thinking are so deeply enmeshed that normal language input is, in effect, a form of immersion training in folk psychology. Via language, children receive multifaceted clues to mentalistic concepts day in and day out.

To illustrate these ideas more concretely, we turn to considering one particular aspect of normal language input: the case of reference to things absent. In the remainder of our chapter, we discuss how we might test our ideas about language as a pervasive facilitator of mentalistic abstraction in the context of linguistic interaction involving reference to the absent.

Absent Reference

Reference to the absent occurs anytime linguistic interaction involves mention of a thing or things at spatial or temporal remove. It is obvious that there is quite a continuum of "distance" in this respect, in that something referred to might be immediately present but simply out of current view and/or hearing (and hence absent only in the sense of not in this particular instant impinging on the senses), while other things referred to might have existed in a different historical epoch on a different continent (and hence have no potential for perceptual access). Regardless, in each and all of these cases, reference is occurring to a thing not immediately accessible.

Although language input to children has frequently been characterized as largely concerned with the "here and now" (e.g., Bloom, 1970; Brown & Bellugi, 1964), children in fact encounter references to the absent at fairly high rates even in infancy. It is certainly true that one does not attempt to talk about topics such as pre-Babylonian politics with 10-month-olds, but talk about absent family members, missing binkies, blankies, cuddly toys, and highly salient prior or anticipated events (a birthday party, a vacation, the visit of a favorite friend) is in fact relatively common.

We conjecture that references to the absent, among many other aspects of linguistic interaction, have the potential to provide important clues to children about the mentalistic arena. The essence of the idea is that hearing a known word in the context of absent reference provides infants with an opportunity for structural alignment across communicative contexts: mapping the use of the known word in the absence of its referent to prior understood uses in contexts in which the referent was present. The process of comparison and structural alignment thus invoked could promote the inference that an *intent to refer* occurs despite the absence of the referent.

Our ideas are most easily conveyed in the context of a concrete illustration. First, imagine a 12-month-old infant who is making normal progress in building a comprehension vocabulary. Among the words she has begun to link to appropriate referents is the word "dog." When dogs (and sometimes other dog-like entities, such as dog toys and pictures of dogs) are present and someone says the word "dog," she is inclined to look toward the dogs, rather than, say, balls or bananas. Let's consider the possibility that this young language learner's actual understanding of the word "dog" simply involves the appreciation that the speaker's /dog/ utterance is related to or "about" the present dog, a level of understanding not genuinely mentalistic. That is, she doesn't yet appreciate that another's utterance of the word "dog" reflects *attention* to dogs or an *intention* to communicate about dogs. She simply recognizes that people's dog utterances are about dogs. She may also have noticed that /dog/ utterances often come along with other dog-related talk or activity and some tendency for the speaker to switch gaze between herself and dogs. This level of understanding might lead her to anticipate seeing dogs on hearing /dog/ utterances and to anticipate /dog/ utterances as most likely when a speaker's gaze has been directed toward a dog.

At this phase, our young language learner has the benefit of a firmly entrenched /dog/-to-dog link, but hearing /dog/ when no dogs are to be found (i.e., absent reference involving the word "dog") should strike her as incongruous. What could the utterance /dog/ be about given the absence of dogs? In such an absent-reference scenario, she has three obvious options: (1) she could ignore what seems to her to be an anomalous utterance, (2) she could question whether the sound pattern /dog/ really should be interpreted as relating to dogs, or (3) she could compare the apparently incongruous dog-absent /dog/ utterances with prior "sensible" scenarios in which /dog/ was heard in the presence of dogs, seeking alignment.

In other words, she could treat her memory and understanding of prior references to immediately present dogs as the source domain (to use the standard terminology for analogical reasoning) toward which she strives to map elements in the initially incongruous absent-reference scenario (the target domain) in which /dog/ is heard in the absence of dogs. What is understood about dog-present dog reference is mapped to dog-absent dog reference, setting the stage for analogical inference to fill in gaps of understanding about dog-absent dog reference. For example, mapping source to target leads to the inference that the sound pattern /dog/ in the target domain is still about dogs, despite their absence. The fact that dog-absent dog reference, like dog-present dog reference, also often precedes discussion of dog-relevant things and activities (e.g., food, fur, breath, walks) supplies a readily mappable source of commonality that would support the source-to-target alignment.

However, a direct, one-to-one, parallel mapping isn't quite possible on the surface. In the target domain, gaze toward dogs (and gaze switching between child and dog) isn't observed (as dogs aren't there). Instead, when dog-absent dog reference occurs, gaze seems typically directed toward the child herself when /dog/ is heard. The urge to achieve parallel mappings from source to target domain can't be met in any simple way, so an inference may be drawn that enables them to be met at a more abstract level.

One such inference that would do the trick is that /dog/ utterances and dog-directed gaze are separate reflections of an unseen, internal dog-related thrust or focus (i.e., intention/attention). Under this inference, /dog/ utterances can reflect dog-related focus even when dogs are absent. This inference would also help the language learner to make sense of there being some gaze switching with dog-present dog references but gaze directed primarily at self with dog-absent dog references. If dog-directed gaze reflects a dog-related focus, gaze switching between self and dog then reflects coordinated focus on self and dog. And then structural alignment would lead to the inference in the target domain that /dog/

utterances (reflecting dog-related focus) accompanied by gaze at self (self-directed focus) also reflects coordinated focus on self and dog.

In this way, the attempt to structurally align dog-present dog reference scenarios with dog-absent dog reference scenarios yields inferences that generate a new, more abstract way of encoding the relations among dog utterances, dog-directed gaze, and self-directed gaze. The structural alignment process thus simultaneously makes possible an interpretation of an otherwise anomalous set of utterances (the dog-absent dog references), as well as generating a higher level, more abstract understanding of the source domain (dog-present dog references). And this is all achieved simply by everyday language input that triggers structural alignment processes that we have real reason to suspect even infants possess.

As infants make progress in aligning dog-present dog references with dog-absent dog references, they, of course, meanwhile have the opportunity to engage in the analogous structure-mapping process for other words (e.g., kitty, Daddy, keys, blankie) that they are beginning to comprehend in the present-reference scenario and may be hearing in the context of absent reference, as well. In each case, structure mapping could promote inferences about an internal focus of attention to make possible alignment across present- and absent-reference scenarios. Over time, as isolated absent references start to be understood in these terms, structure mapping across absent-reference scenarios could occur, yielding generalizations about language conveying others' intent/attentional focus and enabling shared focus with an addressee. In other words, understanding of the concept of an internally mediated intent and focus of attention would initially emerge as a piecemeal explanation for individual utterances of specific words and only over time become consolidated into a general appreciation that language embodies communicative intent and attentional focus. If this is at all correct, it draws an analogy between Akhtar and Tomasello's constructivist account of syntax acquisition (e.g., the verb-island hypothesis, Akhtar, 1998, 1999; Akhtar & Tomasello, 1997; Tomasello, 1992) and the acquisition of mentalistic concepts, opening the door to recruiting those researchers' ingenious methodological techniques in the syntactic domain to this very different domain.

Evidence about Infants' Absent-Reference Understanding

Of course, our extended dog-related structural-alignment narrative is at present nothing more than a "just-so story." It seems at least remotely plausible, but relatively little is yet known about how children at this phase in development actually do respond to references to the absent involving words they already comprehend. Research investigating infants' absent-reference capabilities has focused largely on their own production of absent reference, and what little information was available about absent-reference comprehension was almost entirely anecdotal (e.g., Eisenberg, 1985; Sachs, 1983). Research that we recently conducted provides the first systematic body of information about infants' comprehension of utterances involving reference to the absent (Saylor, 2001; Saylor & Baldwin, in press).

In one group of studies, we presented infants between 12 and 31 months with three different kinds of references to absent things: references to absent familiar people, absent familiar objects, and absent objects for which the infants had just learned a label (Saylor, 2001). We reasoned that an understanding of absent reference should elicit production of relatively unique verbal (e.g., mentioning name of absent thing) and nonverbal (e.g., searching, looking and gesturing toward likely location, looking toward speaker) responses relative to responses elicited by the same utterances in a present reference context. Higher rates of absent-reference communicative behaviors for absent than for present reference was thus our index of comprehension for absent reference.

Clear age differences in infants' comprehension of absent reference emerged. In particular, 12-month-olds showed only the vaguest, and possibly spurious, glimmers of an understanding for absent reference. Twelve-month-olds' failure to engage in communicative behaviors appropriate to absent reference (e.g., gesturing toward a likely location) was striking because the basic gestures themselves were well within their existing repertoire of skills. Underscoring this is the fact that they successfully engaged in analogous behaviors in the context of present reference in this very study.

In contrast to 12-month-olds, 15-month-olds systematically displayed a variety of appropriate responses (e.g., searching for the person, gesturing at a likely location) when the experimenter referred to an absent person that they rarely, if ever, showed in present reference contexts. Interestingly, however, they did so only in response to discussion of absent people and did not show this level of sophistication when absent reference concerned either familiar or novel objects. Infants at 23 months and older displayed appropriate responding when reference was made to all of three kinds of absent objects (familiar people, familiar objects, novel objects). These findings suggest that comprehension of absent reference dawns for highly familiar referents (e.g., an absent caregiver) between 12 and 15 months of age and undergoes significant expansion in the period up through at least 23 months.

A new study by Saylor (2003) provides further support for developmental differences in infants' absent-reference comprehension during the early portion of their second year. Saylor presented 12- to 15-month-old infants with a different type of absent-reference scenario. Infants were introduced to pairs of familiar objects, each with a distinguishing property (e.g., a *red* car and a *blue* shoe). During the critical test phase, the experimenter talked about one of the objects (e.g., the car) when color panels matching the properties of both objects were within infants' line of sight but the objects were absent. Starting at

12 months, infants directed more visual attention (longer looking, frequency of looking) at the color panel that matched the mentioned absent object (e.g., the red panel) than the panel that matched the unmentioned absent object. This looking advantage for the absent-referent color panel might indicate a starting appreciation of absent reference. Alternatively, of course, it could arise from associative mechanisms alone. Interestingly, at 15 months, infants coordinated their looking to the panel with looking to the speaker, in addition to displaying the looking advantage for the absent referent-matching color panel, suggesting, at the very least, that 15-month-olds have a deeper appreciation of the communicative thrust of absent-reference utterances than 12-month-olds.

These findings are interesting in several respects. They provide the first evidence that infants at the beginning of their second year are already responding in discriminating and communicatively responsive ways to another's reference to something absent (e.g., by looking at relevant associated things, and gazing at the speaker when nothing is present to look at). The findings also suggest, however, that changes in infants' understanding of references to absent things are occurring during this period: between 12 and 15 months, infants may be gaining appreciation of the mentalistic, communicative underpinnings of absent-reference utterances. At 15 months, infants regularly look toward the speaker and engage in appropriate communicative behaviors, whereas, at 12 months, all of these pieces do not seem to be in place. In particular, 12-month-olds may look at the speaker or they may look at a relevant associated object, but they do not seem to coordinate the two. It is not simply the case that they are unable to do so, because during present reference they readily coordinate attention to a present object with attention to the speaker. It is only for cases of absent reference that they fail to do so.

Finally, with respect to the issues of central interest in this chapter, it is striking that infants in these studies displayed some level of comprehension to absent reference only a few months after they likely began comprehending references to present objects. Such comprehension of present reference has been documented as emerging in the period between 8 and 12 months (e.g., Benedict, 1979; Huttenlocher, 1974; Oviatt, 1980; Reznick & Goldfield, 1992). In other words, a starting conceptual appreciation of others' absent references seems to emerge in relatively tight time-lock with comprehension of a given word in a present-reference context. This outcome is consistent with what our analogical reasoning account would predict.

Testing Absent Reference as a Folk Psychology Facilitator

Direct evidence in support of our analogical reasoning account is not yet available, but we hope soon to undertake research to investigate some unique predictions of the account. In particular, with regard to the absent-reference scenario that we have been relying on as our example, the account predicts that parental references to the absent will assist infants in constructing mentalistic concepts such as attention, but only to the degree that absent reference involves words that infants already comprehend. That is, only when infants have established comprehension for a particular word can such understanding serve as the source domain in the structure-mapping process needed to make sense of the target domain (e.g., absent references involving that same word). We should expect, then, that infants whose parents frequently refer to absent objects with labels known to infants will show accelerated progress in understanding attention. In contrast, parents who avoid reference to absent objects, or whose references to the absent are relatively insensitive to infants' linguistic knowledge, should display no such acceleration in understanding attention. Testing these predictions involves collecting a corpus of data regarding parental input that captures parent-child conversation in situations where absent reference is likely and also measuring infants' (a) developing comprehension vocabularies and (b) understanding of joint attention via activities such as those used by Carpenter, Nagell, and Tomasello (1998) in their research charting the developmental emergence and coalescence of early joint attentional understanding.

Looking beyond Absent Reference

The case of absent reference is just one specific example of how language could potentially promote structural alignment that facilitates children's construction of mentalistic concepts. The overarching hypothesis predicts that language will frequently serve to trigger comparison, and hence structure mapping, across distinct behavioral scenarios that could support, among other things, inferences about internal, mentalistic causes that underlie others' behavior. The case of acquiring an understanding of "prior intentions" (as opposed to "intentions in action"; see Searle, 1983) furnishes another possible example, and presumably there are many other possible candidates. There is reason to believe that children as young as 12 to 18 months possess a basic appreciation of at least some aspects of "intentions in action," meaning that they seem to understand that another's ongoing actions are purposefully directed toward achieving specific goals (e.g., Baldwin, 2000; Carpenter, Akhtar, & Tomasello, 1998; Csibra, Biro, Koos, & Gergely, 2003; Meltzoff, 1995; Tomasello, 1999; Woodward, 1998). How and when children come to understand prior intentions—intentions formulated well in advance of a sequence of actions—is not well understood (but see Carpenter, Call, & Tomasello, 2002, for seminal work on this question). An appreciation for prior intentions is especially noteworthy as an advance in mentalistic understanding, because such intentions may be imputed in the absence of any actual goal-relevant action. Language could play a key role in helping to trigger inferences about the existence of prior intentions. For one, in everyday language input children hear terms such as "plan" (e.g., "I have a <u>plan</u>!") and "idea" (e.g., "Here's an <u>idea</u>."). The use of a given term across contexts could engender structure mapping that yields identification of commonalities across different uses of "plan" or "idea"—such utterances tend to presage action sequences yielding interesting effects, providing direct evidence for prior intention. Other terms, such as "accident" and "mistake"—also relatively frequent in everyday child-oriented language—provide a different kind of (converging) evidence for prior intention. These terms often occur when highly salient unexpected outcomes occur, accompanied by distinctive emotional responses of amusement or chagrin. Structure mapping across contexts in which these terms are heard could facilitate recognition of the "unexpectedness" (lack of prior intention) element. Finally, reference to absent objects provides additional evidence about prior intentions: talk about things in their absence (e.g., "Oh no! Where are my <u>keys</u>?," "Have you seen the <u>kitty</u>?") sometimes predicts distinctive search activity and ultimate contact with that thing. Once absent reference is understood as an instance of genuine reference to an object in its absence (e.g., absent reference as indicative of the speaker's internal focus on the referred-to thing), then such utterances supply evidence of prior intention regarding the absent referent.

Again, as yet all of these ideas regarding ways in which language could facilitate mentalistic inferences via structural alignment are "just-so stories." We offer them as pure speculations in hopes they have real heuristic value, as each makes testable predictions regarding specific relations between aspects of parental input and conceptual advances on children's part in the mentalistic arena.

Conclusion

A central question about human thought is how children construct convergent mentalistic concepts given the abstractness of the link between such concepts and actual behavior. Like many others, we are inclined to think that language provides significant assistance in fostering abstraction of the mentalistic. In this chapter, we have borrowed Gentner and colleagues' recent theorizing about analogical reasoning as a route to abstraction to make this intuition more explicit. We have focused largely on a particular aspect of language—reference to things absent—as a possible microcosm within which structural alignment processes could give birth to nascent inferences about attention and prior intention. We have tried to articulate at least initial ways in which these ideas could be put to the test. We suspect, however, that absent reference represents just one tiny aspect of a multidimensional spectrum of linguistic—and, more generally, communicative—forces that point toward the mentalistic. From birth, language seems to immerse children in the mentalistic. Their powerful skills for analogizing can assist them in discovering the mentalistic structure latent within everyday linguistic interchange.

Acknowledgments Our sincere thanks to Janet Astington and Jodie Baird for their invitation to participate in the conference and to contribute to this volume. The writing of this chapter was assisted by funds from the National Science Foundation under Grant No. BCS-0214484.

References

Akhtar, N. (1998). Characterizing English speaking children's understanding of SVO word order. In E. Clark (Ed.), *The proceedings of the twenty-ninth annual child language research forum* (pp. 161–169). Stanford, CA: Center for the Study of Language and Information.

Akhtar, N. (1999). Acquiring basic word order: Evidence for data-driven learning of syntactic structure. *Journal of Child Language, 26,* 339–356.

Akhtar, N., & Tomasello, M. (1997). Young children's productivity with word order and verb morphology. *Developmental Psychology, 33,* 952–965.

Baldwin, D. A. (2000). Interpersonal understanding fuels knowledge acquisition. *Current Directions in Psychological Science, 9,* 40–45.

Baldwin, D. A. (2002). The rise of intentional understanding: Analogies to the ontogenesis of language. In T. Givon & B. F. Malle (Eds.), *The evolution of language out of prelanguage* (pp. 285–305), Amsterdam: John Benjamins.

Baldwin, D. A., Markman, E. M., & Melartin, R. L. (1993). Infants' ability to draw inferences about nonobvious object properties: Evidence from exploratory play. *Child Development, 64,* 711–728.

Baron-Cohen, S. (1995). *Mindblindness: An essay on autism and theory of mind.* Cambridge, MA: MIT Press.

Benedict, H. (1979). Early lexical development: Comprehension and production. *Journal of Child Language, 6,* 183–200.

Bloom, L. (1970). *Language development: Form and function in emerging grammars.* Cambridge, MA: MIT Press.

Brown, R., & Bellugi, U. (1964). Three processes in the child's acquisition of syntax. *Harvard Educational Review, 34,* 133–151.

Bullock, M., Gelman, R., & Baillargeon, R. (1982). The development of causal reasoning. In W. J. Friedman (Ed.), *The developmental psychology of time* (pp. 209–254). New York: Academic Press.

Carpenter, M., Akhtar, N., & Tomasello, M. (1998). Fourteen- through 18-month-olds differentially imitate intentional and accidental actions. *Infant Behavior and Development, 21,* 315–330.

Carpenter, M., Call, J., & Tomasello, M. (2002). Understanding "prior intentions" enables two-year-olds to imitatively complete a task. *Child Development, 73,* 1431–1441.

Carpenter, M., Nagell, K., & Tomasello, M. (1998). Social cognition, joint attention, and communicative competence from 9 to 15 months of age. *Monographs of the Society for Research in Child Development, 63*(4, Serial No. 255).

Case, R. (1985). *Intellectual development: Birth to adulthood.* New York: Academic Press.

Cohen, L. B., & Oakes, L. M. (1993). How infants perceive a simple causal event. *Developmental Psychology, 29,* 421–433.

Csibra, G., Biro, S., Koos, K., & Gergely G. (2003). One-year-old infants use teleological representations of actions productively. *Cognitive Science, 27,* 110–133.

Davidson, D. (1980). *Essays on actions and events.* New York: Oxford University Press.

Dennett, D. C. (1991). *Consciousness explained.* Boston: Little, Brown.

Desjardins, R., & Baldwin, D. A. (1992). Infants' understanding that object labels license inferences about underlying properties. Unpublished manuscript, University of Oregon.

Dunn, J., Brown, J., Slomkowski, C., Tesla, C., & Youngblade, L. M. (1991). Young children's understanding of other people's feelings and beliefs: Individual differences and their antecedents. *Child Development, 62,* 1352–1366.

Eisenberg, A. R. (1985). Learning to describe past experiences in conversation. *Discourse Processes, 8,* 177–204.

Ekman, P., & Davidson, R. J. (1994). *The nature of emotion: Fundamental questions.* New York: Oxford University Press.

Forbus, K. D. (2001). Exploring analogy in the large. In D. Gentner, K. J. Holyoak, & B. N. Kokinov (Eds.), *The analogical mind: Perspectives from cognitive science.* Cambridge, MA: MIT Press.

Gentner, D. (1983). Structure-mapping: a theoretical framework for analogy. *Cognitive Science, 7,* 155–170.

Gentner, D. (1999). Abstract from an invited address at the Center for Advanced Study in the Behavioral Sciences, Stanford, CA.

Gentner, D., Holyoak, K. J., & Kokinov, B. N. (2001). *The analogical mind: Perspectives from cognitive science.* Cambridge, MA: MIT Press.

Gentner, D., & Medina, J. (1998). Similarity and the development of rules. *Cognition, 65,* 263–297.

Gentner, D., & Ratterman, M. J. (1991). Language and the career of similarity. In S. A. Gelman & J. P. Byrnes (Eds.), *Perspectives on language and thought: Interrelations in development* (pp. 225–277), Cambridge: Cambridge University Press.

Gick, M. L., & Holyoak, K. J. (1983). Schema induction and analogical transfer. *Cognitive Psychology, 15,* 1–38.

Gordon, R. M. (1987). *The structure of emotions: Investigations in cognitive psychology.* New York: Cambridge University Press.

Goswami, U. (1992). *Analogical reasoning in children.* Hillsdale, NJ: Erlbaum.

Goswami, U. (1996). Analogical reasoning and cognitive development. *Advances in Child Development and Behaviour, 26,* 91–138.

Goswami, U. (2001). Analogical reasoning in children. In D. Gentner, K. J. Holyoak, & B. N. Kokinov (Eds.), *The analogical mind: Perspectives from cognitive science.* Cambridge, MA: MIT Press.

Graham, S. A., Kilbreath, C. S., & Welder, A. N. (2002). The importance of being a FLUM: 12-month-olds rely on shared labels and shape similarity for inductive inferences. Paper presented at the 13th Biennial International Conference on Infant Studies, Toronto, Canada.

Grice, H. (1957). Meaning. *Philosophical Review, 66,* 377–388.

Halford, G. S. (1987). A structure-mapping approach to cognitive development. *International Journal of Psychology, 22,* 609–642.

Halford, G. S. (1993). *Children's understanding: the development of mental models.* Hillsdale, NJ: Erlbaum.

Harris, P. L., & Saarni, C. (1989). Children's understanding of emotion: An introduction. In C. Saarni & P. L. Harris (Eds.), *Children's understanding of emotion: Cambridge Studies in Social and Emotional Development* (pgs. 3–24). New York: Cambridge University Press.

Holyoak, K. J., & Thagard, P. (1995). *Mental leaps: Analogy in creative thought.* Cambridge, MA: MIT Press.

Huttenlocher, J. (1974). The origins of language comprehension. In R. Solso (Ed.), *Theories in cognitive psychology.* Hillsdale, NJ: Erlbaum.

Johnson, S. C. (2000). The recognition of mentalistic agents in infancy. *Trends in Cognitive Sciences, 4,* 22–28.

Klein, K. J. K., Hodges, S. D. (2001). Gender differences, motivation, and empathic accuracy: When it pays to understand. *Personality and Social Psychology Bulletin, 27,* 720–730.

Leslie, A. M. (1984). Spatiotemporal continuity and the perception of causality in infants. *Perception, 13,* 287–305.

Leslie, A. M. (1986). Getting development off the ground: Modularity and the infants' perception of causality. In P. Van Geert (Ed.), *Theory building in developmental psychology* (pp. 406–436). Amsterdam: North-Holland.

Levinson, S. C. (1983). *Pragmatics.* Cambridge: Cambridge University Press.

Marangoni, C., Garcia, S., Ickes, W., & Teng, G. (1995). Empathic accuracy in a clinically relevant setting. *Journal of Personality and Social Psychology, 68,* 854–869.

Meins, E., & Fernyhough, C. (1999). Linguistic acquisitional style and mentalising development: The role of maternal mind-mindedness. *Cognitive Development, 14,* 363–380.

Meins, E., Fernyhough, C., Wainwright, R., Das Gupta, M., Fradley, E., & Tuckey, M. (2002). Maternal mind-mindedness and attachment security as predictors of theory of mind understanding. *Child Development, 73,* 1715–1726.

Meltzoff, A. N. (1995). Understanding the intentions of others: Re-enactment of intended acts by 18–month-old children. *Developmental Psychology, 31,* 1–16.

Oakes, L. M., & Cohen, L. M. (1990). Infant perception of a causal event. *Cognitive Development, 5,* 193–207.

Oviatt, S. L. (1980). The emerging ability to comprehend language: An experimental approach. *Child Development, 51,* 97–106.

Pascual-Leone, J. (1987). Organismic processes for neo-Piagetian theories: A dialectical causal account of cognitive development. *International Journal of Psychology, 22,* 531–570.

Premack, D., & Premack, A. J. (1995). Intention as psychological cause. In D. Sperber (Ed.), *Causal cognition: A multidisciplinary debate.* (pp. 185–199). Oxford: Clarendon Press.

Quine, W. V. O. (1960). *Word and object.* Cambridge: Cambridge University Press.

Ratterman, M. J., Gentner, D., & DeLoache, J. (1987, April). Young children's use of relational similarity in a transfer task. Poster presented at the biennial meeting of the Society for Research in Child Development, Baltimore, MD.

Ratterman, M. J., Gentner, D., & DeLoache, J. (1989, April). Effects of competing surface similarity on children's performance in an analogical task. Poster presented at the biennial meeting of the Society for Research in Child Development, Kansas City, MO.

Reznick, S. J., & Goldfield, B. A. (1992). Rapid change in lexical development in comprehension and production. *Developmental Psychology, 28,* 406–413.

Ruffman, T., Slade, L., & Crowe, E. (2002). The relation between children's and mothers' mental state language and theory-of-mind understanding. *Child Development, 73,* 734–751,

Sabbagh, M. A., & Callanan, M. A. (1998). Metarepresentation in action: 3-, 4-, and 5-year-olds' developing theories of mind in parent-child conversations. *Developmental Psychology, 34,* 491–502.

Sachs, J. (1983). Talking about the there-and-then: The emergence of displaced reference in parent-child discourse. In K. E. Nelson (Ed.), *Children's language,* vol. 4 (pp. 1–28). Hillsdale, NJ: Erlbaum.

Saylor, M. M. (2001). Understanding talk about the absent: An investigation of infants' comprehension of absent reference from 12 to 31 months. Unpublished doctoral dissertation, University of Oregon.

Saylor, M. M. (2003). Infants' recognition of properties of mentioned absent things. Manuscript in preparation.

Saylor, M. M., & Baldwin, D. A. (in press). Discussing things not present: Absent reference comprehension from 12 to 31 months. *Journal of Child Language.*

Schweder, R. A. (1994). "You're not sick, you're just in love": Emotion as an interpretive system. In P. Ekman & R. J. Davidson (Eds.), *The nature of emotion: Fundamental questions.* (pp. 32–44). New York: Oxford University Press.

Searle, J. R. (1983). *Intentionality: An essay in philosophy of mind.* Cambridge: Cambridge University Press.

Spelke, E. (1994). Initial knowledge: Six suggestions. *Cognition, 50,* 431–455.

Tomasello, M. (1992). *First verbs: A case study of early grammatical development.* Cambridge: Cambridge University Press.

Tomasello, M. (1999). *The cultural origins of human cognition.* Cambridge, MA: Harvard University Press.

Welder, A. N., & Graham, S. A. (2001). The influences of shape similarity and shared labels on infants' inductive inferences about nonobvious object properties. *Child Development, 72,* 1653–1673.

Woodward, A. L. (1998). Infants selectively encode the goal object of an actor's reach. *Cognition, 69,* 1–34.

Woodward, A. L., Sommerville, J. A., & Guajardo, J. J. (2001). How infants make sense of intentional action. In B. Malle, L. Moses, & D. Baldwin (Eds.), *Intentions and intentionality: Foundations of social cognition* (pp. 149–169). Cambridge, MA: MIT Press.

8 Language and the Development of Cognitive Flexibility: Implications for Theory of Mind

Sophie Jacques and Philip David Zelazo

It is well established that linguistic ability relates to performance on tests of "theory of mind" (ToM) (Astington & Jenkins, 1999; Happé, 1995; Hughes, 1998; Jenkins & Astington, 1996; Watson, Painter, & Bornstein, 2001). However, the reasons for this correlation are unclear, and questions remain regarding which aspects of language are related to which aspects of ToM, when, and perhaps most important, why. In this chapter, we argue that one aspect of language (labeling) is related to standard preschool measures of ToM (e.g., false-belief, representational-change, and appearance-reality tasks; Flavell, Flavell, & Green, 1983; Gopnik & Astington, 1988; Wimmer & Perner, 1983) because these measures of ToM all require *cognitive flexibility*, which undergoes dramatic changes during the preschool years. In support of this argument, we briefly review the results of recent experimental research on the effects of labeling on tasks that assess cognitive flexibility. The results of these studies indicate that there are widespread changes in the effects of labeling on 4-year-olds' performance on these tasks. We conclude with predictions for future experimental labeling manipulations with ToM tasks that might shed light on the causal nature of the relation between language and ToM.

Relations between Language and Theory of Mind

The link between language and ToM was perhaps first noted by Dunn and her colleagues (Dunn, Brown, Slomkowski, Tesla, & Youngblade, 1991), who found that measures of child discourse at 33 months predicted children's performance on ToM tasks at 40 months and that these relations were significant despite the fact that the sample was very young and that there appeared to be little variability in performance on the ToM tasks due to floor effects. Since Dunn et al.'s early observation, others have examined specifically whether language relates to ToM measures (e.g., Hughes, 1998; Jenkins & Astington, 1996). For example, Jenkins and Astington examined whether performance on false-belief tasks was associated with linguistic ability above and beyond the effects of age and nonverbal memory. Not only were there significant relations between success on false-belief tasks and linguistic ability, but also there appeared to be a threshold effect indicating the minimal linguistic ability that children needed in order to succeed on these false-belief tasks: Only 1 child (out of 50) who passed any of the four false-belief tasks did so with linguistic ability below that of a typical child of 4 years, 1 month, as assessed by the Test of Early Language Development (TELD; Hresko, Reid, & Hammill, 1981).

More recently, a number of longitudinal studies have also been conducted in an attempt to determine whether language predicts ToM longitudinally (and vice versa). For example, Astington and Jenkins (1999) not only found significant relations between language development and performance on standard preschool measures of ToM including false-belief and appearance-reality tasks, but more important, they also found that language development—particularly syntax development—at 40 months of age predicted children's ability to reason on standard preschool ToM tasks at 44 and 47 months even when the variance due to age and ToM performance at 40 months was taken into account (see also Watson, Painter, & Bornstein, 2001). However, the reverse was not true: Performance on ToM tasks at 40 months did not predict scores on later language measures.

Similarly, using a new statistical technique for longitudinal designs developed by Nagin (1999; Nagin & Tremblay, 1999), we sought to determine whether children followed different *patterns* of ToM development across the preschool years and whether children with different patterns of development also differ in terms of their language abilities (Jacques, Séguin, & Zelazo, 2002). To do so, we examined the performance of approximately 400 children who were assessed longitudinally at 42 and 60 months of age on measures of language development and ToM (among other measures). The technique identified two groups of children who showed distinct patterns of developmental change on the ToM tasks across the two ages: One group of children (approximately 70% of the sample) improved significantly on the ToM tasks across the two ages, whereas the other group (approximately 30% of the sample) not only performed more poorly than the former group at both ages but also failed to improve in performance on the ToM tasks across the two ages. We then compared these two groups in terms of their linguistic abilities and found that the two groups could also be differentiated from each other at both 42 and 60 months in terms of their linguistic abilities.

Researchers have also noted relations between language and ToM in atypical development. For example, several researchers have found that individuals with autism, who have marked deficits in language (Tager-Flusberg, 2001), perform poorly on ToM tasks (e.g., Baron-Cohen, Leslie, & Frith, 1985). In addition, their success on ToM tasks is associated with their language abilities (e.g., Happé, 1995; Tager-Flusberg & Joseph, this volume, chapter 14; Yirmiya, Solomonica-Levi, Shulman, & Pilowsky, 1996). Similar results have also been reported for deaf children (e.g., P. de Villiers, this volume, chapter 13; see also J. de Villiers & P. de Villiers, 2000; Garfield, Peterson, & Perry, 2001, for reviews). In general, the performance of deaf children on ToM tasks appears to be related to their signing abilities, irrespective of their chronological age or overall nonverbal cognitive abilities. Interestingly, however, for both deaf children and children with autism, the minimal linguistic abilities required to pass ToM tasks (as assessed by standardized language measures) appear to be much higher than those for typically developing children. For example, Happé (1995) reported that whereas 80% of typically developing children with verbal mental ages of 4.5 years pass false-belief tasks, only 50% of individuals with autism with verbal mental ages of 9.2 consistently pass these tasks (see Garfield et al., 2001, for a review).

Various possible reasons for the correlation between language and ToM have been considered: language affects ToM, ToM affects language, some third variable affects both (see Astington & Baird, this volume, chapter 1; Astington & Jenkins, 1999; J. de Villiers & P. de Villiers, 2000, for discussions). Moreover, although the finding that early language development appears to predict later ToM performance (but not vice versa) is consistent with the idea that language has a direct effect on ToM, there are other reasons why the asymmetrical relation may exist. For example, performance on ToM tasks at an early age may have little variability because of floor effects, and as a result, it may be difficult to detect evidence that early ToM performance predicts later language development. The link between language and ToM may also be indirect; children with more developed language skills may also be more social than less language-proficient children, and as a result of their increased exposure to social experiences, these more language-proficient children could learn to consider other people's mental states—both in their everyday interactions and on tasks assessing this kind of understanding—at an earlier age than less language-proficient children (cf., Dunn & Brophy, this volume, chapter 3).

For all of these reasons, one cannot conclude that language plays a direct causal role in the development of ToM. In addition, part of the problem in interpreting relations between language and ToM is that despite two decades of research on ToM, there is still no consensus regarding how best to characterize it. In the following sections, we recast measures of ToM as measures of cognitive flexibility, and we then review experimental research that assesses whether language plays a causal role in the development of cognitive flexibility.

Recasting ToM as Flexible Perspective Taking

Although ToM undoubtedly involves the acquisition of specific concepts pertaining to mental states and their implications for human behavior, we believe that most of the variance on standard preschool measures of ToM (e.g., false-belief, appearance-reality, and representational-change tasks) can be attributed to the development of flexible perspective taking, or cognitive flexibility more generally. That is, the use of certain mental concepts such as the concept of *belief* necessarily involves cognitive flexibility (both in ToM tests and in everyday experience), and it may be this that develops rapidly during the preschool years. For example, consider the standard false-belief task. In this task, if children can flexibly adopt the perspective of a protagonist who holds a false belief, then they should be able to predict the protagonist's behavior on the basis of that (mistaken) perspective. However, if they cannot reason from more than one perspective, then they will predict the protagonist's behavior on the basis of their own, current perspective. Therefore, in order for children to succeed on the standard false-belief task (or even to have a notion of false belief at all), they necessarily need to be flexible in their thinking, because false belief requires that children consider multiple (or at least two) conflicting representations of a single object or event (presumably in addition to requiring them to have a conceptual understanding of mental states themselves).

Measures of cognitive flexibility exist in both the social and the nonsocial domains (see Jacques & Zelazo, in press; Zelazo & Jacques, 1996, for reviews), and nonsocial measures of cognitive flexibility, such as the Dimensional Change Card Sort (Frye, Zelazo, & Palfai, 1995), have been shown to be correlated with performance on ToM tasks in both typical (e.g., Carlson & Moses, 2001; Frye et al., 1995; see Perner & Lang, 1999, for a review) and atypical development (e.g., Colvert, Custance, & Swettenham, 2002; Hughes & Russell, 1993; Ozonoff, Pennington, & Rogers, 1991; Zelazo, Jacques, Burack, & Frye, 2002). Furthermore, within both domains, we can distinguish between two types of measures of cognitive flexibility. *Deductive* measures of *rule use*, such as the Dimensional Change Card Sort (Frye et al., 1995), the Day-Night Stroop (Gerstadt, Hong, & Diamond, 1994), and "Simon Says" (Strommen, 1973), consist of tasks in which children are explicitly told what to do and asked to act in one way given a certain set of constraints and asked to act in an incompatible way given other constraints, or they are simply asked to act in a way that is incompatible with their habitual response to a particular situation (see Zelazo &

Jacques, 1996, for a review of deductive measures). In contrast, *inductive* measures, such as standard preschool measures of ToM (e.g., Flavell et al., 1983; Gopnik & Astington, 1988; Wimmer & Perner, 1983), the Flexible Item Selection Task (FIST; Jacques, 2001; Jacques & Zelazo, 2001), and the Wisconsin Card Sorting Test (Berg, 1948; Grant & Berg, 1948), also consist of measures in which children must take at least two incompatible perspectives, but in these tasks, children are not told *explicitly* what to do from each perspective (see Jacques & Zelazo, in press, for a review of inductive measures). Both types of measures, however, assess cognitive flexibility because more than one perspective (leading to different outcomes) must be taken in order to succeed.

Language and Cognitive Flexibility

Many theorists, including Vygotsky (1934/1986), Werner (1948), Bruner (1973), and even Piaget (1964/1967), have suggested that language acquisition plays an important role in the development of cognitive flexibility. For example, Piaget conceded that "language confines itself to profoundly transforming thought by helping it to attain its forms of equilibrium by means of a more advanced schematization and a more *mobile* abstraction" (Piaget, 1964/1967, pp. 91–92; italics added). Despite the widespread recognition that language may be involved in the development of cognitive flexibility, however, few theorists have articulated exactly how it might go about doing so. Here we consider briefly two different proposals, both of which predict that one aspect of language, labeling of relevant stimuli, will increase cognitive flexibility, and we then review some of the evidence in support of these proposals.

According to the Levels of Consciousness Model (e.g., Zelazo, 1999), labeling drives the development of self-reflection, which in turn permits increases in flexible thought and action. In particular, labeling one's subjective experiences helps make those experiences an object of consideration at a higher level of consciousness (i.e., what was formerly subjective becomes an object of consideration as one ascends through levels of consciousness). Increases in level of consciousness, in turn, allow for the flexible selection of perspectives from which to reason (i.e., they allow for increases in cognitive flexibility).

In contrast, Jacques (2001) has emphasized the importance of the *arbitrary* nature of linguistic symbols as one of the main characteristics of language that allows for cognitive flexibility.[1] Because labels are arbitrary and generally bear no resemblance whatsoever to the external stimuli that they represent, they provide symbol users with an excellent means of separating themselves from the immediate environment. In other words, linguistic symbols create psychological distance between the symbol user and the external stimuli that the symbols represent. This distance should allow individuals to be better able to control their own thinking because they are no longer bound to respond on the basis of the immediate environment.[2] The idea that symbol use leads to increased psychological distance between the symbol user and the environment is not new (cf. Dewey, 1931/1985; Kendler, 1963; Sigel, 1993; Vygotsky, 1978; Werner & Kaplan, 1963). What is new is the idea that the reason why linguistic symbols are particularly well suited for creating distance is precisely that they are arbitrary. From this perspective, then, the use of iconic (or concrete) symbols should not be as effective in promoting cognitive flexibility (in fact, see DeLoache, 2000; Uttal, Liu, & DeLoache, 1999, for discussions of some of the limitations of concrete symbols for psychological distance).

These two accounts, then, differ in the following way: whereas Zelazo maintains that labeling brings about increases in flexibility indirectly via the effect of labeling on level of consciousness, Jacques argues that it is a particular characteristic of language itself (viz., its arbitrary nature) that allows for distancing, which in turn allows for flexible thinking. That is, thinking that is conducted in linguistic terms (i.e., discursive thinking) is intrinsically (and necessarily) more flexible than thinking that is conducted on the basis of perceptual information, regardless of one's level of consciousness. Irrespective of the differences between these accounts, both suggest that language plays an instrumental role in the development of cognitive flexibility and that it might be possible to reinterpret the relation between language and ToM performance in terms of language-related effects on flexible thinking, more generally—a point to which we return in a later section. First, however, we review experimental evidence for a causal effect of labeling on cognitive flexibility.

Experimental Evidence

Labeling effects on children's performance have been noted on a wide range of tasks, including tasks that assess discrimination-shift learning (e.g., Kendler & Kendler, 1961), transposition (e.g., Kuenne, 1946), memory (e.g., Keeney, Cannizzo, & Flavell, 1967), object categorization and classification (e.g., Deák, Ray, & Pick, 2002; Inhelder & Piaget, 1959/1964; Kotovsky & Gentner, 1996), and self-regulation (e.g., Luria, 1959, 1961). The effects of labeling in several of these tasks may be due to effects on cognitive flexibility (see Jacques & Zelazo, in press). For example, Kendler and Kendler found that 4-year-olds who were asked to label relevant aspects of stimuli during a training phase of a variant of the reversal-shift learning paradigm reached criterion on a subsequent test phase more rapidly than those who were not asked to label or who were asked to label the irrelevant dimension. As another example, to their surprise, Inhelder and Piaget (1959/1964, chap. 7) noted that in a classification task in which items could be classified in multiple ways, children's ability to *change* their classification criteria and to anticipate the classes beforehand was affected by whether or not the items were named initially.

Using a more stringent methodology, Loewenstein and Gentner (2004, Experiments 3 and 4; Gentner & Loewenstein, 2001) recently found labeling effects with preschoolers on a cross-mapped version of a spatial-mapping task, a search task that they devised on the basis of DeLoache's (1987) scale-model search task. From our perspective, this task can also be construed as a measure of cognitive flexibility. Specifically, in this task, a child is shown two boxes (the "experimenter's hiding box" and the "child's finding box"; see figure 8.1) in which a card is placed on an upper shelf (i.e., "on" location), another card is placed on a middle shelf (i.e., "in" location), and a third is placed under the box (i.e., "under" location). The three cards that are placed in the experimenter's box are all different from one another but are all identical with the three cards that are placed in the child's box, although analogous cards are placed in a *different* location across the two boxes. In full view of the child, the experimenter places a sticker behind one of the cards in the experimenter's box; then, out of the child's sight, the experimenter hides another sticker in the corresponding location in the child's box. The child is then told to find his own sticker "in the very same place" in his own box. This task is a measure of cognitive flexibility because it requires that children learn to use spatial relational information to solve the task *while at the same time* refraining from responding on the basis of incompatible object-identity information.[3]

In one experiment (Experiment 3), Loewenstein and Gentner (2004) tested 49-, 55-, and 62-month-old children in one of two conditions that differed in

Experimenter's Hiding Box   Child's Finding Box

Figure 8.1. The cross-mapped version of the spatial-mapping task that Loewenstein & Gentner (2004) used to assess children's ability to use spatial relational information to find a sticker when that information conflicted with object-identity information. (Reproduced with permission from Loewenstein & Gentner, 2004)

how the experimenter referred to the hiding locations when placing the sticker in the experimenter's hiding box. Specifically, in the no-label condition, the experimenter simply stated, "I'm putting the winner right here," whereas in the label condition, the experimenter stated, "I'm putting the winner on/in/under the box." The authors found that the youngest group (i.e., the 49-month-olds) searched at chance in both the label and no-label conditions and that they performed more poorly than the two older age groups. In contrast, for the older age groups, those in the label condition outperformed those in the no-label condition. The authors interpreted their findings by proposing that relational language (e.g., "on," "in," or "under") invites children to think in terms of relations and consequently helps children make relational mappings more easily. Their results, however, are also consistent with our idea that labels help children because they affect children's tendency to be more flexible and thus facilitate selecting spatial information to find the sticker instead of the more compelling object information.

Recently, we set out to investigate specifically whether language contributes to the emergence of cognitive flexibility. In order to do so, we first designed a task, the Flexible Item Selection Task (FIST; Jacques & Zelazo, 2001), which is suitable for use with preschoolers and in which cognitive demands other than cognitive flexibility are minimized. We based this task on the Visual-Verbal Test, a neuropsychological test that Feldman and Drasgow (1951; Drasgow & Feldman, 1957) developed in the 1950s to assess abstraction and cognitive flexibility in individuals with schizophrenia. In subsequent experiments, we then manipulated labels experimentally to see whether we could *cause* a change in flexible thinking through language manipulations (Jacques, 2001; Jacques, Zelazo, Lourenco, & Sutherland, 2005).

More specifically, on each trial of the FIST, children are shown sets of three items on a computer screen (e.g., a large yellow teapot, a large yellow shoe, and a small yellow shoe; figure 8.2). These items can vary on three dimensions (color, shape, and size), and each dimension is represented by one of three possible cues (e.g., for color, the cues were red, blue, and yellow). The sets of three items are designed so that one pair of items is matched on a cue of one relevant dimension (in figure 8.2, the large yellow teapot and the large yellow shoe match on size), and a different pair of items is matched on a cue of a different relevant dimension (in figure 8.2, the large yellow shoe and the small yellow shoe match on shape). So one *pivot item* (i.e., the large yellow shoe) always matches one of the other items on one dimension and at the same time matches the third item on another dimension. The cue of the third dimension is irrelevant and constant across the three items (in the example in figure 8.2, all the items are alike on color). On each trial, children are asked to make two distinct selections. They are first asked to select a pair of items that are alike in some way (i.e., Selection 1). Selection 1 responses provide an index of children's ability to extract a single basis of

Figure 8.2. An example of items presented on a trial of the Flexible Item Selection Task (FIST).

similarity among nonidentical items (i.e., an abstraction component). Once children have made an unambiguous response for Selection 1, they are then asked to select a second pair of items that are alike, but in some other way (i.e., Selection 2). Selection 2 responses also provide a measure of abstraction, but in light of good performance on Selection 1, Selection 2 responses serve primarily as an index of children's ability to switch flexibly between dimensions (i.e., a cognitive-flexibility component). In other words, in order to do well on both selections, children must be able to represent the pivot item in two different ways: according to both size *and* shape in the example in figure 8.2.

In our initial study with a slightly different version of the FIST (Jacques & Zelazo, 2001), we found that 3-year-olds were significantly worse than both 4- and 5-year-olds on Selection 1, suggesting that they had difficulties selecting a pair of nonidentical items that matched on a common dimension. However, despite equivalent and good performance on Selection 1, 4-year-olds had significantly more difficulty than the 5-year-olds on Selection 2, suggesting that they had specific problems with switching flexibly between dimensions (i.e., difficulties with cognitive flexibility).

We then hypothesized that the age-related changes in cognitive flexibility between 4 and 5 years might be due to underlying changes in language development, or, more precisely, in children's spontaneous representation of information in linguistic terms. Consequently, we then conducted two experiments in which we assessed children's performance on the FIST and on an independent measure of language development (i.e., the Peabody Picture Vocabulary Test-Revised; PPVT-R; Dunn & Dunn, 1981). More important, to determine whether language plays a role in the development of cognitive flexibility, we introduced labeling manipulations experimentally to see whether we could change children's tendency to be flexible. In the first of these experiments (Jacques et al., 2005, Experiment 1), we tested 108 children, 41-, 53-, and 65-months old, in one of three conditions that differed in whether or how the children were asked to label on each selection. In a no-label condition, children were simply given the standard version of the task; in a relevant-label condition, children were asked to label the dimension by which they selected items on each selection; and in an irrelevant-label condition, they were asked to label the irrelevant dimension (the dimension that did not vary on that trial, e.g., color in figure 8.2). The irrelevant-label condition was important in that it served as a control condition for possible nonspecific effects of labeling: As in the relevant-label condition, children had to talk about the items, but the labels that they had to provide were irrelevant to their actual selections. We were particularly interested in the effects of labeling on Selection 1 on performance on Selection 2, our measure of cognitive flexibility.

The results of this experiment confirmed the general pattern of age-related changes that we found in our initial study (Jacques & Zelazo, 2001). In addition, as with ToM tasks, we found significant correlations between performance on Selection 2 and overall receptive language development, irrespective of the condition in which children participated and even after chronological age was partialled out ($r = .62$, $p < .01$, unpartialled correlation, and $r = .32$, $p < .01$, partialled correlation). More important, however, we also found that the Selection 2 performance of 53-month-olds could be influenced dramatically by whether or not they were asked to label the relevant dimension on Selection 1. When 53-month-olds were asked to provide labels on Selection 1 that were relevant to their selection, their Selection 2 performance improved significantly compared to 53-month-olds who were not asked to label or who were asked to label irrelevant aspects of the stimuli. Moreover, within the relevant-label condition, children who made fewer labeling errors on Selection 1 did better on Selection 2 than those who made more errors.

In contrast, the Selection 2 performance of 41- and 65-month-olds did not appear to be affected by labeling. On the one hand, given that 41-month-olds failed to select items correctly on Selection 1 in the first place (and consequently, often failed to label accurately on Selection 1), it is not surprising that they did not benefit in terms of their Selection 2 performance. On the other hand, explicit instructions to label the relevant dimension on Selection 1 did not help 65-month-olds because their Selection 2 performance was already high, and presumably they were already spontaneously representing the items linguistically. Indeed, we found that across all conditions, children (more of whom were 5-year-olds) who spontaneously labeled the relevant dimension in preliminary trials that preceded the FIST did better on Selection 2 of the FIST than those who did not label in these preliminary trials. These null effects of labeling for younger and older children are comparable with existing findings in other domains, suggesting that labeling effects may be reserved for *transitional* children who are not too close to floor or to ceiling performance (e.g., Kendler & Kendler, 1961).

The next experiment we conducted (Jacques et al., 2005, Experiment 2) was designed to determine experimentally whether the labels that are provided on Selection 1 actually cause improvements on Selection 2. Unlike previous experiments with the FIST, only 54-month-olds participated, and it was the experimenter who always selected items on Selection 1 (in a predetermined way) and who always labeled the items (differently depending on the condition). This procedure was adopted so that we could present labels in a controlled manner and assess which kinds of labels caused a change in performance. Results showed that as predicted, only labels that referred to the relevant dimension (i.e., the dimension on which items matched each other; e.g., size) helped, but those that referred to the irrelevant dimension (i.e., the dimension that did not vary across the 3 items, e.g., color) did not. This result was obtained both for labels that referred to a dimension (e.g., "size") and also for labels that referred to specific cues of a dimension (e.g., "big").

The labeling effects observed on the FIST are particularly important because our finding that labeling on Selection 1 influenced Selection 2 performance allows us to rule out salience or attention-getting explanations of labeling effects. Specifically, some researchers may argue that labels act only by changing the relative salience of specific information within a given task, without necessarily changing the nature of the *representation* that children hold. In most previous labeling studies, children were asked to respond in a manner consistent with what they had labeled. Thus, in those studies, the claim could be made that labels influence performance because they draw children's attention *toward* relevant information, changing the relative salience of that information. However, such an explanation cannot account for the labeling effects on the FIST. If attention-getting properties of labels were operating on the FIST, children in the relevant-label condition should have had *more* difficulty selecting items correctly on Selection 2. That is, because we asked children (or the experimenter) to label the relevant dimension on Selection 1, we presumably made that dimension more salient. Hence, if labels affected performance on the FIST because they drew children's attention toward that particular dimension, then on this account, Selection 2 performance should have *declined* instead of improving (because the Selection 1 dimension would now be more salient). Thus, the fact that we found that children made significantly fewer errors on Selection 2 suggests that attention-getting properties of labels cannot be responsible for these labeling effects. We return to this point later in the next section.

Labeling on ToM: Predictions of Experimental Manipulations

Even though cognitive flexibility is required to perform well on standard preschool ToM tasks such as the false-belief task, these tasks are not ideal measures of cognitive flexibility per se because several *other* cognitive processes may also be needed to perform well on these tasks (e.g., good understanding of mental-state concepts such as beliefs or desires). However, despite differences in the necessity of other cognitive processes in the tasks used by Loewenstein and Gentner (2004) and by Jacques et al. (2005), the similarities in the labeling effects across both tasks are striking, suggesting that it may be possible to introduce experimental labeling manipulations on standard preschool ToM tasks and obtain comparable results despite the fact that other processes may be involved.

There have been a few attempts to manipulate verbal (and visual) information on ToM tasks. However, those studies in which only visual information was manipulated across conditions and verbal information was held constant, such as those conducted by Johnson and Maratsos (1977) and Zaitchik (1991), do not really address whether language affects ToM performance (see Astington & Baird, this volume, chapter 9, for a similar point). In contrast, Astington and Baird (this volume, chapter 9) describe a recent study that they conducted in which they systematically manipulated both the verbal and visual information that they presented to children. Specifically, in one experiment, they tested 42- and 52-month-olds on three versions of a false-belief task; in one version, children were shown a video of a change-of-location false-belief task and heard the corresponding narrative (standard version); in another version, they heard the narrative but did not see the locations or object during the transfer episode (verbal-only version), and in the third version, they only saw the actions and locations involved without hearing the narrative (visual-only version). The critical comparison for assessing language-related effects on this task is to compare the standard version to the visual-only version, versions that differed from each other only in terms of the verbal information that they provided. However, contrary to our expectations (and theirs), Astington and Baird found only an effect of age. They did not find an effect of task version or an interaction between age and task version, which we would have anticipated (see discussion later in this section). The authors conducted a second experiment with the same versions of the task, but in this experiment they actually acted out the stories (rather than presenting the stories to children on videos). Again, no significant differences between versions were detected.[4]

At first glance, these results appear to be inconsistent with our hypothesis that language should have an effect on this measure of cognitive flexibility. However, it is possible that the entirely nonverbal nature of the visual-only task *forced* children who were capable of doing so to narrate the story themselves so that they could follow the events (see Astington & Baird, this volume, chapter 9, for a similar interpretation). Those children who were able to narrate the story themselves in that version may also have been the same children who were able to benefit from the narrative presented in the other versions. In contrast, those children who may have failed to construct a narrative in the visual-only version may also have failed to benefit from the narratives presented in the other versions. In this respect, it would be useful to know whether some of the children spontaneously and overtly labeled relevant story information during the visual-only version and whether these children were likely to do well in all versions.

We believe that it is perhaps not necessary to construct fully nonverbal versions of false-belief tasks to assess the role of language on these tasks. Instead, we predict that manipulating the use of labels for the two possible perspectives involved would probably be sufficient to obtain language-related effects. By perspectives, we mean naming the two relevant locations in a change-of-location paradigm, the two relevant states in a deceptive-item task, or the two relevant items in an unexpected-contents task. It is important to note that in published versions of the false-belief task that have been used to date, the perspectives *are* labeled, and we believe that this is one reason why 4-year-olds generally do well on these tasks. However, if given a version without explicitly labeled perspectives, we believe that children in this age range are likely to be hindered by the lack of labels. Therefore, we actually predict that 4-year-olds will experience relative difficulties in a nonlabeled version.

For example, an explicit false-belief task like the one used by Wellman and Bartsch (1988; Experiment 3) would be particularly well suited for this kind of labeling manipulation. In Wellman and Bartsch's explicit false-belief task, children are shown props and told, "Jane wants to find her kitten. Jane's kitten is really in *the playroom*. Jane thinks her kitten is in *the kitchen*. Where will Jane look for her kitten? Where is the kitten really?" Various versions of this story could be constructed by manipulating whether specific labels are used to refer to one or both locations ("the playroom" versus "the kitchen"), or whether the location(s) are pointed to and referred to only by some nondescript label such as "here" and "here." On the basis of the labeling-related effects on other measures of cognitive flexibility (see previous section; Jacques & Zelazo, in press), we make several predictions as to how such labeling manipulations might influence performance on each of these versions.

First, as suggested earlier, we predict that 4-year-old children should do worse on the version of the task in which both locations are given the nondescript label "here"[5] than children given versions of the task in which one or both of the locations are actually referred to by name. That is, labeling the child's perspective (i.e., providing the label for the location in which the cat really is) or labeling the protagonist's (false) perspective (i.e., providing the label for the location in which the protagonist believes the cat to be) or both should all be equally effective in improving performance over the nondescript-label version. Second, the performance of 3-year-olds should not differ across the different versions given that their performance is likely to be close to floor on all versions. Likewise, 5-year-olds should also not differ across versions because presumably they are spontaneously coding the information linguistically. Third, as on the FIST, children who spontaneously name one or the other location in the nondescript-label version should outperform those who do not. Finally, we expect that it would not matter whether the experimenter provided the labels for the location(s), or asked children to label them themselves.

Our prediction that labeling the child's perspective (the location in which the object really is) should help performance as much as labeling the protagonist's false perspective (the location in which the object is believed to be) or both is particularly noteworthy because it runs counter to what several other researchers would predict. For example, consider accounts that emphasize the role of visual salience on ToM tasks, such as those proposed by Zaitchik (1991) and others (e.g., Carlson, Moses, & Hix, 1998; Mitchell & Lacohée, 1991; Russell, Mauthner, Sharpe, & Tidswell, 1991). These authors have argued that children have difficulty predicting a protagonist's behavior on the basis of that protagonist's false belief because the perspective of the protagonist is less salient than their own perspective, which they know to be true. On these accounts, labeling the child's own perspective should make it harder for children to disengage from their own perspective and instead reason from the perspective of the protagonist. In contrast, we predict that it would be easier (not harder) for them to do so under these circumstances, because we believe that labeling leads to some kind of qualitative change in how children represent information. It remains to be determined whether this prediction or any of our other predictions are borne out.

Conclusions

In this chapter, we have suggested that relations between language and performance on ToM tasks may result indirectly from the fact that standard preschool measures of ToM tasks such as the false-belief task require cognitive flexibility. We have briefly considered two proposals for why labeling may lead to cognitive flexibility. Future research investigating which labels help under which circumstances may address whether the arbitrary nature of linguistic symbols is the key property or whether objectification through higher levels of consciousness is crucial. Finally, we presented recent experimental data that show that manipulating one aspect of language (i.e., labeling) can affect 4-year-old children's performance on other measures of cognitive flexibility. This kind of experimental manipulation has yet to be done with ToM tasks, although we have suggested one way in which labeling manipulations might be introduced in the false-belief task.

Our hypothesis about the link between language and children's performance on standard preschool measures of ToM does not preclude the possibility that language influences developments in ToM at several levels and in several ways (see Astington & Baird, this volume, chapter 9). For example, developments in symbolic, semantic, syntactic, and pragmatic aspects of language can each independently influence different aspects of ToM development, as other authors in this volume and elsewhere have postulated. Nor does our interpretation preclude the possibility that certain developments in ToM may in turn influence certain aspects of language development. What is evident at this point, however, is that despite the considerable evidence that exists for links between ToM and language development, more research involving experimental manipulations of language must be done before we can gain any further insight into the causal nature of these links.

Acknowledgments The preparation of this chapter was funded by a research grant and a postdoctoral fellowship from the Natural Sciences and Engineering Research Council (NSERC) of Canada.

Notes

1. Jacques (2001) proposed that there are other characteristics of language that may be important for cognitive flexibility, but for the purpose of simplicity, only the arbitrary aspect of language is discussed in the current paper.
2. This argument shares some similarity with the one presented by Astington and Baird (this volume, chapter 9). They argue that language provides a means for representing mental states that conflict with reality and for marking them as such.
3. Loewenstein and Gentner (2004) also used an easier *neutral* version of the spatial-mapping task in Experiments 1 and 2 in which all cards were identical within each box, but differed across the two boxes. However, that version does not require cognitive flexibility because there is no conflicting object-identity information on which children could select items.
4. However, the authors did not separate the children by age group. Performance on the standard version did appear to be somewhat better than performance on the visual-only version (i.e., 37% versus 29% correct, respectively). It would be interesting to know whether this difference would be significant with a larger sample, and, more important, whether it would be significant only for the older age group (as we would predict; see discussion later in this section).
5. The word "here" would have to be used for both locations rather than the contrastive words "here" and "there" because contrast information inherent in distinct labels may be another important characteristic of labels that plays a role in cognitive flexibility (see Jacques, 2001).

References

Astington, J. W., & Jenkins, J. M. (1999). A longitudinal study of the relation between language and theory-of-mind development. *Developmental Psychology, 35,* 1311–1320.

Baron-Cohen, S., Leslie, A., & Frith, U. (1985). Does the autistic child have a "theory of mind"? *Cognition, 21,* 37–46.

Berg, E. (1948). A simple objective test for measuring flexibility in thinking. *Journal of General Psychology, 39,* 15–22.

Bruner, J. S. (1973). The course of cognitive growth. In J. S. Bruner, *Beyond the information given* (J. M. Anglin, Ed.; Ch. 19, pp. 312–323). New York: W. W. Norton.

Carlson, S. M., & Moses, L. J. (2001). Individual differences in inhibitory control and children's theory of mind. *Child Development, 72,* 1032–1053.

Carlson, S. M., Moses, L. J., & Hix, H. R. (1998). The role of inhibitory processes in young children's difficulties with deception and false belief. *Child Development, 69,* 672–691.

Colvert, E., Custance, D., & Swettenham, J. (2002). Rule-based reasoning and theory of mind in autism: A commentary on the work of Zelazo, Jacques, Burack and Frye. *Infant and Child Development, 11,* 197–200.

de Villiers, J., & de Villiers, P. (2000). Linguistic determinism and the understanding of false beliefs. In P. Mitchell & K. Riggs (Eds.), *Children's reasoning and the mind* (pp. 191–228). New York: Psychology Press.

Deák, G. O., Ray, S. D., & Pick, A. D. (2002). Matching and naming objects by shape or function: Age and context effects in preschool children. *Developmental Psychology, 38,* 503–518.

DeLoache, J. S. (1987, December 11). Rapid change in the symbolic functioning of very young children. *Science, 238,* 1556–1557.

DeLoache, J. S. (2000). Dual representation and young children's use of scale models. *Child Development, 71,* 329–338.

Dewey, J. (1985). Context and thought. In J. A. Boydston (Ed.) & A. Sharpe (Textual Ed.), *John Dewey: The later works, 1925–1953* (Vol. 6: 1931–1932) (pp. 3–21). Carbondale, IL: Southern Illinois University Press. (Original work published in 1931.)

Drasgow, J., & Feldman, M. (1957). Conceptual processes in schizophrenia revealed by the Visual-Verbal Test. *Perceptual and Motor Skills, 7,* 251–264.

Dunn, J., Brown, J., Slomkowski, C., Tesla, C., Youngblade, L. (1991). Young children's understanding of other people's feelings and beliefs: Individuals differences and their antecedents. *Child Development, 62,* 1352–1366.

Dunn, L. M., & Dunn, L. M. (1981). *PPVT: Peabody Picture Vocabulary Test-Revised.* Circle Pines, MN: American Guidance Services.

Feldman, M. J., & Drasgow, J. (1951). A Visual-Verbal Test for schizophrenia. *Psychiatric Quarterly, 25(Suppl.),* 55–64.

Flavell, J. H., Flavell, E. R., & Green, F. L. (1983). Development of the appearance-reality distinction. *Cognitive Psychology, 15,* 95–120.

Frye, D., Zelazo, P. D., & Palfai, T. (1995). Theory of mind and rule-based reasoning. *Cognitive Development, 10,* 483–527.

Garfield, J. L, Peterson, C. C., & Perry, T. (2001). Social cognition, language acquisition, and the development of the theory of mind. *Mind & Language, 16,* 494–541.

Gentner, D., & Loewenstein, J. (2001, April). Relational language facilitates the development of relational thought. In S. Jacques & P. D. Zelazo (Chairs), *Language as a tool for thought.* Paper presented at the biennial meeting of the Society for Research in Child Development, Minneapolis, MN.

Gerstadt, C. L., Hong, Y. J., & Diamond, A. (1994). The relationship between cognition and action: Performance of children 3 ½–7 years old on a Stroop-like day-night test. *Cognition, 53,*129–153.

Gopnik, A., & Astington, J. W. (1988). Children's understanding of representational change and its relation to the understanding of false belief and the appearance-reality distinction. *Child Development, 59,* 26–37.

Grant, D. A., & Berg, E. A. (1948). A behavioral analysis of degree of reinforcement and ease of shifting to new responses in a Weigl-type card-sorting problem. *Journal of Experimental Psychology, 38,* 404–411.

Happé, F. (1995). The role of age and verbal ability in the theory of mind task performance of subjects with autism. *Child Development, 66,* 843–855.

Hresko, W. P., Reid, D. K., & Hammill, D. D. (1981). *The Test of Early Language Development (TELD).* Austin, TX: Pro-Ed.

Hughes, C. (1998). Executive function in preschoolers: Links with theory of mind and verbal ability. *British Journal of Developmental Psychology, 16,* 233–253.

Hughes, C., & Russell, J. (1993). Autistic children's difficulty with mental disengagement from an object: Its implication for theories of autism. *Developmental Psychology, 29,* 498–510.

Inhelder, B., & Piaget, J. (1964). *The early growth of logic in the child: Classification and seriation* (E. A. Lunzer & D. Pepert, Trans.). New York: Harper & Row. (Original work published in 1959.)

Jacques, S. (2001). *The roles of labeling and abstraction in the development of cognitive flexibility.* Unpublished doctoral dissertation, University of Toronto.

Jacques, S., Séguin, J. R., & Zelazo, P. D. (2002, April). A longitudinal study of age-related changes in theory of mind: Identifying preschoolers with distinct developmental trajectories and describing their respect language-related profiles. Presented at the International Conference on Why Language Matters for Theory of Mind, Toronto, Canada.

Jacques, S., & Zelazo, P. D. (2001). The Flexible Item Selection Task (FIST): A measure of executive function in preschoolers. *Developmental Neuropsychology, 20,* 573–591.

Jacques, S., & Zelazo, P. D. (in press). On the possible roots of cognitive flexibility. In B. Homer & C. Tamis-Lemonda (Eds.), *The development of social understanding and communication.* Mahwah, NJ: Erlbaum.

Jacques, S., Zelazo, P. D., Lourenco, S. F., & Sutherland, A. (2005). Age- and language-related changes in preschoolers' performance on the Flexible Item Selection Task: The roles of labeling and abstraction in the development of cognitive flexibility. Manuscript in preparation.

Jenkins, J. M., & Astington, J. W. (1996). Cognitive factors and family structure associated with theory of mind development in young children. *Developmental Psychology, 32,* 70–78.

Johnson, C. N., & Maratsos, M. P. (1977). Early comprehension of mental verbs: Think and know. *Child Development, 48,* 1743–1747.

Keeney, T. J., Cannizzo, S. R., & Flavell, J. H. (1967). Spontaneous and induced verbal rehearsal in a recall task. *Child Development, 38,* 953–966.

Kendler, H. H., & Kendler, T. S. (1961). Effect of verbalization on reversal shifts in children. *Science, 134,* 1619–1620.

Kendler, T. S. (1963). Development of mediated responses in children. In J. C. Wright & J. Kagan (Eds.), *Basic cognitive processes in children. Monographs of the Society for Research in Child Development, 28*(2, Serial No. 86), 33–52).

Kotovsky, L., & Gentner, D. (1996). Comparison and categorization in the development of relational similarity. *Child Development, 67,* 2797–2822.

Kuenne, M. R. (1946). Experimental investigation of the relation of language to transposition behavior in young children. *Journal of Experimental Psychology, 36,* 471–490.

Loewenstein, J., & Gentner, D. (2004). Relational language and the development of relational mapping. Manuscript under review.

Luria, A. R. (1959). The directive function of speech in development and dissolution. Part I. Development of the directive function of speech in early childhood. *Word, 15,* 341–352.

Luria, A. R. (1961). *The role of speech in the regulation of normal and abnormal behavior* (J. Tizard, Ed.). New York: Pergamon Press.

Mitchell, P. & Lacohée, H. (1991). Children's early understanding of false belief. *Cognition, 39,* 107–127.

Nagin, D. S. (1999). Analyzing developmental trajectories: A semiparametric group-based approach. *Psychological Methods, 4,* 139–157.

Nagin, D. S., & Tremblay, R. E. (1999). Trajectories of boys' physical aggression, opposition, and hyperactivity on the path to physically violent and nonviolent juvenile delinquency. *Child Development, 70,* 1181–1196.

Ozonoff, S., Pennington, B. F., & Rogers, S. J. (1991). Executive function deficits in high-functioning autistic individuals: Relationship to theory of mind. *Journal of Child Psychology and Psychiatry and Allied Disciplines, 32,* 1081–1105.

Perner, J., & Lang, B. (1999). Development of theory of mind and executive control. *Trends in Cognitive Sciences, 3,* 337–444.

Piaget, J. (1967). Language and thought from the genetic point of view. In J. Piaget, *Six psychological studies* (Ch. 3, pp. 88–98; D. Elkind, Ed.; A. Tenzer, Trans.). New York: Vintage Books. (Original work published in 1964.)

Russell, J., Mauthner, N., Sharpe, S., & Tidswell, T. (1991). The "windows task" as a measure of strategic deception in preschoolers and autistic subjects. *British Journal of Developmental Psychology, 9* (Special Issue: *Perspectives on the Child's Theory of Mind*), 331–349.

Sigel, I. (1993). The centrality of a distancing model for the development of representational competence. In R. R. Cocking & K. A. Renninger (Eds.), *The development and meaning of psychological distance* (pp. 91–107). Hillsdale, NJ: Erlbaum.

Strommen, E. A. (1973). Verbal self-regulation in a children's game: Impulsive errors on "Simon Says." *Child Development, 44,* 849–853.

Tager-Flusberg, H. (2001). Understanding the language and communicative impairments in autism. *International Review of Research in Mental Retardation, 23,* 185–205.

Uttal, D. H., Liu, L. L., & DeLoache, J. S. (1999). Taking a hard look at concreteness: Do concrete objects help young children learn symbolic relations? In L. Balter & C. S. Tamis-LeMonda (Eds.), *Child psychology: A handbook of contemporary issues* (pp. 177–192). Philadelphia: Psychology Press/Taylor & Francis.

Vygotsky, L. S. (1978). *Mind in society: The development of higher psychological processes* (M. Cole, V. John–Steiner, S. Scribner, & E. Souberman, Eds.). Cambridge, MA: Harvard University Press.

Vygotsky, L. S. (1986). *Thought and language* (A. Kozulin, Ed.). Cambridge, MA: MIT Press. (Original work published in 1934.)

Watson, A. C., Painter, K. M., & Bornstein, M. H. (2001). Longitudinal relations between 2-year-olds' language and 4-year-olds' theory of mind. *Journal of Cognition and Development, 2,* 449–457.

Wellman, H. M., & Bartsch, K. (1988). Young children's reasoning about beliefs. *Cognition, 30,* 239–277.

Werner, H. (1948). *Comparative psychology of mental development.* New York: Science Editions.

Werner, H., & Kaplan, B. (1963). *Symbol formation: An organismic-developmental approach to language and the expression of thought.* New York: John Wiley.

Wimmer, H., & Perner, J. (1983). Beliefs about beliefs: Representation and constraining function of wrong beliefs in young children's understanding of deception. *Cognition, 13,* 103–128.

Yirmiya, N., Solomonica-Levi, D., Shulman, C., & Pilowsky, T. (1996). Theory of mind abilities in individuals with autism, Down Syndrome, and mental retardation of unknown etiology: The role of age and intelligence. *Journal of Child Psychology and Psychiatry and Allied Disciplines, 37,* 1003–1014.

Zaitchik, D. (1991). Is only seeing really believing?: Sources of the true belief in the false belief task. *Cognitive Development, 6,* 91–103.

Zelazo, P. D. (1999). Language, levels of consciousness, and the development of intentional action. In P. D. Zelazo, J. W. Astington, & D. R. Olson (Eds.), *Developing theories of intention: Social understanding and self-control* (pp. 95–117). Mahwah, NJ: Erlbaum.

Zelazo, P. D., & Jacques, S. (1996). Children's rule use: Representation, reflection and cognitive control. *Annals of Child Development, 12,* 119–176.

Zelazo, P. D., Jacques, S., Burack, J. A., & Frye, D. (2002). The relation between theory of mind and rule use: Evidence from persons with autism-spectrum disorders. *Infant and Child Development, 11,* 171–195.

9 Representational Development and False-Belief Understanding

Janet Wilde Astington and Jodie A. Baird

> Without the talking intentional systems, of course, there
> would be no ascribing beliefs, no theorizing, no assuming
> rationality, no predicting. The capacity for language is no
> doubt the crowning achievement.
> —Dennett, 1978, p. 17

The importance of language for theory of mind, and more specifi-cally for belief ascription, has become increasingly apparent during recent years. Language is important in many ways for many reasons, as the chapters in this volume clearly show. In this chapter we discuss the question of why language matters for the development of false-belief understanding in particular.

"Language" is a broad term—different structural aspects as well as differ-ent functions fall under the scope of the term, and therefore we first need to be precise about the aspects of language to which we are referring. In the intro-duction (Astington & Baird, this volume, chapter 1), we make two orthogonal distinctions. The first is a functional distinction, between language as an intra-individual representational system, on the one hand, and language as an inter-individual communication system, on the other. The second distinction is made at a structural level between language in general and mentalistic language in particular. With reference to the first distinction, our focus in this chapter is on language as an internal, representational system that can support the develop-ment of false-belief understanding. With reference to the second, we focus on the role of language in general until the final section of the chapter, when we turn our attention to mentalistic language in particular.

Linguistic Representation

Language is crucial for theory of mind because it allows for, and indeed supports, a separation between what is real and what is hypothetical or counterfactual. Language is a medium of representation and, in simple uses, linguistic representations code perceptions. That is, when language is used to represent the currently observed situation, the "same" information is given in linguistic and in perceptual form. Rozeboom (1972) argues, however, that even though the same information may be encoded, there is an important difference between perceptual and linguistic representation, in that only the latter allows for articulation of the content and mode of belief. On his view, percepts directly give rise to beliefs—the "seeing is believing" of folk lore. However, this is not the case for linguistic representation. That is, if someone tells you something, you do not necessarily believe it, although generally you do believe, otherwise human communication would be impossible. But in contexts where one is disinclined to believe, one may be led to sever content and mode, that is, to separate the propositional content of the utterance from the attitude one takes toward it, whether conjecture, doubt, disbelief, or whatever. The linguistic form provides the propositional content, while other features such as intonation and context determine the mode or attitude. Context affects the nonlinguistic cases, too, of course; for example, hearing the sound of thunder might not lead to a belief that it is raining if there is heavy construction work going on nearby. Nevertheless, on Rozeboom's view, the crucial point is this:

> In nonlinguistic elicitation of a [belief], the same stimulus configuration whose occurrence determines the [belief's] content *also* has a primary effect, by virtue of its occurrence, on the [belief's] mode. In contrast, content and mode effects are causally decoupled in linguistic arousal through their respective control by cleanly separable components of the eliciting complex. In this way, language is able to present (convey, evoke in thought) a proposition without prejudicing any particular valuation of it. . . . It is not that propositions with distant reference cannot be thought without words, but that when unverbalized they are likely to be evoked only by stimuli which also control the degree to which they are believed. Language is what makes *contemplative* thought a practical possibility. (Rozeboom, 1972, p. 46, italics in original)

That is to say: perception fixes content and mode/attitude together. Seeing rain establishes the content "it is raining" and the attitude of belief that it is raining. Hearing the utterance "it is raining" ordinarily does both, as well. However, language allows one to separate content and attitude such that one can hear a content and not necessarily believe it, especially if it is contrary to perception or expectation. This occurs because the content can be conveyed in the words uttered while at the same time the attitude can be conveyed prosodically (e.g., with a questioning or joking intonation) or extralinguistically (e.g., with a wink or a gesture).[1]

This separation of content and mode/attitude allows one to go beyond the simple representation of what is the case to consider what might be the case and what is not the case. Language can represent negation and falsity (importantly, these are not the same thing), and it can represent possibility; in sum, language can mean without referring. It provides the resources to represent alternative hypothetical and counterfactual situations.

The argument that language allows for the separation of content and mode does not claim that a language-learning child has to be able to represent content and mode in object complement structures. It is closer to Perner's (1988) argument that, from the start, linguistic information is treated differently from perceptual information in that it is "semantically evaluable." It also reflects Karmiloff-Smith's (1992) argument that representations that are not available to conscious access until later in development may be available earlier in data structures. Almost as soon as they start to acquire language, children can evaluate linguistic information and are able to reject false assertions (Pea, 1982) and to treat pretense utterances as hypothetically true (Harris & Kavanaugh, 1993). However, at this stage the child cannot form embedded propositions in which mode and content are explicitly represented, as discussed in the final section of the chapter. Nonetheless, even at this early stage, language can be used to establish a linguistic representation in contrast to the perceptual display.

False-Belief Tasks

In false-belief tasks, language provides a means for representing mental states in contradistinction to the evidence given in reality. In standard change-in-location false-belief tasks, an object is moved from one place to another while the story protagonist is off the scene. As the story unfolds, the child needs some way of keeping track of what is in the absent character's mind when the object is moved from the first location to the second. Linguistic representation is crucial because it allows the child to represent the character's representation of the situation, in the face of the conflicting situation in the visual display. Children usually achieve this ability around 4 years of age.

Nonetheless, as Plaut and Karmiloff-Smith (1993) (as well as many others, cf. Lewis & Mitchell, 1994) pointed out, children younger than 4 years of age can pass false-belief tasks under some conditions, while under other conditions, children may not achieve success until 5 or 6 years of age. On the one hand, Plaut and Karmiloff-Smith (1993; cf. also Karmiloff-Smith, 1992, p. 130) cite Zaitchik's (1991) finding that the false-belief task is easier if the salience of the real situation is reduced by telling but not actually showing children the location of the object. Zaitchik compared 3-year-olds' performance in three conditions. The first was a standard change-in-location false-belief story. In the second condition, a story protagonist tells the child that an object is in location A but that he is going to tell another story character that it is in location B, which he does when the other character appears. The third condition is the same as the second, but the protagonist not only tells the child that the object is in location A but actually shows it to the child. In each case, the child is asked where the character who holds a false belief thinks the object is. Performance in the condition where children did not actually see the object was significantly better than performance in the other two conditions (72% versus 44% and 44%).

On the other hand, Plaut and Karmiloff-Smith also cite a conference paper (Norris & Millan, 1991) that used a silent-movie version of a false-belief task in which there was a visual representation of the story but no verbal telling of it. Children were not successful on this task until close to 6 years of age.

On the basis of these data, Plaut and Karmiloff-Smith describe a developmental pattern of performance: children younger than 4 are able to achieve success with solely verbal input and no conflicting visual display, 4-year-olds are successful when they receive visual and verbal input together, and children older than 4 years are successful even when given only visual input. They argue:

> Theory-of-mind tasks require the ability to simultaneously represent conflicting information: the protagonist's (or one's own) belief about a past situation and the current true situation. We believe the developmental results are best interpreted in terms of increasing capability in using and generating symbolic representations that are sufficiently well elaborated to override the otherwise compelling interpretations generated by direct experience. Furthermore, language is central to theory-of-mind processes precisely because it provides particularly effective "scaffolding" for symbolic representations. Critically, it requires less cognitive sophistication to merely maintain and use symbolic representations provided by others (in the form of verbal description) than it does to generate the appropriate representations oneself. (Plaut & Karmiloff-Smith, 1993, p. 70)

That is, symbolic representation, in particular linguistic representation, can hold onto the earlier scenario when the scene changes, for example when Maxi's chocolate is moved from a cupboard to a drawer ("chocolate *is* in cupboard" → "chocolate *was* in cupboard"). The child can also code the fact that Maxi was present when the chocolate was put into the cupboard and was absent when it was moved to the drawer. In order to predict where Maxi will look for the chocolate when he returns, the child has to recognize that there is a mismatch between what is now the real state of the world and what was the state when Maxi was last on the scene. Linguistic representation is crucial because it allows the child to represent the past situation, in the face of the conflicting situation in the visual display. Further, it is easier for children if they are given the linguistic representation as a verbal description than it is if they have to create it themselves from what they see.

Thus, Plaut and Karmiloff-Smith argue that language is crucial to false-belief understanding because it provides a symbolic representation that can prevail over direct perception. First, children can understand false belief when they are given a verbal representation of the false-belief scenario and are not misled by direct perception, that is, by the salience of reality. Second, children can understand false belief, even in the face of the real situation, when they are given the verbal representation, that is, the experimenter tells the story and they see the action, as in the standard version of the task. Third, children can understand false belief, even when they have to construct their own verbal representation of the story from changing perceptual representations of the situation. However, the evidence Plaut and Karmiloff-Smith cite in support of this developmental sequence is rather weak insofar as it depends on rather meagre findings from different tasks with different populations. Moreover, the Zaitchik (1991) task is unlike a standard false-belief story task because there is no transfer of an object from one location to another; instead, a character is simply misinformed about its location. Nevertheless, the proposal is interesting and the evidence suggestive. Therefore, we decided to put it to a more rigorous test.

Experimental Investigation

We designed a study with three different versions of the same false-belief task. The first version was a standard change-in-location false-belief task, in which children watched the action while hearing the story. In the second version, children did not witness the transfer of the object from one location to the other, although the narrator described the transfer in telling them the story. The third version was exactly the same as the first, but children only watched the action; they were not told the story. We hypothesized that the "verbal-only" version, where children did not actually see the object moved to the new location, would be easier than the standard version. And the "visual-only" version, where children had to construct their own linguistic representation of the false-belief situation in conflict with the perceptual representation of the real situation, would be more difficult than the standard version.

Study 1

We presented 23 three-year-olds (mean age = 3;6) and 21 four-year-olds (mean age = 4;6) with these three different versions of the false-belief task. All versions were depicted on video with child actors as the story characters. In the Standard version, children saw the initial object placement and the transfer of the object from one location to another. Meanwhile, a female voice-over narrated the story. For example, as the action unfolded, the narrator described the first character's placement of a toy into a box and, following his departure, the second character's transfer of the toy to a basket. The Verbal-only version was identical to the standard, but the camera angle was changed to obscure the object and the two locations during both the initial placement and the subsequent transfer of the object. In this version, children did not actually see the object being moved—rather, they heard about it from the voice-over narration. By telling but not showing the object's transfer, we aimed to reduce the salience of the object's final location. The Visual-only version was identical to the standard in that children saw all of the action, including the object placement and transfer, but without any voice-over narration. Instead, the narration was replaced by classical piano music. Without the narration, children had to construct their own representation of the story. It is important to note that—aside from the key manipulations—the three versions were exactly parallel.

Three different false-belief stories were used, each with a different set of characters, objects, and locations: in one, a boy puts a toy into a box and a girl moves it to a basket; in another, a girl puts a cake into her lunchbox and a boy moves it to his backpack; and in the third, a boy puts a drum into a drawer and a girl moves it to underneath some pillows. We prepared videotapes of each story in each of the three conditions.

Each child viewed the three different versions of the false-belief task (Standard, Verbal-only, Visual-only), with a different story for each version, and with presentation order and condition/story combination counterbalanced across participants. The same test question was asked the end of each false-belief task: "Where will [the first character] look for [the object]?" For example, "Where will the boy look for the toy?"

In alternation with the three false-belief tasks, children received three standard language tests: a semantic measure (the Peabody Picture Vocabulary Test, PPVT-III; Dunn & Dunn, 1997) and two syntax measures (the Sentence Structure and the Word Structure subtests of the Clinical Evaluation of Language Fundamentals, CELF-Preschool; Wiig, Secord, & Semel, 1992).

As expected, our results showed a clear age effect in children's false-belief understanding, with 3-year-olds' performance 19% correct, compared with 62% for 4-year-olds. Summing across the three false-belief tasks, 4-year-olds ($M = 1.86$, $SD = 1.35$) significantly outperformed 3-year-olds ($M = .57$, $SD = 1.08$)

overall, $t(42) = 3.52$, $p < .001$. Of greater interest, however, was whether children's performance differed by false-belief condition. As figure 9.1 illustrates, we found absolutely no condition differences. The results are quite striking: children were not at all affected by watching the video in the absence of a story narrative (Visual-only), nor were they affected by hearing the story in the absence of witnessing the actions (Verbal-only). In fact, of the 44 children who participated, 37 passed or failed all three false-belief tasks. That is, only seven children showed any differential responding across the three versions, and there was no hint of condition or order effects in these seven.

Thus, the data do not support the hypothesis that the false-belief task is easier if the child does not actually see conflicting information in the visual display (i.e., Verbal-only), or that the task is harder if the child has to construct and maintain her own verbal representation of the past situation (i.e., Visual-only). Rather, it seems that once children understand false belief, they have no difficulty constructing a representation of the story for themselves.

Does this mean that language does not matter for false-belief understanding? Not necessarily. The development of false-belief understanding may be crucially tied to language, but once children can understand false belief, these particular task manipulations do not make any difference to their performance. In fact, the language data we collected revealed that false-belief task performance is correlated with both semantic ability (PPVT-III) and syntactic ability (an aggregate of the two CELF measures), $rs(42) = .38$ and $.34$, respectively, $ps < .05$. It must be acknowledged, however, that the correlations between false-belief understanding and language are not as strong as is typically found, and they are nonsignificant when age is controlled. Moreover, age explains 21% of the variance in false-belief scores after accounting for the variance due to language

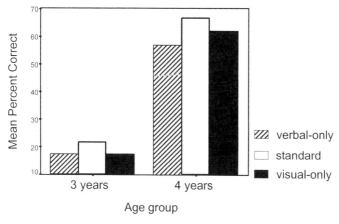

Figure 9.1. Children's performance in the three false-belief conditions in Study 1.

ability—insofar as age "explains" anything. What we mean is that some matura-tional factor other than language is driving false-belief task performance, and/ or children who succeed on the task have had more experience with some ex-ternal factor that underlies their success.

What might the factor(s) be? One possibility is that children's TV-viewing experience influenced their performance. With the video format we used, chil-dren received the false-belief narrative in a disembodied voice-over, rather than in the context of contingent interaction with the experimenter. That is, because we used a video presentation, we were unable to pace the narrative to suit the child. This may have disadvantaged younger children, who have less experience than older children in retrieving information from a prepackaged format. The video presentation also may have influenced the false-belief condition differ-ences (or, rather, the lack thereof). In particular, because of the video presenta-tion, the salience of reality may not have been sufficiently different across conditions. That is, even in the standard version, the object and hiding loca-tions were not actually present—they were distanced by TV. Thus, our attempts to manipulate the salience of reality may have been thwarted as a result of the video format.

Study 2

We therefore conducted a second study to investigate the possible influence of presentation format on children's performance in our false-belief task. We used the same measures and design as the first study, but, instead of using videos, we acted out the false-belief stories using small dolls and toys in a dollhouse, and the story narration (when provided) was given in contingent interaction with the child. Thus, in the Standard version of the task, the experimenter both acted out the story with the dolls and narrated the action as it unfolded. In the Verbal-only version, the experimenter manipulated the dolls while telling the story, but a curtain obscured children's view of the object, the locations, and the action; all that they could see throughout the narration were the tops of the dolls' heads bobbing up and down above the curtain. To justify the obscured view, children were told, "It's nighttime now, so the curtains are closed," and then the curtain was opened at the end of the story when the test question was asked. In the Visual-only version, children watched as the experimenter acted out the story in full view, but, instead of providing a narration, the experimenter just hummed along while manipulating the dolls. Eighteen 3-year-olds (mean age = 3;6) and 17 4-year-olds (mean age = 4;5) participated in this study. As in the first study, children received all three versions of the false-belief task, with a different story (characters, ob-jects, locations) for each version and with presentation order and condition/story combination counterbalanced across participants. As before, we administered the three language measures (PPVT-III, CELF Sentence Structure, CELF Word Structure) in alternation with the three false-belief tasks.

Successful performance across the three false-belief tasks was fairly low in both age groups (30% for 3-year-olds and 33% for 4-year-olds).[2] There was no significant difference between the two groups, and so we treated the whole sample as one group in the subsequent analysis. As in Study 1, we found no effect of condition or of presentation order on performance: 19 children failed all three tasks, and 7 passed all three; only 9 of the 35 children scored 1 or 2 out of 3. Overall performance on the three conditions was: Verbal-only 29%, Visual-only 29%, Standard 37%. Although children's performance appears to be somewhat better on the standard version, this difference is not significant, but perhaps it hints at the possibility that the false-belief task is easiest when both perceptual and linguistic input are provided and that reducing either one makes it more difficult.

Summary

We hypothesized that the false-belief task would be easier if children did not actually see the object in the new location because they would not be misled by the salience of reality, and we hypothesized that the false-belief task would be more difficult if children had to construct their own linguistic representation of the false belief, in conflict with the perceptual representation of the real situation. However, the data from these two studies do not provide the support that we had anticipated. Nonetheless, other researchers have found the hypothesis interesting and suggestive and wonder whether we have not yet used the right manipulation. For example, Annette Karmiloff-Smith (personal communication, April 12, 2002) suggested that it may be too much to expect accuracy differences among the three conditions, but the hypothesized differences may show up in reaction times, and Michael Tomasello (personal communication, April 27, 2002) suggested that the effect may be obtained between subjects but not within subject.

However, it may be the hypothesis that is at fault, not the data. It may be that the manipulations that we used really do have no effect on children's false-belief task performance. In the next section we examine existing studies that address this issue.

Are "Verbal-Only" Tasks Easier?

Zaitchik's (1991) study suggested that the verbal-only task would be easier, but is the Zaitchik finding robust? It is replicated (actually, it is foreshadowed) in an earlier study of children's understanding of the mental terms *think* and *know*

(Johnson & Maratsos, 1977), which included a quasi false-belief task as a pretest, with a manipulation similar to Zaitchik's, that yielded a similar result. In the Johnson and Maratsos study, stories were acted out for the children: for example, a hider played a trick on a seeker and while the seeker was not looking, the hider took his toy and hid it under box A, but the hider told the seeker it was under box B. There were two conditions; in one condition, children saw the toy being hidden under box A, whereas in the second condition they did not actually see the toy being hidden but were simply told about it. The pretest question (which came before the children were asked about what the hider and the seeker thought and knew) was, "Where will [the seeker] look for the toy?" Three-year-olds' performance was worse in the condition where they saw the toy being hidden than in the one where they were merely told about it (29% correct versus 53%; and on a second try, after the story was repeated, 39% correct versus 86%). That is, just as in Zaitchik's study, performance was better when children did not see the object.

Robinson, Mitchell, and Nye (1995) attempted to replicate Zaitchik's (1991) finding using a similar story frame with different content and a reversed order of questioning; they asked the test question first ("Where does [the character] think [the object] is?") and then the reality control question ("Where is [the object] really?"). Unlike Zaitchik, who obtained 100% correct performance on the reality control question (asked first), only 62% of children in the Robinson et al. study were correct on the control (asked second). Nonetheless, they replicated the Zaitchik effect; that is, they found a significant difference between children's performance on standard false-belief and on the modified task where the object was not seen (32% versus 62%, excluding those who failed the reality control question; 29% versus 61% including all participants).

Thus, these two studies (Johnson & Maratsos, 1977; Robinson et al., 1995) confirm the effect Zaitchik (1991) found. Her task is sometimes reported in the literature as a demonstration that if children are told about but do not actually witness the object's transfer in a change-in-location story, then the false-belief task is easier (e.g., Plaut & Karmiloff-Smith, 1993). However, all of these tasks (Johnson & Maratsos, 1977; Robinson et al., 1995; Zaitchik, 1991) are different from the standard false-belief task (Wimmer & Perner, 1983) in that the object is not moved from one place to another but the child is simply told that a character is misinformed about its location. Importantly, it is likely that this has some bearing on the findings. To succeed on the task, the child does not need to consider where the character *thinks* the object is located, merely where the character is told the object is located. That is, all the child needs to know is that people tend to follow instructions—they will look for an object where they are told it is. This clearly is a departure from the standard change-in-location false-belief task, in which successful performance hinges on the child's ability to consider a character's outdated belief about the location of an object.

In our study, this critical aspect of the task was retained, and care was taken to ensure that the different versions of the false-belief task were exactly parallel, apart from the manipulation of verbal and visual information.

Robinson et al. (1995) also compared seen and unseen conditions in an unexpected-contents type of false-belief task (the "Smarties-box" task; Perner, Leekam, & Wimmer, 1987). Children were asked what they thought was in a familiar container (e.g., a toy car box), and when they answered with the expected content (a car), the experimenter looked into the box and told them it was actually something different (a teddy). In a second condition, they were also allowed to see the unexpected different content as in the standard version of this task. Later, a second experimenter asked children what was in the box, and if they updated their belief to accord with what they had been told or seen, they were asked what they had thought was in the box before it was opened. Robinson et al. found that it was no easier for children to acknowledge their earlier false belief if they had only been told and had not seen what was really inside the box. Robinson et al. conclude that in the Zaitchik (1991) task, children are not really recognizing false beliefs—because they have no original belief about the object's location, what they are told does not update an earlier belief, as it does in the unexpected-contents task. Therefore, Robinson et al. argue, if children accept what the experimenter says (i.e., update their belief) in the unexpected-contents task, they take it as true, because if they were uncertain they could keep their original belief. However, in the Zaitchik task there is no original belief, and so children are acknowledging alternative beliefs (as in Wellman & Bartsch, 1988), not false beliefs.

Nonetheless, more recently and more forcefully, Wellman, Cross, and Watson's (2001) meta-analysis of false-belief studies demonstrates that the task *is* easier if the true state of affairs is not instantiated by a real and present object (e.g., if Maxi's chocolate is eaten, or if the Smarties box is empty). That is, if perceptual reality is less compelling, then it is easier to acknowledge another person's false belief about a situation.

Thus, there is some evidence besides Zaitchik's (1991) study to support the hypothesis that the "verbal-only" task would be easier. Moreover, there is already an explanation for the finding that the false-belief task is easier when reality is less compelling. A number of researchers have argued that 3-year-olds' failure on false-belief tasks is due in part to a lack of inhibitory control (Carlson & Moses, 2001; Hughes, 1998), that is, the ability to suppress a prepotent response. In the false-belief task, reality—the new location of the object—is compelling. Success on the task requires the ability to suppress a prepotent response to indicate (e.g., by pointing) the real location of the object in favor of the location where the story character merely thinks that the object is. That is, children have to inhibit the tendency to respond on the basis of reality, which they find easier to do if reality is made less compelling, as in Zaitchik's (1991) task. Conversely, if the inhibitory control demands of the task are increased, even 4-year-olds' performance suffers, and success is not achieved until 5 years of age or later (Leslie & Polizzi, 1998).

However, Perner, Lang, and Kloo (2002) argue strongly against the suggestion (Carlson & Moses, 2001) that children's difficulty with standard false-belief tasks is a result of difficulties with inhibitory control. Recall that Zaitchik's task is unlike the standard false-belief task because the object is not transferred. The task used in our study is exactly the same as the standard task except that the object and hiding places are masked during the transfer, and we found no difference in performance on the standard and modified tasks. Moreover, Robinson et al. (1995) also found no difference in performance between the standard unexpected-contents false-belief task and their modified version in which children did not actually see the unexpected content but were merely told about it. It seems that "reality masking" has no effect when the tasks are exactly parallel, which supports Perner et al.'s (2002) argument against the explanation that false-belief task failure is due to a lack of inhibitory control.

Are "Visual-Only" (Nonverbal) Tasks More Difficult?

Plaut and Karmiloff-Smith (1993) also pointed to a situation where the false-belief task is harder than in the standard version. They claimed that the task is more difficult when children have to construct the false-belief story themselves from a nonverbal presentation, citing Norris and Millan's (1991) conference paper that described the use of a silent-movie version of a false-belief task, in support of their argument. We refer to the silent-movie version of our task as "visual-only" to correspond to "verbal-only" in the version that reduces the salience of perceptual reality. However, such visual-only tasks are usually referred to in the literature as nonverbal tasks, and that is the label we will use henceforth.

We first need to be clear about the different ways in which the false-belief task could be modified to create a nonverbal task, or a "less-verbal" one, as these tasks are sometimes called, indicating that language is reduced but not completely removed from the task. In fact, our nonverbal (visual-only) task should strictly be called a less-verbal task: the test question was posed in verbal form, and children could respond verbally or by pointing. This illustrates the fact that any or all of the three parts of the false-belief task—presentation, question, response—may be nonverbal.

Researchers have developed nonverbal tasks for a variety of reasons. Some argue that children younger than 4 years of age have an understanding of false belief that is obscured in the standard version of the task because the task itself relies heavily on language (e.g., Chandler, Fritz, & Hala, 1989; Fodor, 1992). They contend that if the task demands less linguistic ability, younger children will perform correctly. Although Wellman et al. (2001) did not include the feature "verbal versus nonverbal" in their meta-analysis of false-belief tasks, there is some evidence from individual studies in favor of this argument. For example, 3-year-olds can act out a doll's search when the doll holds a false belief, even though they cannot make a verbal prediction of where the doll will look (Freeman, Lewis, & Doherty, 1991). More strikingly, children just turning 3 years of age will look to the correct location, where the story protagonist thinks the object is, even though they give an incorrect response to the verbal test question (Clements & Perner, 1994). Although these tasks allow the child to respond nonverbally, they still rely on the child's receptive language ability to follow the story and comprehend the test question. Thus, and important in relation to Plaut and Karmiloff-Smith's (1993) hypothesis, the story is narrated to children, providing them with a symbolic representation of the situation. The hypothesis that nonverbal tasks will be more difficult depends on nonverbal *presentation* of the false-belief situation, requiring children to generate and maintain their own symbolic representation of the situation. This was the case in the nonverbal (visual-only) tasks used in our experiments.

P. de Villiers and Pyers (2001; see also P. de Villiers, this volume, chapter 13) also developed a task that is more relevant to the Plaut and Karmiloff-Smith hypothesis. They used a modification of the unexpected-contents (Smarties box) task to develop a false-belief task for deaf children, in which the presentation of the situation is less verbal. The child is shown picture sequences in which the typical contents of a box are replaced with something unexpected, while a character sees or does not see the transfer (depending on condition). The final picture shows the character, with blank face, opening the box. The child's task is to choose one of two faces—showing either a surprised or a neutral expression—to place over the blank face. For both deaf and hearing children, success on the task (i.e., choosing the surprised face for a character who did not see and one with a neutral expression for a character who did see) is correlated with standard false-belief task performance, although the task is somewhat harder than standard false-belief, as Plaut and Karmiloff-Smith's hypothesis would predict. However, the reason for this may be because the child has to infer emotion based on belief, not because the task is nonverbal (Harris, Johnson, Hutton, Andrews, & Cooke, 1989; Wellman & Liu, 2004).

Obviously, experimental investigation of the ability of nonhuman primates to attribute mental states requires nonverbal tasks. Call and Tomasello (1999) designed a nonverbal false-belief task for chimpanzees and orangutans and also tested human children. The experimenter hides a sticker in one of two identical boxes and the child's task is to find it, helped by another adult. The helper watches the hiding process, which is screened from the child, and then the two identical boxes are revealed. After the helper leaves the room, the location of the two boxes is switched. The helper returns to the room and indicates which box the child should open to find the sticker. In order to succeed on the task, the child has to recognize that the helper has a false belief about the location of the sticker because the boxes were switched in his absence and therefore the other box is the one containing the sticker. A series of training and control trials preceded the test trials in order to make it clear that success on the test trials is evidence of false-belief understanding. The success rate over four test trials was 40% for young 4-year-olds and 82% for young 5-year-olds. Call and Tomasello also included what they refer to as a verbal task, which is modeled on the nonverbal one. Screened from the child, the helper watches the experimenter hide the sticker, then the two identical boxes are revealed and the helper leaves the room. Watched by the child, the experimenter opens the boxes and transfers the sticker from one box to the other. The boxes are closed again, and the experimenter asks the child which box the helper will indicate as containing the sticker. Children's performance on this task is similar to their performance on the completely nonverbal version (45% for the 4-year-olds and 78% for the 5-year-olds over two trials). Moreover, the two tasks are highly correlated. However, in both tasks children are not provided with a verbal description of the situation but have to construct their own representation of the situation from the visual input. It is just the test question that is verbal in the "verbal" version. Performance over the two tasks is slightly lower than performance on standard tasks (Wellman et al., 2001), perhaps suggesting that the Call and Tomasello task is more difficult, although it is hard to compare across populations. Moreover, Lunn (2003) used both versions of the Call and Tomasello tasks and reported that older 3-year-olds scored above 70% on both versions of the task, whereas their performance on a standard unexpected-contents false-belief task (Perner et al., 1987) was below 40%. A slightly modified version of the Call and Tomasello tasks was given to deaf children of hearing parents (Figueras-Costa & Harris, 2001) with the expectation that they would achieve success because of the reduced verbal demands. However, only children 6 years and older (mean age = 9;7) were successful, while performance in a younger group (mean age = 5;6) was not above chance. Overall, the evidence in support of the hypothesis that nonverbal tasks are more difficult than verbal ones is at best equivocal.

Summary of the Evidence

Along with Plaut and Karmiloff-Smith (1993), we hypothesized that the standard false-belief task would be easier if children were provided with a verbal description of the situation while reality was masked in the visual display and would be more difficult if children had to construct and maintain their own symbolic representation of the situation from the visual display in the absence of a verbal narration of the story. We conducted two studies and a review of the literature in order to seek support for this hypothesis (see summary in table 9.1).

There is some evidence that masking reality does make the task easier (Johnson & Maratsos, 1977; Robinson et al., 1995 [story task]; Zaitchik, 1991). This is somewhat ambiguous, however, in that these tasks are not the same as the standard task because the object is not actually transferred. In other tasks (e.g., Wimmer & Perner, 1983, Experiment 2), the object transfer is not masked but the salience of reality is reduced by eliminating the object from the scene when the test question is asked (e.g., Maxi's chocolate is used to make a cake that is taken away)—and this too makes the task easier. An explanation for these findings is that they place less demand on the child's mastery of inhibitory control, which correlates with successful performance on the standard task (Carlson & Moses, 2001; Hughes, 1998). However, Perner et al. (2002) argue against this explanation, and the data from the Studies 1 and 2 in the present chapter support their argument. We used a reality-masked task exactly the same as the standard task, except that the transfer and final location of the object were hidden, and it was no more and no less difficult than the standard task. Similarly, children in Robinson et al.'s (1995) study did not find the reality-masked version of the unexpected-contents task any easier than the typical unexpected-contents task. Thus, the evidence that masking reality makes the task easier is equivocal.

Table 9.1 Summary of Findings Using Modified False-Belief Tasks with Normal Populations

Reality-Masked Tasks	Comparison with Standard False-Belief Task Performance
Astington & Baird (this chapter)	
Verbal-only condition, Study 1	same
Verbal-only condition, Study 2	same
Johnson & Maratsos (1977)	easier
Robinson, Mitchell, & Nye (1995)	
Study 1 (Zaitchik task)	easier
Study 2 (unexpected contents task)	same
Zaitchik (1991)	easier
Nonverbal Tasks	
Astington & Baird (this chapter)	
Visual-only condition, Study 1	same
Visual-only condition, Study 2	same
Call & Tomasello (1999)	same
Lunn (2003)	easier
Norris & Millan (1991)	more difficult
P. de Villiers & Pyers (2001)	more difficult

At the other end of the hypothesized developmental sequence, there is little evidence that nonverbal tasks are more difficult. We should stress that the tasks to which we refer may or may not include a nonverbal question and response but, importantly, the presentation of the situation is nonverbal, as the Plaut and Karmiloff-Smith (1993) hypothesis requires. The greater difficulty of one task that was harder (P. de Villiers & Pyers, 2001) is perhaps explained by the fact that, unlike in the standard task, children had to infer the story character's emotional state (Harris et al., 1989; Wellman & Liu, 2004). The nonverbal task that has been used in several studies is no more difficult (Call & Tomasello, 1998) and indeed may be easier (Lunn, 2003) than standard tasks, although this task is somewhat unlike the standard task. The nonverbal task used in Studies 1 and 2 in the present chapter was exactly the same as the standard task, except that no narrative was provided, and it was no more and no less difficult than the standard task.

In sum, our data and our review of other studies do not lend much support to our original hypothesis. We thus conclude that children's false-belief task performance is not affected by variation of the mode in which the critical information is conveyed to them. In the final section of the chapter we seek to explain this conclusion.

Representation and Mental Models

Our reading of Rozeboom (1972) and our interpretation of the Plaut and Karmiloff-Smith (1993) hypothesis has implied that the child maintains two representations of a narrated scenario, one that records the perceptual features and another that records the verbal narrative. When language is used to represent the current situation, the same information is given in both perceptual and verbal form and is similarly recorded in perceptual and linguistic representations. However, in the case of the false-belief scenario, as the episode proceeds, the linguistic representation preserves a record of the former situation (and the protagonist's belief in it) when the actual situation changes. The perceptual representation, on the other hand, is updated to represent the current true state of affairs.

Harris (2002) denies such a possibility. Rather, he argues that in watching and talking about a scene, perceptual information and verbal information are integrated into the same situational model, which is updated as the scene changes, and as the narrative or conversation proceeds (see also Harris, 2000, chapter 9). Consequently, there is no possibility for linguistic and perceptual representations to preserve different information. On Harris's view, therefore, one would not expect to find differences in performance caused by the manipulation of visual or verbal input in different versions of the false-belief task (Harris, personal communication, April 27, 2002). It is certainly the case that

3-year-old children do not differentiate among different sources of information that they have just received (Gopnik & Graf, 1988; Wimmer, Hogrefe, & Perner, 1988). They can, for example, remember what is inside a box but fail to distinguish between whether they were shown or told about its contents, which may suggest that they would also be indifferent to the mode of presentation of the false-belief task scenario.

Moreover, Nelson et al. (2003) provide evidence that directly supports Harris's claim. In Nelson's experiment, children put an object into a box before leaving a room, they were subsequently told that it had been moved to another box, and when they returned to the room they had to find the object and were also asked which box they had first put the object into, how they knew where to find it, and where their parent, who had not been informed of the transfer, would think the object was. The task was plausibly contextualized so that leaving the room, returning, and needing to find the object all made sense to the child. Most 4-year-olds and some 3-year-olds succeeded on the task. Among the remaining 3-year-olds, a majority found the object where they had been told that it was, but they could not remember where they had originally put it. Only one child showed the reverse pattern, that is, he remembered where he had put the object but not where he had been told that it was. That is, in this admittedly small sample, among younger children who failed the task, perceptual memory was displaced by later verbal information. This implies, as Harris suggests, that the verbal information was integrated into the same situational model, updating the earlier model. Indeed, in the first report of 3-year-olds' difficulty remembering their own false beliefs (Gopnik & Astington, 1988), we suggested that old information might be overwritten by new: "It seems plausible that very young children simply update their beliefs as they receive new information, writing over their past beliefs. This would make their memory rather different from the memory of adults, who continue to retain information about their past beliefs even when those beliefs turn out to be false" (Astington & Gopnik, 1988, p.205).

The question now is: if there is a single situational model that is updated by both perceptual and verbal information, what is the difference between the 3-year-old's and the 4-year-old's model such that the older children can update without losing track of their earlier beliefs? Certainly 3-year-olds can retain some information, including that which is no longer true. For example, in Wimmer and Hartl's (1991) "change-of-state" condition in the unexpected-contents false-belief task, the candy box actually does contain candy when the child is first asked about it; then the candy is replaced by a different content while the child watches, and then the box is closed and the test question is asked, as in the standard version of the task. Here, 3-year-olds have little difficulty remembering what they had thought was in the box when they were first asked about it, even though it is now false because the box contents have been changed. The problem for 3-year-olds occurs when what they first thought is false. That is to say, they can remember changed states of the world, but not changed states of mind. Why cannot 3-year-olds remember their former beliefs or understand others' false beliefs, whereas 4-year-olds can? What changes occur in the structure of the model that supports the development of false-belief understanding?

Perner's (1988, 1991) theory provides one answer to these questions. He describes three stages in the development of the mental model that is needed. At first, the infant's mental model is a perceptual representation of the world, a single updating model of the real situation, referred to as a primary representation (Perner, 1991), which does not incorporate any linguistic information. Children's mental modeling power increases in their second year, when they can use linguistic information and can entertain multiple models of situations, secondary representations, that allow them to compare past and future, or real and pretend (Perner, 1991). These models are different from primary representations in important ways, because they are "decoupled" from the primary representation of reality (Leslie, 1987) and do not carry the same truth and existence implications that primary representations do. By 2 years of age, children must be able to produce such secondary representations, because in pretend play they can link their actions to what another person is pretending, not to what he or she is actually doing (Harris & Kavanaugh, 1993). Two-year-olds relate persons to situations. If the situation is different from the real situation, they think of it as an alternative situation, and they relate the person to the alternative situation. Four-year-olds, on the other hand, relate the person to a representation of the situation (Perner, 1991) (see figure 9.2).

These two ways of looking at a situation do not seem very different, until we come to the case where the person has a false belief. The 2-year-old sees the false-belief situation not as the person's representation of the world but just as an alternative possible situation, as in pretense. However, in order to understand false belief, one has to see that the person takes the alternative situation to be the way the world is. Perner (1991) argues that the only way one can do this is by understanding it as a representation and separating the content of the representation—that is, the thought—from its reference—that is, the situation. This distinction between content and reference cannot be made for situations, only for representations of situations. The 2-year-old can relate Maxi to the hypothetical situation "chocolate in cupboard" but cannot see that he would look for the chocolate in cupboard. Because it is just an alternative situation, not the true one, the 2-year-old thinks Maxi would look in the drawer, where the chocolate really is. The child cannot predict that Maxi would look for the chocolate in the cupboard, without the ability to see the alternative situation as his representation. That is, the only way in which the child can understand false belief is by constructing a situation model that is sophisticated enough to model the protaganist's view of the real situation as the protagonist's representation—that is, a meta-representation (Perner, 1988, 1991).

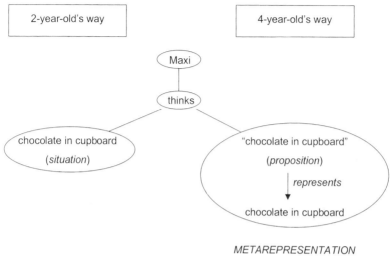

Two ways of understanding: "Maxi thinks the chocolate is in the cupboard"
(the chocolate is really in the drawer)

Figure 9.2. Understanding mental states as situations or as representations.

Hence, the crucial point is that a meta-representational model is needed in order to represent false belief. It is now that we can shift our focus from the role of language in general to that of mentalistic language in particular. Language itself allows for the separation of the attitude and content of a proposition (Rozeboom, 1972), as argued at the beginning of the chapter. It may be the further development of language, specifically the acquisition of mental terms, that allows the distinction between propositional attitudes and propositional contents to be explicitly represented.

Karmiloff-Smith (1992) proposes a theory of representational redescription whereby information that is in the mind becomes explicit knowledge to the mind. The redescriptive process allows for the re-representation of knowledge in a new representational format. In this case, the implicit representation of attitude and proposition is made explicit. On Karmiloff-Smith's view, the development of the 4-year-old's meta-representational understanding of mental states depends on mental verbs:

The RR (Representational Redescription) model posits that it is not the language capacity per se that explains development, but rather the redescriptive processes which allow for re-representation of knowledge in different (often linguistic) representational formats. However, the theory-of-mind domain may be one area where the translation into natural-language terms (e.g., the use of mental-state verbs such as "pretend that", "think that", "believe that", and "know that") is an essential part of the redescriptive process. (Karmiloff-Smith, 1992, p. 130)

Language itself allows for the separation of propositional attitudes and propositional contents (Rozeboom, 1972), which is at first represented only implicitly. Mentalistic language allows this separation to be explicitly represented. Thus, language supports false-belief understanding because it supports the metarepresentational model that underlies the understanding. It is not the acquisition of the mental terms themselves which is crucial, because these terms may be used in a situational model. Rather, it is the use of these terms in a metarepresentational model that is decisive, at least in regard to the role of language as an internal, representational system that supports the development of false-belief understanding.

Acknowledgments We are grateful to Chris Moore, David Olson, and Josef Perner for their comments on an earlier version of this chapter. We also thank the child actors in the videotaped scenarios; the children who participated in the studies and their teachers; Marla Endler and Karen Milligan, for assistance with data collection; and the Natural Sciences and Engineering Research Council of Canada, for financial support.

Notes

1. Content and mode can also be disconnected solely within language, for example, by using modals or verbs which convey psychological attitude (e.g., it might be raining; I doubt it's raining). This is essential in written language, where there are no paralinguistic or extralinguistic features. However, discussion of such matters would stray too far from the current topic.

2. We do not have a good explanation for the low performance of 4-year-olds in Study 2. In all three tasks, they were 100% correct on both the memory and the reality control questions, and their scores on the language measures were typical for their age. There were no significant differences between the 4-year-olds in Study 1 and Study 2 in age or on any of the language measures ($ts = -0.18—0.19$, $ps > .10$). However, the difference in false-belief task performance between 4-year-olds in the two studies was quite apparent: $t_{(36)} = 1.99$, $p = .054$. Because of the low performance of the 4-year-olds in Study 2, the false-belief measure was not correlated with the language measures in this study. Nonetheless, because their performance was similarly low in all three false-belief conditions (paired sample $ts = -1.0 – 0.0$, $ps = .33 – 1.0$), we include them in the analysis of Study 2 data, where the focus of our interest is condition differences.

References

Astington, J. W., & Gopnik, A. (1988). Knowing you've changed your mind: Children's understanding of representational change. In J. W. Astington, P. L. Harris, & D. R. Olson (Eds.), *Developing theories of mind* (pp. 193–206). New York: Cambridge University Press.

Call, J., & Tomasello, M. (1999). A nonverbal false belief task: The performance of children and great apes. *Child Development, 70,* 381–395.

Carlson, S. M., & Moses, L. J. (2001). Individual differences in inhibitory control and children's theory of mind. *Child Development, 72,* 1032–1053.

Chandler, M. J., Fritz, A. S., & Hala, S. M. (1989). Small scale deceit: Deception as a marker of 2–, 3– and 4–year-olds' early theories of mind. *Child Development, 60,* 1263–1277.

Clements, W. A., & Perner, J. (1994). Implicit understanding of belief. *Cognitive Development, 9,* 377–395.

de Villiers, P., & Pyers, J. (2001). Complementation and false-belief representation. In M. Almgren, A. Barrena, M.-J. Ezeizabarrena, I. Idiazabal, & B. MacWhinney (Eds.), *Research on child language acquisition: Proceedings of the 8th Conference of the International Association for the Study of Child Language* (pp. 984–1005). Somerville, MA: Cascadilla Press.

Dennett, D. C. (1978). *Brainstorms: Philosophical essays on mind and psychology.* Montgomery, VT: Bradford Books.

Dunn, L. M., & Dunn, L. M. (1997). *Peabody Picture Vocabulary Test—Third Edition (PPVT-III).* Circle Pines, MN: American Guidance Service.

Figueras-Costa, B., & Harris, P. (2001). Theory of mind development in deaf children: A nonverbal test of false-belief understanding. *Journal of Deaf Studies and Deaf Education, 6,* 92–102.

Fodor, J. A. (1992). A theory of the child's theory of mind. *Cognition, 44,* 283–296.

Freeman, N. H., Lewis, C., & Doherty, M. J. (1991). Preschoolers' grasp of a desire for knowledge in false-belief prediction: Practical intelligence and verbal report. *British Journal of Developmental Psychology, 9,* 139–157.

Gopnik, A., & Astington, J. W. (1988). Children's understanding of representational change and its relation to the understanding of false belief and the appearance-reality distinction. *Child Development, 59,* 26–37.

Gopnik, A., & Graf, P. (1988). Knowing how you know: Young children's ability to identify and remember the sources of their beliefs. *Child Development, 59,* 1366–1371.

Harris, P. L. (2000). *The work of the imagination.* Oxford: Blackwell.

Harris, P. L. (2002). What do children learn from testimony? In P. Carruthers, M. Siegal, & S. Stich (Eds.), *Cognitive bases of science* (pp. 316–334). New York: Cambridge University Press.

Harris, P. L., Johnson, C. N., Hutton, D., Andrews, G., & Cooke, T. (1989). Young children's theory of mind and emotion. *Cognition and Emotion, 3,* 379–400.

Harris, P. L., & Kavanaugh, R. D. (1993). Young children's understanding of pretense. *Monographs of the Society for Research in Child Development, 58*(1, Serial No. 231).

Hughes, C. (1998). Executive function in preschoolers: Links with theory of mind and verbal ability. *British Journal of Developmental Psychology, 16,* 233–253.

Johnson, C. N., & Maratsos, M. P. (1977). Early comprehension of mental verbs: Think and know. *Child Development, 48,* 1743–1747.

Karmiloff-Smith, A. (1992). *Beyond modularity: A developmental perspective on cognitive science.* Cambridge, MA: MIT Press.

Leslie, A. M. (1987). Pretense and representation: The origins of "theory of mind." *Psychological Review, 94,* 412–426.

Leslie, A. M., & Polizzi, P. (1998). Inhibitory processing in the false belief task: Two conjectures. *Developmental Science, 1,* 247–253.

Lewis, C., & Mitchell, P. (Eds.). (1994). *Children's early understanding of mind.* Hove, UK: Erlbaum.

Lunn, J. A. (2003, April). Is Call and Tomasello's (1999) nonverbal false belief task a test of precocious mental state understanding? Paper presented at the Biennial Meeting of the Society for Research in Child Development, Tampa, FL.

Nelson, K., Skwerer, D. P., Goldman, S., Henseler, S., Presler, N., & Walkenfeld, F. F. (2003). Entering a community of minds: An experiential approach to "theory of mind." *Human Development, 46,* 24–46.

Norris, R., & Millan, S. (1991). Theory of mind: New directions. Social Psychology Seminar, cited by Plaut & Karmiloff-Smith, 1993.

Pea, R. D. (1982). Origins of verbal logic: Spontaneous denials by two- and three-year-olds. *Journal of Child Language, 9,* 597–626.

Perner, J. (1988). Developing semantics for theories of mind: From propositional attitudes to mental representation. In J. W. Astington, P. L. Harris, & D. R. Olson (Eds.), *Developing theories of mind* (pp. 141–172). New York: Cambridge University Press.

Perner, J. (1991). *Understanding the representational mind.* Cambridge, MA: Bradford Books/MIT Press.

Perner, J., Lang, B., & Kloo, D. (2002). Theory of mind and self control: More than a common problem of inhibition. *Child Development, 73,* 752–767.

Perner, J., Leekam, S., & Wimmer, H. (1987). Three-year-olds' difficulty with false belief: The case for a conceptual deficit. *British Journal of Developmental Psychology, 5,* 125–137.

Plaut, D. C., & Karmiloff-Smith, A. (1993). Representational development and theory-of-mind computations. *Behavioral and Brain Sciences, 16,* 70–71.

Robinson, E. J., Mitchell, P., & Nye, R. (1995). Young children's treating of utterances as unreliable sources of knowledge. *Journal of Child Language, 22,* 663–685.

Rozeboom, W. W. (1972). Problems in the psycho-philosophy of knowledge. In J. R. Royce & W. W. Rozeboom (Eds.), *The psychology of knowing* (pp. 25–55). New York: Gordon & Breach.

Wellman, H. M., & Bartsch, K. (1988). Young children's reasoning about beliefs. *Cognition, 30,* 239–277.

Wellman, H. M., Cross, D., & Watson, J. (2001). Meta-analysis of theory of mind development: The truth about false-belief. *Child Development, 72,* 655–684.

Wellman, H., & Liu, D. (2004). Scaling theory-of-mind tasks. *Child Development, 75,* 523–541.

Wiig, E. H., Secord, W., & Semel, E. (1992). *Clinical Evaluation of Language Fundamentals—Preschool (CELF-Preschool).* San Antonio, TX: Psychological Corporation, Harcourt Brace Jovanovich.

Wimmer, H., & Hartl, M. (1991). Against the Cartesian view on mind: Young children's difficulty with own false belief. *British Journal of Developmental Psychology, 9,* 125–138.

Wimmer, H., Hogrefe, G.-J., & Perner, J. (1988). Children's understanding of informational access as source of knowledge. *Child Development, 59,* 386–396.

Wimmer, H., & Perner, J. (1983). Beliefs about beliefs: Representation and constraining function of wrong beliefs in young children's understanding of deception. *Cognition, 13,* 103–128.

Zaitchik, D. (1991). Is only seeing really believing?: Sources of true belief in the false belief task. *Cognitive Development, 6,* 91–103.

10 Can Language Acquisition Give Children a Point of View?

Jill G. de Villiers

I begin with an illustration of the nature of the problem of other minds in a concrete context, to show how the "reading" of another person's beliefs involves representations of a special kind. The chapter then discusses a circumscribed variety of linguistic determinism. This requires an elaboration of an account of the process by which children acquire complement-taking verbs, to clarify how syntax and semantics are intertwined in this area, and why desire and belief verbs develop along radically different trajectories. I then respond to three different challenges that have been made to the linguistic determinism theory that I propose. At the end, I provide a speculative theory of the linguistic structures involved, using a notion of Point of View domains.

An Illustration: What Is It to Have a Full Theory of Mind?

Several years ago, we spent some happy hours with our students viewing old silent movies to find suitable scenes that portrayed a false belief and its consequences. Charlie Chaplin movies are full of illustrations. Take, for example, the scene in *The Gold Rush* where a grimy Charlie Chaplin is at an outdoor sink washing his hands and face vigorously. Next to the sink is a table, and another man has laid out bread and a slab of cheese on the same table for a sandwich. Reaching across with his eyes closed, Chaplin first finds the hunk of cheese and attempts to wash with it, but it crumbles. Reaching out again, he finds his soap but then sets it down on the bread. A moment later, the other man closes the sandwich and takes a large bite of it, soap and all, then splutters bubbles.

Consider the language that we need to explain what happened. For example:

(1) The man thought *the soap was cheese.* or
(2) Chaplin thought *the cheese was soap.* or
(3) The man thought *he was eating a cheese sandwich.*

Each one of these sentences involves a verb of belief and an embedded tensed complement (in italics) that contains a false statement such as "the cheese was soap." Perhaps this is more elaborate than necessary? Couldn't we just capture it in a lexical item, such as:

(4) The man made a mistake.
(5) Chaplin was deluded.

But those expressions neither predict what will happen nor explain the particulars—why on earth does Chaplin wash with cheese? Why does his partner eat soap? Can we say at least:

(6) The man was deluded about the soap.

Again, that fails to predict why he *ate* it, instead of carving it or using it as a paperweight. But once we have the full propositional content:

(7) The man thought the soap was cheese.

then we can predict exactly what he is likely to do with it: eat it, slice it, put it back in the fridge, and so forth.

The propositional complexity is necessary to fully explain the scene to others, but is it not equally necessary to read the scene for ourselves? Fodor (1975), Segal (1998), and other philosophers of mind have said that the reasoning we engage in around the contents of other minds must have the same degree and precision of propositional complexity as is contained in our natural language descriptions of such events. Anything less precise won't fit the bill, that is, it will not allow us to predict behavior.

Language and the Development of False-Belief Understanding: The Linguistic Determinism Theory

This volume elaborates on several theories in which language plays a more central role than a simple crutch for the false-belief task; that is, language is causally involved in the *development* of false-belief understanding, not just in task *performance*. The semantics of mental-state verbs alone provides a way to draw the child's attention to certain classes of events and reify them, which should help in just the way any words help to "invite" the formation and differentiation of concepts (Brown, 1957). However, I have argued that lexical meaning isn't enough, that the syntax of mental-state verbs also plays a vital role. The syntax claim is the one I take responsibility for, aided and abetted by Helen Tager-Flusberg (e.g., Tager-Flusberg & Joseph, this volume, chapter 14) and Peter de Villiers (this volume, chapter 13), neither of whom is to blame for its shortcomings. On this position, it is not just learning the concepts coded in the verb meanings but the special syntax that verbs of belief project that gives the child the scaffolding for false-belief representation. But the arguments here are subtle, because it is undeniable that the child also attends to the meaning of the verbs, namely the particular lexical items, to get the syntax right! Thus, the current chapter evolved as a way to spell out what the argument is, to address critiques of the position, and to propose a specific developmental path for false-belief development guided by language.

Complement Syntax, Mental Verbs, and False-Belief Reasoning

We have argued that the language of propositional attitudes opens up a classification into worlds, or different points of view on reality. Without such forms, there is no way to represent alternatives as belief states of individuals. Verbs of mental state take complements, and these have special semantic and syntactic status. Children cannot make the appropriate semantic/syntactic distinctions immediately, because they are subtle and because the verbs and complementizers have to be classified in particular languages according to their uses, and there is huge lexical variety in English (Roeper & de Villiers, 1994). Around age 3, children begin to acquire the lexical items for mental states and then the attached clauses. However, the production of such a form is no guarantee of its adult status.

Complement Comprehension Task

If we give the child a story such as:

(8) The Mom said she bought apples, but look, she really bought oranges.

(9) What did the Mom say she bought?

Three-year-old children say "oranges," but 4-year-olds say "apples." It is as if the younger children do not yet know that the *what* question in (9) must take both verbs into account, that is, the *what* question is the object of "bought," but both verbs take scope over it:

(10) The Mom said *she bought apples*

(11) The Mom said *she bought **what**?*

(12) What did the mom say *she bought (trace)?*

Four-year-old children can hold the complement structure in memory and make the appropriate computation across the structure, falsehood and all. At the point at which children can do this reliably, we consider the complement structure mastered, although their spontaneous speech may contain sporadic well-formed cases earlier than this. The actual understanding of minds is minimized by this simple task—all we ask is memory for a form and syntactic operations across it. This argument is even stronger if we use verbs of communication, that is, *say* rather than *think*, as in the case given.

If *understanding false beliefs* requires a propositional structure of this degree of complexity, then we predicted that children might not understand them unless they could also handle *language* of this propositional complexity. But that could reflect almost any of the alternative theories of the relationship between language and false belief, even one in which the conceptual distinction is just *manifest* first in language. If we strip away all the language requirements of the usual false-belief task, so that the information and the response requirements are relatively language-free, then the concept-first theories should not predict that language is necessary to pass such tasks, but we do. And we predicted that language-delayed deaf children would be delayed in false-belief reasoning until they had the equivalent mastery of think/ say sentences in their natural language, whether spoken or signed. The details of these findings are discussed further by Peter de Villiers (this volume, chapter 13).

Evidence for the Linguistic Determinism Theory

What we know so far:

1. Preschool children pass both standard and nonstandard false-belief tests after acquiring the structures of mental or communication verbs with complements. The best gauge of this development is a task that removes the requirement to understand false beliefs but demands that the child understand that the object is under the scope of both verbs: the Complement Comprehension task as described earlier (de Villiers & Pyers, 2002).

2. Oral deaf children and ASL-learning deaf children who are delayed in learning language because of access problems show a concomitant delay in false-belief reasoning. Their performance on both standard and nonverbal false-belief tests is most closely predicted by their performance on the Complement Comprehension task, which shows that mastery of tensed complements under mental or communication verbs is delayed to the same degree (de Villiers & de Villiers, 2000, 2003; P. de Villiers, this volume, chapter 13).

3. Children with deaf parents who acquire ASL as a first language at the same age as hearing children acquiring spoken language achieve mastery of mental verb complements and false beliefs on a normal timetable and linked in the same ways, despite the radically different form in that language (P. de Villiers, de Villiers, Schick, & Hoffmeister, 2001; Schick, Hoffmeister, de Villiers & de Villiers, in preparation).

4. Children exposed to no formal well-developed signed language, such as first-generation Nicaraguan signers, reach adulthood with no formal marking of complementation in their language, and such signers fail nonverbal false-belief tasks. Their peers who acquired more developed or evolved versions of Nicaraguan sign language pass such tasks with ease (Pyers, 2001).

5. Two training studies have demonstrated that training on false complements with communication verbs can increase children's performance on standard false-belief tasks, as much as or more than direct training on false belief or nonverbally alerting them to discrepancy (Hale & Tager-Flusberg, 2003; Lohmann & Tomasello, 2003; Lohmann, Tomasello, & Meyer, this volume, chapter 12). Exposure to other complex syntactic forms with no false complements, namely relative clauses, is ineffective (Hale & Tager-Flusberg, 2003).

6. The evidence of false-belief understanding in nonhuman primates is equivocal and may represent local behavioral strategies (Hare & Wrangham, 2002; Hauser, 1999; Povinelli, Bering, & Giambrone, 2000; Premack & Woodruff, 1978; Tomasello, 1996). Their lack of complements under mental verbs is unequivocal.

Critiques of the Linguistic Determinism Position

There are several specific empirically based critiques of our central argument, and these take three forms:

1. Studies showing cross-linguistic variation in complement forms that call into question whether "tensed complements" are necessary (e.g., Perner, Sprung, Zauner, & Haider, 2003; Perner, Zauner, & Sprung, this volume, chapter 11; Tardif & Wellman, 2000).

2. Studies that either fail to find that complements predict false-belief understanding or pit complement development against broader measures of language skill and show that more general language measures work as well as complements do as predictors of false-belief understanding (e.g., Ruffman, Slade, Rowlandson, Rumsey, & Garnham, 2003).

3. Hints in the training studies that suggest other routes (such as discourse about deceptive objects) are possible for the child's devel-

opment of false-belief understanding (e.g., Lohmann & Tomasello, 2003; Lohmann et al., this volume, chapter 12).

Each of these critiques is addressed in this chapter. First, however, it is necessary to look more closely at the path of linguistic development for complements. This serves two purposes: it details the mechanism and reveals why the problem is a deep and central one in language acquisition. This exposition aims to make clear why it is not so easy to separate syntax from semantics and why linguists find it necessary to invoke underlying structures instead of surface structures.

The Acquisition Problem for Complement Syntax and Mental Verbs

How do children acquire the complements under mental verbs? Gleitman (1990) has argued cogently that verb meaning is not learned by ostension (see also Montgomery, this volume, chapter 6). Gleitman (1990; Gleitman & Gleitman, 1992) and Tomasello (1995) argue that verb learning is a challenging task because the events that verbs name are rarely simultaneous with the verb's use, and there is considerable ambiguity about how to carve up events. Gleitman and others place a large burden on the syntax of the verb's argument frame to narrow down the possible meaning, a process called "syntactic bootstrapping." That is, they claim that the argument structure of the verb—how many arguments it has and how they are arrayed—plays a vital role in cueing the child to its meaning. For instance, an intransitive verb has only one argument and usually refers to some inherent activity of an object, with cause unmentioned; for example:

(13) John sneezed
       The cup fell

In contrast, transitive verbs with two arguments refer to a causal event:

(14) Bill pushed the train
       Maria enthralled Ramon

If these "linking rules" between syntax and meaning were innate, or at least acquired early, the child could hear a new verb used in such a frame, examine the situational context, and use the syntax to guess which action was referred to. For example:

(15) Big Bird meeped
(16) Big Bird meeped Grover

(15) should mean something Big Bird did alone, but the act in (16) is whatever is being done to Grover. In a series of careful studies, this contrast has been shown

for young children ages 2 and 3 years (Fisher, Hall, Rakowitz, & Gleitman, 1995; Naigles, 1990).

Gleitman and her colleagues (Fisher, Gleitman, & Gleitman, 1991; Landau & Gleitman, 1985; Lederer, Gleitman, & Gleitman,1995) extend this argument to claim that adults and children could use complements to figure out that a verb is a mental-state (or communication) verb, because of the unique syntax. That is, hearing a form such as:

(17) Big Bird meeped that Grover was here

or

(18) Big Bird meeped Grover to be here

should allow the listener to infer some mental state or communication of Big Bird about Grover.

Three recent experiments have shown that 4- to 6-year-old children can indeed "fast map" novel mental-state verbs from complement syntax, although not perfectly (Asplin, 2002; Johnson, 2001; Johnson, de Villiers, D'Amato, Deschamps, & Huneke, 2002). In particular, they need the framework of concrete nouns and a scene to guide them and cannot succeed with "empty" nouns. Johnson (2001) considered whether children could pick out the right verb from a complex scene for either:

(19) The clown meeped the woman to send the apple

or

(20) The woman meeped the apple to the clown

Here, (19) must refer to a mental or communication verb, and (20) to a transfer verb. Three- to 6-year-old children were able to pick out the right action above chance level, but not when the clues from the nouns were removed (Johnson et al., 2002), as in:

(21) Somebody meeped somebody to send something

Six-year-olds, and most adults, failed to attach consistent meaning to the verb "meep" for (21) with a single ambiguous exposure.

Asplin (2002) gave children three different occasions to pick out the meaning, using a complement frame:

(22) Somebody meeped the raccoon to eat the corn

After three exposures across varying content scenarios, 4- and 5-year-olds could figure out which character did the action of meeping. But when exposed to the form:

(23) Somebody meeped that the raccoon ate the corn

even 6-year-olds chose correctly only 50% of the time.

To summarize, the complement may let the child guess that the verb is a mental-state or communication verb, as Gleitman and her colleagues have argued. But the experimental evidence shows also that a *that*-complement as in (23) is not in itself enough to determine what *kind* of reading a complement receives under a novel mental-state verb. With an *unknown* verb, it remains ambiguous without further evidence (Asplin, 2002). But evidence of what kind? That question is at the heart of this chapter, and the answer is a long one.

Complement Clauses: Varieties

What is a complement clause? Figure 10.1 shows the structure, vastly simplified,[1] that represents how complements are attached to verbs (e.g., Radford, 1988). Some verbs (e.g., "ate" in Figure 10.1a) take only noun phrases (NP) as their "complements" in the object position. Verbs of mental state and communication (e.g., "said" in Figure 10.1b) take whole clauses in that same position. These subordinate clauses are called complementizer phrases (CP). The CP may contain the specific sentence connectives—*that, for, which*, and so on introducing the clause—although these are often optional. Compare the complement with the case of an adjunct clause, such as "because he ate the bread" (Figure 10.1c) adjoined as a sister to the inflectional phrase (IP) "she had nothing." It should be evident that the structures are distinct and that the contents of the adjunct clause are not embedded under the verb "had." Finally, compare the relative clause in Figure 10.1d: the same propositional structure is embedded under a noun, not a verb. Importantly, only in the case of (10.1b) does the possibility arise that the clause can be false while the whole remains true. But that is only the beginning.

Traditionally, the complement clause is held to be selected by the verb that it is embedded under ("said" in Figure 10.1b) and is particular to that type of verb. This is why it is not usually feasible to talk about the syntax of complements in isolation from the verb classes to which they are attached. So, *verbs of perception* can take special clauses with no tense, called "small clauses," as in:

(24) She saw *him* fall

Notice that the accusative case "him" on the subject of fall is unusual compared to the *that*-clause:

(25) She saw *that* he fell

Causative clauses also take similar untensed forms like perception verb small clauses (Felser, 2002):

(26) She made *him* fall

194   WHY LANGUAGE MATTERS FOR THEORY OF MIND

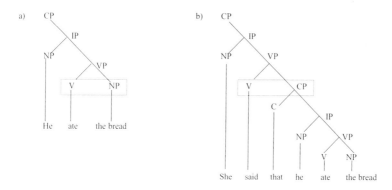

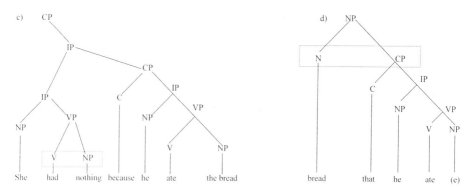

Figure 10.1. Various configurations of clauses in a simplified version of X′ syntax: (a) a simple transitive verb; (b) a complement-taking verb; (c) a verb with an adjunct clause; (d) a relative clause.

However, there are numerous differences between the complements, as Felser points out. For example, expletive subjects can occur with causatives but not with perception complements:

(27) She made *it seem likely that he fell*

(28) *She saw *it seem likely that he fell*

So the complements may look alike, but they are underlyingly distinct.

Factive verbs (*forget, remember, know*) (Kiparsky & Kiparsky, 1970) require their tensed complements to be true, so:

(29) She forgot *that he arrived late*

presupposes that he did arrive late. This is unlike *nonfactive* verbs such as *think* and *say*:

(30) She thought *that he arrived late*

This is fortunate, or we wouldn't be able to use the latter type to describe false beliefs! Furthermore, factives and nonfactives belong to different verb classes that do not behave alike syntactically (Cattell, 1978). For example, wh-movement is allowed from nonfactives (31) but not from factives (32):

(31) When did she think that he arrived?
(32) *When did she forget that he arrived?

Cattell (1978) made a division among types of predicate-taking verbs, distinguishing response stance, nonstance, and volunteered stance. Response stance includes *deny, accept, confirm, verify,* and *admit.* Nonstance includes factives: *realize, know, regret, remember, surprise, notice,* and so on. Finally, volunteered stance includes *think, believe, suspect, allege, assume, claim,* and similar verbs. Cattell argued that the first two classes generally block wh-adjunct (e.g., *when, how, why*) extraction.

In addition, the relation in time between the complement and the verb it is embedded under is determined by the verb class. Verbs of desire take complements that have the property that their tense is "forward" from the time of the desire, captured in English by a to-infinitive:

(33) He wanted *to go to the party*

and in many languages by a subjunctive (Avrutin & Wexler, 2000), which has the appearance of a tensed clause but is still tense-dependent, rather like an infinitive is.

Linguists have also classified complement types into *realis* and *irrealis* "mood" forms, which are sometimes, but not always, marked explicitly on the surface. Bickerton (1981, p. 284) writes: "the realis/irrealis distinction codes events that are observable with those that are unobservable, at least at the time of speech." In English, *realis* is usually expressed via a tensed complement (e.g., "he said she left") and *irrealis* most often by an infinitive (e.g., "he wants to go") or marked by a modal (*should, would*). In other languages, including Spanish, indicative marks *realis* and subjunctive verb forms mark *irrealis.* Bickerton argued that marking complements as *realis* or *irrealis* is an essential part of the human language "bio-program" and a common property of Creole languages.

It is essential to notice that the syntax of a single sentence does not always betray the special semantics that it has, as shown by comparing (24) and (26) or (29) and (30). Instead, rephrasings, syntactic operations, and other tests reveal that two superficially similar forms are underlyingly different. Invisible properties are standard assumptions in linguistics, though they may seem like sleight of hand to the uninitiated. Chomsky is fond of reminding us that many sciences go through a stage of positing hidden properties, or forces, some of which are then detected with new instrumentation. Genes, bacteria, molecules, electrons, and black holes were all posited before being observed, but then so were phlogiston, ether, and the id!

What does this mean for the story here? The verb classes in a language are defined by noting similarities across *sets* of syntactic forms, not a single form. So, in an oft-cited paradox from Baker (1979) examined at length by Pinker (1989), take the verbs *donate* and *give*. On comparing:

(34) He gave the book to the class

and

(35) He donated the book to the class

one would be inclined to think they were identical, but compare:

(36) He gave the class the book
(37) *He donated the class the book

Obviously, despite the virtual identity of meaning and the appearance in the same transfer construction, they belong to different syntactic classes, with widespread consequences. That is why hearing a new verb in a single syntactic construction may not be sufficient to fine-tune its class. Instead, exposures to it in multiple syntactic contexts may be needed (Fisher et al., 1994). However, even that exposure does not tell you the exact lexical meaning without other rich clues (Asplin, 2002; Pinker, 1994).

The Path of Linguistic Development for Complements

The crucial point is that the child must put three important pieces together to get the full representation of a verb like *think*. The first is its lexical meaning, referring to some hidden activity or state of the mind but offering no potential clues as to its propositional nature: it could be a mirroring of reality, as Perner (1991) proposed. The second is its syntactic structure, assessed across a range of different contexts, which provide clues that *think* takes propositions as its *content*. The third is discovering that these embedded propositions can be false compared to the world.

It is this last "breakthrough" that completes mastery of the verb *think*, and it is the point at which everyone balks at my account. The most common objection is that here the story has slipped into attributing to language acquisition a step that is properly part of the conceptual development story (Perner et al., this volume, chapter 11; Ruffman et al., 2003). One example given earlier is provided to show that semantics and syntax intertwine here: the case of factives, in which there are syntactic consequences of the obligatory true requirement on the complement (examples 29–32). How to capture this relationship is far from clear, but it is evident that we need a solution inside linguistic theory itself. As soon as something has a clear effect on syntax, it needs to be incorporated into the linguistic account.

I have argued previously (de Villiers, 1999) that the complementizer position (C) heading the clause (CP) contains some kind of special marker that indicates its status. It had been commonplace to assume that factive complements had such a marker, but I argued that nonfactives needed a marker to indicate that their clauses "could be false." This has to be posited as an abstract feature because the complementizer itself (e.g., "that") may be absent.

But postulating a "marker" hardly solves the acquisition problem. How does a child recognize that *think* falls in such a class? This is where the analogy across verb classes starts to do some work. De Villiers (1995) argued that the verbs of communication might provide a bootstrap for figuring out the syntax/semantics of complements, because acts of speaking are overt: "He said that he was eating cheese" can be checked against events, but "He thought that he was eating cheese" is an inference and an attribution from subtle clues. So one ingredient in the solution may be the overt evidence from described acts of speech as follows:

1. The converging surface syntactic evidence allows the child to place *think* in the same subclass as *say*,
2. There is overt evidence that *say* can take false complements,
3. The child extends this to treat *think* complements analogously: their logical underlying form is equivalent.

Notice the explicit work that syntax does in this progression: it provides the bootstrap between the overt evidence of truth/falsity for the verb say and the attribution of potential falsehood to the complement of think. However, this story was designed for English, and recent studies have pointed to the need for a tighter line of reasoning to consider the cross-linguistic variation.

In the following section I describe a possible path that children could follow in differentiating among different classes of mental-state verbs. It is necessarily speculative, as much is unknown about the generalizations possible in the world's languages as a whole and so it is ambitious to try to make a universal claim (Baker, 1996; Evans, 2003; Hanson, 1992). There is great variation in the structure of mental verbs across languages, but it seems plausible that all languages make a realis/irrealis distinction and that surface similarity among forms of complementation may belie important structural differences.

Challenges to the Linguistic Determinism Theory

I now turn to address three different challenges that have been made against the linguistic determinism theory proposed here.

Challenge 1: Differentiating Want and Think

Perner et al. (2003; this volume, chapter 11), suggest that cross-linguistic variation in complement forms challenges the developmental course I have charted
for English. In English, *want* and *think* take a different set of structures:

(38) He wants ice cream   *He thinks ice cream
      He wants to leave   *He thinks to leave
      He wants her to leave   *He thinks her to leave

However, in other languages, the syntactic complement under *want* is the same
on the surface as the one with *think:*

German:

(39) Mutter will dass Andreas ins Bett geht
      Mother wants that Andy in bed goes
(40) Mutter glaupt dass Andreas ins Bett geht
      Mother thinks that Andy in bed goes

Cantonese:[2]

(41) Mama jiu dzaidzai fangau
      Mother want son   sleep
(42) Mama jiwai dzaidzai   fan   (dzo)   gau
      Mother think son   sleep (PAST) 2ndpartofsleepverb
      (i.e. the tense is an infix, and somewhat optional)

In German, Mandarin, and Cantonese, children master the syntactic form
under *want* before they master it under *think*, even though the surface forms
are similar. In the Chinese languages, the evidence is from production; children
produce the forms under *want* verbs before *think* verbs (Tardif & Wellman,
2000). Since there is no marking of complementation, it is hard to assess from
production alone how sophisticated this syntax is: the clauses could be adjoined
rather than embedded. No examples are provided to assess whether children
use the right aspect markers at this age.

However, in German, the evidence comes from comprehension, and thus
it is clearer that the verb takes scope over its complement, that is, it is a true
embedded form. As Perner et al. (this volume, chapter 11) argue, this gap between *want* and *think* complements cannot be syntactic, since the forms are the
same, but instead the gap must be "conceptual." Thus, they argue that only when
children get the full *conceptual* understanding of belief, as opposed to desire,
can they master the complement of the *think* verb form.

Yet we have seen that the data from deaf children (P. de Villiers, this volume, chapter 13) are difficult to reconcile with a simple concept-first model of the relationship of language and false belief: given the special difficulty deaf children have with syntax, shouldn't they show mastery of false beliefs in nonverbal tasks long before they master the equivalent linguistic forms? Of course, one could retreat to the more moderate position that deaf children still need sufficient exposure to linguistic discourse to build the *conceptual* theory about false beliefs (Harris, this volume, chapter 4; Perner, 2000). But that is also insufficient to explain the very tight relationships we have found between complement mastery and false-belief understanding in those populations. "Discourse" is needed to build the language just as much as to build the theory and may be ineffective if it does not contain the right syntax clues (Lohmann et al., this volume, chapter 12).

Given these considerations, I am motivated to find a way to reconcile the gap between *want* and *think* forms linguistically, not just conceptually. What this requires is a reason that *want* is never considered analogous to *think*, even in languages where the single complement structure has a surface resemblance, as in German. Notice that the children who fail to understand *think* in Perner et al. do not treat *think* as *want*; instead, they answer with the truth, not counter to current reality. What allows them to make the next step? In other words, what is the source, for Perner, of the conceptual breakthrough in understanding thinking, and thus *think*? I contend that it is language, that is, learning *think*, and thus thinking.

The progression needs to consider:

1. the source of the lexical meaning of the verbs
2. the syntax of the complement
3. the nature of the analogies used to form verb classes that dictate further semantic consequences.

A Proposed Developmental Progression

The problem of acquiring the meaning of mental verbs has been pointed out repeatedly, and Gleitman and others (Gleitman, 1990; Landau & Gleitman, 1985) have emphasized the important role that complement structure plays as a clue to the meaning. However, Maratsos and Deak (1995) have countered that there are also false analogues in this domain that could trip up the child equipped with "innate linking rules": how is the child to recognize complements in the language? Pinker (1994) has also criticized Gleitman's bootstrapping approach by saying that lexical meaning is not available from the syntax. So this is tricky territory, and most agree that the child needs multiple sources of information to acquire the full meaning and structures of a mental verb.

Want Take the case of *want*. The verb is on the list of the most common first 50 words in English (Communicative Development Inventory; Fenson et al., 1993), and it is undoubtedly heard frequently (Bartsch & Wellman, 1995; Shatz, Wellman, & Silber, 1983). The child undoubtedly experiences it first in connection to her own desires but also hears it used about others. The behavioral evidence must look something like this: a person exhibits "yearning" toward an object, and the verb *want* occurs in such a context. When that object is obtained, the person exhibits satisfaction and ceases yearning. If it is not obtained, the yearning increases in urgency. I use the word "yearning" rather than "state of desire" to focus on it as a behavior: reaching, pointing, struggling to get, displaying rage or despair at its removal, and so on. That's what it is to want something.

Once a partial mapping has occurred for the verb meaning, the unusual thing about *want* is that it extends to invisible objects (Baldwin & Saylor, this volume, chapter 7). The child will hear the verb in sentences such as "she wants her bottle" when a baby is crying, no bottle in sight. Undoubtedly, too, the child has by this time herself experienced desire for objects out of sight. So *want* is different from verbs like *kick* and *carry*: it is used for a future goal. Its objects are not *realis*, but *irrealis*, potential. Even if possession of the object is not achieved, it is still true that the person wanted it.

This *irrealis* property of the verb *want* is linked to its conceptual character: desires have a different fit between state of mind and reality than do beliefs. We change the world to match our desire; we change our beliefs to match the world (Schwitzgebel, 1999).

The verb *want* has three complement types in English:

(43) He wants a car
(44) He wants to buy a car
(45) He wants Jane to buy a car

Work on spontaneous speech has shown that language development proceeds in that order, with the last type becoming prevalent only at 3 years of age or later (Bartsch & Wellman, 1995; Bloom, Rispoli, Gartner, & Hafitz, 1989). All are undoubtedly common in parental speech, and the child must extend her understanding to allow the verb not only to take an NP complement but also a state of affairs. In each case, the complement is *irrealis*: the event is in the future, or potential, not actual. In English, this is marked by the infinitival form, in Spanish by the subjunctive, in Russian with a special complementizer, but in German and Cantonese with no unique marker. Yet it is probable that the child extends from the understanding that the object is *irrealis* to the understanding that all complements of the desire verb are *irrealis*. In essence, how could it be otherwise? That is the nature of desire, and it has been given overtly. In this case, there is *no* reason to believe that the language creates the understanding. I suspect that many of our mammalian relatives have propositional understanding of desire to the same degree as young children (see also Witt & de Villiers, 2001), though it remains to be fully tested. That is, do babies, or chimpanzees, clearly understand nonverbal scenes where someone wants someone to do something, as opposed to where someone wants an object?

Say Now consider the case of *say*. Here the child's evidence is fairly straightforward: people speak, and the verb *say* is employed about these acts of speaking. But it is not just like the word *speak*, because *say* refers to the words or sounds that emerge from their mouths: saying has *content*. (Is it an accident that a very common routine for young children just learning to talk in the West is the endless requesting of "what does the dog say?"—"woof!" and similar expressions?). However, saying is not just in terms of generics ("the dog says 'woof'") but also describing present and past events:

(46) Mom said you liked the movie

and *irrealis* events:

(47) Mom said you should clean up

The child experiences through the verb *say* the opportunity to sort the complements into the different moods. And the mapping is overt, since speech is experienced and enduring and the relation between what is said and what happened can be experienced directly.

In time, experiences will accumulate of mismatches: people will say false things (de Villiers, 1995). Of course, disagreements start very early, long before the verb *say* is fully understood. In some households, teasing is a natural occurrence, with deliberate misnaming of objects or attributes that the child has already mastered. Or the child will hear people saying things that do not match his understanding. Suppose his mother says, "Look at this nice blue apple." The child might at an early age respond, "No, it's red!" The next step is hearing this event described as "She said it was blue." The child might still respond, "No, it's red!" But with time and exposure, the child establishes that this is a permissible sentence of the language, that the sentence "She said it was blue" is not itself false, though it contains a falsehood. That is the step at which the child understands the special nature of nonfactive complements and fixes the class of verbs to which *say* belongs. At this point, the *say* verb splits off from other verbs as a special class of *realis*, with the possibility of a false complement.

Even if the linking rules between argument structure and meaning are innate, the form the complement takes in the language in question, and the particular lexical items that fit in that class, must each be learned. The child's work is still not over, because it is necessary to establish the marking for indirect and direct speech, which is as variable cross-linguistically as most other things, and is still a matter of confusion late in the preschool years (Hollebrandse, 1999, 2000).

Think Now we come to the case of *think*, the heart of the matter. Unlike desires, beliefs have no immediate behavioral manifestation. People inhabiting a world in which all beliefs were true might never invent the concept of belief. Beliefs must be inferred from behavioral cues, such as mistakes. To the young child, mistakes must just be baffling bits of misbehavior, like slipping on a banana peel. Adults don't bother to attribute to the hapless faller the belief that the ground was clear, or to the dropper of a glass the belief that his grip was secure. But Charlie Chaplin washing with cheese? In the case of apparently intentional, purposive behavior that seems weird, adults (at least in many cultures; Vinden & Astington, 2000) feel the need to invoke contents of beliefs. The young child apparently does not (de Villiers, Pyers, Broderick, & Eddy, 2002).

What brings the child to the state of inferring false beliefs? The verb *think* appears in children's spontaneous speech considerably later than *want* (Bartsch & Wellman, 1995). The child must begin to form a lexical meaning for *think* that is something to do with private, inner events that have no obvious immediate behavior associated with them. Like *say*, *think* will have both *realis* and *irrealis* uses:

(48) He thinks you did a good job
(49) He thinks you should go tomorrow

The overlap in syntactic and discourse use between *think* and *say* must be a help in cracking these meanings: in either context, *say* could also have occurred, but *think* can occur even without overt acts of speech. The child who hears someone say the apple is blue could easily hear the act described as "She thinks it's blue!" Now imagine that nothing is said but that the child sees her baby brother eating a bar of soap. Someone laughs and says, "He thinks it's food!" The child who has sorted *think* into the special *realis* subclass with *say* on the basis of its syntactic behavior now has an interpretation of such an utterance, namely that the verb *think* allows a false complement, and the analogy completes her meaning for *think*. This linguistic achievement, that the verb *think* allows a false complement, is the step that permits the representation of false beliefs in the absence of overt labeling, and hence reasoning about how others will act and why they acted the way they did.

I have argued that *want* is not a likely analog for *think* because it is irredeemably *irrealis*, regardless of the syntactic forms it manifests across languages. *Say*, however, is an overtly mappable lexical item that provides key information to the child about how *irrealis* and *realis* forms are differentiated and, ultimately, how false complements can be accommodated. *Say* provides the crucial analogy for cracking *think*. There is one more pretender to this role, and it is the case of the verb *pretend*.

Garfield, Peterson, Garson, Nevin, and Perry (2002) make an exactly parallel argument to Perner et al. (2003), namely that the child masters false complements with *pretend* before she masters them with *think* (see also Custer, 1996). Therefore, the whole linguistic complement solution is in place early, and the gap to understanding false beliefs as opposed to pretense is therefore conceptual not syntactic. The authors make a nice argument for the important role not just of pretense but of discourse about pretense as playing a real role in cognitive development: talk about pretending, not saying, is a crucial step for them, but not the final one. They agree that complements scaffold false beliefs but argue that the pretense-belief gap is conceptual, not linguistic.

It is tempting to draw the parallels among *say*, *think* and *pretend*: each takes a tensed complement that is "false" with respect to the world:

(50) He pretended that the block was a car
(51) He said that the block was a car
(52) He thought that the block was a car

But *pretend* breaks from the others in allowing infinitivals:

(53) He pretended to be a bunny
(54) ? He said to be a bunny (note: we can get a reading but not if he is the bunny)
(55) *? He thought to be a bunny

Neither does *pretend* enter passivized infinitival forms like these:

(56) He was thought to be a miser
(57) He was said to be a miser
(58) *He was pretended to be a miser

Pretend also doesn't easily allow direct complements:

(59) He said, "Come here, you villain!"
(60) He thought, "Come here, you villain!"
(61) *He pretended, "Come here, you villain!"

In conclusion, the child would be unwise to make an analogy on syntactic grounds between *think* and *pretend*. *Pretend*, like *want*, is the wrong verb type.

In case a diagram would help, I have tried something Darwinian in figure 10.2. The tree represents differentiation in verb type over the child's development, within this domain. I am assuming that the child begins with all verbs having the same status, as *realis*, connected to ongoing events. This is undoubtedly a brief period, because we know *want* is an early verb of the *irrealis* type. *Want*-NP splits off, and from that branch grow the extensions into propositional

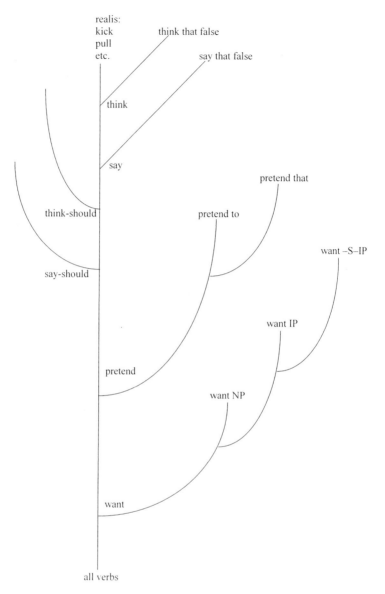

Figure 10.2. A proposed developmental progress of complement-taking verbs.

forms under *want*. Slightly later, *pretend* does the same thing, with the more frequent form *pretend to* leading to the still *irrealis* form *pretend that*. Soon thereafter, the child recognizes the distinction between the *irrealis* and *realis* forms of *say*, and then *think*. But the realis forms of *say* and *think* are still not separated from other verbs. Penultimately, *realis* "say that" splits off, and the form is marked as special, in that false complements are now possible. By analogy, "think that" (*realis*) also splits off and is absorbed into that verb class.

But is there any evidence of this progression, for example, that children have *irrealis* complements sorted out before *realis* for *think*? Or that *think* is never understood as *want*? Or that children do not use *pretend* as the analogue for *think*? In the next section, I discuss the preliminary data in support of these conjectures.

Evidence for the Developmental Progression

A critical claim about how *want* is learned is that children recognize early that *want* takes an intensional object in its scope, namely an object that refers not to something in the immediate world but to something in the world of ideas. At a young age, children hear, understand, and produce forms such as:

(62) I want a candy

when there is no candy in evidence, at the same time that they normally say, for example:

(63) I am eating a candy

when the very candy is present.

Importantly, in addition, Witt and de Villiers (2001) showed that even 3-year-old children recognize the NP under *want* as intensional even in the face of competing evidence. In our study, a character wanted an object that looked like one thing but was really something else. For example, a child was shown a Piglet puppet and a transparent tennis ball can with a green apple partly visible inside and told the following brief story: "Piglet really wants this. Know why? Because it looks like a tennis ball." Piglet was then put under the table, the tennis ball can was opened, and the experimenter continued: "But, look, it's really an apple!" The child was then asked three test questions:

1. Does Piglet want a tennis ball? (correct answer = yes)
2. Does Piglet want an apple? (correct answer = no)
3. Does Piglet want the apple? (correct answer = no)

Children 3 through 6 years of age were tested on three different scenarios. The 3- and 4-year-olds were well above chance on all three questions, and the 5- and 6-year-olds were virtually at ceiling. That is to say, all children clearly took the verb *want* as *irrealis*, hence the noun as intensional: they rejected the true description of the desired object as *apple* in favor of the puppet's conception of it: *tennis ball*. By extending this, children might quite early understand complements under *want* and *pretend* even though the clause contents are discrepant with the world in front of them.

At the same time, I claimed earlier that children treat *say* and *think* complements as if they were true, *realis* clauses. If children encounter a statement about a false statement or belief, they reject the truth of the whole and fail to integrate the information across both clauses. At no point should they think that the verbs *say* and *think* are inherently *irrealis*. To test whether children recognize this difference with respect to truth value, I have begun a study that attempts to pit *realis/irrealis* mood against the form of verb+complement in a complement-comprehension paradigm, a partial replication of Perner et al. (2003), though in English and with yes/no questions. The study asks how much of the force of the *realis/irrealis* reading is given by the introduction of the event. Two different lead-ins are used, either: "Mom says, 'Tell X to . . . VP [verb phrase]'" or "Mom says, 'I'm so happy because . . . p [proposition]'" The child is shown a picture in which the VP directive is unfulfilled or the proposition is false and is then asked a series of questions using the verbs *want* and *think*, with two different complement forms for each verb (see table 10.1).

Notice the strong parallel across circumstances. If children were blind to the *realis/irrealis* quality of the forms, one might expect them at some stage either:

1. to take a *realis* position: to reject any question that mentions an event not currently true and accept any one that is, or

Table 10.1 Lead-in, Questions, and Complement Forms for Verbs *want* and *think*

Lead-in	Picture	Question—Yes	Question—No
Mom says, "Tell Bella to play on the computer."	Bella is painting	Does Mom **want** Bella **to play** on the computer?	Does Mom **want** Bella **to paint** a picture?
		Does Mom **think** Bella **should play** on the computer?	Does Mom **think** Bella **should paint** a picture?
Mom says, "I'm so happy because Bella is playing on the computer."	Bella is painting	Does Mom **want** Bella **playing** on the computer?	Does Mom **want** Bella **painting** a picture?
		Does Mom **think** Bella **is playing** on the computer?	Does Mom **think** Bella **is painting** a picture?

    2. to take an *irrealis* position in which all questions are judged inde-
    pendent of current reality. This would mean, ironically, that all dis-
    agreeing circumstances would get a "yes" response and all agreeing
    would get a "no."

Further:

    1. If the lead-in matters, (i.e., *tell to* . . . versus *I'm so happy because*
    . . .) then *want* . . . *to* and *think* . . . *should* will behave differently
    from *want* . . . *ing* and *think* . . . *is.*
    2. If the child takes the verb *want* to be obligatorily *irrealis*, then *want*
    . . . *to* and *want* . . . *ing* will pattern together, despite the difference
    in lead-in.
    3. If the child considers *think* to be obligatorily *realis, think should* and
    think . . . *is* will pattern together.

Figure 10.3 shows some preliminary data (N=15 3-year-olds; 2 stories each)
and the results look very striking. Three-year-olds, even very young 3-year-olds,
have no trouble judging the three *irrealis* cases, but they fail dramatically on
the *realis* case of *think* . . . *is.* Furthermore, the lead-in is clearly irrelevant for
want, suggesting that the verb is irreducibly *irrealis.* It is not yet clear what is
cueing the children to the *irrealis* nature of *think* . . . *should*, but clearly something is. It is either the modal *should*, or it is the lead in *tell* . . . *to.*

But, importantly, the children never take *think* . . . *is* to mean *think* . . .
should, so they never generalize *irrealis* to *think* verbs in general. Instead, these

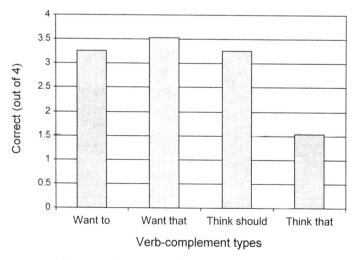

Figure 10.3. Preliminary data on how 3-year-old children judge the truth of
different kinds of verb-complement combinations.

young 3-year-olds treat *think . . . is* as *realis* and obligatorily true and judge by correspondence with what Bella is currently doing as shown in the picture.

Finally, a recent report suggests that training false complements with pretense has no carryover to false-belief understanding (Rakoczy, 2003), which was presented as a strong piece of counterevidence to the view that training syntactic tensed complements can improve theory of mind. I hope it is clear to the reader why I have not made such a generic claim and why these data on pretense, namely that training with verbs of pretense fails to enhance false-belief reasoning, are what the current theory would in fact *predict*.

Challenge 2: Language in General versus Complementation in Particular

The second empirical challenge to the account presented here comes from studies that pit more general measures of language development against complements and show that the general measures work better in predicting false-belief development. Here one must pay careful attention to the measures used, as well as to more general measurement issues.

To address the model I have proposed, it is necessary to use an adequate test of complementation. Spontaneous speech evidence is the weakest, because one cannot tell from the surface form whether children have reached the final underlying form. Wh-movement of the object from the complement as in our Complement Comprehension test (described earlier) is a secure way to tell whether the child considers the form embedded. Production judged by surface forms is a weak substitute for that test. Ruffman et al. (2003) take issue with the Complement Comprehension test as confounding false-belief reasoning and language; they contend that a child will be confused by such situations without understanding the motivation behind someone telling a lie or making a mistake in speech. I do not think this is a necessary assumption, as I discussed earlier, but I also agree that such situations involving speech are critical in the progression.

It is also important not to add additional requirements to the complement task. Perner et al. (2003) cite work by van der Lely, Hennessey, and Battell (2001) showing that children with severe forms of Specific Language Impairment (SLI) could pass false-belief tasks while failing on a complement task, a serious contradiction to the story here. However, the complement test in that study was one that the normally developing children also could not pass until age 6 or so, being a rather elaborate truth-judgment task that must have taxed memory or attention in addition to grammatical knowledge (see P. de Villiers, Burns, & Pearson, 2003, for different evidence about SLI).

The complement test should involve the particular verbs being addressed, namely the most common word for *think* or *say* in the language that has the right kind of meaning and structure to allow description of false beliefs. Other verbs take complements but introduce new complications such as certainty (*guess, know, bet*: see Moore, Bryant, & Furrow, 1989; Ziatas, Durkin, & Pratt, 1998), or factivity (*forget, remember, know*) or monotonic inferences (de Villiers, Curran, Philip, & DeMunn, 1998) that amplify the problems the child has to solve to get the full semantics. One would not expect all this to be achieved before false-belief understanding, and it is not.

The argument is not about "syntax being better than semantics." There is no reason to expect "syntax," even general embedded clauses (Ruffman et al., 2003) in general, to predict anything, unless it is a proxy for how far along the developmental progression the child is.

Finally, there are important measurement issues. In the studies we have reported, we have used at least six examples in the Complement Comprehension test—in the longitudinal study we used twelve; six with communication and six with belief verbs. We have also always ensured that there was a battery, not a single test, of false-belief questions, again usually six. Changes in children's performance are continuous, not all-or-none, and one wants to decide a standard for "passing" that takes the variability across examples into account. A very small number of test questions cannot compete in accounting for variance in false-belief measures with a large battery of standardized language measures, even in the best of worlds. If either the dependent variable or the predictor variables being tested have too little variance, then regression analyses are uninterpretable.

Challenge 3: Discourse versus Grammar

Note that the mechanism described here is specific, not general. Rich discourse is required to build the understanding of beliefs, but via the precise analogical mechanisms described here, which operate inside the child's grammar. It depends on exposure to particular facts about parallels across verbs, and exposure to such things as mistakes, teasing, disagreements, jokes, and so on, that are commented on by others using verbs like *say* and *think*. If conversation were devoid of these clues, it shouldn't work. This brings us back to the condition in Lohmann and Tomasello (2003, see also Lohmann et al., this volume, chapter 12) in which the child is exposed to discrepancy that is commented on without the use of mental or communication verbs and complements. In their "discourse only" training condition, the child is exposed to the discrepancy between the deceptive object's appearance and its function, but the experimenter says only the equivalent of "This is an X, it looks like an X; now it's a Y, it's really a Y." Children in this group gained in false-belief understanding despite demonstrating no gains in the language of belief, as measured on a complements posttest. This leads Lohmann and Tomasello to conclude that while the syntax of false complements may be a more effective way to increase false-belief understanding, gains can occur in the absence of the mastery of such forms if the child gets exposed to people who notice and describe "discrepancy" without mental terms. Harris underlines this point in his chapter (this volume, chapter 4).

However, a few aspects of the study need attention. First, the gains are quite small for "discourse only." On the representational change task, the average posttest score is 40% of the questions correct, compared to 75% correct for the group trained on false complements (*say* or *think* combined). In the ANOVA analyses, the only significant group difference on the posttest is the full training condition with false complements compared to all the other conditions, including no-language. It is only when one looks at change from pretest to posttest that the discourse group showed improvement, but the planned comparison showed that it did not improve more than the no-language condition. Furthermore, it is not clear that 40% is significantly greater than chance on two questions, each with a 50/50 chance of the right answer.

Unlike Hale and Tager-Flusberg (2003), who pretested children in their training study to ensure that they did not understand false complements with *say*, Lohmann and Tomasello (2003) did not filter subjects on this basis on the pretest, and inspection of the complement comprehension pretest mean scores suggests the children were already fairly well along in complement mastery to begin with (average 2.4/4, and enough variance to suggest some children may have even have had 4 right). Neither did they do a regression analysis to test whether the gains in false-belief reasoning could be predicted by the variation in this linguistic competence at the start of the study. They did find improvement in complement understanding in the group trained on true sentential complements, and that improvement predicted who passed the false-belief tasks. But, overall, it is hard to assess whether any children were passing the false-belief tasks at the end without "knowing" complements.

Despite these misgivings, it still seems to be the case that in both training studies, some children *improved* in false-belief reasoning without *improving* on the complement comprehension task. It remains a possibility that training of either sort, linguistic or conceptual, on the cusp of this mastery, could tip the child into competence. The training studies are not done in a vacuum: the children continue daily life between sessions, and the experience of being in such a study might bring outside discourses and structures to a new level of awareness. In the focus on the doubts, it is important not to lose sight of the fact that brief training on false complements with *say* boosted false-belief performance to passing levels, a fact that solidly supports the present theory.

One Final Conjecture: Point of View Marking

In this final section, I propose a semiformal account of how the complements under *say* and *think* might be "marked" as taking false complements. I have argued that they fall into a special class of nonfactives and hence pattern together and distinct from other forms with other special characteristics, such as *want, pretend, know,* and *forget.* "Marking" the complement ensures that the logical form is distinct for this class, as it must be, and provides a new view of some very ancient and venerable questions concerning *referential opacity.* Referential opacity refers to the long-noted problem that in ordinary sentences, we can substitute terms and retain the truth value, as long as they refer to the same thing (Frege, 1892/ 1960; Larson & Ludlow, 1993; Quine, 1960). The sentences that follow show that this is not the case for complements under mental-state verbs.

(64) Oedipus married *Jocasta*
      → Oedipus married *his mother*
(65) Oedipus thought he married *Jocasta*
      —//→ Oedipus thought he married *his mother*

The problem is that although we know that *Jocasta* and *Oedipus's mother* refer to the same individual, Oedipus does not represent his beloved that way. *His mother* is our term for her. Evidence is accumulating that understanding the appropriate use of noun phrases in mental verb complements is a late development, delayed beyond false-belief understanding (Apperly & Robinson, 1998; de Villiers & Fitneva, 1995; de Villiers, Pyers, & Broderick, 1997; Kamawar & Olson, 1999; Russell, 1987).

In recent work, my colleagues and I have argued that Point of View (PoV) is a pervasive aspect of language, found at several levels in different guises across languages. Crucially, PoV is involved in the relation between a verb and its *complement.* We represent this as a PoV feature on the clause or complementizer phrase (CP). Complements introduce a different PoV, the subject's-PoV, depending upon the verb chosen:

(66) Peter thinks $_{\text{PoV-subject}}$ CP[a unicorn is dancing in the garden]

Assume the verb *think* assigns a PoV to the complement, that is, the PoV of the subject, *Peter.* This captures the fact that when we say (66), even though from our perspective the embedded proposition is false, the whole sentence can still be used as a true sentence about Peter's false belief. In other words, we can consider subject PoV to be the distinctive feature dictated by this subclass of say/think *realis* verbs. So each clause is associated with a Point of View. For main clauses it is the Speaker's PoV;[3] for these special embedded clauses called complements it must be the Subject's:

(67) $_{\text{PoV-speaker}}$ CP [Peter thinks $_{\text{PoV-subject}}$ CP[a unicorn is dancing in the garden]]

Suppose that the Point of View on a clause dictates the noun phrases that can be used within its scope. In sentence (67), *a unicorn* is Peter's representation, not the speaker's. If what he actually saw was a mule with an ice cream cone glued on its head, we are not entitled to say:

(68) Peter thought that a mule was dancing in the garden

That term "a mule" reflects the Speaker's PoV, but the clause that contains it has the subject's Point of View.

However, a long-noticed fact of complement clauses is that under certain circumstances, they do permit the Speaker's perspective to intrude (the *de re* reading). Notice that with a definite article as in (69), the proposition in (68) begins to sound acceptable:

(69) Peter thought that the mule was dancing in the garden

Why should the determiner make a difference? Recently we have postu-lated that indefinite NPs inherit the PoV of the clause, that is, that of the CP. Definite noun phrases (DPs)[4] have their own PoV, so do not inherit the PoV from the CP. So the child must not only attend to the PoV on clauses but also monitor the PoV of nominals inside the clauses: whose word is this? Is it Peter's word (unicorn in [67]) or our word (mule in [68])? Is it definite (in 69), sug-gesting specific reference, or indefinite (in 68), suggesting a kind? A child who fails to grasp this intricacy will still fail at referential substitution even after mastering complementation: exactly what the results show.

If we adopt a series of indices for convenience to mark PoV on clauses and noun phrases, this can be illustrated. In (70), the first CP has the PoV set to "speaker" (default), and the second CP under *thought* has its PoV set to the sub-ject of the verb *thought*, namely *Peter*. Now truth in that clause is relative to Peter, to his mental world. This allows us to represent his false beliefs. If nominals in a clause are not full DPs but instead NPs, then they inherit the PoV of that clause. In (70) the NP *a unicorn* inherits the subject PoV from its CP (i.e., Peter's PoV) and is appropriate where *a mule* (the speaker's conception of the crea-ture) would not be:

(70) $_{POV\text{-}speake}CP[_rPeter$ thought $_{POV\text{-}subject}CP[that _{NP}[a$ unicorn$]$ was dancing in $_{DP}[$ the garden$]]]$

The final representation of a *de re* reading looks like (71), where the DP *the mule* is our representation:

(71) $_{POV\text{-}speake}CP[_rPeter$ thought $_{POV\text{-}subject}CP[that _{POV\text{-}speaker}DP[_rthe$ mule$]$ was dancing in $_{DP}[$the garden$]]]$

Being definite, the full DPs under the scope of the CP are independent PoV domains; hence they can revert to the speaker's POV.

The notation works to capture some puzzles about opacity, *de re* versus *de dicto*, the way deixis and proper names behave under complementation, and so forth (de Villiers, 2001; de Villiers & Roeper, in preparation). It is at the cost of proposing a feature—Point of View—that is considerably more abstract than a "that" complementizer to mark factuality. But we have seen that it is more in keeping with cross-linguistic facts in which the syntactic marking may be very lean on the surface, like Cantonese or ASL, and with languages, such as German, that have two superficially identical complements under *want* and *think* that must be distinguished. Furthermore, it is carried by the nature of the verb: not all verbs open up possible worlds with attendant truth values, only a special set concerned with belief and communication.

Is PoV on clauses a semantic property? Of course it is, but it is also linked to particular syntactic configurations specified by particular lexical classes. In this ambiguity of what module it belongs to it does not differ from other aspects of language, such as a referential index. Is a referential index a semantic property? Linguistics papers are full of these examples, with indices to mark which nominals co-refer:

(72) The man$_1$ told the boy$_2$ to help him$_1$

Obviously the referential index is semantic: it is about how words point to referents. Yet it can occur only on certain types of phrase (nominals), and the conditions of its behavior are central to syntactic theory (Binding Theory; Chomsky, 1991). In a similar way, the PoV index is crucially part of syntax. It occurs only on certain kinds of phrases (e.g., CP and DP), and it may have effects on wh-extraction. Cattell's (1978) division among types of predicate-taking verbs (response stance, nonstance, and volunteered stance) is relevant here. Notice that the last class, "volunteered stance," is what I have suggested carries a PoV feature, and only that class permits wh-extraction (Hegarty, 1992).

Conclusion

The path toward mastery of mental-state verbs is a complex one, not easily allocated to any single one of:

1. Conceptual development (the concept seems to need linguistic input);
2. Lexical development (the meaning of the word alone isn't the issue);
3. Syntactic development (the surface forms of the complement vary);
4. Semantic development (because syntax provides the bootstrap across *say* and *think*).

I have argued that full mastery of mental verbs and their complements entails a step-wise development, with its final manifestation being a full syntactic structure with complements marked by a PoV. The surface forms may vary, but the path of development is designed to accommodate the variations that occur. What is crucial is that *want* and *irrealis* forms be separated out from *realis,* and that *say* then serve as the syntactic analog for *think* (in those languages in which *say* does not cover both meanings).

However it is arrived at, the final mastery of think PoV complements provides the appropriate representational structure for handling false beliefs, and here there are several alternatives. Some argue that natural language itself is the medium of thinking about such things (Garfield, Peterson, & Perry, 2001; Vygotsky, 1962), though perhaps never reaching phonological form and therefore not conscious (Carruthers, 2002; Jackendoff, 1996). The alternative is a language of thought (Fodor, 1975) independent of language's dissolution (see Varley, 1998, on aphasia) but perhaps triggered by natural language achievements (de Villiers & de Villiers, 2000). This is an exciting frontier of research, and solutions will take great ingenuity.

Acknowledgments I am very grateful to the participants in the Toronto conference, and the excellent feedback from audiences at Carleton University in Ottawa, the University of Massachusetts, Harvard University, and the Society for Research in Child Development in Tampa, Florida. Many thanks to Janet Astington and Jodie Baird, Josef Perner, Tom Roeper, Peter de Villiers, Angelika Kratzer, Deepthi Kamawar, Jennie Pyers, Matthew Phillips, Kristen Asplin, and Valerie Johnson for their persistent and probing questions and suggestions. All remaining errors are of course my own.

Notes

1. The syntax contains the right phrases, but there is a good deal of intervening X' syntax not represented. Linguists reading this will recognize it as a caricature.

2. Thanks to Twila Tardif for the translations.

3. Main clauses have a CP, too, needed as the landing site for wh-movement and auxiliary movement.

4. Once again, this is a drastic simplification for expository purposes. See Schafer and de Villiers (2000).

References

Apperly, I. A., & Robinson, E. J. (1998). Children's mental representation of referential relations. *Cognition, 63,* 287–309.

Asplin, K. (2002). Can complement frames help children learn the meaning of abstract verbs? Unpublished doctoral dissertation, University of Massachusetts, Amherst.

Avrutin, S., & Wexler, K. (2000). Children's knowledge of subjunctive clauses; obviation, binding and reference. *Language Acquisition, 1,* 67–100.

Baker, C. L. (1979). Syntactic theory and the projection problem. *Linguistic Inquiry, 10,* 533–581.

Baker, M. C. (1996). *The polysynthesis parameter.* New York: Oxford University Press.

Bartsch, K., & Wellman, H. M. (1995). *Children talk about the mind.* New York: Oxford University Press.

Bickerton, D. (1981). *The roots of language.* Ann Arbor, MI: Karoma.

Bloom, L., Rispoli, M., Gartner, B., & Hafitz, J. (1989). Acquisition of complementation. *Journal of Child Language, 16,* 101–120.

Brown, R. (1957). Linguistic determinism and the part of speech. *The Journal of Abnormal and Social Psychology, 55,* 1–5.

Carruthers, P. (2002). The cognitive functions of language, *Behavioral and Brain Sciences, 25,* 657–675.

Cattell, R. (1978). On the source of interrogative adverbs. *Language, 34,* 61–77.

Chomsky, N. (1991). *Lectures on government and binding.* Dordrecht: Foris.

Custer, W. (1996). A comparison of young children's understanding of contradictory representations in pretense, memory and belief. *Child Development, 67,* 678–688.

de Villiers, J. G. (1995, March). Steps in the mastery of sentence complements. Paper presented at the Biennial Meeting of the Society for Research in Child Development, Indianapolis, IN.

de Villiers, J. G. (1999). On acquiring the structural representations for false complements. In B. Hollebrandse (Ed.), *New perspectives on language acquisition* (pp. 125–136). Amherst: University of Massachusetts Occasional Papers in Linguistics.

de Villiers, J. G. (2001). Extension, intension and other minds. In M. Almgren, A. Barrena, M-J. Ezeizabarrena, I. Idiazabal, & B. MacWhinney (Eds.), *Research in child language acquisition: Proceedings of the 8th Conference of the International Association for the Study of Child Language* (pp. 1015–1025). Somerville, MA: Cascadilla Press.

de Villiers, J. G., Curran, L., Philip, W., & DeMunn, H. (1998). Acquisition of the quantificational properties of mental predicates. In A. Greenhill, M. Hughes, H. Littlefield, & H. Walsh (Eds.), *Proceedings of the 22nd Annual Boston University Conference on Language Development* (pp.153–164). Somerville, MA: Cascadilla Press.

de Villiers, J. G., & de Villiers, P. A. (2000). Linguistic determinism and the understanding of false beliefs. In P. Mitchell & K. Riggs (Eds.), *Children's reasoning and the mind* (pp. 189–226). Hove, UK: Psychology Press.

de Villiers, J. G., & de Villiers, P. A. (2003). Language for thought: Coming to understand false beliefs. In D. Gentner & S. Goldin-Meadow (Eds.), *Language in mind: Advances in the study of language and thought* (pp. 335–384). Cambridge, MA: MIT Press.

de Villiers, J. G., & Fitneva, S. (1995, September). Language, reference and truth: The child's developing consciousness of other minds. Paper presented at the Conference on Language and Consciousness, Varna, Bulgaria.

de Villiers, J. G., & Pyers, J. E. (2002). Complements to cognition: A longitudinal study of the relationship between complex syntax and false-belief understanding. *Cognitive Development, 17,* 1037–1060.

de Villiers, J. G., Pyers, J. E., & Broderick, K. (1997, November). A longitudinal study of referential *opacity*. Paper presented at the 22nd Annual Boston University Conference on Language Development, Boston, MA.

de Villiers, J. G., Pyers, J., Broderick, K., & Eddy, N. (2002, July). A longitudinal study of explanations of action. Paper in symposium on *The language of mental state explanations: Conceptual, semantic and syntactic issues in normal and delayed development*, presented at the IASCL/SCRLD meeting, Madison, WI.

de Villiers, J. G., & Roeper, T. (in preparation). Point of View in language acquisition.

de Villiers, P. A., Burns, F., & Pearson, B. (2003). The role of language in the Theory of Mind development of language-impaired children: Complementing theories. In B. Beachley, A. Brown, & F. Conlin (Eds.), *Proceedings of the 27th Annual Boston University Conference on Language Development* (pp. 232–242). Somerville, MA: Cascadilla Press.

de Villiers, P. A., de Villiers, J. G., Schick, B., & Hoffmeister, R. (2001, April). Theory of mind development in signing and non-signing deaf children: The impact of sign language on social cognition. Poster presented at the biennial meeting of the Society for Research in Child Development, Minneapolis, MN.

Evans, N. (2003). *Bininj Gun-wok: a pan-dialectal grammar of Mayali, Kunwinjku and Kune*. Canberra: Pacific Linguistics.

Felser, C. (2002). *Verbal complement clauses: A minimalist study of direct perception constructions*. Philadelphia: John Benjamins.

Fenson, L., Dale, P. S., Reznick, J. S., Thal, D., Bates, E., Hartung, J. P., Pethick, S., & Reilly, J. S. (1993). *The MacArthur Communicative Development Inventories: User's guide and technical manual*. San Diego: Singular Publishing Group.

Fisher, C., Gleitman, H., & Gleitman, L. R. (1991). On the semantic content of subcategorization frames. *Cognitive Psychology, 23*, 331–392.

Fisher, C., Hall, D. G., Rakowitz, S., & Gleitman, L. R. (1994). When it is better to receive than give: Syntactic and conceptual constraints on vocabulary growth. *Lingua, 92*, 333–375.

Fodor, J. (1975). *The language of thought*. New York: Crowell.

Frege, G. (1892/1960). On sense and reference. In P. Geach and M. Black (Eds.), *Philosophical writings of Gottlob Frege* (pp. 56–78). Oxford: Basil Blackwell.

Garfield, J. L., Peterson, C. C., Garson, B., Nevin, A., & Perry, T. (2002). Let's pretend! The role of pretence in the acquisition of theory of mind. Unpublished manuscript, Smith College and University of Tasmania.

Garfield, J. L., Peterson, C. C., & Perry, T. (2001). Social cognition, language acquisition and the development of the theory of mind. *Mind and Language, 16*, 494–541.

Gleitman, L. (1990). The structural sources of verb meanings. *Language Acquisition, 1*, 3–55.

Gleitman, L., & Gleitman, H. (1992). A picture is worth a thousand words, but that's the problem: The role of syntax in vocabulary acquisition. *Current Directions in Psychological Science, 1*, 31–35.

Hale, C. M., & Tager-Flusberg, H. (2003). The influence of language on theory of mind: A training study. *Developmental Science, 6*, 346–359.

Hanson, C. (1992). *A Daoist theory of Chinese thought: A philosophical interpretation*. Oxford: Oxford University Press.

Hare, B., & Wrangham, R. (2002). Integrating two evolutionary models for the study of social cognition. In M. Bekoff, C. Allen, & G. M. Burghardt (Eds.), *The cognitive animal* (pp. 363–369). Cambridge, MA: MIT Press.

Hauser, M. D. (1999). Primate representations and expectations: Mental tools for navigating in a social world. In P. D. Zelazo, J. W. Astington, & D. R. Olson (Eds.), *Developing theories of intention* (pp. 169–194). Mahwah, NJ: Erlbaum.

Hegarty, M. (1992). Adjunct extraction without traces. In D. Bates (Ed.), *The Proceedings of the 10th West Coast Conference on Formal Linguistics* (pp. 209–222). Stanford, CA: CSLI.

Hollebrandse, B. (1999). The acquisition of Sequence of Tense. Unpublished doctoral dissertation, University of Massachusetts, Amherst.

Hollebrandse, B. (2000). The acquisition of Sequence of Tense and Point of View. In M. Almgren, A. Barrena, M-J. Ezeizabarrena, I. Idiazabal, & B. MacWhinney (Eds.), *Research in Child Language Acquisition: Proceedings of the 8th Conference of the International Association for the Study of Child Language* (pp. 1038–1045). Somerville, MA: Cascadilla Press.

Jackendoff, R. (1996). How language helps us think. *Pragmatics and Cognition, 4,* 1–34.

Johnson, V. (2001). Fast mapping verb meaning from argument structure. Unpublished doctoral dissertation, University of Massachusetts, Amherst.

Johnson, V., de Villiers, J .G., D'Amato, K., Deschamps, C., & Huneke, S. (2002, July). Can syntax give you complements? Poster presented at the IASCL/SCRLD meeting, Madison, WI.

Kamawar, D., & Olson, D. R. (1999). Children's representational theory of language: The problem of opaque contexts. *Cognitive Development, 14,* 531–548.

Kiparsky, P., & Kiparsky, C. (1970). Fact. In M. Bierwisch & K. E. Heidolph (Eds.), *Progress in linguistics* (pp. 143–173). The Hague: Mouton.

Landau, B., & Gleitman, L. (1985). *Language and experience: Evidence from the blind child.* Cambridge, MA: Harvard University Press.

Larson, R. K., & Ludlow, P. (1993). Interpreted logical forms. *Synthese, 95,* 305–355.

Lederer, A., Gleitman, H., & Gleitman, L. R. (1995). Verbs of a feather flock together: Semantic information in the structure of maternal speech. In M. Tomasello & W. E. Merriman (Eds.), *Beyond names for things: Young children's acquisition of verbs* (pp. 277–297). Hillsdale, NJ: Erlbaum.

Lohmann, H., & Tomasello, M. (2003). The role of language in the development of false belief understanding: A training study. *Child Development, 74,* 1130–1144.

Maratsos, M., & Deak, G. (1995). Hedgehogs, foxes and the acquisition of verb meaning. In M. Tomasello & W. E. Merriman (Eds.), *Beyond names for things: Young children's acquisition of verbs* (pp. 377–401). Hillsdale, NJ: Erlbaum.

Moore, C., Bryant, D., & Furrow, D. (1989). Mental terms and the development of certainty. *Child Development, 60,* 167–171.

Naigles, L. (1990). Children use syntax to learn verb meanings. *Journal of Child Language, 17,* 357–374.

Perner, J. (1991). On representing that: The asymmetry between belief and desire in children's theory of mind. In D. Frye & C. Moore (Eds.), *Children's theories of mind* (pp. 139–155). Hillsdale, NJ: Erlbaum.

Perner, J. (2000). About + belief + counterfactual. In P. Mitchell & K. Riggs (Eds.), *Children's reasoning and the mind* (pp. 367–397). Hove, UK: Psychology Press.

Perner, J., Sprung, M., Zauner, P., & Haider, H. (2003). *Want that* is understood well before *say that, think that,* and false belief: A test of de Villiers' linguistic determinism on German-speaking children. *Child Development, 74,* 179–188.

Pinker, S. (1989). *Learnability and cognition: The acquisition of argument structure.* Cambridge, MA: MIT Press.

Pinker, S. (1994). How could a child use verb syntax to learn verb meanings? *Lingua, 92*, 377–410.

Povinelli, D. J., Bering, J., & Giambrone, S. (2000). Toward a science of other minds: Escaping the argument by analogy. *Cognitive Science, 24*, 509–541.

Premack, D., & Woodruff, G. (1978). Does the chimpanzee have a theory of mind? *Behavioral and Brain Sciences, 1*, 515–526.

Pyers, J. (2001, June). Three stages in the understanding of false belief in Nicaraguan signers: The interaction of social experience, language emergence, and conceptual development. In R. Senghas (Chair), The Emergence of Nicaraguan Sign Language: Questions of development, acquisition, and evolution. Invited symposium conducted at the 31st annual meeting of the Piaget Society, Berkeley, CA.

Quine, W. V. O. (1960). *Word and object.* Cambridge, MA: MIT Press.

Radford, A. (1988). *Transformational grammar.* Cambridge: Cambridge University Press.

Rakoczy, H. (2003, April). The role of experience and discourse in the developing understanding of pretense: A training study. Paper presented at the biennial meeting of the Society for Research in Child Development, Tampa., FL.

Roeper, T., & de Villiers, J. G. (1994). Lexical links in the Wh-chain. In B. Lust, G. Hermon, & J. Kornfilt (Eds.), *Syntactic theory and first language acquisition: Cross linguistic perspectives,* Vol. II: *Binding, dependencies and learnability* (pp. 357–390). Hillsdale, NJ: Erlbaum.

Ruffman,T., Slade, L., Rowlandson, K., Rumsey, C., & Garnham, A. (2003). How language relates to belief, desire, and emotion understanding. *Cognitive Development, 18*, 139–158.

Russell, J. (1987). "Can we say . . . ?" Children's understanding of intensionality. *Cognition, 2*, 289–308.

Schafer, R., & de Villiers, J. (2000). Imagining articles: What *a* and *the* can tell us about the emergence of DP. In S. C. Howell, S. A. Fish, & T. Keith-Lucas (Eds.), *Proceedings of the 24th Boston University Conference on Language Development* (pp. 609–620), Somerville, MA: Cascadilla Press.

Schick, B., Hoffmeister, R., de Villiers, P. A., & de Villiers, J. G. (in preparation). Theory of Mind: Language and cognition in deaf children.

Schwitzgebel, E. (1999). Representation and desire: A philosophical error with consequences for theory-of-mind research. *Philosophical Psychology, 12*, 157–180.

Segal, G. (1998). Representing representations. In P. Carruthers and J. Boucher (Eds.), *Language and thought* (pp. 146–161). Cambridge: Cambridge University Press.

Shatz, M., Wellman, H. M., & Silber, S. (1983). The acquisition of mental verbs: A systematic investigation of the first reference to mental state. *Cognition, 14*, 301–321.

Tardif, T., & Wellman, H. M. (2000). Acquisition of mental state language in Mandarin- and Cantonese-speaking children. *Developmental Psychology, 36*, 25–43.

Tomasello, M. (1995). Pragmatic contexts for early word learning. In M. Tomasello and W. E. Merriman (Eds.), *Beyond names for things: Young children's acquisition of verbs* (pp. 114–147). Hillsdale, NJ: Erlbaum.

Tomasello, M. (1996). Chimpanzee social cognition (Commentary on Povinelli & Eddy). *Monographs of the Society for Research in Child Development, 61*(3, Serial no. 247), pp. 161–173.

van der Lely, H., Hennessey, S., & Battell, J. (2001). Linguistic determinism and false belief: Insight from children with specific language impairment. Unpublished manuscript, University College, London.

Varley, R. (1998). Aphasic language, aphasic thought. In P. Carruthers and J. Boucher (Eds.), *Language and thought* (pp. 128–145). Cambridge: Cambridge University Press.

Vinden, P. G., & Astington, J. W. (2000). Culture and understanding other minds. In S. Baron-Cohen, H. Tager-Flusberg, H., & D. J. Cohen (Eds.), *Understanding other minds: Perspectives from developmental cognitive neuroscience* (pp. 503–519). Oxford: Oxford University Press.

Vygotsky, L.S. (1962). *Thought and language.* Cambridge, MA: MIT Press.

Witt, J., & de Villiers, J. G. (2001, April). Understanding desires: Preschoolers' limitations. Poster presented at the biennial meeting of the Society for Research in Child Development, Minneapolis, MN.

Ziatas, K., Durkin, K., & Pratt, C. (1998). Belief term development in children with autism, Asperger syndrome, specific language impairment, and normal development: Links to theory of mind development. *Journal of Child Psychology and Psychiatry and Allied Disciplines, 39,* 755–763.

What Does "That" Have to Do with Point of View? Conflicting Desires and "Want" in German

Josef Perner, Petra Zauner, and Manuel Sprung

At the age of about 4 years, noticeable changes occur in children's understanding of the mind, in particular the understanding that a person can have a false belief about some state of affairs (Perner, Leekam, & Wimmer, 1987; Wimmer & Perner, 1983)—a development that has been intensively researched (Wellman, Cross, & Watson, 2001). This development has been found to relate strongly to children's growing linguistic competence. It relates to measures of verbal intelligence in typical development (Astington & Jenkins, 1995, 1999; Jenkins & Astington, 1996), as well as in children with autism and other developmental disorders (Happé, 1995; Tager-Flusberg, 1993, 1996; Tager-Flusberg & Sullivan, 1994). Also, the language delay surrounding deafness seems to delay theory-of-mind development in its wake (Gale, de Villiers, de Villiers, & Pyers, 1996; Peterson & Siegal, 1995, 1999). This relationship between theory of mind and linguistic development seems particularly strong for children's mastery of the false-belief test, their syntactic competence in producing complement constructions (using the Index of Productive Syntax; Scarborough, 1990), and their memory for complements in statements about mistakes (de Villiers & de Villiers, 2000, p. 200ff; de Villiers & Pyers, 1997).

Two Theories of the Relation between Language and Theory of Mind

Jill de Villiers (1995) had anticipated these developmental links between theory of mind and language development with the specific theory that thinking about mental states requires certain syntactic features in one's language of thought that originate from the spoken language. De Villiers (this volume, chapter 10; see also de Villiers & de Villiers, 2000) suggests that the critical syntactic element is a point-of-view (PoV) feature on complement phrase (CP) headings, also occurring on other syntactic elements, that gives children an understanding of points of view (perspective). This claim makes de Villiers's theory very similar, in several essential points, to what one of us has been claiming for some time about children's intellectual change around 4 years of age (Perner, 1991, 1995; Perner, Stummer, Sprung, & Doherty, 2002).

The core developmental assumption is the same in the two theories. Perner (1991) saw that the ability to understand belief depends on the ability to realize that things in the world (states of affairs, external referents, or—we now like to use the most neutral terminology—"targets") can be represented as being different than they are (known to the child). Frege (1892/1960) called this "sense" or "mode of presentation," which is in essence the same as the *perspective* or *point of view* taken on the external referent. Perner, Brandl, and Garnham (2003) analyze perspective problems as problems where the difference between perspectives needs to be confronted and where some representational element must be taken into account in order to maintain a coherent view of the world.

J. de Villiers (this volume, chapter 10) makes the same developmental claim by suggesting that around 4 years of age, children acquire PoV markers on particular syntactic elements, and it is the way these markers function that allows children to keep distinct differences in point of view. As a consequence of their core claims, the two theories share the important consequence that they are opposed to theory of mind as a domain specific module, as most radically formulated by Leslie (1994). In opposition to modularity, both theories deny theory of mind the modular feature of being impenetrable (see Fodor, 1975), because substantial changes in theory of mind are considered to be due to domain general changes in understanding perspective (Perner, Stummer, et al., 2002) or to changes in a different, language module, that is to say, changes in syntax (J. de Villiers, this volume, chapter 10).

Despite these core similarities, there are, of course, interesting differences. The main difference is that we have described the changes as a conceptual advance without further specifying its particular nature. One consequence of our view is that children who have acquired this understanding should be able to talk about it. However, there is usually some gap between children's ability to make correct behavioral predictions in a false-belief test and their ability to explain the erroneous behavior in a sensible way (Clements & Perner, 1994; Perner, Lang, & Kloo, 2002; Wimmer & Mayringer, 1998). Moreover, Clements and Perner (1994, 2001) found that, almost a year before children can make correct predictions, they show some understanding of the protagonist's mistaken action in their visual orienting behavior (see also Carpenter, Call, & Tomasello, 2002; Happé & Loth, 2002; Ruffman, Garnham, Import, & Connolly, 2001).

De Villiers's theory might hold an elegant solution to this early "implicit" understanding of perspective differences, because her proposed mechanism is a syntactic procedure for managing contradictory contents of different perspectives that is not explicitly addressable and usable for justifications. Rather than being a threat to her theory (de Villiers & de Villiers, 2003), these findings of early implicit understanding may follow naturally from her theory.

Another difference between de Villiers's theory and ours concerns the developmental relationship between theory of mind and language development. We have no great theoretical commitment on this point and see the link by default in the role of language as provider of information that is required for building a theory of mind (e.g., Perner, 2000, p. 378), a position that de Villiers characterizes as language-as-communication (de Villiers & de Villiers, 2000, 2003). De Villiers, in contrast, has a substantial theoretical stake in that developmental link. Growing linguistic competence, in particular syntactic competence, shapes the thoughts with which one thinks about the mind. Without this particular syntactic device of PoV markers, there could be no understanding of false beliefs and other cases of perspective differences. We can see further theoretical mileage in de Villiers's more detailed account, although we also encounter some conceptual problems in need of clarification, as well as empirical evidence, that together ask for an elaboration of her theory.

Realis, Irrealis, and Point of View

Perner (1991) described the development of children's understanding of truth in the following way. By 2 years of age (and probably earlier), children can evaluate the truth of a statement (Hummer, Wimmer, & Antes, 1993; Pea, 1980); that is, they recognize the *realis* force of a statement and check whether it is appropriate. They can also relate statements to fictitious worlds (e.g., pretend scenarios; Harris & Kavanaugh, 1993); that is, they understand that they are meant to be *irrealis.* In contrast, 2-year-olds cannot understand that something that is false can be mistaken as *realis,* which is exactly what is required for understanding false belief in distinction to pretense, or a sincere but mistaken statement based on a false belief as opposed to a pretend statement. Only around 4 years of age, when they understand perspectival relativity (as a core feature of representations), can children understand that within a different perspective, a proposition that is evidently false from the child's perspective (i.e., not an appropriate description of reality) can be *realis.*

De Villiers's theory adds an interesting twist to this developmental description: The *realis-irrealis* distinction is clearly signaled by syntactic constructions. Tensed sentences or complements (sentential phrases) carry the *realis* force. Belief sentences (in English) can be formulated only with tensed that-clauses;

hence, children take the complement information as *realis*. So, if someone says about a Smarties box filled with pencils, "There are Smarties in this box," children take it as a description of the box's true contents and reject it as false, if they know better. Before they understand perspective—before the age of 4 years without PoV markers—they have no means for remembering this inappropriate *realis* claim, since they have no way of distinguishing a *realis* claim from their point of view from a *realis* claim within someone else's perspective. Hence, when asked, "What did she say was in the box?" they can answer only in terms of their own perspective that she said (*realis*) what they themselves know to have been in the box. The same holds for questions about that person's beliefs.

In contrast, language conducive of leading children into pretense and fictitious scenarios avoids straight factive statements. Let us take an example from Harris and Kavanaugh (1993, pp. 46–47). The experimenter introduced a toy monkey: "The monkey likes to eat chocolate. Let's give him some chocolate." A brown block was placed on a paper plate and put in front of the monkey. . . . "Oh, dear! Watch what naughty Teddy does," spoken as Teddy was "pouring" pretend tea from an empty teapot over the "chocolate." Then several questions were asked, in particular: "Is the chocolate wet or dry?" And almost all 2- to 3-year-olds (Table 28, p. 52) interpreted this question within the pretend mode and answered "wet," despite the blatantly obvious fact that there was not a single drop of liquid anywhere.

Presumably, the results would have been much less successful if the experimenters had started: "This is a tea party. Teddy pretends that this (empty) pot is full of tea, and that this (block) is a piece of chocolate. Now, Teddy pours some tea on this chocolate. Is the chocolate now wet or dry?" Plausibly, this seems a much less genuine way of introducing a pretend mode because of the extensive use of tensed sentential complements, which were completely avoided in the actual version used by Harris and Kavanaugh. Use of tensed clauses might explain why Leekam and Perner (briefly reported at the first theory-of-mind conference in Toronto, June 1986) had no success in showing children's ability to adjust their answers to a pretend scenario in view of a contrasting reality. Leekam and Perner worked with a toy dog that was so fluffy that one could not tell head from tail until one searched for its eyes under the hair. The objective was to have a tightly controlled comparison between a pretend and a false-belief condition. For that reason, the pretend story was introduced by stating that the story protagonist knows where the head really is but that *he pretends that the head is where the tail is*, in contrast to the belief story, in which children were told that *he thinks that the head is where the tail is*. Then he goes out to get milk and when he comes back, children were asked: "Where will he put the bowl of milk?" The children had to indicate the tail end of the dog. Children found this as difficult for pretense as for the false-belief story. No wonder! We were probably too insensitive to the use of appropriate linguistic cues, including avoiding tensed that-complements, in our pretend instructions. In any case, the to-infinitive form is preferred by young children when talking about pretense.

Some Useful Terminological Distinctions

Although our view of children's relevant development meshes nicely with de Villiers's description, her terminology makes this sometimes difficult to see. Let us clear these terminological obstacles.

The Proposition and the Attitude

The verbs that describe mental states, acts of communication, or informational relations (e.g., *imply, indicate*) can be characterized as *propositional attitudes*. That is, they describe the specific way in which a person or other sentient organism relates to a proposition. These verbs allow for the special grammatical construction of embedded clauses, which express the relevant proposition. These syntactic constructions are special because they create an *opaque* or *intensional* context for the embedded clause, which gives that clause a certain semantic independence from the embedding sentence. One such feature is that they are *not truth functional*; that is, the truth of the embedding sentence is not determined by the truth of the embedded clause. De Villiers emphasizes a particular case, in which an embedded proposition can be "false" without upsetting the truth of the embedding sentence: "young children have an 'underarticulated' clause structure that lacks some crucial feature, namely, whatever it is that allows the embedded proposition to be false without disturbing the overall truth value. Interestingly only embedded complements have the property that they can be false yet the sentence that contains them can still be true" (de Villiers & de Villiers, 2000, p. 197).

It is important to note that verbs of desire (*want*) are also propositional attitudes with embedded clauses that express propositions whose truth is independent of the embedding sentence, and not only cognitive verbs (*know, think, forget*) or verbs of communication (*say* and other assertoric speech acts). There is, of course, an important difference between these groups of verbs in terms of the fundamental kind of *attitude* they express. As Searle (1983), following Anscombe (1957), pointed out, the embedded propositions specify the satisfaction conditions for each attitude; there are two fundamentally different kinds of attitude that differ in their *direction of fit*. Following the classical tripartite division of psychological processes into cognitive, conative, and affective (Hilgard, 1980), the two fundamental attitudes could be labeled *cognitive* and *conative attitudes*. The function of cognitive attitudes is to capture the state of the world accurately. These attitudes satisfy their purpose only if the proposition they relate to is true of the world. For instance, when I *say* that I own a piece of chocolate, then this is a satisfactory speech act only if the proposition *I own a piece of chocolate* is true.

In contrast, conative attitude verbs denote mental states or speech acts whose function is to specify how the world is desired to be. These states are satisfied only when the world conforms to what is being desired. For instance, when I *want* to own a piece of chocolate, then my desire is satisfied only if the proposition *I own a piece of chocolate* is true.

Notably, to understand the fundamental meaning of what is being said with "He *thinks/says* that he owns a piece of chocolate" as well as with "He *wants* to own a piece of chocolate" requires an appreciation that the statements can be true even though the embedded proposition is false. For the think/say statement, this is required to judge whether what he says is correct, and for the want-statement, it is necessary to judge whether or not his desire is satisfied. In sum, we can say that "whatever it is that allows the embedded proposition to be false without disturbing the overall truth value" (de Villiers & de Villiers, 2000, p. 197) is required for understanding desires as well as beliefs.

The Falsity of Propositions and the "Falseness" of Attitudes (Mental States)

We have seen that it is necessary for understanding statements about cognitive attitudes (thinking, saying), as well as about conative attitudes (wanting), to appreciate the potential *falsity* of embedded propositions, that is, the possibility that the statement about the attitude can be true even when the embedded proposition is false.

However, we have also seen that the function of these attitudes is fundamentally different. The function of cognitive attitudes is to represent the world truthfully. Beliefs and sincere assertions contain, therefore, an (implicit, practical) claim to truth. For this reason, we tend to transfer the *falsity* of the embedded proposition to the *falseness* of the attitude when speaking of "false beliefs" and "false statements." When de Villiers and de Villiers (2000, p. 198) say that "only complements of mental and communication verbs can be 'false' propositions," they presumably speak of this *falseness* of the attitude.

In contrast, the function of desires is not to represent the world truthfully but to stipulate how the world is desired to be. The falsity of the embedded proposition, therefore, translates not into a "false desire" but into a "unsatisfied desire." In that sense, de Villiers and de Villiers are right to reserve "falseness" for mental (i.e., cognitive) and communication verbs. However, strictly speaking, their denying that the complement propositions of desire verbs can be false is not warranted. It is important to keep these attributions of falsity (of propositions) and "falseness" of attitudes distinct and to realize that the problem of false embedded propositions is common to verbs of both belief and desire. Hence, the syntactic mechanism, postulated by de Villiers (1997, as cited in de Villiers & de Villiers, 2000, p. 198), that PoV markers relativize truth to possible worlds is critical for understanding desires, as well as beliefs. Further, what is critical for beliefs is to relativize the claim to truth (*realis* force) about the real world to a different perspective. This is not required for desires, because the proposition embedded in statements of desire has no *realis* force.

Understanding "Want" in German

We now turn to some data that speak partly for and partly pose some problem for de Villiers's theory. A central claim by de Villiers is her "linguistic determinism," the idea that thinking about mental states comes from internalizing the language with which these states are expressed in the child's linguistic environment. Our data on German-speaking children's understanding of "want" are relevant to this claim.

German grammar is analogous to English grammar with respect to verbs of belief (*glauben, denken*), both languages requiring finite complements (for third-party belief ascription they are in fact *necessary*). German is also analogous in its rules for expressing desires concerning one's own actions. They can be expressed by using an infinitive complement (1a) just as in English (1b).

(1) a. Mutter will ins Bett gehen.
     b. Mom wants to go to bed.

Importantly, German differs from English in its grammar for verbs of desire (*wollen, mögen*) that something happen or that someone else do something. In English, a nonfinite, infinitive phrase *must* be used as complement (2a). It *cannot* be a finite complement phrase (2b).

(2) a. Mom wants Andy to go to bed.
     b. *Mom wants that Andy goes to bed.

In German, on the contrary, a finite *that*-complement must be used in these cases—and the *that* (*dass*) is strictly obligatory (3a). Use of an infinite complement (3b) is illegal, in contrast to English (2a).

(3) a. Mutter will, dass Andreas ins Bett geht.
        [*Mom wants *that* Andy goes to bed].
     b. * Mutter will Andreas ins Bett gehen.
        [Mom wants Andy to go to bed].

Perner, Sprung, Zauner, and Haider (2003) tested children's memory of false complements in statements (verb of communication: "say"), their ability to infer the false complement of false beliefs from false assertions and false complements of unfulfilled desires from statements of what was desired. In all stories, a hand puppet was used, together with a cardboard screen that prevented puppet and child from seeing the scene on the other side. This target scene was different for each sketch. For example, in the *rabbit sketch* there was a rabbit and a small box. The rabbit was sitting in its box, behind the cardboard screen, and so child and hand puppet couldn't see what the rabbit was doing. Now, in the *WANT condition* of this sketch, the experimenter asked the puppet what the rabbit *should do*, and the puppet responded: "The rabbit should jump out of the box." After the puppet's response, the puppet was removed and put under the table, and then the experimenter removed the cardboard screen so that the child could see what the rabbit was actually doing (i.e., sitting in its box) and asked the child the critical test question and control questions:

> WANT-question: "What does the puppet *want* the rabbit to do?".
> ["Was *will* die Puppe, *dass* der Hase tut?"]
> (i.e., *What does the Puppet *want that* the rabbit does?)

In the *SAY and THINK conditions* the experimenter asked the puppet what the rabbit *is doing* and the puppet responded: "The rabbit is jumping out of the box." Then the experimenter put the puppet under the table, removed the cardboard screen, and asked the critical test question:

> SAY-question: "What did the puppet *say* that the rabbit was[1] doing?"
> ["Was *hat* die Puppe *gesagt, dass* der Hase tut?"]
> THINK-question: "What does the puppet *think* that the rabbit is doing?"
> ["Was *glaubt* die Puppe, *dass* der Hase tut?"]

Children were also given two traditional false-belief tests (Wimmer & Perner, 1983).

The results are shown in figure 11.1. Statistical analysis confirms the picture that children's memory for complements is much better for unfulfilled desire statements than for belief statements, which goes hand in hand with their ability to pass the false-belief task. Memory for complements of false statements, though significantly worse than memory for desires, is also substantially better than memory for beliefs. In an earlier study (Perner, Sprung, et al., 2003, Experiment 1) that used material similar to that used in this experiment, in de Villiers and Pyers (1997), and in Hale and Tager-Flusberg (2003), memory for belief complements and for false statements tended to be nearly equal. One reason for this discrepancy may be the fact that the stories in the present study were enacted, whereas in our earlier experiment and in the other studies only pictorial support was used. Enactment may give characters' speech a manifestation

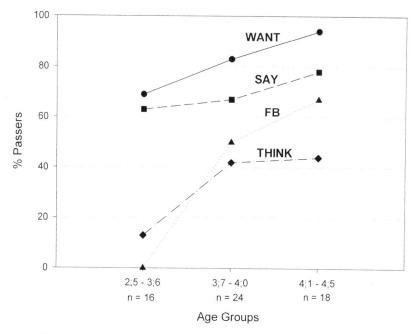

Figure 11.1. Percentage of children per age group passing each of the four complement tests. (Data from Perner, Sprung, Zauner, & Haider, 2003).

independent of what the speech is about. And this may have helped some children to simply remember what the character had said.

The fact that memory for desire complements is so much better than memory for belief complements in German-speaking children poses a problem for de Villiers's theory about the function of complement phrase (CP) markers. Let us briefly review the argument. As we have seen, the CP marker cannot just bring in the means for representing (in one's language of thought) the idea that someone can actually believe something even though the proposition that characterizes this content is false. If this were all, then children should also have problems understanding unfulfilled desires. But as data with English-speaking children (Wellman & Banerjee, 1991; Wellman & Woolley, 1990; Yuill, 1984; Yuill, Perner, Pearson, Peerbhoy, & van den Ende, 1996) and also our data on German children show, children understand unfulfilled desires substantially earlier than false beliefs. Hence, we argued, supported by de Villiers's suggestion that desires are not "false" but only *irrealis*, that there must be a particular difficulty with CP markers in those grammatical constructions that are used with verbs of belief and communication. And de Villiers suggests that this is indeed the case, because these cognitive verbs take that-complements, whereas verbs of desire take to+infinitive complements. This, however, implies that German-speaking children should have the same problems with complements of desire. As the data show, this is clearly not the case.

A similar problem for de Villiers's CP-marker theory is also posed by English-speaking children. They can deal noticeably earlier with complements of the verb "pretend," which also takes a that-complement, than with complements of "say" and "think" (Custer, 1996; Garfield, Peterson, Garson, Nevin, & Perry, 2002). It is also interesting to note the English "pretend" behaves grammatically like "want" in German. It takes a to+infinitive complement when one pretends to be or to do something (e.g., "I pretend to be a king."). It requires a finite that-complement when one pretends that something else is or does something (e.g., "I pretend *that* this banana is a telephone.").

A slightly different problem for de Villiers's theory is raised by data from Tardif and Wellman (2000). In both Mandarin and Cantonese, it is possible to use the same relatively simple grammatical construction to talk about beliefs and desires. Yet, in Tardif and Wellman's (2000) report, there was a much earlier and a higher frequency of desire terms than talk about belief, as was also the case with the English data (Bartsch & Wellman, 1995). This result raises the question of what delays Chinese children's understanding of (talk about) belief if it isn't the CP markers attached to finite that-complements.

At a more general level, the findings on German and Chinese children make a very simple point against linguistic determinism of theory of mind. Regardless of how desires and beliefs are expressed in a particular language—neither requiring complicated finite that-complements (Chinese), both requiring that-complements (German), or only belief but not desire requiring that-complements (English)—children understand and talk about desire substantially earlier than belief.

Using "That" in German to Express Desire and Belief

In the study by Perner, Sprung, et al. (2003), we added an informal exploratory test after children had answered our test questions in order to see whether they would use an explicit "that" in their response to prompts like: "And what did the puppet want/say/think . . . ?" The data are incomplete, and we didn't record how children who didn't use "that" answered. That's why we didn't even analyze these data until after we had published the report. When we did look at the data recently, they were not as incomplete as we had originally thought, though they are still limited in their value, especially because what matters is not the use of "that" as much as whether a tensed complement was used, that is, responses like "she thought the rabbit was jumping out of the box" (a tensed complement) was not counted as it should have been simply because no "that" was used. Nevertheless, we think the data are still interesting and give some support to de Villiers's theory.

As with memory for complements (figure 11.1), where we scored children as "passers" and "failers," we scored children as "users" if they used a "that" on both occasions and as "nonusers" otherwise. Figure 11.2 shows the percentage of "that" users (broken lines) in relation to the complement data (full lines). Interestingly, the percentage of "that" users is practically the same for the three conditions—whether children completed a want-, a say- or a think-sentence with "that". Moreover, all three lines crowd around the percentage of children passing the memory for think-complements. This looks like good evidence for de Villiers's theory that the use of "that" provides the basis for thinking with that-clauses.

This evidence is further strengthened by a significant correlation between memory for think-complements and passing or failing *that*-use ($r = .58$). This correlation remains strong even after age and verbal intelligence scores (KABC; Kaufman & Kaufman, 1994) are partialed out: $pr = .52$, $p < .01$.

Another impressive aspect is the consistency with which children (scored on a pass-fail basis) use "that" across the want-, say-, and think-tasks. All three correlation coefficients are between .57 and .70. For further analysis, we formed a general *that*-use score of 0 to 6 for each child to see how well the score corre-

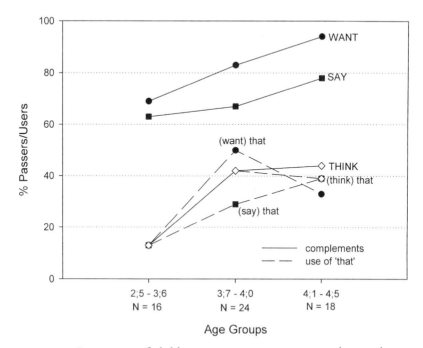

Figure 11.2. Percentage of children per age group passing each complement test and using "that."

lates with their ability to remember complements and to pass the false-belief task. These correlations are shown in table 11.1. Although the correlations are not as impressive as the ones between memory for think-complements and use of "that" in think sentences, there is still a notable correlation between the general that-use score and memory for think-complements, even after age and verbal intelligence (KABC scores) are partialed out. However, there is no sizable correlation between *that*-use and passing the false-belief test, and the correlation reduces absolutely to zero when age and verbal intelligence are partialed out.

In sum, these data provide quite strong evidence that there is a link between children's use of "that" and their answers to think-questions based on what people said. The age at which children start to use "that" also coincides quite closely with the age at which they become able to pass the false-belief test. However, the lack of correlations among these abilities leaves open the question how close a link there might be. In any case, we can say that "that" has to do with memory for what people think on the basis of what they had said. However, and more important—what does "that" have to do with point of view?

What Are Points of View—Can They Be *Irrealis*?

J. De Villiers (this volume, chapter 10, p. 211) proposes that "the verb *think* assigns a PoV to the complement." The main function of these PoV markers on CPs is to make clear that the tensed that-complement is not to be taken *realis* of the speaker's world but is to be taken relative to a possible world. One problem with this position is that what someone is said to believe to be the case,

Table 11.1 Correlations (Pearson's r) above Main Diagonal and Partial Correlations with Children's Age and Verbal Intelligence Scores (KABC) Accounted for [in Brackets] Below the Main Diagonal

	KABC	Want	Say	Think	"that"	FB
Age	.57**	.23	.28*	.14	.42**	.45**
KABC	—	.32*	.00	−.05	.28*	.32*
Memory for Complements						
WANT	—	—	.35**	.31*	.41**	.33*
SAY	—	[.37**]	—	.38**	.31*	.28*
THINK	—	[.34*]	[.34*]	—	.38**	.27*
Use of "that"	—	[.35**]	[.19]	[.37**]	—	.19
False belief	—	[.24]	[.15]	[.25]	[.00]	—

* p < .05
** p < .01

even when it is a false belief, is *realis* about the speaker's world and not about some other possible world. And that's the reason why it is a Point of View (PoV) marker and not a Possible World (PW) marker. It gives a different (in the case of false belief, a wrong) perspective on that world.

Moreover, we have another problem with de Villiers's restrictive application of the PoV-marker, because a difference of perspective can occur not just about reality but also about possible states of the world, in particular about desired states. A perspective difference between desires becomes explicit, for instance, in the case of competition and in the subjective satisfaction about a wicked deed. There is increasing evidence that children understand these cases at the same time as they understand belief. And that fact raises a question for de Villiers's theory: why are perspective differences of desire understood at the same age as those of belief, even though there is no syntactic backup for a PoV marker in *irrealis* complements of desire statements (e.g., "I want myself to win and him to lose, while he wants himself to win and me to lose")? To explain this may not be an insurmountable hurdle for the theory, but the developmental data ought to be a relevant area of application for the theory, as discussed later. However, before we report on these data, we make some clarifications on what we think points of view (perspectives) are.

Perspective Differences

We are faced with a difference in perspective when we encounter two different representations (e.g., pictures, sentences) that show (are about) the same *thing* (representational target). One way of testing that they have the same target is to check whether their different contents can be integrated into a unified representation without contradiction. For instance, figure 11.3 illustrates Abe and Bea looking at the same scene of a squat rock and a long pole between them. Now, let us assume that Abe says, "the pole is long," and Bea says, "the rock is squat"; then both descriptions can be simply conjoined: "The pole is long AND the rock is squat." Figure 11.3 gives the pictorial equivalent of these two statements and their conjunction. This indicates that the two original statements are descriptions of different parts of a scene, that is, they have different representational targets. In contrast, if Abe says, "the rock is behind the pole," and Bea, "the pole is behind the rock," then these two statements cannot be integrated without contradiction: "the rock is behind the pole AND the pole is behind the rock." This indicates that the two people describe not different parts of the scene but one and the same part (the spatial relations between the two objects) from different perspectives. Integration of these two statements is possible only when they are augmented by some reference to being representational contents, as in *"From person A's point of view* the rock

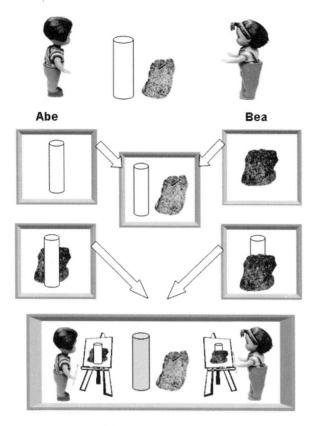

Figure 11.3. Perspective problems.

is behind the pole AND *from person B's point of view* the pole is behind the rock." Again, figure 11.3 gives a pictorial version of this problem and a metapictorial solution to the integration problem: a picture of Abe and Bea each making a picture of the objects. In this case, we speak of a *perspective problem* or *perspective task* when such a meta-representational addition is required to coherently represent the task at hand.

Simple Desires

Understanding people's desires does not usually create a perspective problem—not even the understanding that people have different desires. For instance, if Abe wants to have an apple and Bea wants to have a banana, then the following two statements express what each of them wants: "Abe has an apple," and "Bea has a banana." If I need to understand what both want, then I can simply conjoin the two statements into one: "Abe has an apple AND Bea has a banana."

Incompatible Desires

Such simple conjunction of what is being desired is not possible when people desire different states of the world that are mutually exclusive (within the powers of our imagination). Competitive, zero-sum games are prototypical. Take the good old penny-hiding game. I hide the penny behind my back and then show you my two fists. You have to point to the fist with the penny in it. So, you want to find the penny, while I want you not to find the penny. The description of the states that we desire, "you find the penny" and "you do not find the penny," cannot be conjoined without contradiction: "you find the penny AND you do not find the penny." There is evidence that children do not understand this until they can handle false belief between 3 and 5 or even 6 years, as we show in the following section.

Conflicting Desires

Competition

Gratch (1964) investigated at what age children display competitive behavior in the hand-guessing game, that is, whether they bothered to conceal the penny properly, didn't help the opponent guess the right hand, and showed disappointment when the opponent guessed correctly. The proportion of children in three age groups who displayed competitive spirit in the hand-guessing game in Gratch's (1964) classical study are shown in figure 11.4.

Conflicting Desires

Moore, Jarrold, Russell, Sapp, and MacCallum (1995, Experiment 2) looked at 3- to 4-year-olds' understanding of other people's desire in a competitive game at a point where the child wanted the next card to be turned over to be blue (in order to complete the next step in the puzzle), while the opponent, Fat Cat, wanted it to be red. When asked which color Fat Cat wanted now, only 7 of 20 answered correctly, and about the same percentage (8 of 18) passed a traditional false-belief task. Figure 11.4 shows that these percentages fit nicely the age trend described by Gratch's (1964) data.

Moore et al. (1995) interpreted their data as showing that young children cannot inhibit their preoccupation with their own desire and own knowledge of the world and that failure makes it difficult to focus on what someone else wants or believes. This explanation, however, is at odds with Gratch's finding. If young children were simply preoccupied with their own desires, then they

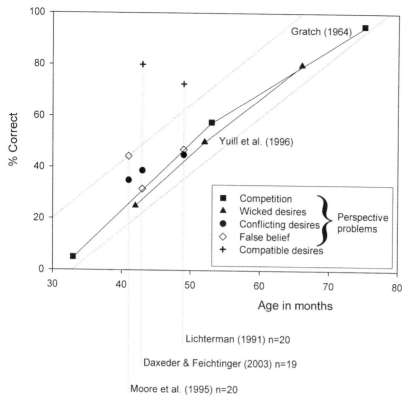

Figure 11.4. Beam of perspective: Proportions of children passing perspective problems.

should have come out as hypercompetitive in Gratch's hand-guessing game, but the opposite was the case. Our interpretation of Moore et al.'s data is consistent with Gratch's finding. The younger children cannot represent that Fat Cat wants the card to be drawn to be red when they themselves want that card to be blue. The younger children can't do this because it is a perspective problem, which we can see by the fact that what both players want (i.e., "this card will be blue" and "this card will be red") cannot be integrated without bringing in points of view. Children's error consisted in responding to the question about Fat Cat with their own desire. This may happen either because the desire is their own or because they were asked about it first. But if the conflict didn't raise a perspective problem, then they could answer the question about Fat Cat correctly, as well as the question about their own desire.

Compatible Desires Control

If ours is the correct explanation of these data, then children's difficulty should be alleviated if each player has his own deck of cards to draw from. Then the desired states of the world can be easily integrated: "The card from his deck should be red AND the card from my deck should be blue." In a recent student project, Daxeder and Feichtinger (2003) had children play against a confederate. Each player had a prince who wanted to climb his flight of stairs to get to the princess at the meeting point of the staircases. Each player's prince could advance only if the die to be thrown showed the color of the next step. On two occasions, the colors of the princes' next steps differed and children were asked which color they wanted the die to show and then what color the confederate wanted the die to show. Figure 11.4 shows that the percentage of correct specifications (39%, n = 9) of the other player's *incompatible* desire again fits the age trend of Gratch's data and the percentage of children passing the false-belief task (32%, n = 19)—fully replicating the finding by Moore et al. (1995). In addition, figure 11.4 also shows that children did much better (80%, n = 10) with *compatible* desires (Fisher's Exact Test of Significance $p < .05$, contrasting none correct with 1 or 2 correct answers). Here, the only change from the incompatible condition consisted in the child and the confederate each being given their own die to throw, which made their respective desires compatible: for example, "Child's die shows blue AND confederate's die shows red."

Emotional Reaction to Desire Satisfaction

A similar pattern of results was also found in an earlier study by Lichterman (1991; Perner, Peerbhoy, & Lichterman, 1991) that tested understanding of the emotional state resulting from a match and a mismatch between desire and outcome. Compatible desires were contrasted with incompatible desires and false belief. Stories like the following boat scenario were used. In the independent desire stories, a boy and a girl are traveling, each in his or her own boat, down a river that bifurcates into two branches. The girl wants to go in her boat along the left branch, and the boy wants to go in his boat along the right branch. Now, note that these are independent desires in that the desired states are compatible: "The girl goes in her boat along the left branch AND the boy goes in his boat along the right branch."

In contrast, in the conflicting desire story, the boy and the girl are traveling in the same boat. He wants to go left, but she wants to go right. These desires are clearly dependent. If her desire is satisfied, his will necessarily remain unsatisfied, and vice versa. They are perspective problems because the desired states are not compatible: "They go along the right branch AND they go along the left branch," is contradictory. Unlike in the Moore et al. (1995) study, children were not asked to specify what each character's desire was (if they had been asked, they would presumably have had problems with the incompatible desires). Instead, they were shown each character's desire and the outcome of the story, which conformed to one character's desire but not to the other character's. They had first to indicate which character was happy about this outcome. They had little problem with this; that is, in both stories most children answered correctly with the character to whose desire the outcome conformed. However, when asked the follow-up question whether the other character was also happy, most children gave the correct answer—"not happy"—only for independent stories. In the conflict story, the majority said incorrectly that (s)he was happy, too. Moreover, there was a strong correlation between children's ability to answer the conflict stories and a traditional false-belief test correctly ($\Phi = .73, p < .001$). Figure 11.4 shows that the percentage of correct answers on the conflict story and the false-belief task again fall within the developmental trend described by the tasks that require an understanding of perspective.

The correlation between understanding conflicting desires and false belief is underlined by the difficulty that children with autism have with conflicting desires, and they are also known to have problems with false belief. Only about 20% of those with a mental age of more than 4 years tend to pass the false-belief task (Baron-Cohen, Leslie, & Frith, 1985; Perner, Frith, Leslie, & Leekam, 1989). These children seemed to have similar problems with conflicting desires (Harris & Muncer, 1988, reported in Harris, 1991, pp. 296–297): when one child wants the family to go to the zoo and the other child wants the family to go to the lake, only about 30% of their answers were correct that one child was happy but the other not. Most of them thought both children happy.

Wicked Desires

In addition, data by Yuill et al. (1996; see also Rieffe, Terwogt, Koops, Stegge, & Oomen, 2001; Yuill, 1984) on children's understanding of the emotional consequences of achieving neutral or wicked desires (i.e., wanting objectively undesirable outcomes) fits the *developmental beam of perspective* in figure 11.4. Even 3-year-olds are quite good at understanding happiness as a function of goal satisfaction if the goals are basically neutral events, but not if they are wicked desires. Yuill et al. explained this difficulty with 3-year olds' understanding being limited to an "objectivist" notion of desire and emotion. For instance, they understand that a story protagonist who wants to throw a ball to one (A) of two people will be happier if that person (A) catches the ball than if the other person (B) catches it (Wellman & Banerjee, 1991; Yuill, 1984). The information that the protagonist wants person A to catch the ball makes *A catching the ball* an "objectively" desirable outcome and leaves *B catching the ball* neutral. Consequently, when A catches the ball, the protagonist finds himself in a more desirable situation and, therefore, will be judged as happier than when B catches the ball. Now consider wicked desires: the protagonist wants to hit A on the head with the ball. Three-year-olds are very clear about bodily hurt being unnegotiably bad (Nucci & Turiel, 1978; Smetana, 1981, 1993). Hence, being told what the wicked protagonist wants, does not change the "objectively" negative value of what the protagonist wants. So, whether person A, as intended, or person B gets hit on the head, the protagonist is involved in an "objectively" undesirable situation and won't be happy. Most 3-year olds made this judgment in the study by Yuill et al. (1996). To be able to see that achieving a wicked desire can make a wicked person happy, children need to understand that desirability depends on the person's perspective. Even though hitting someone on the head is (from our point of view) undesirable, if the wicked protagonist wants it, it is desirable from his point of view. As we can see in figure 11.4, the number of children who see a difference in the protagonist's reaction to person A's versus person B's being hit describes the same developmental trend as the proportion of children who understand other perspective problems (conflicting desires, false belief) and who display competitive spirit.

In sum, figure 11.4 provides an impressively consistent developmental trend. From 3 to 6 years, the proportion of children who understand point of view increases steadily as demonstrated by a variety of different tasks. However, before we can accept that the common denominator of these tasks is an appreciation of perspective differences, we need to consider and clarify seemingly clear counterevidence that much younger children appreciate the subjectivity of desire.

Subjective Preferences

Bartsch and Wellman (1995, p. 86) report, for instance, the following deliberations of a child 3;0 years old: "I don't like shaving cream. . . . Daddy like shaving cream." This indeed suggests that objects are not objectively attractive or repugnant for such young children but that these children do understand that attractiveness is a matter of subjective preference. However, we need to point out that this kind of subjectivity need not be understood as a difference in point of view. Rather, it can be captured by different individuals being part of situations, which then can be seen as "objectively" desirable or undesirable. In other words, the logical form of the 3-year-old's statement in Bartsch and Wellman's corpus can be given as something like: *Shaving cream applied to daddy's cheeks is something good* [objectively desirable], *while shaving cream applied to my cheeks is something bad* [objectively undesirable] (Perner et al., 1991). This means that no understanding of point of view is required. The two statements of objective value can be integrated into a coherent view.

The same argument applies to the demonstration of subjectivity of preference by Repacholi and Gopnik (1997) in 18-month-old infants. The infants were presented with two kinds of food, yummy crackers and yucky broccoli (most infants conformed to this opinion). In a control condition, when another person asked them for something to eat, they almost always gave that person a cracker, rather than a piece of broccoli. However, in the discrepant desire condition, the other person first demonstrated deviant preferences. Tasting the crackers, she exclaimed: "Yuck, that's awful!" underlined by the appropriate facial expression. When tasting the broccoli, she looked pleased and also said so: "Mmm, that's good!" Now, when this person later asked the infant for something to eat, most children younger than 18 months still handed her crackers, but most children over 18 months handed her the broccoli. Again, this suggests very early understanding of subjective taste preferences. Nevertheless, this kind of subjectivity does not require an understanding of point of view because the subjective nature can be captured within objectively good person-food combinations (broccoli in her mouth is good) and objectively bad ones (broccoli in my mouth is bad).

PoV and "That"

Perhaps we have been dwelling overly long on the topic of conflicting desires, but the topic is relevant for de Villiers's claims that the syntactic form of how we talk about the mind forms the basis for thinking about the mind. Central to her argument is the idea that, with the acquisition of the syntax for tensed that-complements, children acquire PoV markers that allow them to relativize the truth of the embedded propositions to a particular person's point of view, for example:

(1) $_{\text{PoV-speaker CP}}$[Max thinks $_{\text{PoV-subject CP}}$ [that the chocolate is still in the old location]].

In order to explain why this development seems to coincide with the understanding of conflicting desires, the theory needs to be expanded. Perhaps the most straightforward extension is to posit PoV markers for to-infinitive complements:

(2) $_{\text{PoV-speaker CP}}$[Fat Cat wants $_{\text{PoV-subject CP}}$ [to draw a red card]].

J. De Villiers (this volume, chapter 10) would presumably reject this because she posits Point-of-View marking only on CPs under verbs like *say* and *think*: "I have argued that they fall into a special class of nonfactives and hence pattern together and distinct from other forms with other special characteristics, such as *want*, *pretend*, *know*, and *forget*. 'Marking' the complement ensures that the logical form is distinct for this class, as it must be" (pp. 210–211). But, perhaps, in view of the data, linguistic analysis could accommodate PoVs for *irrealis* complements. If this can be done, we would have to conclude that "that" has nothing much to do with point of view.

Another solution might be to assume that understanding of perspective of desires requires thinking in terms of what *ought* to be done or to happen relative to a person's point of view. This would bring back tensed that-complements in conjunction with PoV to explain children's grasp of conflicting desires:

(3) $_{PoV\text{-speaker}}$ CP[*Fat Cat* thinks $_{PoV\text{-subject}}$ CP [that the card to be drawn ought to be *red*]].

(3') $_{PoV\text{-speaker}}$ CP[*I* think $_{PoV\text{-subject}}$ CP [that the card to be drawn ought to be *blue*]].

If children come to understand conflicting desires in this way, de Villiers's theory would also require that they come to it by talking about desire in this way. Is there any evidence for that?

Overall Evaluation

- Our findings on German children's understanding of desire in conjunction with data from Chinese children (Tardif & Wellman, 2000) provide a very simple challenge for linguistic determinism of theory of mind. Regardless of how desires and beliefs are expressed in a particular language, when neither requires complicated finite that-complements (Chinese), both require that-complements (German), or only belief but not desire requires that-complements (English), children understand and talk about desire substantially earlier than belief. This raises this question: what does "that" have to do with theory of mind?

- In contrast to the preceding point, our data on German children's production of that-complements show an intriguing correlation between the use of "that" and inference of what someone mistakenly thinks from what they said. Also, the ages at which children start to use "that" and at which they pass the false-belief test are similar. Unfortunately, there is no correlation between these two abilities. Nevertheless, there seems to be some evidence that "that" has to do with inferring and remembering think-complements.

- The finding that children understand differences of point of view in the context of conflicting desires at the same time as they understand it with belief raises the question how understanding of point of view can be linked to understanding the that-complements of belief. What "that" has to do with point of view remains a mystery.

Acknowledgments We would like to express our appreciation to the heads and children of the following kindergartens for their cooperation and valuable time participating in our study on children's understanding of "want": Pfarrkindergarten Herrnau and St. Vitalis, the Betriebskindergarten LKH, and the Sportkindergruppe Monika Eder. We are also very grateful to Dr. Lisa Schirl-Leitgeb and the members and children of the TEZ (Zentrum für Tageseltern). The project was financially supported by the Austrian Science Fund (project P14495-SPR). We acknowledge Hubert Haider's invaluable advice on grammatical issues and Hannes Rakoczy's helpful comments on conflicting desires.

Note

1. In the German version the embedded proposition was in present tense, which corresponds literally to the English sentence "What did the puppet *say* that the rabbit is doing?" Unlike in German, however, this wording is permissible in English only if at the time of the puppet's statement the puppet assumed that the rabbit's doing would still be true at the later time at which the question is being asked. Since this assumption cannot be claimed, we used the past tense in the English translation.

References

Anscombe, G. E. (1957). *Intention*. Cambridge: Cambridge University Press.

Astington, J. W., & Jenkins, J. M. (1995, March). Language and theory of mind: A theoretical review and a longitudinal study. Paper presented at the biennial meeting of the Society for Research in Child Development, Indianapolis, IN.

Astington, J. W., & Jenkins, J. M. (1999). A longitudinal study of the relation between language and theory-of-mind development. *Developmental Psychology*, 35, 1311–1320.

Baron-Cohen, S., Leslie, A. M., & Frith, U. (1985). Does the autistic child have a "theory of mind"? *Cognition, 21*, 37–46.

Bartsch, K., & Wellman, H. M. (1995). *Children talk about the mind*. Oxford: Oxford University Press.

Carpenter, M., Call, J., & Tomasello, M. (2002). A new false belief test for 36-month-olds. *British Journal of Developmental Psychology, 20*, 393–420.

Clements, W. A., & Perner, J. (1994). Implicit understanding of belief. *Cognitive Development, 9*, 377–397.

Clements, W. A., & Perner, J. (2001). When actions really do speak louder than words—but only implicitly: Young children's understanding of false belief in action. *British Journal of Developmental Psychology, 19*, 413–432.

Custer, W. L. (1996). A comparison of young children's understanding of contradictory representations in pretense, memory, and belief. *Child Development, 67*, 678–688.

Daxeder, U., & Feichtinger, V. (2003). *Verstehen von unterschiedlichen subjektiven Wünschen—ein Problem in Konfliktsituationen*. Experimentelle Übungen Sommersemester 2003, Institut für Psychologie, Universität Salzburg.

de Villiers, J. G. (1995). Questioning minds and answering machines. In D. MacLaughlin & S. McEwen (Eds.), *Proceedings of the 19th Boston University Conference on Language Development* (pp. 20–36). Somerville, MA: Cascadilla Press.

de Villiers, J. G., & de Villiers, P. A. (2000). Linguistic determination and the understanding of false beliefs. In P. Mitchell & K. J. Riggs (Eds.), *Children's reasoning and the mind* (pp. 191–228). Hove, UK: Psychology Press.

de Villiers, J. G., & de Villiers, P. A. (2003). Language for thought: Coming to understand false beliefs. In D. Gentner & S. Goldin-Meadow (Eds.), *Language in mind: Advances in the study of language and thought* (pp. 335–384). Cambridge, MA: MIT Press.

de Villiers, J. G., & Pyers, J. (1997). Complementing cognition: The relationship between language and theory of mind. In E. Hughes, M. Hughes, & A. Greenhill (Eds.), *Proceedings of the 21st annual Boston University Conference on Language Development*. Somerville, MA: Cascadilla Press.

Fodor, J. A. (1975). *The language of thought*. Cambridge, MA: Harvard University Press.

Frege, G. (1892/1960). On sense and reference. In P. Geach & M. Black (Eds.), *Philosophical writings of Gottlob Frege* (pp. 56–78). Oxford: Basil Blackwell.

Gale, E., de Villiers, P., de Villiers, J., & Pyers, J. (1996). Language and theory of mind in oral deaf children. In A. Stringfellow, D. Cahana-Amitay, E. Hughes, & A. Zukowski (Eds.), *Proceedings of the 20th Annual Boston University Conference on Language Development*. (Vol. 1, pp. 213–224). Somerville, MA: Cascadilla Press.

Garfield, J. L., Peterson, C., Garson, B., Nevin, A., & Perry, T. (2002). Let's pretend! The role of pretense in the acquisition of theory of mind. Unpublished manuscript, Smith College and University of Tasmania.

Gratch, G. (1964). Response alternation in children: A developmental study of orientations to uncertainty. *Vita Humana, 7,* 49–60.

Hale, C. M., & Tager-Flusberg, H. (2003). The influence of language on theory of mind: A training study. *Developmental Science, 6,* 346–359.

Happé, F. (1995). The role of age and verbal ability in the theory of mind task performance of subjects with autism. *Child Development, 66,* 843–855.

Happé, F., & Loth, E. (2002). "Theory of mind" and tracking speakers' intentions. *Mind and Language, 17,* 24–36.

Harris, P. L. (1991). The work of imagination. In A. Whiten (Ed.), *Natural theories of mind: evolution, development and simulation of everyday mindreading* (pp. 283–304). Oxford: Basil Blackwell.

Harris, P. L., & Kavanaugh, R. D. (1993). Young children's understanding of pretense. *Monographs of the Society for Research in Child Development, 58(1, Serial No. 231).*

Harris, P. L., & Muncer, A. (1988, September). Autistic children's understanding of beliefs and desires. Paper presented at the British Psychological Society Developmental Section Conference, Coleg Harlech, Wales.

Hilgard, E. R. (1980). The trilogy of mind: Cognition, affection, and conation. *Journal of the History of the Behavioral Sciences, 16,* 107–117.

Hummer, P., Wimmer, H., & Antes, G. (1993). On the origin of truth functional negation. *Journal of Child Language, 20,* 607–618.

Jenkins, J., & Astington, J. W. (1996). Cognitive factors and family structure associated with theory of mind development in young children. *Developmental Psychology, 32,* 70–78.

Kaufman, A., & Kaufman, N. (1994). Kaufman Assessment Battery for Children (2d ed.). Frankfurt, Germany: Swets & Zeitlinger.

Leslie, A. M. (1994). Pretending and believing: issues in the theory of ToMM. *Cognition, 50,* 211–238.

Lichterman, L. (1991). *Young children's understanding of desires: 3rd- year project report.* Laboratory of Experimental Psychology, University of Sussex.

Moore, C., Jarrold, C., Russell, J., Sapp, F., & MacCallum, F. (1995). Conflicting desire and the child's theory of mind. *Cognitive Development, 10,* 467–482.

Nucci, L. P., & Turiel, E. (1978). Social interactions and the development of social concepts in preschool children. *Child Development, 49,* 400–407.

Pea, R. D. (1980). The development of negation in early child language. In D. R. Olson (Ed.), *The social foundations of language and thought: Essays in honor of Jerome S. Bruner* (pp. 156–186). New York: W. W. Norton.

Perner, J. (1991). *Understanding the representational mind.* Cambridge, MA: MIT Press.

Perner, J. (1995). The many faces of belief: Reflections on Fodor's and the child's theory of mind. *Cognition, 57,* 241–269.

Perner, J. (2000). About + belief + counterfactual. In P. Mitchell & K. J. Riggs (Eds.), *Children's reasoning and the mind* (pp. 367–401). Hove, UK: Psychology Press.

Perner, J., Brandl, J., & Garnham, A. (2003). What is a perspective problem? Developmental issues in belief ascription and dual identity. *Facta Philosophica, 5,* 355–378.

Perner, J., Frith, U., Leslie, A. M., & Leekam, S. R. (1989). Exploration of the autistic child's theory of mind: Knowledge, belief and communication. *Child Development, 60,* 689–700.

Perner, J., Lang, B., & Kloo, D. (2002). Theory of mind and self–control: More than a common problem of inhibition. *Child Development, 73,* 752–767.

Perner, J., Leekam, S. R., & Wimmer, H. (1987). Three-year-olds' difficulty with false belief: The case for a conceptual deficit. *British Journal of Developmental Psychology, 5,* 125–137.

Perner, J., Perrbhoy, D., & Lichterman, L. (1991, April). Objective desirability: Bad outcomes, conflicting desires and children's concept of competition. Paper presented as discussant of the symposium "Intention in the Child's Theory of Mind" at the biennial meeting of the Society for Research in Child Development, Seattle, WA.

Perner, J., Sprung, M., Zauner, P., & Haider, H. (2003). *Want that* is understood well before *say that, think that,* and false belief: A test of de Villiers's linguistic determinism on German-speaking children. *Child Development, 74,* 179–188.

Perner, J., Stummer, S., Sprung, M., & Doherty, M. (2002). Theory of mind finds its Piagetian perspective: Why alternative naming comes with understanding belief. *Cognitive Development, 17,* 1451–1472.

Peterson, C. C., & Siegal, M. (1995). Deafness, conversation and theory of mind. *Journal of Child Psychology and Psychiatry, 36,* 459–474.

Peterson, C. C., & Siegal, M. (1999). Representing inner worlds: Theory of mind in autistic, deaf, and normal hearing children. *Psychological Science, 10,* 126–129.

Repacholi, B. M., & Gopnik, A. (1997). Early reasoning about desires: Evidence from 14– and 18–month-olds. *Developmental Psychology, 33,* 12–21.

Rieffe, C., Terwogt, M. M., Koops, W., Stegge, H., & Oomen, A. (2001). Preschoolers' appreciation of uncommon desires and subsequent emotions. *British Journal of Developmental Psychology, 19,* 259–274.

Ruffman, T., Garnham, W., Import, A., & Connolly, D. (2001). Does eye gaze indicate implicit knowledge of false belief? Charting transitions in knowledge. *Journal of Experimental Child Psychology, 80,* 201–224.

Scarborough, H. S. (1990). Index of producitve syntax. *Applied Psycholinguistics, 11,* 1–22.

Searle, J. (1983). *Intentionality.* Cambridge: Cambridge University Press.

Smetana, J. G. (1981). Preschool children's conceptions of moral and social rules. *Child Development, 52,* 1333–1336.

Smetana, J. G. (1993). Understanding of social rules. In M. Bennett (Ed.), *The child as a psychologist* (pp. 111–141). New York: Harvester/Wheatsheaf.

Tager-Flusberg, H. (1993). What language reveals about the understanding of minds in children with autism. In S. Baron-Cohen, H. Tager-Flusberg, & D. J. Cohen (Eds.), *Understanding other minds: Perspectives from autism* (pp. 138–157). Oxford: Oxford University Press.

Tager-Flusberg, H. (1996, July). Relationships between language and thought: Cognition verbs and theory of mind. Paper presented at the meeting of the International Association for the Study of Child Language, Istanbul, Turkey.

Tager-Flusberg, H., & Sullivan, K. (1994). Predicting and explaining behavior: A comparison of autistic, mentally retarded and normal children. *Journal of Child Psychology and Psychiatry, 35,* 1059–1075.

Tardif, T., & Wellman, H. M. (2000). Acquisition of mental state language in Mandarin- and Cantonese-speaking children. *Developmental Psychology, 36,* 25–43.

Wellman, H. M., & Banerjee, M. (1991). Mind and emotion: Children's understanding of the emotional consequences of beliefs and desires. *British Journal of Developmental Psychology, 9,* 191–124.

Wellman, H. M., Cross, D., & Watson, J. (2001). Meta-analysis of theory of mind development: The truth about false belief. *Child Development, 72,* 655–684.

Wellman, H. M., & Woolley, J.D. (1990). From simple desires to ordinary beliefs: The early development of everyday psychology. *Cognition, 35,* 245–275.

Wimmer, H., & Mayringer, H. (1998). False belief understanding in young children: Explanations do not develop before predictions. *International Journal of Behavioral Development, 22,* 403–422.

Wimmer, H., & Perner, J. (1983). Beliefs about beliefs: Representation and constraining function of wrong beliefs in young children's understanding of deception. *Cognition, 13,* 103–128.

Yuill, N. (1984). Young children's coordination of motive and outcome in judgements of satisfaction and morality. *British Journal of Developmental Psychology, 2,* 73–81.

Yuill, N., Perner, J., Pearson, A., Peerbhoy, D., & van den Ende, J. (1996). Children's changing understanding of wicked desires: From objective to subjective and moral. *British Journal of Developmental Psychology, 14,* 457–475.

12 Linguistic Communication and Social Understanding

Heidemarie Lohmann, Michael Tomasello, and Sonja Meyer

> But there is nothing odd about the product of a given process
> contributing to, or even becoming an essential factor in, the
> further development of that process.
> —George Herbert Mead, 1934, p. 226

"Language" and "theory of mind" are both global terms that cover a wide array of phenomena. Therefore, to be precise about a link between the two, it is first necessary to clarify which aspects of language and which aspects of theory of mind are at issue. We focus here less on Language as an abstract representational medium and more on linguistic communication as the process by which people use linguistic conventions to pursue communicative goals. And we focus not on Theory of Mind, narrowly defined as the understanding of false beliefs, but rather on children's growing understanding of other persons more generally—what we shall call simply social understanding.

In particular, we are concerned here with two levels of social understanding that we have previously differentiated (Tomasello, 1999): (1) the understanding of other persons as intentional agents, whose behavior is governed by goals and perceptions, and (2) the understanding of other persons as mental agents, whose behavior is governed by goals (desires) and beliefs, including ones that are false. Our central claim is that the relationship between linguistic communication and social understanding is different depending on which of these two levels is involved. Fundamentally, understanding others as intentional agents is necessary for human beings to comprehend and acquire the use of linguistic symbols and conventions in the first place. So, in this case, language arises from certain skills of social understanding—and this would be the case both phylogenetically (historically) and ontogenetically. But then the use of these intentionally constituted linguistic conventions in communicative interactions (discourse) with other persons leads young children (and perhaps led prehistoric humans) to an understanding of beliefs. More specifically, children come to understand beliefs as a result of participating in various kinds of linguistic interactions in which their interlocutor shifts perspectives in various ways—including taking various perspectives and modal attitudes both on the child's and on her own linguistically expressed beliefs (e.g., in propositional attitude constructions). In the case of understanding beliefs, then, linguistic interactions help to create new forms of social understanding.

Early Intention Reading and Language

Dogs understand verbal commands, parrots produce English words and phrases, and vervet monkeys give different alarm calls for different predators. Why are these not language? They are not language because they do not have the requisite psychological dimension. These animals are not trying to understand or manipulate the intentional or mental states of others; rather, they are focused on the behavior (or perhaps motivational states) of others. They are therefore comprehending and using communicative signals—either not learned or learned associatively—not linguistic symbols. Operating with linguistic symbols requires a certain kind of social understanding.

We can see this most clearly if we look at the process of word learning. Most theories of word learning hold that a linguistic symbol is simply a sound (or possibly a hand sign) that "stands for" something in the world (or else a concept). What it means for one thing to stand for another is never really addressed. The implicit assumption is that it is just an association—which makes it pretty much like what dogs and parrots do. But if we look at children's earliest comprehension and production of real-life linguistic utterances, we see that something very different is going on. The child encounters an adult making funny noises at her. What is she to make of this odd behavior? She could simply associate these noises with ongoing experiences, like a dog. But if she understands the other person as an intentional being, she will attempt to determine the purpose for which that person is making these funny noises. One possibility is that the adult is attempting to communicate with her, and so the child must attempt to determine her communicative intentions.

This is not a process of association. This is a process of establishing joint attention, and it relies on intention reading—and indeed a special form of intention reading at that (Tomasello, 1999, 2001). It requires the child to understand not just the adult's intentions to some outside entity but also his intentions toward her (the child's) attention to some outside entity—that is, his communicative intentions (Tomasello, 1998). This is what a linguistic convention or symbol is. It is a sound (or other behavior) that two or more individuals use with each other to direct each other's attention and thereby to share attention—and they both know this is what they are doing. If you do not have this, then you may have something like the family pet knowing that the sound "dinner" means that food is coming, but you do not have an intersubjectively understood linguistic symbol used to follow into, direct, and share attention with other persons. This is the essence of what has been called the social-pragmatic theory of language (especially word) learning (Bruner, 1983; Nelson, 1985; Tomasello 1992).

This way of viewing early language acquisition explains in a way that no other theory of early language does—especially all of those relying on simple association—why language acquisition begins when it does in the months just after the child's first birthday. Thus, children begin to develop nonverbal joint attentional skills at around 9 to 12 months of age, including such things as following the gaze direction and gestures of adults, imitating adult actions on objects, and directing adult attention to outside objects using various kinds of gestural signals (see Tomasello, 1995, for a review). Many children also show their first signs of comprehending language at this same age, with the first linguistic productions coming soon after (Fenson, Dale, Reznick, et al., 1994). Most important, in a recent longitudinal study, Carpenter, Nagell, and Tomasello (1998) found that children's comprehension and production of language correlated highly with their skills of joint attentional engagement with their mothers. The reason that linguistic skills are so highly correlated with joint attentional skills is that language is nothing more than another type—albeit a very special type—of joint attentional skill; people use language to influence and manipulate one another's attention.

The social understanding required for word learning can be seen especially clearly in some recent studies in which children learn new words in the ongoing flow of social interaction in which both they and the adult are trying to do things. For example, here are five different situations—all requiring some kind of intention reading—in which 18- to 24-month-old children learned new words with some facility.

- In the context of a finding game, an adult announced her intention to "find the toma" and then searched in a row of buckets, all of which contained novel objects. Sometimes she found it in the first bucket searched. Sometimes, however, she had to search longer, rejecting unwanted objects by scowling at them and replacing them in their buckets until she found the one she wanted. Children of 18 and 24 months of age learned the new word for the object the adult intended to find (indicated by a smile and termination of search) regardless of whether or how many objects were rejected during the search process (Tomasello & Barton, 1994; Tomasello, Strosberg, & Akhtar, 1996).

- Also in the context of a finding game, an adult had the child find four different objects in four different hiding places, one of which was a very distinctive toy barn. Once the child had learned which objects went with which places, the adult announced her intention to "find the gazzer." She then went to the toy barn, but it turned out to be "locked." She thus frowned at the barn and then proceeded to another hiding place, saying, "Let's see what else we can find" (taking out an object with a smile). Later, children of 18 and 24 months of age demonstrated that they had learned "gazzer" for the object they knew the experimenter wanted in the barn, even though they had not seen the object after they heard the new word and even though the adult had frowned at the barn and smiled at a distractor object (Akhtar & Tomasello, 1996; Tomasello et al., 1996).

- An adult set up a script with the child in which a novel action was performed always and only with a particular toy character (e.g., Big Bird on a swing, with other character-action pairings demonstrated, as well). She then picked up Big Bird and announced, "Let's meek Big Bird," but the swing was nowhere to be found—so the action was not performed. Later, using a different character, 24-month-old children demonstrated their understanding of the new verb even though they had never seen the referent action performed after the novel verb was introduced (Akhtar & Tomasello, 1996).

- An adult announced her intention to "dax Mickey Mouse" and then proceeded to perform one action accidentally and another intentionally (or sometimes in reverse order). Twenty-four-month-old children learned the word for the intentional, not the accidental, action, regardless of which came first in the sequence (Tomasello & Barton, 1994).

- A child, her mother, and an adult played together with three novel objects. The mother then left the room. A fourth object was brought out, and the child and adult played with it, noting the mother's absence. When the mother returned to the room, she looked at the four objects together and exclaimed, "Oh look! A modi! A modi!" Understanding that the mother would not be excited about the objects she had already played with previously but that she very well might be excited about the object she was seeing for the first time, 24-month-old children learned the new word for the object the mother had not seen previously (Akhtar, Carpenter, & Tomasello, 1996).

No theory of associative learning can explain these results. Although any one of these studies might be explained in other ways, when they are considered as a group the most plausible explanation is that, by the time they are 18 to 24 months of age, children have developed a deep and flexible understanding of other persons as intentional beings, and so they are quite skillful at determining the adult's communicative intentions in a wide variety of relatively novel communicative situations.

And so linguistic communication is made possible by a certain form of social understanding, namely the understanding of the intentions and communicative intentions of other persons. Other animal species do not operate with this kind of understanding, and so while they can learn to associate sounds with experiences, they do not acquire the use of linguistic symbols as social conventions for manipulating the intentional and mental states of others. So, at this level of analysis, social understanding enables, indeed is in an important sense constitutive of, language.

Language and the Development of False-Belief Understanding

Once children have begun communicating with other people using historically evolved linguistic conventions, they are exposed to all of the different categories and perspectives that previous individuals in their linguistic community have found it useful to employ communicatively. And, in Vygotskian fashion, as they internalize these linguistic symbols, they begin to develop concepts and social-cognitive skills similar to those of other persons in their linguistic community, as well.

A social-cognitive skill currently of great interest to many developmentalists, including many of the authors in this volume, is the understanding of false beliefs. Arguably, the acquisition of language plays a central role in the ontogeny of this understanding. Thus, language development and false-belief understanding are relatively strongly correlated, as established by Dunn, Brown, Slomkowski, Tesla, and Youngblade (1991), Astington and Jenkins (1999), Gale, de Villiers, de Villiers, and Pyers (1996), de Villiers and de Villiers (2000), Watson, Painter, and Bornstein (2002), and Farrar and Maag (2002).

In addition, some investigators have used training studies in an attempt to go beyond correlations and to demonstrate specific causal relations between children's experience during training and their false-belief understanding. Relevant studies of this kind are Appleton and Reddy (1996), Swettenham (1996), Slaughter and Gopnik (1996), Slaughter (1998), McGregor, Whiten, and Blackburn (1998), Clements, Rustin, and McCallum (2000), and Hale and Tager-Flusberg (2003). The type of training was different in each of these studies, but in all cases in the key conditions children experienced some kind of deceptive scenario involving issues of appearance-reality and/or false belief (including in some cases training on false-belief tasks directly), along with linguistic descriptions of that scenario, typically including mental-state talk. The problem is that none of these studies had a control condition in which children experienced some kind of deceptive scenario during training but without any linguistic description at all. Such a control condition is necessary to unconfound deceptive experience and language and thus to determine whether language influences false-belief understanding over and above training involving deceptive experiences.

Beyond the question of whether or not language plays a role in false-belief understanding, very little research has been aimed at identifying specifically the nature of this role. There are four global hypotheses. The first is that language has no special role to play. The idea is that children are constantly forming theories about other people and their minds and that any and all data are relevant. Data from linguistic sources may be used, but they have no special status. Although it is unclear whether anyone espouses this view in its pure form, the theory-theory certainly tends in this direction (Gopnik & Wellman, 1992). The second hypothesis is that learning mental-state terms such as *think*, *know*, and *believe* plays a key role in the development of false-belief understanding (see, e.g., Olson, 1988). The idea here is that these particular linguistic symbols are used by adults to indicate the relevant mental states, and so in learning the referents of these terms children form, in Whorfian fashion, the relevant concepts. Again, it is unclear whether anyone espouses this as the exclusive, or even as the single most important factor involved. But Bartsch and Wellman (1995) discuss in detail the possible importance of this language learning process, and Astington (2000) also seems to accord it some importance.

Third, de Villiers and de Villiers (2000; see also Gale et al., 1996) proposed that the syntax, that is, the grammatical form, of the way adults talk about beliefs and related mental states provides children with a necessary representational format for dealing with false beliefs. Specifically, what is said to be crucial is the syntax of complementation, in which a sentence takes a full clause as its object complement (sentential complements). For example, consider *Peter thinks Mommy's home* or *You know that I'm not coming to the party*. This hypothesis has recently received support from a training study in which children trained with sentential complement sentences subsequently improved in their false-belief understanding (Hale & Tager-Flusberg, 2003). However, it is important to point out that the sentences in this training study were given in talking about deceptive experiences, and so it is possible that it was these experiences, and not the sentences themselves, that led to the increase in false-belief understanding (i.e., there was no control condition without deceptive experience).

A fourth hypothesis, put forward by Harris (1996, 1999), proposed that it is not the semantic content of mental-state terms or the syntax of complementation that are key linguistic influences on the understanding of false beliefs but rather that the key is the process of linguistic interchange that children experience in discourse with other people. The idea here is that the whole notion of "belief" as a mental state makes sense only in the context of alternative possible beliefs about a situation, including one that is "true" (implying that others may be false). Harris claims that it is in the to-and-fro of discourse that the child comes to appreciate that other people know things she does not know, that they do not know things they ought to know, and that they have different perspectives on things (see also Tomasello, 1999; Siegal, 1999). Most training studies have employed rich discourse interactions as a part of the training (see preceding discussion), and so it is possible that these studies provide support for the discourse view. But, again, these training conditions typically involved a number of other factors in addition, including mental-state terms and sentential complements.

We report here two training studies. The first study attempted to establish both (1) whether language causally influences false-belief understanding (with the appropriate control group), and (2) if so, the nature of this influence with respect to the various hypotheses previously proposed (with the appropriate comparison groups).

Study 1: Training False-Belief Understanding

In this study, 3-year-old German children (mean age = 42.6 months) experienced pretests, intervention training, and then posttests. Children who had not yet acquired false-belief understanding (and who showed linguistic development within the norms of their age group) took part in the intervention training. All of the details are reported in Lohmann and Tomasello (2003), from which the following section is abstracted.

Pretests

Each child was given three pretests: (a) a vocabulary test, (b) a false-belief task (the representational change task; Gopnik & Astington, 1988), and (c) two tests of the child's comprehension of sentential complement constructions (a modification of Swettenham's (1996) Tom test, and the memory for complements test of de Villiers and de Villiers, 2000; see also J. de Villiers, this volume, chapter 10).

Training

There were four different training conditions. All involved adult-child interactions with deceptive objects (e.g., children see an object that looks like an apple but is really a candle). Training in the different groups was as follows:

Full Training In this condition, the deceptive aspect of the training objects was highlighted and the experimenter (E) talked about this using either mental-state verbs (*think, know*) or communication verbs (*say*) within sentential complement constructions. Thus, for each object, E showed the child the object and asked her what she thought the object was, using psychological verbs (e.g., *think*) and sentential complement constructions. Then the object was handed to the child so that she could see its "real" function, which was highlighted by E. Then the child was asked to recall her previous belief and her current knowledge of the object's nature, which was possibly corrected and summarized once more by E. The child was also asked to predict a third person's reaction to the deceptive object. A hand puppet, Schnuffi, was used to represent a third person, and the child watched as E informed Schnuffi of the real function of the object. Children could observe the surprise reactions of the puppet and assist the puppet in finding out the real function of the object. Finally, the children were asked about the puppet's new (changed) belief about the object. (To see whether specific verbs made a difference, half the children in this condition were trained using only mental-state verbs such as *think* and *know*, and half were trained using only the communication verb *say*. Since these options turned out to produce the same results, they were subsequently collapsed).

Discourse Only Training In this condition, the deceptive aspect of the training objects was highlighted, but E did this without using either mental-state verbs or sentential complement constructions. Thus, for example, instead of asking, "What do you think this is?" E asked the child, "What is this?"; instead of saying, "You thought it was a flower," E said, "A flower."

No Language Training In this condition, the deceptive aspect of the training objects was highlighted, but E did this essentially nonverbally. Thus, children were first shown an object, and E said, "Look!" and then their attention was drawn to the real function by E's showing it and saying, "But now look!" The appearance/reality distinction of the objects was highlighted twice by E with appropriate nonverbal emotional expressions; no questions were asked, and no feedback was given to the child. For the third-person perspective, the hand puppet was brought out and shown the object: "Look, Schnuffi." The child observed the puppet's reactions to the object, which showed surprise reactions to the real function of the object: "Oh!," "All right," and the like.

Sentential Complements Only Training In this condition, the deceptive aspect of the training objects was *not* highlighted for the child in any way. E simply talked about them as normal objects, using mental verbs or communication verbs and sentential complements. Four short stories were designed so that E could talk about the objects without referring to their deceptive nature. Thus, children were asked what they thought the object was and about certain attributes of the object, while the deceptive nature of the objects was never revealed. To avoid contrasting mental states, children's answers were not contradicted. In order to stimulate the children's acquisition/comprehension of sentential embeddings, the children were also asked to help E clarify what the protagonist of the story had done or said. For example, a handpuppet Ernie says: "This chair belongs to my grandfather. I know that!" E then asks the child: "What does Ernie know?" To answer the question appropriately, children had to use one clause as a sentential complement of the other: "He knows that the chair belongs to his grandfather." The same number of sentential complement sentences with mental verbs was used in feedback and questions as in the Full Training group, but without referring to any kind of contrasting deceptive experiences.

During training, each child interacted with an adult experimenter on each of four occasions within a two-week period. The basic training procedure was modeled on that of Slaughter and Gopnik (1996). Children in all training groups were exposed to 16 objects. Each was brought out singly and replaced after discussion of it was completed. Order was randomized across children (except in the Sentential Complements Training condition, in which a fixed order was used so as to tell a story). Twelve of the objects were deceptive objects in the sense that on first glance they appeared to be one thing (e.g., a flower) but on closer inspection they had another function (e.g., a writing pen). Four objects did not have a deceptive aspect and were used randomly among the 12 deceptive ones to prevent children from expecting every object we showed them to be something other than what it appeared to be. Training for each group consisted of discussion of each object, with the experimenter providing feedback and corrections to the child's comments where appropriate (except for the No Language Training group, where no feedback was given and no questions asked). The child's first session consisted of the pretests and training with 3 deceptive objects. In the second session, 5 deceptive objects were discussed; in the third session, 4 deceptive objects were discussed; and in the final session the posttests were administered.

Posttests

As outcome, we measured three different types of false-belief understanding (one appearance-reality test similar to the training and two transfer tests).

- The appearance-reality task with deceptive objects (Flavell, 1986) was similar in format to the training procedure. In order to look for influences of the different training elements on children's understanding of the appearance-reality distinction, the test was scored with three points: one point was given for the reality, one for the appearance, and one for the third-person prediction question.

- The representational change task (Gopnik & Astington, 1988) was similar in structure to the pretest, but with different content (this served as one transfer task—one point was given for each of the two questions concerning the child's own and a third person's mental state).
- The change-of-location task (Wimmer & Perner, 1983) served as another test of transfer of training (one point was given for a correct answer to the test question "Where will the protagonist look for the object?").

Children were also given sentential complement posttests. The format of the complement pretests was used again for the posttest, but with different story content in both cases.

Results

Preliminary analyses established that all four training groups were equivalent on all relevant measures at pretest. With regard to posttests, a significant effect of group was found for the first transfer test of false-belief understanding: Representational Change Task. The Full Training group outperformed each of the other groups on this task at posttest, and none of the paired comparisons among these other three groups revealed significant differences. Converted to percentages, the Full Training group was correct on average on 75% of the posttest questions; the Discourse Only and Sentential Complements Only groups averaged about 40% correct; and the No Language group averaged only about 25% correct answers. No difference between first- and third-person test questions was found. Pretest and posttest scores on the Representational Change Task are presented in table 12.1. Testing each group individually against chance, it was found that all groups except the No Language group increased their performance significantly compared to their pretest scores.

The other transfer task is the Location Change task. There was also a significant group difference for this task. Post hoc tests showed that the Full Training group was significantly better on the Location Change task than the No Language group, with no other groups differing from one another.

The Appearance-Reality task measured outcome on a task similar in structure to the training itself. No significant effect of group was found on the sum of questions in this "training-related" false-belief task. It appears that any training with experience of appearance-reality objects helped children to pass this test. But it should also be noted that even children with no deceptive experience but linguistic training on sentential complements did well on this task; this may be a result of the fact that the test uses test questions with sentential embeddings (similar to training). However, further analyses revealed group differences on the third-person prediction question of the test. Results of a logistic

Table 12.1 Means Scores on the Representational Change Task at Pretest and
Posttest for Each Training Group

	Full Training	Discourse Only	No Language	Sentential Complements
Pretest				
False Belief (0-1) mean:	.33	.23	.27	.33
Posttest				
False Belief (0-2) mean:	1.5**	.80*	.53	.77*

Note: Children could not get 2 points in the pretest because passing the test was used as an
exclusion criterion for the training.
*indicates a significant improvement from pretest to posttest score. Sign test:
* = p < .05
** = p < .01

regression showed a significant group effect for this question. Post hoc tests
showed that the Full Training led to significantly more correct answers on this
question than the No Language Training, once again duplicating the finding for
the Representational Change task.

These analyses of the individual posttests provided evidence that the Full
Training condition was most effective in producing social-cognitive gains, but
the Discourse Only and Sentential Complements Only also produced gains on
some tasks. In a final, most general analysis, we summed across all false-belief
posttest tasks to look for an overall effect of training. This analysis confirmed a
group effect on false-belief understanding between the training groups. Figure
12.1 shows that the Full Training group performed better at posttest than each
of the other groups on the sum of false-belief scores.

We also looked in more detail at the different training conditions, with a
focus on (1) the Discourse Only group and how it compared with the others,
and (2) the Sentential Complements Only group and how it compared with
the others. First, the Discourse Only group provided children with differing
perspectives on the deceptive objects using nouns, whereas the Full Training
group did something similar, but using the language of sentential complements
with mental verbs. The comparison between these groups is thus informative
about the role of sentential complements over and above perspective-shifting
discourse. Contrasts of the Full Training against the Discourse Only condition
showed a significant effect of the Full Training. Thus, the use of sentential
complements facilitated children's false-belief understanding beyond that provided by the Discourse Only condition. Nevertheless, a planned contrast between the Discourse Only and the Sentential Complements groups found no

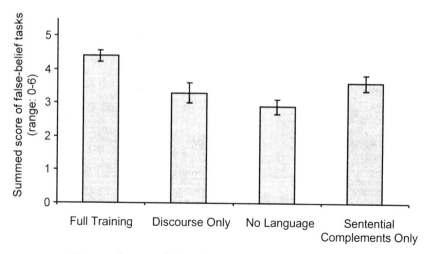

Figure 12.1. Means of sums of three false-belief posttest scores by training group. (Reprinted with permission of the Society for Research in Child Development)

difference, suggesting that the deceptive experience in the Full Training condition was an important factor, as well. In a final planned contrast, the Discourse Only group did not differ significantly from the No Language group.

Second, the Sentential Complements group was similar to the Full Training group, except that there was no deceptive experience involved. That is, the children in the Full Training group experienced deceptive objects and perspective-shifting talk about them (including both first- and third-person perspectives), whereas children in the Sentential Complements group did not experience deceptive objects or talk of contrasting mental states during the training. The results of a planned orthogonal contrast showed that the group with deceptive experience (Full Training) outperformed the group without deceptive experience (Sentential Complements). Thus, the experience of changing perspectives on deceptive objects seems to be an important factor in the acquisition of false-belief understanding. Comparing the Sentential Complements with the No Language condition again revealed a significant difference in favor of the Sentential Complement training. Moreover, combining those conditions that used sentential complements in the training (Full Training and Sentential Complements) and comparing them with those conditions that did not (Discourse and No Language) also showed that the groups with sentential complements in the input outperformed the groups that did not use this specific linguistic construction in the training. The use of sentential complements thus seems to be an important factor in the acquisition of false-belief understanding independent of deceptive experience and perspective-shifting discourse.

Supportive of this last finding, another important result is that the use of sentential complements in training was correlated with improved scores on false-belief understanding. Analysis of children's improvement on the sentential complement tasks at post-test showed that the most improvement came in the Sentential Complements training group. More importantly, table 12.2 shows the correlation between the change scores of false-belief understanding and the change scores on sentential complements (Test 1) of all training groups. A significant correlation was found for the Sentential Complements training group. This indicates that those children who improved their linguistic skills also improved their false-belief scores in this condition. In contrast, in the Full Training group, children's improvement in false-belief understanding was not reliably associated with improved linguistic scores, presumably indicating the role of other effective factors (such as perspective-shifting discourse) in this condition.

Discussion

This study had three main findings. First, language was a necessary condition for young children to make progress in false-belief understanding. Simply experiencing deceptive objects was not sufficient; children needed to have that experience structured by some language from other persons—for example, different nouns indicating different possible perspectives on these objects (mediated perspective-shifting discourse). Second, training in the syntax of sentential complements, including mental-state predicates as matrix verbs, was sufficient by itself to facilitate children's false-belief understanding. This effect was evident even in a condition in which children had no experience with deceptive objects. Third, these two effects—of perspective-switching discourse and sentential complement syntax—seem to be relatively independent of each other. The strongest facilitator of children's false-belief understanding in this study was a training condition that incorporated both of these factors, and the correlational findings provided further support for the independence of these two factors.

The difference between the No Language training and the Discourse Only condition suggests that in our training it was the explicit labeling of the different

Table 12.2 Correlation of Pretest to Posttest Improvements on Both False-Belief and Sentential Complements Understanding for Each Training Group

	Change Scores on False Belief			
	Full Training	Discourse Only	No Language	Sentential Complements
Change scores on sentential complements	r = -.18 p = .22	r = .08 p = .68	r = -.01 p = .95	r = .39 p = .035

perspectives that helped children to learn from the training. In the Discourse Only condition, the two perspectives were encoded in contentful linguistic symbols, such as "First it is a flower, and now it is a pen." And so the effect of language had to do with the adult using conventionalized symbols (mainly in the form of common nouns) to highlight the different perspectives. It is important that the explicit encoding in this training condition did not involve reference to mental states themselves—nor did it use any sentential complements—and so the effective factor in this condition was the process of perspective-shifting discourse, rather than any explicit reference to mental states using mental-state language or any syntactic format for symbolizing propositional attitudes.

Sentential complements (even without experience with deceptive objects or perspective-shifting discourse) were also an important factor. In the only other training study to investigate this question (Hale & Tager-Flusberg, 2003), the training of sentential complements always occurred in conjunction with deceptive experience, and so the current findings are the first to establish the important role of sentential complement syntax by itself in promoting the understanding of false beliefs. The current findings thus support the hypothesis of de Villiers and de Villiers (2000) that sentential complement constructions provide children with a convenient (if not necessary) representational format for conceptualizing and talking about false beliefs. It is also important to note that the sentential complement sentences in this training condition contained mental-state verbs, and so these might have played an important role in producing the training effect. However, in an explicit comparison of the two versions of the Full Training condition—one containing mental-state verbs (e.g., *think, know*) and one containing a communication verb (*say*)—no difference was found. This is at least indirect evidence that the main effect in the Sentential Complements condition was primarily tied not to the semantics of mental verbs but to the structure of sentential complement syntax (e.g., see Diessel & Tomasello, 2001). However, although a sufficient factor for false-belief understanding in this study, sentential complement syntax might not be a necessary factor for this understanding (see also Perner, Sprung, Zauner, & Haider, 2003; Perner, Zauner, & Sprung, this volume, chapter 11).

In virtually all analyses, the largest training effect was observed in the Full Training condition, which, like most previous training studies, contained both perspective-shifting discourse and sentential complement syntax, but no more overall talk than the other conditions. In combination with the findings that demonstrate the effectiveness of these two factors by themselves, the superiority of the Full Training condition implies that both perspective-shifting discourse and sentential complement syntax make relatively independent contributions to children's false-belief understanding.

The current study thus provides the strongest evidence to date that language plays a central role in children's development of false-belief understanding.

Specifically, perspective-switching discourse that uses contentful linguistic symbols (not necessarily mental-state language) and the ready availability of sentential complement syntax as a representational format both seem to make independently important contributions to the ontogenetic process. Further evidence for this general proposal comes from research with profoundly deaf children born to hearing families, who have almost no available means in their early years of conversing with their hearing family members, especially about topics such as mental states, which may have no obvious visual referent (de Villiers & de Villiers, 2000; Gale et al., 1996; Peterson & Siegal, 1995, 1998, 1999, 2000). These children, who are of normal intelligence, presumably experience as many situations as typically developing children do in which they observe others in surprise reactions or experience their own false beliefs. But these children struggle with false-belief tasks up to the age of 16 years. In contrast, deaf children born to signing parents, who share a communicative system and thus have much richer linguistic experiences, develop concepts of false belief at the same age as do hearing children (Peterson & Siegal, 1999, 2000).

Study 2: The Difference between First- and Third-Person Experience

Does the facilitating effect of perspective-switching discourse and sentential complement syntax hold also for younger children? In order to investigate this question, the following study used a modified version of the training procedure in Study 1 with children just turning 3 years of age. Another question is the possible role of self versus others' experience—that is, whether children need themselves to engage in discourse about deceptive experiences or whether they can merely observe others in these kinds of interactions. On the basis of the claims of simulation theory (Harris, 1991), it might be suggested that children would benefit most from having deceptive experience and talking about it themselves. Therefore, in this study, first- and third-person experience was separated into two conditions.

Method

Forty-eight German children between 2 years 10 months and 3 years 2 months of age (M = 3;0) participated in the study. All children failed a pretest of false-belief understanding before training began. As in Study 1, training consisted of a pretest, three training units with the first one starting immediately after pretest, and finally a posttest. Each child was given at pretest the same false-belief task and vocabulary test that was used in Study 1. In addition, all children received practice in forced-choice questions, which were regarded as central to the training. For this practice, children were shown 6 pictures of common content and then each time asked a forced-choice question with the correct answer alternately mentioned at the beginning or at the end. For instance, a picture of a dog was presented, and then the child was asked: "Is this a dog or is this a cat?" After the training (described later), each child was given the same 3 false-belief posttests that were used in Study 1.

The training procedure was a modification of the training in Study 1. The structure was parallel in length and feedback to the most complex training condition of Study 1, the Full Training condition. As in Study 1, children were exposed to a total of 12 deceptive and 4 nondeceptive objects within the three training units. However, two training conditions were designed, a *first-person* and a *third-person condition,* as described in this section.

First the experimenter presented the appearance form of one object to the child and asked: "What do you think this is?" Then the real function was shown with the question: "But look, what is it really?" The procedure was then repeated with the child answering both questions again. Three fillers, such as "Have you ever seen such an object?," were included to adapt the present training to Study 1 in length, without referring to another person's perspective. The two training conditions differed in the following way: in the *first-person condition,* children experienced their initial misconception of the objects during the training sessions and received appropriate feedback to their answers, whereas in the *third-person condition,* the children observed a doll being trained by the experimenter and assisted in presenting the nondeceptive objects to the doll. In order to minimize first-person experience in this training condition, the child was introduced to the appearance and the reality form of the deceptive objects at the beginning of the doll's training unit. In this version, only the doll received feedback to its answers; the child's own comments on the questions were ignored by the experimenter.

Results and Discussion

To evaluate the overall performance of children at a mean age of 3;0 in false-belief tasks, both training conditions were first combined to form one group of 48 children. Only children with correct control questions were given credit for a correct answer on a test question. Results on the Representational Change task showed a significant improvement in the self question, while children's answers to the question about the other's belief did not improve from pretest to posttest. In the Appearance-Reality task, 23% of the children gave correct answers to all three questions, and in the Change of Location task, 15% of the children gave correct answers. These values are roughly equivalent to those found for children in this age range without any training experience (Wellman, Cross, & Watson, 2001).

As for differences between training conditions, in the Representational Change task, children in the first-person condition outperformed children in the third-person condition on the self question; however, there were no differences between groups on the question about the other's belief. There were no significant differences in overall performance between children in the two conditions on the Appearance-Reality or Change of Location task. Interestingly, on the Representational Change task, it was found that children who succeeded on the question about the other's belief also succeeded on the self question (Kappa = 0.38, p = 0.001).

Thus, there are two main findings from this study. First, the study is the first to explicitly compare training conditions with self and others' experience separated in a training setting. A significant difference between training conditions was found for the self question in the Representational Change task, with the first-person condition outperforming the third-person condition. This result might suggest that having the experience of being deceived, with discourse about that deception, focuses children's attention on beliefs. However, the difference between the two conditions might also have been influenced by the type of engagement during the training (see also Wellman et al., 2001). The third-person group mostly observed a doll being trained. To keep the children interested and engaged in the training of a third person, children of this group assisted the experimenter and were asked questions irrelevant to the training. This more "passive" engagement did not lead to results comparable to those from the first-person training.

Second, an interesting issue is the question of age. Children at the age of 3;0 who were trained in perspective-shifting discourse and sentential complement syntax showed between 15% and 23% correct performance in transfer tasks that are very different in type and linguistic form from the training tasks. Wellman et al. (2001) found that similar numbers of children in this age group passed without any prior training experience. With regard to sentential complement syntax, the present results show that, at an age at which German-speaking children have already mastered some complement sentence constructions, this knowledge is not sufficient to permit the children to apply it in solving specific cognitive tasks such as false-belief situations.

Language and Social Understanding: A Developmental Progression

Young children depend on their skills of intention reading—knowing important things about what others see, do, intend, and attend to—to acquire and use linguistic conventions from soon after their first birthdays. In doing this, they come to understand something of the intentional structure of language and the way it can provide different perspectives and descriptions of things: the very same animal is a dog, an animal, a pet, or a pest; the very same action is running, fleeing, chasing, or exercising. They thus come to form, in a way that other animals do not, perspectival cognitive representations (Tomasello, 1999).

But, sometime after their second birthday, many children begin to command linguistic skills advanced enough to enable them to engage in more sophisticated discourse interactions with a real give-and-take of perspectives, that is, those involving not just the different perspectives implicit in the use of linguistic symbols but the explicit perspectives that interlocutors linguistically express toward each other in propositions—sometimes concerning each other's previously expressed propositions. As children engage in such discourse, they are constantly simulating the perspective of the other person and relating that perspective to their own (Harris, 1996; Tomasello, 1999). There are several forms of discourse that seem especially important in children's coming to understand that others have beliefs. One is disagreements and misunderstandings in which one person expresses the view that X is the case, and the other disputes this and claims that Y is the case. Also important may be (a) misinterpretations, in which the adult interprets the child's utterance in a way that she did not intend, and (b) clarification requests, in which the child says something that the adult does not understand and so the adult asks for clarification. These situations lead the child to try to discern why the adult does not comprehend the utterance—perhaps she did not hear it, perhaps she is not familiar with this specific linguistic formulation, and so forth. In all, it seems that these kinds of disagreements, misunderstandings, and repairs are an extremely rich source of information about how one's own understanding of a linguistically expressed perspective on a situation may differ from that of others.

But perhaps of the greatest importance is reflective discourse in which the adult and child comment on the ideas contained in the discourse turn of the other (or the self). For example, a child may make some statement, and then either her interlocutor or she herself will make some evaluative comment about that statement. Relatedly, during the period from age 2 to age 4, for most languages, children also master sentential complement constructions (propositional attitude constructions) in which the speaker symbolically indicates both a proposition and some epistemic or modal attitude toward it, all in one construction. These could also then be considered, in a sense, reflective discourse, but in this case the state of affairs and the attitude toward it are all bound up in a single representational format in the form of a syntactic construction (de Villiers & de Villiers, 2000). Syntactic constructions are nothing other than grammaticalized (compressed and automated) strings of discourse (Bybee, 2003; Givon, 1979, 1995), and so looser discourse interactions and tighter syntactic constructions are all a part of the same process. It is thus natural that some kinds of syntactic constructions—specifically those that automate and compress *reflective* discourse—would be especially helpful in encouraging children to see both a state of affairs and a psychological attitude toward it all in one glance, as it were.

There is thus no conflict, in our view, between the view that discourse is crucial for developing an understanding of false beliefs and the view that mastering propositional attitude constructions is crucial. The recent work of Perner and colleagues (2003; see also this volume, chapter 11) demonstrates that mastery of the syntax of propositional attitude constructions per se is not sufficient to engender false-belief understanding—since young German-speaking children master such constructions well before they pass false-belief tasks. However, the training study reported here shows that for children who are already on the cusp of understanding false beliefs, training with propositional attitude constructions is sufficient. We propose to think of these constructions as simply grammaticized discourse that, by being compressed and automated, contributes in special ways to a more general process of discourse in which children are constantly confronted with different perspectives and attitudes on different things, including their own perspective. Discourse is everything, but grammaticized discourse, that is, syntactic constructions, may influence children's cognition in special ways.

Certain forms of social cognition—reading communicative intentions—are thus prerequisite for the acquisition and use of linguistic conventions, and the use of linguistic conventions, including syntactic constructions, in discourse is prerequisite for certain other forms of social cognition—understanding false beliefs. There is nothing odd about this; it is simply another manifestation of the dialectic in which children are biologically prepared for culture, but it is participation in culture—whose artifacts embody the cognitive skills and attitudes of past members of the culture—that takes their cognitive skills to new places (Tomasello, 1999; Vygotsky, 1978). To be precise about how all of this takes place, we must break down both language and theory of mind into more basic components.

References

Akhtar, N., Carpenter, M., & Tomasello, M. (1996). The role of discourse novelty in early word learning. *Child Development, 67,* 635–45.

Akhtar, N., & Tomasello, M. (1996). Two-year-olds learn words for absent objects and actions. *British Journal of Developmental Psychology, 14,* 79–93.

Appleton, M., & Reddy, V. (1996). Teaching three-year-olds to pass false belief tests: A conversational approach. *Social Development, 5,* 275–291.

Astington, J. W. (2000). Language and metalanguage in children's understanding of mind. In J. W. Astington (Ed.), *Minds in the making: Essays in honor of David R. Olson* (pp. 267–284). Oxford: Blackwell.

Astington, J. W., & Jenkins, J. M. (1999). A longitudinal study of the relationship between language and theory-of-mind development. *Developmental Psychology, 35,* 1311–1320.

Bartsch, K., & Wellman, H. (1995). *Children talk about the mind.* New York: Oxford University Press.

Bruner, J. (1983). *Child's talk.* New York: W. W. Norton.

Bybee, J. (2003). Sequentiality as the basis of constituent structure. In T. Givón & B. Malle (Eds.), *From pre-language to language* (pp. 107–134). Amsterdam: John Benjamins.

Carpenter, M., Nagell, K., & Tomasello, M. (1998). Social cognition, joint attention, and communicative competence from 9 to 15 months of age. *Monographs of the Society for Research in Child Development, 63(4, Serial No. 255)*.

Clements, W. A., Rustin, C., & McCallum, S. (2000). Promoting the transition from implicit to explicit understanding: A training study of false belief. *Developmental Science, 3,* 88–92.

de Villiers, J., & de Villiers, P. (2000). Linguistic determinism and the understanding of false beliefs. In P. Mitchell & K. J. Riggs (Eds.), *Children's reasoning and the mind* (pp. 191–228). Hove, UK: Psychology Press.

Diessel, H., & Tomasello, M. (2001). The acquisition of finite complement clauses in English: A corpus-based analysis. *Cognitive Linguistics, 12,* 97–141.

Dunn, J., Brown, J., Slomkowski, C., Tesla, C., & Youngblade, L. (1991). Young children's understanding of other people's feelings and beliefs: Individual differences and their antecedents. *Child Development, 62,* 1352–1366.

Farrar, M. J., & Maag, L. (2002). Early language development and the emergence of a theory of mind. *First Language, 22,* 197–213.

Fenson, L., Dale, P. S., Reznick, J. S., D., T., Bates, E., Harters, J. P., Pethick, S., & Reilly, J. S. (1993). *The MacArthur Communicative Development Inventories: A guide and technical manual.* San Diego, CA: Singular Publishing Group.

Flavell, J. H. (1986). The development of children's knowledge about the appearance–reality distinction. *American Psychologist, 41,* 418–425.

Gale, E., de Villiers, P., de Villiers, J., & Pyers, J. (1996). Language and theory of mind in oral deaf children. Paper presented at the 20th Boston University Conference on Language Development, Somerville, MA.

Givón, T. (1979). *On understanding grammar.* New York: Academic Press.

Givón, T. (1995). *Functionalism and grammar.* Amsterdam: John Benjamins.

Gopnik, A., & Astington, J. W. (1988). Children's understanding of representational change and its relation to the understanding of false belief and the appearance-reality distinction. *Child Development, 59,* 26–37.

Gopnik, A., & Wellman, H. (1992). Why the child's theory of mind is really a theory. *Mind & Language, 7,* 145–171.

Hale, C. M., & Tager-Flusberg, H. (2003). The influence of language on theory of mind: A training study. *Developmental Science, 6,* 346–359.

Harris, P. (1991). The work of the imagination. In A. Whiten (Ed.), *Natural theories of mind.* (pp. 283–304). Oxford: Blackwell.

Harris, P. (1996). Desires, beliefs, and language. In P. Carruthers & P. K. Smith (Eds.), *Theories of theories of mind* (pp. 200–220). Cambridge, UK: Cambridge University Press.

Harris, P. (1999). Acquiring the art of conversation: Children's developing conception of their conversational partner. In M. Bennett (Ed.), *Developmental psychology: Achievements and prospects* (pp. 89–105). Philadelphia: Psychology Press.

Lohmann, H., & Tomasello, M. (2003). The role of language in the development of false belief understanding: A training study. *Child Development, 74,* 1130–1144.

Mc Gregor, E., Whiten, A., & Blackburn, P. (1998). Teaching theory of mind by highlighting intention and illustrating thoughts: A comparison of their effectiveness with 3-year-olds and autistic individuals. *British Journal of Developmental Psychology, 16,* 281–300.

Mead, G. H. (1934). *Mind, self, and society.* Chicago: University of Chicago Press.

Nelson, K. (1985). *Making sense: The acquisition of shared meaning.* New York: Academic Press.

Olson, D. R. (1988). On the origins of beliefs and other intentional states in children. In J. W. Astington & P. Harris & D. R. Olson (Eds.), *Developing theories of mind* (pp. 414–426). New York: Cambridge University Press.

Perner, J., Sprung, M., Zauner, P., & Haider, H. (2003). *Want-that* is understood well before *say-that, think-that*, and false belief: A test of de Villiers's linguistic determinism on German-speaking children. *Child Development, 74*, 179–188.

Peterson, C. C., & Siegal, M. (1995). Deafness, conversation and theory of mind. *Journal of Child Psychology and Psychiatry and Allied Disciplines, 36*, 459–474.

Peterson, C. C., & Siegal, M. (1998). Changing focus on the representational mind: Deaf, autistic and normal children's concepts of false photos, false drawings and false belief. *British Journal of Developmental Psychology, 16*, 301–320.

Peterson, C. C., & Siegal, M. (1999). Representing inner worlds: Theory of mind in autistic, deaf and normal hearing children. *Psychological Science, 10*, 126–129.

Peterson, C. C., & Siegal, M. (2000). Insights into theory of mind from deafness and autism. *Mind & Language, 15*, 123–145.

Siegal, M. (1999). Language and thought: The fundamental significance of conversational awareness for cognitive development. *Developmental Science, 2*, 1–34.

Slaughter, V. (1998). Children's understanding of pictorial and mental representations. *Child Development, 69*, 321–332.

Slaughter, V., & Gopnik, A. (1996). Conceptual coherence in the child's theory of mind: Training children to understand belief. *Child Development, 67*, 2767–2988.

Swettenham, J. (1996). Can children with autism be taught to understand false belief using computers? *Journal of Child Psychology and Psychiatry and Allied Disciplines, 37*(2), 157–165.

Tomasello, M. (1992). The social bases of language acquisition. *Social Development, 1*, 67–87.

Tomasello, M. (1995). Joint attention as social cognition. In C. Moore & P. J. Dunham (Eds.), *Joint attention: Its origins and role in development* (pp. 103–129). Hillsdale, NJ: Erlbaum.

Tomasello, M. (1998). Reference: Intending that others jointly attend. *Pragmatics and Cognition, 6*, 219–234.

Tomasello, M. (1999). *The cultural origins of human cognition.* Cambridge, MA: Harvard University Press.

Tomasello, M. (2001). Perceiving intentions and learning words in the second year of life. In M. Bowerman & S. Levinson (Eds.), *Language Acquisition and Conceptual Development* (pp. 132–158). Cambridge: Cambridge University Press.

Tomasello, M., & Barton, M. (1994). Learning words in non-ostensive contexts. *Developmental Psychology, 30*, 639–650.

Tomasello, M., Strosberg, R., & Akhtar, N. (1996). Eighteen-month-old children learn words in non-ostensive contexts. *Journal of Child Language, 23*, 157–176.

Vygotsky, L. (1978) *Mind in society: The development of higher psychological processes.* Ed. M. Cole. Cambridge, MA: Harvard University Press.

Watson, A., Painter, K., & Bornstein, M. (2002). Longitudinal relations between 2-year-olds' language and 4-year-olds' theory of mind. *Journal of Cognition and Development, 2*, 449–457.

Wellman, H. M., Cross, D., & Watson, J. (2001). Meta-analysis of theory-of-mind development: The truth about false belief. *Child Development, 72*, 655–584.

Wimmer, H., & Perner, J. (1983). Belief about beliefs: Representation and constraining function of wrong beliefs in young children's understanding of deception. *Cognition, 13*, 103–128.

13 The Role of Language in Theory-of-Mind Development: What Deaf Children Tell Us

Peter A. de Villiers

Introduction

The question that frames this book—"Why language matters for theory of mind"—presumes that language indeed plays a significant role in children's ToM (Theory of Mind) development, especially in the conceptual changes that occur when preschoolers between ages 3 and 5 come to understand false beliefs. There is now a great deal of empirical support for this presumption, much of it established by the research of many of the contributors to this volume (see Astington & Baird, this volume, chapter 1).

But, of course, the real issue under debate here is *why* and *how* language works to facilitate or enable the conceptual changes needed for a representational ToM. A mature ToM allows children to represent and reflect on the content of their own beliefs, distinguish them from those of others, and accurately judge their truth and falsity in relation to shared reality. They can then use this meta-representation to predict what others will do and to explain the underlying mental causes of their behavior.

Positions on these issues vary in both the properties and aspects of language that they stress and on the strength of the causal relation that they posit between language and ToM. Some suggest that talk about mental states constitutes the "best evidence" that children have about the unobserved mental causes of behavior, especially cognitive states (e.g., Brown, Donelan-McCall, & Dunn, 1996; Dunn, Brown, Slomkowski, Tesla, & Youngblade, 1991; Hughes & Dunn, 1997; Meins & Fernyhough, 1999; Perner, 2000; Peterson & Siegal, 2000).

Others propose that language plays a crucial scaffolding role in the broader social engagement of the child with others and so is a central part of the fabric of interaction between the child, caregivers, and siblings in which social-cognition is situated (Nelson, 1996). General language skills may be a necessary means of encoding events and bearing them in mind when the situation changes and there is a discrepancy between the new reality and the past situation as it is represented in the mind of another person—the classic false-belief situation (Astington, 2000). In this sense, language is a crucial scaffold for symbolic representations of events in memory (Karmiloff-Smith, 1992; Nelson, this volume, chapter 2). Conversation can also illuminate speakers' and listeners' intentions, beliefs, and states of knowledge as the participants learn to read communicative goals and presuppositions and to avoid or repair breakdowns in communication (Harris, 1996; Peterson & Siegal, 1995, 2000).

These approaches propose broad cognitive and social functions for language in general, and they are supported by global relationships between language and ToM reasoning. But other theorists have focused on specific aspects of language and argued for a more particular role for language. Some stress the role that learning labels for mental states or communication events plays as a meta-language that invites the formation and elaboration of the underlying concepts (Bartsch & Wellman, 1995; Olson, 1988, 1994). This role for linguistic labels has been proposed as a fundamental way in which language interacts with and facilitates conceptual development in other domains, too, such as object and event categorization (Gopnik & Meltzoff, 1993), and number and spatial understanding (Spelke, 2003).

Finally, the importance of syntactic development for false-belief understanding has been posited by J. de Villiers (1995, 2000; and this volume, chapter 10) and Tager-Flusberg (1997; Tager-Flusberg & Joseph, this volume, chapter 14). De Villiers suggests that children's mastery of the syntax of embedded false-complement clauses and their attendant marking of points of view provides the means for representing propositional attitudes and their contents. She argues that *realis* false-complement clauses with verbs of communication are mastered first because there is a clearer relationship between the content of communication and reality. These provide a syntactic model for *realis* mental-state verbs, such as "think" and "believe," whose propositional content can be true or false.

There is some empirical support from longitudinal studies (Astington & Jenkins, 1999; J. de Villiers & Pyers, 2002) for mastery of both general and specific features of language predicting later ToM reasoning, but some cross-sectional studies have reported that general language measures overwhelm any specific effects of the syntax of complementation (Ruffman, Slade, Rowlandson, Rumsey, & Garnham, 2003). The general problem in trying to separate the effects of different components of language is that so many cognitive, social, and linguistic advances are made in such a short time in normally developing preschoolers between ages 3 and 5, many of them highly correlated with each other. So often the overwhelmingly significant predictor variable in statistical analyses turns out to be just age as a proxy for general development or maturity.

Why Study Deaf Children?

Deaf children provide a strong test of a causal role for language in ToM development. Many deaf children have significantly delayed language acquisition, but they have age-appropriate nonverbal intelligence and active sociability. Studying their ToM reasoning can therefore tease out the effects of language acquisition from those of cognitive maturation and engagement in social interaction—to the extent that the latter do not themselves depend on language acquisition. Furthermore, the entire language acquisition process tends to be stretched out in deaf children, and they have differential difficulty with embedded sentence structures. Mastery of complex syntactic forms is usually more impaired than pragmatics and conversational skills (P. de Villiers, 2003), and so it may be possible to tease out the relative contribution of different elements of language to the development of ToM. In addition, wide variations in linguistic abilities can be observed at a given age, so age per se becomes a weaker predictive factor in regression analyses.

A subgroup of deaf children who have deaf parents are exposed to a full language from birth in the form of a natural sign language, so their language acquisition follows the normal timetable (P. de Villiers & Pyers, 2003). They therefore provide a control for any effects of deafness per se. If language acquisition plays a central causal role in ToM development, then deaf children with delayed language will experience corresponding delays in their understanding and reasoning about mental states. However, deaf children acquiring a natural sign language from birth should develop a representational ToM on the same timetable as normally hearing children.

In this chapter I first summarize the findings of previous studies of ToM development in deaf children. These provide suggestive evidence that language acquisition is a fundamental contributor to children's mastery of reasoning about false beliefs. However, there are a number of flaws in the earlier studies, varying from small sample sizes to weaknesses in the measurement of ToM reasoning and especially of language acquisition in the deaf children. I therefore describe the findings of a more comprehensive study of the relationship between language and false-belief reasoning in deaf children that was designed to eliminate these weaknesses.

The findings of recent studies of how deaf children acquire an understanding of false belief can be broken down into six broad categories:

1. Deaf children with language delay show a delay of up to several years in their reasoning about the cognitive states (thoughts, beliefs, and

knowledge) of others (Courtin, 2000; J. de Villiers & P. de Villiers, 2000; P. de Villiers & Pyers, 2001; Gale, P. de Villiers, J. de Villiers, & Pyers, 1996; Jackson, 2001; Peterson & Siegal, 1995, 1997, 1999; Russell, Hosie, Gray, et al. , 1998; Steeds, Rowe, & Dowker, 1997).

2. Deaf children show comparable levels of performance on the highly verbal standard tests of false-belief reasoning (e.g., the unexpected-contents task) and much less verbal or essentially nonverbal tests of reasoning about cognitive states. Therefore, their delayed perfor-mance on standard tests of false-belief reasoning do not result from the language demands of the tasks themselves—for example, the linguistic complexity of the questions the children are asked or the need to follow a verbal narrative (J. de Villiers & P. de Villiers, 2000; P. de Villiers & Pyers, 2001; Figueras-Costas & Harris, 2001; Gale et al., 1996; Woolfe, Want, & Siegal, 2002).

3. Deaf children's performance on tasks assessing their reasoning about false beliefs and states of knowledge is differentially predicted by their language levels (Jackson, 2001; Woolfe et al., 2002), specifi-cally their mastery of language about the mind and the syntax of complementation that goes with it (P. de Villiers & Pyers, 2001). This is true for both the highly verbal standard tasks and for less verbal or essentially nonverbal tests that involve similar types of reasoning about cognitive states (J. de Villiers & P. de Villiers, 2000; P. de Villiers & Pyers, 2001).

4. Deaf children are good at predicting simple emotional reactions from stereotypical situations (P. de Villiers, Hosler, Miller, Whalen, & Wong, 1997; Pyers & P. de Villiers, 2003) and readily appeal to desires and other mental states as explanations of emotion (Rieffe & Terwogt, 2000). In contrast, their performance on tasks involv-ing judgments about emotions based on characters' false beliefs is delayed to the same degree as their reasoning about false beliefs on the classic tasks (P. de Villiers et al., 1997; Pyers & P. de Villiers, 2003). P. de Villiers et al. (1997) found that oral deaf children's judgments about characters' emotional reactions in different causal situations were predicted by different background and language measures. The children's understanding of simple emotions based on stereotypical situations was predicted by nonverbal IQ and age, not by language measures or by their reasoning on standard ToM tests. However, their judgments of emotions based on false beliefs were predicted by mastery of cognitive state verbs and the syntax of complementation.

5. Deaf children with deaf relatives who acquire a natural sign lan-guage from an early age do not appear to be delayed in their ToM

development (Courtin, 2000; Deleau, 1996; Jackson, 2001; Peterson & Siegel, 1999).

6. Deaf children's delay in ToM reasoning is specific to the representation of cognitive states that do or do not correspond to perceived reality. They do not have any problem in judging the contents of a physical representation (a photograph) that no longer reflects the scene that is in front of them (P. de Villiers & Pyers, 2001; Peterson & Siegel, 1997, 1998). In fact, their performance on the "false photographs" test (Zaitchik, 1990) matched that of hearing peers of the same age (P. de Villiers & Pyers, 2001). Thus, their failure on traditional false-belief reasoning tasks is not the result of general meta-representational problems or an inability to detach themselves from the tendency to answer the test questions with reality.

Although the bulk of these findings support the conclusion that language-delayed deaf children are also delayed in their understanding of false beliefs and that the degree of language delay determines the degree of conceptual delay, a few studies have argued that in many other aspects of ToM, deaf children and adolescents are not different from hearing peers in their social cognition (e.g., Marschark, Green, Hindmarsh, & Walker, 2000; Rhys-Jones & Ellis, 2000; Rieffe & Terwogt, 2000). In fact, they may be more likely than hearing children to explain actions and emotions by reference to desires (Rhys-Jones & Ellis, 2000; Rieffe & Terwogt, 2000).

Limitations and Weaknesses of These Studies

Most studies of ToM in deaf children suffer from major weaknesses in design. Very few studies examined the ToM reasoning of the same deaf children in both standard verbal tasks and in nonverbal or less verbal tasks involving the same reasoning about states of knowledge or belief. Most of the studies did not directly assess the children's language skills, or did so in a very general way (typically by rating scales) that could not determine which aspects of language make a difference in the development of ToM (e.g., Lundy, 2002; Peterson & Siegal, 1995, 1999). Many of the studies with signing deaf children used interpreters to administer the ToM tasks, a source of possible distraction or confusion for the children (Peterson & Siegal, 1995, 1999, 2000).

Sample sizes in almost all of the studies are too small for researchers to be confident about correlational or regression analyses of the relationship between language and ToM measures. In the few studies that examined the performance of native signing children, sample sizes were particularly small, and almost all of the deaf children were a few years older than the age at which hearing children consistently master the standard tests of false-belief reasoning (Peterson &

Siegal, 1999, 2000). So the extent to which the native signing children were delayed or not in their ToM development could not be assessed accurately; all that could be said was that their performance was significantly better than that of the nonnative signers.

Study 1: A Comprehensive Study of the Relationship between Language and False-Belief Understanding in Oral and ASL Signing Deaf Children

In a study designed to eliminate most of these weaknesses (P. de Villiers, J. de Villiers, Schick, & Hoffmeister, 2001; Schick, J. de Villiers, P. de Villiers, & Hoffmeister, in preparation), we investigated the performance of two groups of deaf children with varying degrees of language delay on standard verbal tasks that assess false-belief reasoning and on "low-verbal" or essentially nonverbal tests of similar reasoning about cognitive states. One group of deaf children (the oral group) came from hearing families and educational settings in which only spoken and written English input was provided, with no formal exposure to sign language. Access to auditory information was maximized through hearing aids and cochlear implants, and the children were acquiring spoken English. The other group of deaf children (the ASL group) was being exposed to intensive signed input in both the home and the school setting in the form of ASL. A little more than half of these children had ASL-signing deaf parents, and all of them had signing deaf teachers at school. So all of these children were acquiring ASL as their primary "through-the-air" language. The performance of the various groups of deaf children was compared with that of normally hearing children of the same ages on the same tasks. In addition, we examined the relationships between several aspects of the deaf children's language (vocabulary, general syntax, and complementation) and their reasoning about cognitive states when the effects of background variables (age, hearing loss, and nonverbal intelligence) were statistically controlled for. The language assessments were of spoken English for the oral deaf children and normally hearing children and of ASL for the signing deaf children.

Participants

Oral Participants

Eighty-six deaf children from oral-only educational settings with hearing teachers participated in the study. They ranged in age from 4;0 to 8;3, with a mean age of 6 years 1 month, and there were approximately equal numbers of 4-, 5-, 6-, and 7-year-olds. Their average unaided hearing loss was 92dB (range 47dB to 120dB). Fifty-three of the children wore hearing aids, and 33 had cochlear implants. All of the children had experienced their hearing loss prior to 18 months of age, and they all had normal nonverbal IQs and normal nonverbal sequence memory.

ASL-Signing Participants

Ninety deaf children from intensive ASL educational settings with deaf teachers participated. Ages ranged from 3;11 to 8;0 with a mean of 6 years 1 month, and they were roughly equally divided among the age groups (4, 5, 6 and 7 years). Average unaided hearing loss was 90dB (range 45dB to 120dB), and all of the children had experienced their hearing loss before the age of 18 months. Forty-nine children had deaf parents (DoD—Deaf of Deaf) and had been exposed to ASL since birth; 41 had hearing parents (DoH—Deaf of Hearing) and so had been exposed to ASL at a later point in development. Although all of the hearing parents had received instruction in ASL and were attempting to sign with their offspring, they varied in their fluency in sign language. All of the children received a great deal of input in ASL from deaf teachers and aides in the school settings. As with the oral deaf children, the signing group all had normal nonverbal IQs and age-appropriate nonverbal sequence memory.

Statistical analyses showed that the three groups of deaf children (oral, ASL-DoD, and ASL-DoH) were well matched in age, unaided hearing loss, nonverbal IQ, and sequence memory.

Normally Hearing Control Participants

The 42 normally hearing control children came mostly from working-class communities to match the SES of the group of ASL-signing children with deaf parents with whom they were to be compared on ToM. They ranged in age from 4;0 to 6;8, with approximately equal numbers of 4-, 5-, and 6-year-olds. Statistical analyses showed that the hearing children matched the age distribution of the three groups of 4- through 6-year-old deaf subjects.

Procedure

Each of the children was tested individually and received a battery of nonverbal intelligence, language assessments, and ToM tasks across several testing sessions. For the oral deaf children, the testing was carried out by hearing examiners highly familiar with the speech of deaf children. All of the oral children were using the most appropriate individualized amplification systems for their deafness (typically some combination of FM systems, hearing aids, and cochlear implants). The ASL-signing children were all tested by deaf examiners with native level skills in ASL. None of the testing was done through interpreters.

Background Measures

General cognitive abilities were assessed with the Pattern Construction subtest of the Differential Ability Scales (DAS; Elliott, 1990), a test of pattern matching with colored blocks that is standardized for ages 3;6 to adults, and the Knox's Cube Test of nonverbal sequence memory (Stone & Wright, 1979). On Knox's Cube Test, the child has to imitate the examiner in tapping one wooden cube against a set of four identical cubes in an increasingly complex order. It is standardized on children ages 3 years to adult and has been widely used with deaf children.

Theory-of-Mind Measures

Standard Verbal False-Belief Reasoning Assessments

There were three *change-in-location* narratives in a picture-storybook format (P. de Villiers & Pyers, 2001; Wimmer & Perner, 1983). After each story, the child was asked memory control questions to make sure that he knew where the object had first been placed and where it was moved to. When the character returned and wanted to get the hidden object, the children were asked both "Where will X *first* look for his Y?" (Siegal & Beattie, 1991) and "Why will he look there?" Gale et al. (1996) argued that the picture-book format was better for testing deaf children because it was more familiar and less distracting for them than the act-out procedure usually used with hearing preschoolers, especially if sign language was being used. P. de Villiers and Pyers (2001) showed that the storybook procedure was equivalent in difficulty to the more usual acted-out story for hearing children.

The children were also tested on two familiar containers with *unexpected contents* (e.g., a Crayola crayon box that turned out to contain a plastic spoon) (Perner, Leekam, & Wimmer, 1987). They were asked both about their own belief prior to looking in the box and about what a friend of theirs would think was in the box before she looked in it.

Two Low-Verbal Tasks Involving Reasoning about
the Cognitive States of Another Person

To control for any effects of the language required by the FB tasks themselves, we developed two low-verbal tasks that tapped into reasoning about cognitive states similar to that for the standard verbal tasks.

A *sticker-finding hide-and-seek game* was adapted from research by Povinelli and deBlois (1992) with children and chimpanzees. In the game, the experimenter hid a sticker in one of four identical white boxes while a pull-down screen obscured the hiding from the child. On the crucial test trials, two "helping" adults each pointed to a box after the screen was raised, and the child had to choose whose advice to follow to find the hidden sticker. One adult had sat next to the experimenter and watched the sticker being hidden, while the second was sitting next to the child (screened off from the hiding) and also wearing a blindfold as the sticker was hidden. In essence, the child had to determine which helper knew where the sticker was on the basis of their visual access to the event. In previous studies, this game was mastered by hearing children at approximately the same age that they passed the standard location change false-belief task. It was as difficult as the verbal tasks for oral deaf children, even though it uses minimal language. And it was highly correlated with performance on the standard unseen-location-change task (P. de Villiers & Pyers, 2001; Gale et al., 1996).

The *surprise face game* was a picture-sequence-based task in which the child had to complete a picture at the end of the story sequence by putting a "surprised" or "not-surprised" (neutral) face on a character depending on the character's expectations and state of knowledge about the contents of a familiar container. It was designed as a low-verbal analogue of the standard verbal unexpected-contents task. In the picture sequences, the crucial character either did or did not observe another character substitute an unusual object for the familiar contents of a container (e.g., a key placed in a Crayola crayon box, or a dollar bill placed in a Band-aid box). Minimal language was used in introducing and playing this game. The child was just told what the objects were (e.g., key, crayons, dollar, Band-aids). The pictures specified the actions and whether the character saw the object substitution or not. P. de Villiers and Pyers (2001) reported that mastery of the surprise face game was accomplished at approximately the same age as mastery of the standard false-belief reasoning tasks in hearing preschoolers and that the game was as difficult as the standard unexpected-contents task for oral deaf children, despite the huge difference in the complexity of the language of the task.

More details about these games and how they were administered and scored are given in P. de Villiers and Pyers (2001) and Schick et al. (in preparation).

Language Measures

All of the deaf children were given an extensive battery of language assessments. The measures relevant for this chapter are as follows (for a fuller specification and analysis of the language measures, see Schick et al., in preparation).

Oral Deaf Children

Spoken one-word vocabulary comprehension and production were assessed by the Peabody Picture Vocabulary Test-Revised (PPVT-R; Dunn & Dunn, 1981) and the Elicited One-Word Picture Vocabulary Test (EOWPVT; Gardner, 1990). These are standard picture-based tests of word knowledge that are widely used with both hearing and deaf children.

General spoken English syntax comprehension was tested on the Sentence Structure subtest of the Clinical Evaluation of Language Fundamentals for preschoolers (CELF-Preschool) (Wiig, Secord, & Semel, 1992). This subtest consists of 22 sentences that vary in complexity from simple active declaratives to sentences with embedded relative clauses. It does not include any sentences that contain complement clauses. The stimulus sentences were presented orally, and the child had to choose which of three pictures best depicted the meaning of the sentence.

Comprehension of false-complement clauses with communication verbs ("tell") and cognition verbs ("think") was tested on a memory for complement clauses task (J. de Villiers & Pyers, 1997, 2002). The child was shown two colored photographs that depicted the events of a brief two-sentence anecdote in which a character was described as making a mistake, telling a lie, or having a false belief. Four sequences involved what the character "thought," four sequences involved what the character "told" someone (e.g., "She told the girl there was a bug in her hair [picture 1]). But it was only a leaf [picture 2, close up])." After each sequence, the child was asked, "What did she tell X?" or "What did she think?," depending on the act depicted.

To answer correctly, the child had to process the syntax and remember the embedded false complement with the verb of communication or cognition in the story. The communication items do not require any understanding of mental states for their comprehension, and even in the case of the "think" verbs a child could correctly answer the "What think?" question without a well-developed concept of false belief as long as she had processed the complement clause correctly (J. de Villiers & Pyers, 2002). In their longitudinal study of hearing preschoolers, J. de Villiers and Pyers (2002) showed that performance on the communication verb items on this task around age 3;4 was the primary predictor of later levels of false-belief reasoning (around age 3;8). Indeed, memory for complements was a separate and stronger predictor than other more general measures of language.

ASL-Signing Children

Since there are no standardized tests of ASL comprehension or production currently available, assessment procedures were developed specifically for this study to evaluate the signing children's ASL. The design of the tests and items was based on existing research on which features of ASL show systematic developmental change over this age range. The tests of ASL that parallel the English language assessments carried out for the oral children included a test of ASL sign vocabulary based on the structure and format of the PPVT, a test of general ASL syntax comprehension that did not include complement clauses, and an ASL version of the false-complement comprehension test.

The general syntax test consisted of 16 signed stimulus sentences that represented several fundamental features of ASL sentence syntax. These included sentences involving topicalization in which the object of the sentence was moved to utterance-initial position and marked as the topic by means of nonmanual grammatical markers (see P. de Villiers & Pyers, 2003; Liddell, 1980). Other stimulus sentences involved complex forms of verb agreement with pronominal arguments, another distinctive aspect of the syntax of signed languages such as ASL (Klima & Bellugi, 1979; Wilbur, 1987). The format of the syntax comprehension test was parallel to that of the CELF-Preschool used with the oral deaf children; the examiner signed the stimulus sentence, and the child had to choose which one among three or four pictures best depicted the distinctive meaning of the sentence. An additional test assessed the children's comprehension of classifiers in ASL, semantic and syntactic forms characteristic of sign languages.

To test the signing children's understanding of false-complement clauses in their language, the processing of complement clauses procedure (described earlier) was translated into ASL (by native signers) and administered the same way as for the oral deaf and hearing children.

Key Features of the Study

This study improved upon the previous research on deaf children in several aspects:

1. First, it tested a substantial sample of young deaf children comparable in age to participants in studies of hearing children.
2. Second, it tested substantial numbers of native-signing DoD children at each age level in the ASL group. Most important, it tested native signers who were young enough for us be able to make direct comparisons of their performance with that of hearing control children on the same ToM tasks.
3. For the signing children, the tasks were all translated into ASL and administered directly by deaf researchers with native or near-native ASL skills, not through interpreters. The normally hearing controls and the oral deaf children were tested by examiners very familiar with the speech patterns of young deaf children.
4. Both standard verbal false-belief reasoning tasks and low-verbal tasks were used to assess ToM understanding in the same children.
5. Finally, there was extensive and specific assessment of language skills for all groups of deaf children, regarding both semantic and syntac-

tic features of language and focusing on complement clauses with verbs of communication and cognitive state. In this way, different theories about the role of language could be addressed by the data.

Results

For the following analyses, two measures of ToM reasoning were calculated for each child: a verbal false-belief reasoning score and a measure of mastery of the low-verbal tasks involving states of knowledge and ignorance. The verbal FB score consisted of the number of false-belief questions across the several standard verbal tasks that the child answered correctly (range 0–7). Each of the low-verbal tasks was scored pass-fail on the basis of the number of test trials on which the child was correct. The criterion for passing was >7 out of 10 on the sticker hide-and-seek game and 5 or 6 out of 6 on the surprise face game. The number of low-verbal tasks that each child passed was then calculated (range 0–2).

Mastery of ToM Reasoning in Hearing Controls versus ASL versus Oral Deaf Children

Figure 13.1 shows the average total score on the standard verbal false-belief tasks for each experimental group across the different age groups and figure 13.2 shows the average number of low-verbal games passed by the children in the different experimental groups, by age.

ANOVAs compared the average performance of the different experimental groups on the standard verbal false-belief tasks and the average number of

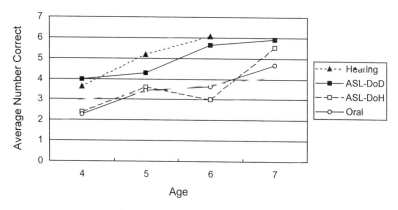

Figure 13.1. Mean total score of the children in each group on the standard verbal false-belief tasks (out of 7 false-belief questions).

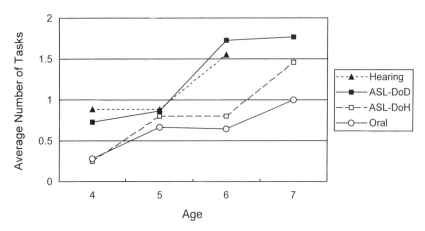

Figure 13.2. Average number of low-verbal tasks passed by the children in each group.

low-verbal tasks that they passed. Only the data from the children ages 4 through 6 were considered for this analysis so that the performance of the deaf children could be compared with that of the hearing controls matched for age.

There were no differences among the four groups in average age or age distribution. However, for the children's performance on the false-belief questions, there was a significant main effect for experimental group ($F(3,164) =7.42$, $p<.001$). Post hoc t-tests demonstrated that the hearing control children and the native signing ASL children with deaf parents (ASL-DoD) were indistinguishable on these verbal ToM tasks, but both of those groups performed significantly better than the two groups of language-delayed deaf children with hearing parents: Hearing versus ASL-DoH ($t = 3.07$, df = 64, $p<.01$), Hearing versus Oral Deaf ($t = 3.39$, df = 102, $p<.001$), ASL-DoD versus ASL-DoH ($t = 3.43$, df = 62, $p<.001$), ASL-DoD versus Oral Deaf ($t = 3.42$, df = 96, $p<.001$). The performance of the two groups of deaf children with hearing parents was equivalent on the verbal tasks, so at these ages there was no significant effect of the predominant language of school instruction, ASL versus oral English.

On the low-verbal tasks there was again a significant main effect for group ($F(3,160) = 3.49$, $p<.001$). The two groups with normal language acquisition (hearing controls and ASL children with signing deaf parents) were equivalent in their performance, and they did significantly better than the children in the two groups with hearing parents who were delayed in their language acquisition: Hearing versus ASL-DoH ($t = 2.18$, df = 64, $p<.05$), Hearing versus Oral Deaf ($t = 3.47$, df = 98, $p<.001$), ASL-DoD versus ASL-DoH ($t = 2.20$, df = 62, $p<.05$), ASL-DoD versus Oral Deaf ($t = 3.47$, df = 96, $p<.001$). Again, no significant difference was observed between the ASL and the Oral Deaf groups who had hearing parents.

To summarize:

1. Language-delayed deaf children, whether signing or oral, are significantly delayed relative to age-matched hearing controls in their reasoning about false beliefs and states of knowledge and ignorance.
2. The magnitude and pattern of delay is similar whether the children are tested by verbal tasks that involve complex language (e.g., the unexpected contents task) or by low-verbal tasks that involve minimal vocabulary or almost no language at all (e.g., the sticker hide-and-seek game). So the language of the task is not a major determining factor in performance.
3. The performance of native-signing deaf children who have age-appropriate language development, albeit in a visual rather than a spoken language, is indistinguishable from that of age-matched hearing children, right down to age 4.

Predictors of the Performance of the Deaf Children on ToM Tasks

Another way to determine the role of language in ToM development in deaf children is to examine whether the various measures of the children's language development differentially predict the children's performance on the various high-verbal and low-verbal tasks when the effects of background variables such as age, hearing loss, and nonverbal intelligence are controlled for. This analysis also allows the different features of language to be pitted against each other. Multiple regression analyses were carried out for both the oral deaf group and the full ASL-signing group. For each analysis, similar predictor variables were entered into the regression equation. The background measures were age, hearing loss, nonverbal IQ on the Pattern Construction subtest of the DAS, and nonverbal sequence memory on the Knox's Cubes Test. Three language measures were entered for each group of children—vocabulary, general syntax comprehension, and the processing of false-complement clauses with verbs of communication in the memory for complements task. The multiple-regression analyses revealed very similar patterns of independent predictors of performance on the two derived measures of ToM reasoning for the oral and the signing deaf groups.

The verbal false-belief reasoning of the *oral deaf children* was independently predicted by vocabulary (p = .001) and the processing of false complement clauses (p = .02), but not by age, hearing loss, nonverbal IQ, or general English syntax comprehension. Similarly, the number of low-verbal ToM tasks that the oral deaf children passed was independently predicted by vocabulary (p = .013) and processing of false-complement clauses (p = .015), but not by any other variable.

Verbal false-belief reasoning in the *ASL-signing children* was also predicted independently by the processing of false complement clauses (p = .039) and by vocabulary comprehension (p = .005). Again, hearing loss, nonverbal IQ, and comprehension of general ASL syntax were not significant predictors. However, for the low-verbal ToM reasoning tasks, the performance of the ASL-signing children was differentially predicted by processing of false complement clauses (p = .004) and by age (p = .012), although vocabulary also approached significance (p = .08).

Conclusions

Taken together with the results of previous studies of deaf children's reasoning about false beliefs, the results of this study argue for a strong causal role of language in the development of a representational ToM.

Deaf children with deaf parents who acquire fluent ASL *early* from a natural input are significantly better in their reasoning about cognitive states than language-delayed deaf children with hearing parents who are being educated in either intensive ASL or oral settings. Indeed, the development of ToM in these fluent-signing DoD children is comparable with that of hearing peers (see also Courtin, 2000).

Language delay leads to a significant delay in DoH children's reasoning about the contents of cognitive states (especially false beliefs and states of knowledge). This is true for highly verbal tasks as well as for ones with minimal language requirements—compare, for example, the language demands of the unexpected-contents task with its complex question ("Before X looks in the box, what will X think is in the box?") and those of the surprise-face game ("Which face?"). Thus, the explicit language of the tasks is not the cause of the delay in reasoning.

Both general semantic features of language (vocabulary) and specific syntactic features (the processing of false-complement clauses) are independently predictive of false-belief reasoning for both oral and ASL-signing children. These language predictors are found for both the highly verbal standard tasks and the low-verbal games. This supports *both* theories that argue for the facilitative effects of semantic or pragmatic (conversational) features of language (e.g., Harris, 1996, this volume, chapter 4; Olson, 1988, 1994; Peterson & Siegal, 1999, 2000) and the theory that mastery of the syntax of complements with verbs of communication and mental state (and, crucially, their truth and falsity conditions) may provide the representational mechanism for reasoning about false beliefs (J. de Villiers, 1995, 2000, this volume, chapter 10). Indeed, it suggests that these theories may be more complementary than exclusive.

Language or Executive Functioning Constraints?

An alternative account of the cognitive processes underlying the mastery of false-belief tasks appeals to the development or maturation of executive functions (EF) between the ages of 3 and 5. Executive functions include cognitive processes required to monitor, control, and plan thought and action. The three aspects of EF that have received the most attention in research on ToM are:

1. Inhibitory control and resistance to interference by competing tasks or behavioral tendencies (Carlson & Moses, 2001; Carlson, Moses, & Hix, 1998; Hughes, 1998a, 1998b; Leslie & Polizzi, 1998);
2. Flexible rule following in situations where there are hierarchical or conditional rules, especially if a competing well-learned rule of action has to be inhibited in the process (Frye, Zelazo, & Palfai, 1995; Zelazo, Carter, Reznick, & Frye, 1997);
3. Working memory to enable the child to maintain and reflect on the competing alternatives in short-term memory (Davis & Pratt, 1995; Gordon & Olson, 1998; Keenan, 1998, 2000).

Logical analyses of the standard tests of false-belief reasoning—unseen change in location, unexpected contents, and appearance-reality judgments—suggest that each of these executive processes is involved in passing the tasks. Furthermore, there seems to be a common developmental time course for EF and representational ToM between the ages of 3 and 5, and several studies have shown that mastery of EF tasks is significantly correlated with performance on ToM tasks in this age range, even when age and basic verbal ability are partialed out (Carlson et al., 1998; Carlson & Moses, 2001; Davis & Pratt, 1995; Frye et al., 1995; Gordon & Olson, 1998; Hughes, 1998a, 1998b; Keenan, 1998, 2000; Moses, 2001). Finally, areas of the prefrontal temporal cortex have been implicated in both EF and ToM performance in brain imaging and brain damage studies, and autistic individuals are notably deficient in both EF and ToM (Ozonoff, Pennington, & Rogers, 1991; Russell, 1997).

On the other hand, the direction of effect between EF maturation and ToM conceptual development has not always been clear. In a longitudinal study, Hughes (1998b) found inhibitory control to be a better predictor of later ToM, especially performance in deception games, than the reverse prediction, from ToM to EF. However, Carlson and Moses (2001) found as many children who were high on ToM and low on EF as children high on EF and low on ToM in a multivariable cross-sectional study, though the latter profile should dominate if EF development has a causal effect on ToM. So, while most theorists posit that EF development leads to later ToM, Perner and his colleagues (Perner & Lang, 2000; Perner, Lang, & Kloo, 2002; Perner, Stummer, & Lang, 1999) have argued for the opposite direction of the relationship. They suggest that the meta-representational skills that are fundamental to ToM are necessary for volitional control over actions and hence EF. They argue that to succeed at EF tasks, children must be able to represent both their goals and impediments to those goals (e.g., from prior learning or habitual tendencies). So self-monitoring requires a means of expressing higher order mental states, that is, ToM.

Although some theorists have implicated language as a causal factor in EF development (see Zelazo, 1999), most have regarded language level just as a background variable to be controlled for. Several studies of the relation between EF and ToM in children have therefore measured general verbal skills on a standard test of vocabulary or semantics and syntax (such as the Test of Early Language Development, TELD; Hresko, Reid, & Hammill, 1991).

The study of oral deaf children who have delayed language but normal nonverbal intellectual development should enable us to separate the relative contributions of EF from those of specific components of language acquisition to the children's mastery of false-belief reasoning in the traditional tasks.

Study 2: Teasing Apart the Relative Effects of Executive Functioning and Language on the Mastery of False-Belief Reasoning by Oral Deaf Children

We (P. de Villiers, Freedman, & Friedman, 2001) hypothesized that deaf children would be far less impaired in their executive functioning than they were in their language and their understanding of false beliefs. So, while EF development might be a cognitive prerequisite for the development of a representational ToM, in deaf children it would be less predictive of the children's actual mastery of the false-belief tasks. That would depend more directly on their language skills, in particular their mastery of false complements with verbs of communication.

Participants

Thirty-one orally taught deaf children participated in the study. Their ages ranged from 3;11 to 8;8, with a mean of 6 years 1 month. Fourteen of the children wore hearing aids, and 17 had cochlear implants. The average aided hearing loss was 31.9dB, with a range of 18 to 57dB. All the children scored in the normal range of nonverbal IQ on the DAS Pattern Construction subtest (Elliott, 1990). Spoken English vocabulary age levels on the Expressive Vocabulary Test (EVT; Williams, 1997) ranged from 1;11 to 6;3, with a mean of 4 years 7 months, so most of the children had substantial language delays.

Procedure

In three one-on-one testing sessions over a period of about two weeks, the children received a battery of assessments of their reasoning about false beliefs, their level of executive functioning, and their language. The testing was carried out by an adult experienced at interacting with oral deaf children and familiar with their speech patterns.

Theory-of-Mind Measures

The children were tested on two standard change-in-location false-belief stories in picture-book format. Following the memory control questions at the end of the story, they were asked both where the character would first look for the object and then why she would first look there.

All of the children also received two unexpected contents tasks with familiar containers. For one container, the children were asked what they thought was in the box before they looked inside; for the other container, they were asked what a friend of theirs would think was in the box before they looked inside.

There were therefore six questions about false beliefs: two about what a person first thought or would think was in a container that the child knew contained an unexpected object, two about where a character would first look for a desired object that was moved without her knowledge, and two justifications for why the character would look in the wrong place.

Measures of Executive Functioning

All three aspects of executive functioning were assessed, that is, working memory, inhibitory control, and flexible, conditional rule following.

Backward Color Span

In this verbal working memory task, the children listened to a spoken list of familiar color words varying from two up to five words long and then had to repeat the list of words backward. The children were first trained on two-word lists with colored flashcards accompanying the words until they understood the task of saying the words in the order opposite to the one in which they were presented. All except one of the youngest deaf children understood the task by the end of this training phase. The test phase proceeded in blocks of four trials. The first four lists consisted of pairs of color words, the next four trials were three-word lists, and so on. Testing stopped when the child made four consecutive errors. This task taxes working memory because it requires the child to remember the color-words that were said and then to manipulate those words in order to say them in backward order. Performance on the task was scored as the number of color-word sequences that were correctly repeated backward. This task was comparable to the backward number repetition test used by Davis and Pratt (1995) that was significantly correlated with performance on standard ToM tasks in hearing children.

Exhaustive-Search Task

One nonverbal working memory task was a sticker-finding game in which the children had to search exhaustively for stickers that they themselves had placed in 8 boxes of identical size and shape but with different color lids. Once the child had put a sticker in each box, the boxes were placed on a "lazy Susan" turntable and covered with a cloth. The turntable was spun to change the orientation of the boxes relative to the child, the cloth was removed, and the child was told to find a sticker. Following each trial, the boxes were spatially rearranged and covered with the cloth, and the turntable was spun. When the boxes were exposed for the next trial, the child was told to "Choose a box you did not look in before." The game continued until the child had found all 8 stickers or until 15 trials were completed. Since the arrangement and orientation of the boxes was changed after each trial, the child had to keep updating in working memory which color box he had looked inside (or not yet looked inside). Efficiency of working memory was scored as the number of stickers that the child found in the first 9 trials. This measure was less distorted than the total number of trials taken in the game, because some children did very well at first but then got stuck with just one sticker that they could not find. This game was similar to one used by Hughes (1998a).

Knox's Cube Test

This is a test of nonverbal memory for action sequences standardized on hearing children ages 3 years to adult (Stone & Wright, 1979; see Study 1 for a description).

Day/Night Stroop Test

The children's inhibitory control was assessed by the day/night version of the Stroop test developed for use with young children (Gerstadt, Hong, & Diamond, 1994). The test used a set of cards on which was drawn either a colored picture of the sun (with diverging rays of sunlight) or a picture of a slivered moon and a few stars. The child was first trained with one example of each card to say the opposite of what was depicted—"night" for the sun and "day" for the moon. The child was then shown a random sequence of 16 cards containing suns and moons, to which she responded with either "night" or "day." This task tested the child's ability to inhibit the usual response of matching the word to the depicted object, producing instead the opposite label. Scores were calculated as the number of correct responses out of 16. Several studies have shown that this task correlates significantly with hearing preschoolers' performance on false-belief reasoning tasks (e.g., Carlson et al., 1998; Carlson & Moses, 2001).

Dimensional-Change Card Sort

Conditional rule following with inhibitory control was tested by a simple version of the dimensional-change card sort task, developed to test preschoolers (Frye et al., 1995). In this task, 8 cards were used. These depicted 2 red circles, 2 red squares, 2 blue circles, and 2 blue squares. In the practice phase of the task, the children demonstrated that they could sort the cards into two boxes according to their color (the "color game") and according to their shape (the "shape game"). The two practice sortings were separated in time so that they did not interfere with each other. In the test phase later in the testing session, once the children had sorted by one dimension (e.g., the "color game"), the game immediately changed to the other dimension (e.g., the "shape game") and then back to the first dimension again (the "color game"). After each switch was announced, the child was reminded about the rules for the new game (e.g., "Remember, in the color game all of the red ones go here, and all of the blue ones go there."). No feedback was given for either correct or incorrect trials in the test phase. So there were 24 cards to be sorted in the test phase, and each child's dimensional change card sort score was calculated as the number of cards correctly sorted out of the 24 trials. This task has been widely used in studies of the relationship between EF and ToM in hearing children (e.g., Carlson & Moses, 2001; Frye et al., 1995).

Language Measures

Vocabulary

All of the children received a standard picture-naming test of vocabulary, the Expressive Vocabulary Test (EVT). It is standardized for hearing children from age 30 months on. Scores were given as vocabulary age, based on the test norms.

General English Syntax

Syntax comprehension was assessed with a subset of 22 sentence syntax items from the Rhode Island Test of Language Structure (RITLS; Engen & Engen, 1983), varying from simple (e.g., subject-verb-object and subject-verb-prepositional phrases) to complex structures (e.g., sentence-initial adverbial and center-embedded relative clauses), but not including any complement structures. The children were given a spoken sentence and had to pick out from a set of three pictures the one that corresponded to the meaning of the sentence. The RITLS was standardized on deaf and hearing children and is widely used with deaf children in both oral and total communication educational settings. Scores were calculated as the number of sentences out of the 22 that were correctly comprehended.

Complement Comprehension

The children's processing of tensed false-complement clauses with verbs of communication ("tell") and cognition ("think") was tested by the same complement comprehension procedure used in Study 1 and adapted from J. de Villiers and Pyers (1997, 2002). There were 8 stimulus sentences, 4 with "tell/told" and 4 with "think."

Results

Each child received a false-belief reasoning score out of 6, which served as the dependent measure in the following statistical analyses.

Predictors of FB Reasoning Scores

Table 13.1 provides the bivariate correlations and partial correlations between each of the independent variables and the false-belief reasoning scores of the children. The partial correlations controlled for the effects of the background variables of age, aided hearing loss, and nonverbal IQ on the DAS.

Of the executive function measures, only the verbal working memory task (Backward Color Span) was significantly correlated with the children's performance on the standard false-belief tasks. The day/night Stroop, the dimensional-change card sort, and the nonverbal memory tasks were not related to the ToM measures, even in the bivariate correlations.

On the other hand, the three language measures were significantly correlated with the false-belief scores and remained so even when the effects of age, hearing loss, and nonverbal IQ were partialed out. For this analysis, only the comprehension of complement clauses with the "tell" verbs was used as a predictor so that the false-complement processing score did not involve the understanding of cognition verbs.

A mixed hierarchical and stepwise linear regression analysis pitted the different language measures and verbal memory measure against each other to determine which were the strongest independent predictors of the children's false-belief reasoning scores (see table 13.2). Background control variables (age, aided hearing loss, and nonverbal IQ) were entered first, and then the various

Table 13.1 Bivariate Correlations and Partial Correlations between False-Belief Reasoning Scores (Out of 6 FB Questions) and the Language and Executive Function Measures[1]

Language and Executive Function Measures	Bivariate Correlations with False-Belief Scores	Partial Correlations with False-Belief Scores
Processing of False Complement Clauses (Communication Verb)	.65***	.68***
Vocabulary (EVT)	.61***	.59***
General Syntax (RITLS items)	.43**	.40*
Backward Color Span	.59***	.56**
Exhaustive Visual Search	−.11	−.15
Nonverbal Sequence Memory (Knox's Cubes)	.27	.21
Dimensional Change Card Sort (total score)	.11	.04
Inhibitory Control (Day/Night Stroop)	.04	.05
Age	.19	
Nonverbal IQ (DAS Pattern Construction)	−.03	

[1]Partial correlations controlled for age, aided hearing loss, and nonverbal IQ on the DAS.
* = p<.05,
** = p<.01,
*** = p<.001 (two-tailed)

language measures were entered in a stepwise fashion. The criterion for order of entry was the wish to maximize the percentage of variance in false-belief scores accounted for by the regression equation.

Pass-Fail Contingency Analyses

The deaf children were scored as passing or failing the complement processing task (≥ 7/8), the dimensional-change card sort (≥ 19/24), and the day/night Stroop (≥ 13/16). A pass-fail contingency analysis with their performance on the false-belief reasoning tasks revealed that the skills involved in each of these measures could be considered as necessary but not sufficient for the children's mastery of the standard false-belief tasks. The strongest contingency relationship was with the complement processing measure; no child passed false-belief reasoning but failed the complements task. For the dimensional-change card sort there was one child and for the Stroop there were two children who passed false-belief reasoning but failed the executive function task. Most of the deaf children

Table 13.2 Mixed Hierarchical and Stepwise Regression Analysis Predicting False-Belief Reasoning Scores

Control Variables Entered First	Beta	T	p
Age	.20	1.00	.33
Nonverbal IQ (DAS)	.08	0.40	.69
Aided Hearing Loss	−.14	−0.73	.47
Percentage of Variance Accounted for by Control Variables = 6.5%			

Predictor Variables Then Entered in Stepwise Fashion (by statistical significance)[1]

	Beta	T	p
"Tell" Complement Clause Processing	.66	4.75	.000***
Additional % of Variance Accounted for by Complement Processing = 43.5%			

	Beta	T	p
Backward Color Span	.36	2.32	.029*
Additional % of Variance Accounted for by Backward Color Span = 8.8%			

[1] RITLS general syntax score and EVT expressive vocabulary did not add significantly to the variance accounted for, so they were not entered.

passed both the dimensional-change card sort and the day/night Stroop but still failed the standard false-belief tasks.

Conclusions

This study of oral deaf children confirms the results of Study 1 that processing of false-complement clauses with communication verbs is the primary language predictor of the mastery of FB reasoning in the standard ToM tasks for deaf children. The other general syntax and vocabulary measures were also significantly correlated with ToM performance, even when age, hearing loss, and nonverbal IQ were partialed out, but they were weaker predictors than the comprehension of false complements in the regression analyses.

With respect to executive functioning, only the most verbal of the working memory measures was related to false-belief reasoning, but that relationship may be mediated by the verbal rather than the memory component of the task. In particular, the nonverbal exhaustive-search game, no less a working memory task, was relatively easy for the deaf children and their performance on this task was unrelated to their ToM performance.

Neither conditional rule following nor inhibitory control as measured by tasks widely used in the study of executive functioning was significantly related to FB reasoning in the deaf children (see Woolfe et al., 2002, for a similar finding with signing and hearing children, showing equivalent performance on the dimensional-change card sort task). However, the contingency analysis suggests that these EF skills may still be necessary but not sufficient for mastery of the FB reasoning tasks. Very few deaf children failed the dimensional-change card sort or the day/night Stroop test and passed the false-belief tests. The study therefore can be accommodated by a theory of the role of EF in ToM development that argues that EF is a cognitive factor (or set of factors) required for the later conceptual developments in ToM (a competence model). But the results are much less easily assimilated by an account of EF constraints on performance in the standard false-belief tasks (a performance model) that suggests that it is simply the demand characteristics of the tasks that determine their relationship with EF measures. The EF tasks were mastered by the deaf children long before the false-belief tasks, and it was the set of language measures that was the proximal predictor of progress on the ToM tasks.

The results provide no support for Perner's proposal that the meta-representational skills inherent in the false-belief tasks are prerequisites for mastery of the EF tasks. It was very clear that the EF tasks were much easier for the deaf children than the standard false-belief tasks.

One limitation of the present study is that it examined only verbal false-belief tasks, and, especially for deaf children, the use of less verbal or nonverbal tasks would be important in future research. However, in Study 1, performance on less verbal tasks involving reasoning about knowledge and expectations was just as delayed as the false-belief reasoning in the standard verbal tasks and was also predicted by processing of false-complement clauses with verbs of communication.

The Role of Language in Theory-of-Mind Development

Taken as a whole, the research on deaf individuals supports three important conclusions about the role of language in ToM development.

First, the effects of language appear to be multifaceted. The tie between delayed false-belief reasoning in both signing and oral deaf children and a general delay in language acquisition in these children is in keeping with the belief that several aspects of language play a causal role in the mastery of a representational ToM. In both of the studies described in this chapter, vocabulary emerged as a strong predictor of the understanding of cognitive states and false beliefs, though general basic syntax was less significant, both for ASL signing children and for oral children. This supports the semantic theory outlined in the introduction (e.g., Olson, 1988, 1994), although specific mastery of the vocabulary for mental states was not directly measured in the vocabulary assessments and vocabulary may here be serving as a proxy for underlying general language development in the children (Astington, 2000). Recently, Moeller (2003) has shown that false-belief understanding in signing deaf children (using signed English in total communication) is predicted by the mothers' use of mental-state terms to describe and explain events involving mistakes and deception and, independently, by the children's own sign language skills.

Second, there is support for the argument that comprehension of false complement clauses serves as a specific causal factor in the understanding of the content of others' cognitive states and false beliefs. In both studies, processing of complements with "tell" verbs emerged as a separate and powerful predictor of the deaf children's reasoning about false beliefs, expectations, and states of knowledge in highly verbal and less verbal ToM tasks. This is in keeping with the position argued by J. de Villiers (this volume, chapter 10; see also J. de Villiers, 2000; J. de Villiers & P. de Villiers, 2003), and the findings of Tager-Flusberg and Joseph (this volume, chapter 14) on autistic children.

However, the overall research also suggests that, in many respects, deaf individuals are not like autistic children in their ToM development (although some researchers have made comparisons between deaf and autistic children; e.g., Peterson & Siegal, 1995, 2000). Complex language may play a crucial role in the mastery of explicit reasoning about unobservable cognitive states that have propositional content, but with much less complex language, other aspects of ToM appear to be developed by deaf children much as they are in hearing children. Thus, reasoning about desires and intentions is less delayed or not delayed at all in signing and oral deaf children (Marschark et al., 2000; Rhys-Jones & Ellis, 2000; Rieffe & Terwogt, 2000; Steeds et al., 1997). In sharp contrast to autistic children, who are considerably impaired in their playing of hide-and-seek deception games like the "penny-in-the-hand" game (Baron-Cohen, 1992), oral deaf children are comparable to hearing children in hiding information and misleading their opponent in a sticker-in-the-hand game (P. de Villiers, Freedman, & Shlasko, 2003). Futhermore, the performance of the deaf children in this game was predicted not by language or false-belief scores on the standard tasks but by age and memory. This suggests that interactive "deception" games like the penny-hiding game that appear on the surface to involve manipulation of beliefs may actually be solved at a far more implicit level of reasoning about other people's behavior based on extraction of behavioral regularities in social interaction (see Dienes & Perner, 1999).

Emerging research on Nicaraguan deaf signers by Pyers (2001, 2003) supports the notion that adult deaf signers may acquire elaborate social interactional skills and function well in the real world, but, unless they have acquired an appropriately complex syntax in their sign language, they may still fail explicit false-belief reasoning tasks. Pyers tested 12 deaf adults who had acquired the Nicaraguan Sign Language (NSL) that evolved over a period of some 15 years when deaf individuals from villages and towns all over Nicaragua were brought together into a new school for the deaf in Managua (Kegl, Senghas, & Coppola, 1999; Senghas, 2000). Six of the adult participants had been in the first cohort of young children who entered the school prior to age 5 in the early 1980s. They took the input of several disparate gestural systems (homesign) used by the older students and elaborated it into a more complete sign language. Another 6 participants were in a later cohort, who had also entered the school prior to age 5, but in the early 1990s, some 10 years into the evolution of a full natural Nicaraguan Sign Language. They took the more elaborate input from the older students and made it still more complex and formal. Although the two groups are now teenagers or young adults and have been using their sign language for many years, the signing of the second cohort is still syntactically more complex than that of the first cohort (Kegl et al., 1999; Senghas, 2000). Both groups were given a nonverbal test of false-belief understanding based on the change-in-location scenario. The second cohort all passed the task, but the first cohort, though older, all failed the task. This suggests that a mature understanding of false beliefs depends on the acquisition of a complex linguistic system; without it, no amount of social experience is enough, though an extensive and effective repertoire of social behaviors may be acquired. It remains to be shown what particular aspects of the syntax and semantics of Nicaraguan Sign Language distinguish the linguistic systems of participants from the first and second cohorts who were tested in this study and how those might be involved in mediating or enabling the development of a representational theory of mind. However, Pyers (2003) reported that later signers used complex utterances with cognitive state verbs and complement clauses to describe and explain mistakes and deceptive actions in videotaped vignettes (see P. de Villiers & Pyers, 2001, for a description of this explanation of action task). In contrast, the first cohort signers used more causal language that involved physical or desire explanations but no language about cognitions and no false-complement clauses.

Similarly, Pyers and P. de Villiers (2003) tested oral deaf children from the United States and the same group of adult Nicaraguan signers on an emotion judgment task based on the procedure developed by Harris, Johnson, Hutton, et al. (1989). The participants had to judge the emotion of a character in three types of pictured narrative in which they could not see the character's facial expression. In some, the emotion could be read off the stereotypical situation (e.g., a vicious dog is shown barking at a boy, leading to fear). In others, the emotion was based on the characters' desires or preferences (e.g., a boy likes snakes, so he is happy when he finds a snake, even though his mother is shown to be afraid of the snake). In the crucial set of stories, the character's state of knowledge or belief has to be computed to determine his emotion (e.g., if a thirsty boy thinks there is orange juice in the container, he will be happy, but if he knows that his brother has poured a disliked drink into the container, he will be angry or sick). Both groups of Nicaraguan signers and the oral deaf children were very good at the stereotypical situation-based emotions and the desire- or preference-based emotions. But, in keeping with their performance on the non-verbal analogue of the change-in-location false-belief task, the first cohort of signers all failed the knowledge- or belief-based items on the emotion-judgment test. In contrast, the later signers, who had more complex sign language, all passed the nonverbal false-belief test and were very good at judging emotions on the basis of the knowledge state of the character. The performance of the oral deaf children on this part of the emotion task was similarly predicted by their ability to pass the standard change-in-location ToM task.

In summary, these studies of deaf individuals suggest that the language of false-complement clauses and verbs of communication and mental state may be centrally involved in the conceptual reasoning that underlies explicit representation of the content of cognitive states. However, other aspects of theory of mind, such as the reading of desires and intentions, or the understanding of simple emotions on the basis of triggering situations and preferences, may be far less dependent on complex language and more accessible from social interaction with more minimal linguistic requirements.

Acknowledgments Several individuals contributed to the research that this chapter describes. They include Jill de Villiers, Sarah Freedman, Jennifer Friedman, and Roberta Giordano, from Smith College; Robert Hoffmeister, Lana Cook, Patrick Costello, Sarah Hafer, Marie Philip, and Marcia Unger, from Boston University; Brenda Schick, Elaine Gale, Jenny Lin, and Gene Mirus, from the University of Colorado at Boulder; and Jennie Pyers, from the University of California at Berkeley. The research was supported by NIDCD Grant #DC02872 to Peter de Villiers, Jill de Villiers, Brenda Schick, and Robert Hoffmeister.

References

Astington, J. W. (2000). Language and metalanguage in children's understanding of mind. In J. W. Astington (Ed.), *Minds in the making: Essays in honor of David R. Olson* (pp. 267–284). Oxford: Blackwell.

Astington, J. W., & Jenkins, J. M. (1999). A longitudinal study of the relation between language and theory-of-mind development. *Developmental Psychology, 35*, 1311–1320.

Baron-Cohen, S. (1992). Out of sight or out of mind? Another look at deception in autism. *Journal of Child Psychology and Psychiatry, 33*, 1141–1155.

Bartsch, K., & Wellman, H. M. (1995). *Children talk about the mind.* New York: Oxford University Press.

Brown, J., Donelan-McCall, N., & Dunn, J. (1996). Why talk about mental states? The significance of children's conversations with friends, siblings, and mothers. *Child Development, 67*, 836–849.

Carlson, S. M., & Moses, L. J. (2001). Individual differences in inhibitory control and children's theory of mind. *Child Development, 72*, 1032–1053.

Carlson, S. M., Moses, L. J., & Hix, H. R. (1998). The role of inhibitory processes in young children's difficulties with deception and false belief. *Child Development, 69*, 672–691.

Courtin, C. (2000). The impact of sign language on the cognitive development of deaf children: The case of theories of mind. *Journal of Deaf Studies and Deaf Education, 5*, 266–276.

Davis, H., & Pratt, C. (1995). The development of children's theory of mind: The working memory explanation. *Australian Journal of Psychology, 47*, 25–31.

Deleau, M. (1996). L'attribution d'états mentaux chez les enfants sourds et entendants: Une approche du role de l'experience langagière sur une Theorie de l'Esprit. *Bulletin de Psychologie, 3*, 1–20.

de Villiers, J. G. (1995, March). Steps in the mastery of sentence complements. Paper presented at the biennial meeting of the Society for Research in Child Development, Indianapolis, IN.

de Villiers, J. G. (2000). Language and theory of mind: What are the developmental relationships? In S. Baron-Cohen, H. Tager-Flusberg, & D. Cohen (Eds.), *Understanding other minds: Perspectives from developmental cognitive neuroscience* (pp. 83–123). Oxford: Oxford University Press.

de Villiers, J. G., & de Villiers, P. A. (2000). Linguistic determinism and the understanding of false beliefs. In P. Mitchell & K. Riggs (Eds.), *Children's reasoning and the mind* (pp. 189–226). Hove, UK: Psychology Press.

de Villiers, J. G., & de Villiers, P. A. (2003). Language for thought: Coming to understand false beliefs. In D. Gentner & S. Goldin-Meadow (Eds.), *Language in mind: Advances in the study of language and cognition* (pp. 335–384). Cambridge, MA: MIT Press.

de Villiers, J. G., & Pyers, J. (1997). Complementing cognition: The relationship between language and theory of mind. In E. Hughes, M. Hughes, & A. Greenhill (Eds.), *Proceedings of the 21st Annual Boston University Conference on Language Development* (pp. 136–147). Somerville, MA: Cascadilla Press.

de Villiers, J. G., & Pyers, J. (2002). Complements to cognition: A longitudinal study of the relationship between complex syntax and false-belief understanding. *Cognitive Development, 17*, 1037–1060.

de Villiers, P. A. (2003). Language of the deaf—acquisition of English. In R. Kent (Ed.), *The MIT Encyclopedia of Communication Disorders*. Cambridge, MA: MIT Press.

de Villiers, P. A., de Villiers, J. G., Schick, B. & Hoffmeister, R. (2001, April). Theory of mind development in signing and nonsigning deaf children: The impact of sign language on social cognition. Poster presented at the biennial meeting of the Society for Research in Child Development. Minneapolis, MN.

de Villiers, P. A., Freedman, S., & Friedman, J. (2001, April). Complex language but not executive functioning predicts false-belief reasoning in oral deaf children. Paper presented at the biennial meeting of the Society for Research in Child Development, Minneapolis, MN.

de Villiers, P. A., Freedman, S., & Shlasko, G. (2003, April). Deception and ToM in oral deaf children. Poster presented at the biennial meeting of the Society for Research in Child Development, Tampa Bay, FL.

de Villiers, P. A., Hosler, E., Miller, K., Whalen, M. & Wong, J. (1997, April). Language, theory of mind, and reading other people's emotions: A study of oral deaf children. Poster presented at the biennial meeting of the Society for Research in Child Development. Washington, DC.

de Villiers, P. A., & Pyers, J. (2001). Complementation and false-belief representation. In M. Almgren, A. Barrena, M-J. Ezeizabarrena, I. Idiazabal, and B. MacWhinney (Eds.), *Research on child language acquisition: Proceedings of the 8th Conference of the International Association for the Study of Child Language* (pp. 984–1005). Somerville, MA: Cascadilla Press.

de Villiers, P. A., & Pyers, J. (2003). Language of the deaf—Sign Language. In R. Kent (Ed.), *The MIT Encyclopedia of Communication Disorders*. Cambridge, MA: MIT Press.

Dienes, Z., & Perner, J. (1999). A theory of implicit and explicit knowledge. *Behavioral and Brain Sciences, 22,* 735–808.

Dunn, J., Brown, J., Slomkowski, C., Tesla, C., & Youngblade, L. (1991). Young children's understanding of other people's feelings and beliefs: Individual differences and their antecedents. *Child Development, 10,* 483–527.

Dunn, L., & Dunn, L. (1981). *Peabody Picture Vocabulary Test-Revised*. Circle Pines, MN: American Guidance Service.

Elliott, C. (1990). *Differential Ability Scales*. San Antonio, TX: Psychological Corporation.

Engen, E., & Engen, T. (1983). *Rhode Island Test of Language Structure*. Austin, TX: Pro-Ed.

Figueras-Costas, B., & Harris, P. (2001). Theory of mind development in deaf children: A nonverbal test of false-belief understanding. *Journal of Deaf Studies and Deaf Education, 6,* 92–102.

Frye, D., Zelazo, P. D., & Palfai, T. (1995). Theory of mind and rule-based reasoning. *Cognitive Development, 10,* 483–527.

Gale, E., de Villiers, P. A., de Villiers, J. G., & Pyers, J. (1996). Language and theory of mind in oral deaf children. In A. Stringfellow, D. Cahana-Amitay, E. Hughes, & A. Zukowski (Eds.), *Proceedings of the 20th Annual Boston University Conference on Language Development* (Vol. I, pp. 213–224). Somerville, MA: Cascadilla Press.

Gardner, M. (1990). *Expressive One-Word Picture Vocabulary Test*. Austin, TX: Pro-Ed.

Gerstadt, C. L., Hong, Y. J., & Diamond, A. (1994). The relationship between cognition and action: Performance of children 3.5–7 years old on a Stroop-like day-night test. *Cognition, 53,* 129–153.

Gopnik, A., & Meltzoff, A. (1993). Words and thoughts in infancy: The specificity hypothesis and the development of categorization and naming. *Advances in Infancy Research, 8,* 217–249.

Gordon, A. C., & Olson, D. R. (1998). The relations between acquisition of a theory of mind and the capacity to hold in mind. *Journal of Experimental Child Psychology, 68,* 70–83.

Harris, P. (1996). Desires, beliefs and language. In P. Carruthers & P. Smith (Eds.), *Theories of theories of mind* (pp. 200–220). Cambridge: Cambridge University Press.

Harris, P., Johnson, C., Hutton, D., Andrews, G., & Cooke, T. (1989). Young children's theory of mind and emotion. *Cognition and Emotion, 3,* 379–400.

Hresko, W., Reid, K., & Hammill, D. (1991). Test of Early Language Development (2d ed.). Austin, TX: Pro-Ed.

Hughes, C. (1998a). Executive function in preschoolers: Links with theory of mind and verbal ability. *British Journal of Developmental Psychology, 16,* 233–253.

Hughes, C. (1998b). Finding your marbles: Does preschoolers' strategic behavior predict later understanding of mind? *Developmental Psychology, 34,* 1326–1339.

Hughes, C., & Dunn, J. (1997). Understanding mind and emotion: Longitudinal associations with mental-state talk between young friends. *Developmental Psychology, 34,* 1026–1037.

Jackson, A. L. (2001). Language facility and theory of mind development in deaf children. *Journal of Deaf Studies and Deaf Education, 6,* 161–176.

Karmiloff-Smith, A. (1992). *Beyond modularity: A developmental perspective on cognitive science.* Cambridge, MA: MIT Press.

Keenan, T. (1998). Memory span as a predictor of false belief understanding. *New Zealand Journal of Psychology, 27,* 36–43.

Keenan, T. (2000). Mind, memory, and metacognition: The role of memory span in children's developing understanding of the mind. In J. W. Astington (Ed.), *Minds in the making: Essays in honor of David R. Olson* (pp. 233–249). Oxford: Blackwell.

Kegl, J., Senghas, A., and Coppola, M. (1999). Creation through contact: Sign language emergence and sign language change in Nicaragua. In M. DeGraff (Ed.), *Language creation and language change: Creolization, diachrony, and development.* Cambridge, MA: MIT Press.

Klima, E., & Bellugi, U. (1979). *The signs of language.* Cambridge, MA: Harvard University Press.

Leslie, A. M., & Polizzi, P. (1998). Inhibitory processing in the false belief task: Two conjectures. *Developmental Science, 1,* 247–253.

Liddell, S. (1980). *American Sign Language syntax.* The Hague, Netherlands: Mouton.

Lundy, J. (2002). Age and language skills of deaf children in relation to theory of mind development. *Journal of Deaf Studies and Deaf Education, 7,* 41–56.

Marschark, M., Green, V., Hindmarsh, G., & Walker, S. (2000). Understanding theory of mind in children who are deaf. *Journal of Child Psychology and Psychiatry, 41,* 1067–1073.

Meins, E., & Fernyhough, C. (1999). Linguistic acquisitional style and mentalising development: The role of maternal mind-mindedness. *Cognitive Development, 14,* 363–380.

Moeller, M. P. (2003). *Mothers' mental state input and theory of mind understanding in deaf and hearing children.* Doctoral dissertation, University of Nebraska at Lincoln.

Moses, L. J. (2001) Executive accounts of theory of mind development. *Child Development, 72,* 688–690.

Nelson, K. (1996). *Language in cognitive development: Emergence of the mediated mind.* New York: Cambridge University Press.

Olson, D. R. (1988). On the origins of beliefs and other intentional states in children. In J. W. Astington, P. L. Harris, & D. R. Olson (Eds.), *Developing theories of mind* (pp. 414–426). New York: Cambridge University Press.

Olson, D. R. (1994). *The world on paper.* Cambridge: Cambridge University Press.

Ozonoff, S., Pennington, B. F., & Rogers, S. J. (1991). Executive function deficits in high-functioning autistic individuals: Relationship to theory of mind. *Journal of Child Psychology and Psychiatry, 32,* 1081–1095.

Perner, J. (2000). About + belief + counterfactual. In P. Mitchell & K. Riggs (Eds.), *Children's reasoning and the mind* (pp. 367–401) Hove, UK: Psychology Press.

Perner, J., & Lang, B. (2000). Theory of mind and executive function: Is there a developmental relationship? In S. Baron-Cohen, H. Tager-Flusberg, & D. Cohen (Eds.), *Understanding other minds: Perspectives from autism and developmental cognitive neuroscience* (pp. 150–181). Oxford: Oxford University Press.

Perner, J., Lang, B., & Kloo, D. (2002). Theory of mind and self-control: More than a common problem of inhibition. *Child Development, 73*, 752–767.

Perner, J., Leekam, S., & Wimmer, H. (1987). 3-year-olds' difficulty with false belief: The case for a conceptual deficit. *British Journal of Developmental Psychology, 5*, 125–137.

Perner, J., Stummer, S., & Lang, B. (1999). Executive functions and theory of mind: Cognitive complexity or functional dependence? In P. D. Zelazo, J. W. Astington, & D. R. Olson (Eds.), *Developing theories of intention: Social understanding and self-control* (pp. 133–152). Mahwah, NJ: Erlbaum.

Peterson, C. C., & Siegal, M. (1995). Deafness, conversation and theory of mind. *Journal of Child Psychology and Psychiatry, 36*, 459–474.

Peterson, C. C., & Siegal, M. (1997). Domain specificity and everyday biological, physical, and psychological thinking in normal, autistic, and deaf children. In H. M. Wellman & K. Inagaki (Eds.), *The emergence of core domains of thought: Children's reasoning about physical, psychological, and biological phenomena* (pp. 55–70). San Francisco: Jossey-Bass.

Peterson, C. C., & Siegal, M. (1998). Changing focus on the representational mind: Deaf, autistic, and normal children's concepts of false photos, false drawings, and false beliefs. *British Journal of Developmental Psychology, 16*, 301–320.

Peterson, C. C., & Siegal, M. (1999). Representing inner worlds: Theory of mind in autistic, deaf, and normal-hearing children. *Psychological Science, 10*, 126–129.

Peterson, C. C., & Siegel, M. (2000). Insights into theory of mind from deafness and autism. *Mind and Language, 15*, 77–99.

Povinelli, D. J., & deBlois, S. (1992). Young children's (*Homo sapiens*) understanding of knowledge formation in themselves and others. *Journal of Comparative Psychology, 106*, 228–238.

Pyers, J. (2001, June). Three stages in the understanding of false belief in Nicaraguan signers: The interaction of social experience, language emergence, and conceptual development. Paper presented in R. Senghas (Chair), *The emergence of Nicaraguan Sign Language: Questions of development, acquisition, and evolution*. Invited symposium at the 31st Annual Meeting of the Piaget Society, Berkeley, CA.

Pyers, J. (2003, April). Emerging complements: The relation between false belief and language in adult signers of Nicaraguan Sign Language. Paper presented at the biennial meeting meeting of the Society for Research in Child Development, Tampa Bay, FL.

Pyers, J., & de Villiers, P.A. (2003, April). Theory of mind and understanding emotions: What is the role of complex language? Poster presented at the biennial meeting of the Society for Research in Child Development, Tampa Bay, FL.

Rhys-Jones, S., & Ellis, H. (2000). Theory of mind: A comparison between deaf and hearing children's comprehension of picture stories and judgements of social situations. *Journal of Deaf Studies and Deaf Education, 5*, 248–265.

Rieffe, C., & Terwogt, M. M. (2000). Deaf children's understanding of emotions: Desires take precedence. *Journal of Child Psychology and Psychiatry, 41*, 601–608

Ruffman, T., Slade, L., Rowlandson, K., Rumsey, C., & Garnham, A. (2003). How language relates to belief, desire, and emotion understanding. *Cognitive Development, 18*, 139–158.

Russell, J. (1997). How executive disorders can bring about an inadequate theory of mind. In J. Russell (Ed.), *Autism as an executive disorder* (pp. 256–304). Oxford: Oxford University Press.

Russell, P. A., Hosie, J. A., Gray, C. D., Scott, C., Hunter, N., Banks, J. S., & Macaulay, M. C. (1998). Development of theory of mind in deaf children. *Journal of Child Psychology and Psychiatry, 39*, 903–910.

Schick, B., de Villiers, J. G., de Villiers, P. A., & Hoffmeister, R. (in preparation). Language and theory of mind in oral and signing deaf children.

Senghas, A. (2000). The development of early spatial morphology in Nicaraguan Sign Language. In S. C. Howell, S. Fish, and T. Keith-Lucas (Eds.), *Proceedings of the 24th annual Boston University conference on language development.* Somerville, MA: Cascadilla Press.

Siegel, M., & Beattie, D. (1991). Where to look first for children's knowledge of false belief. *Cognition, 38*, 1–12.

Spelke, E. S. (2003). What makes us smart: Core knowledge and natural language. In D. Gentner & S. Goldin-Meadow (Eds.), *Language in mind: Advances in the study of language and thought* (pp. 277–311). Cambridge, MA: MIT Press.

Steeds, L., Rowe, K., & Dowker, A. (1997). Deaf children's understanding of beliefs and desires. *Journal of Deaf Studies and Deaf Education, 2*, 185–195.

Stone, M., & Wright, B. (1979). *Knox's Cube Test.* Wood Dale, IL: Stoelting.

Tager-Flusberg, H. (1997). Language acquisition and theory of mind: Contributions from the study of autism. In L. B. Adamson & M. A. Romski (Eds.), *Communication and language acquisition: Discoveries from atypical development* (pp. 135–160). Baltimore, MD: Paul Brookes Publishing.

Wellman, H. M. (1990). *The child's theory of mind.* Cambridge, MA: Bradford Books.

Wiig, E., Secord, W., & Semel, E. (1992). *Clinical Evaluation of Language Fundamentals-Preschool.* San Antonio, TX: Psychological Corporation.

Wilbur, R. (1987). *American Sign Language: Linguistics and applied dimensions* (2nd ed.). Columbus, OH: Merrill.

Williams, K. (1997). *Expressive Vocabulary Test.* Circle Pines, MN: American Guidance Service.

Wimmer, H., & Perner, J. (1983). Beliefs about beliefs: Representation and constraining function of wrong beliefs in young children's understanding of deception. *Cognition, 13*, 103–128.

Woolfe, T., Want, S., & Siegal, M. (2002). Signposts to development: Theory of mind in deaf children. *Child Development, 73*, 768–778.

Zaitchik, D. (1990). When representations conflict with reality: The preschooler's problem with false beliefs and "false" photographs. *Cognition, 35*, 41–68.

Zelazo, P. D. (1999). Language, levels of consciousness, and the development of intentional action. In P. D. Zelazo, J. W. Astington, & D. R. Olson (Eds.), *Developing theories of intention: Social understanding and self-control* (pp. 95–117). Mahwah, NJ: Erlbaum.

Zelazo, P. D., Carter, A., Reznick, J. S., & Frye, D. (1997). Early development of executive function: A problem-solving framework. *Review of General Psychology, 1*, 1–29.

14 How Language Facilitates the Acquisition of False-Belief Understanding in Children with Autism

Helen Tager-Flusberg and Robert M. Joseph

Theory of Mind in Autism

Within the field of cognitive development, theoretical debate on the origins and development of theory of mind has been strongly influenced by research on children with autism (Baron-Cohen, Tager-Flusberg, & Cohen, 1993, 2000). Baron-Cohen and his colleagues were the first to demonstrate that children with autism fail the false-belief task at a significantly higher rate than matched controls (Baron-Cohen, Leslie, & Frith, 1985), and their findings have been replicated many times by different research groups around the world (see Baron-Cohen, 2000, for a review). Studies of theory of mind in autism have used a wide range of tasks and have compared the performance of children with autism to different control groups, including children with Down syndrome, mental retardation of unknown origin, or specific language impairment and normally developing preschoolers (e.g., Baron-Cohen et al., 1985; Baron-Cohen, Leslie, & Frith, 1986; Perner, Frith, Leslie, & Leekam, 1989; Tager-Flusberg & Sullivan, 1994; Yirmiya, Erel, Shaked, & Solomonica-Levi, 1998). Across all studies, the most consistent findings are that children with autism perform significantly worse than controls, even though in many studies participants with mental retardation or specific language impairment do not perform as well as normally developing preschoolers (Benson, Abbeduto, Short, Bibler-Nuccio, & Maas, 1993; Cassidy & Ballaraman, 1997; Miller, 2001; Zelazo, Burack, Benedetto, & Frye, 1996). This body of research is taken as support for the "theory-of-mind hypothesis" of autism, which proposes that this neurodevelopmental disorder is characterized by core deficits in theory of mind (Baron-Cohen et al., 1993).

The significance of this hypothesis is that it provides a unified explanation for the deficits in reciprocal social interaction, communication, and pretend play that are central to autism (Baron-Cohen, 1988; Leslie & Roth, 1993). It also has provided new directions for research on the neurobiological abnormalities that underlie the behavioral symptoms in people with autism (e.g., Frith & Frith, 2000). The theory-of-mind hypothesis of autism has had a profound impact on how we understand people with autism and their difficulties in everyday life. It has also led to the development of intervention programs designed to teach children with autism how to impute mental states to other people and how to use mental-state information to predict and interpret the actions and reactions of others in various situations (e.g., Howlin, Baron-Cohen, & Hadwin, 1999; Ozonoff & Miller, 1995; Swettenham, 1996).

Yet, despite the pervasive influence of the theory-of-mind hypothesis in the field of autism, one key paradox is the fact that in every published study on theory of mind in autism, there are some participants who pass the tasks, including 20% of the children in the original study on false belief by Baron-Cohen and his colleagues (Baron-Cohen et al., 1985). In this chapter, we focus on the question of how children with autism are able to pass theory-of-mind tasks, with specific emphasis on false-belief tasks that tap a meta-representational understanding of mental states. We review evidence for the importance of language in performance on false-belief tasks for individuals with autism, presenting evidence for the special role played by sentential complements in false-belief understanding among children with autism.

Language and False Belief in Autism

Most reviews on the theory-of-mind hypothesis of autism have focused on its significance for understanding the primary *communication deficits* found in autism (e.g., Baron-Cohen, 1988; Happé, 1993, 1994; Tager-Flusberg, 1993, 1999). This work emphasizes how theory-of-mind deficits in autism can explain problems in language use, such as restricted range-of-speech acts, and impairments in conversational discourse, in narrative discourse, and in interpreting intended meaning (Tager-Flusberg, 2000b). In autism, deficits in these aspects of communication are universal and are among the core diagnostic symptoms that define the syndrome. At the same time, the acquisition of other aspects of language is much more variable, and, although delays in the development of language are also part of the diagnostic criteria for autism, some children with high-functioning autism do acquire a rich vocabulary and master the grammar of their native language (Kjelgaard & Tager-Flusberg, 2001). This variability in linguistic knowledge has been viewed as determining, rather than reflecting, performance on theory-of-mind tasks in autism, as in normally developing preschoolers (cf. Astington & Jenkins, 1999; de Villiers & de Villiers, 2000). On this view, differences in linguistic ability among children with autism may provide a partial explanation for why only some children are able to pass standard experimental tasks such as false belief.

Across many studies on false belief in children with autism, performance is significantly correlated with standardized measures of language. One of the first studies to identify the link between language and false belief was conducted by Eisenmajer and Prior (1991), who found that both verbal mental age and pragmatic ability were superior among children with autism who passed theory-of-mind tasks. Happé (1995) conducted a relatively large-scale analysis of children who had participated in a number of different false-belief experiments in England and found an age-independent relationship between performance on false-belief tests and scores on the British Picture Vocabulary Scale (BPVS; Dunn, Dunn, Whetton, & Pintilie, 1982), which is the British counterpart of the widely used Peabody Picture Vocabulary Test (PPVT; Dunn & Dunn, 1981), for both normally developing preschoolers and children with autism. Similar findings have been reported by other groups that have investigated theory of mind and vocabulary knowledge in children with autism (Dahlgren & Trillingsgaard, 1996; Sparrevohn & Howie, 1995). Tager-Flusberg and Sullivan (1994) also found that PPVT scores correlated with false-belief performance in children with autism; however, in their study, a stronger connection to theory of mind was found for a sentence comprehension measure of syntactic knowledge (the Sentence Structure subtest on the Clinical Evaluation of Language Fundamentals [CELF]; Semel, Wiig, & Secord, 1987). Using a different measure of syntactic comprehension (the Test for Reception of Grammar [TROG]; Bishop, 1983), these findings were replicated in a recent study that included a large sample of children with autism (Fisher, 2002). Findings from these studies on the connection between language, particularly syntax, and theory of mind in children with autism parallel the findings from studies with normally developing preschoolers (Astington & Jenkins, 1999; Cutting & Dunn, 1999; de Villiers & Pyers, 2002; Jenkins & Astington, 1996). Some researchers have not found a significant correlation between language and theory of mind in autism (e.g., Baron-Cohen et al., 1985; Perner et al., 1989). However, their studies included relatively small samples of children who varied widely in age and may therefore have lacked the statistical power to detect significant relationships between these two domains.

The strong connection between language and theory of mind in autism has been interpreted in different ways. Some have argued that general language ability is important in order to comprehend the highly verbal tasks used to test false belief and, furthermore, that children with autism are especially dependent on language for solving theory-of-mind problems (e.g., Happé, 1995). Others have suggested that the semantic-conceptual understanding of cognition verbs (e.g., *think, know*) provides the key to the relationship between language and theory of mind in normally developing preschoolers and children with autism (Moore & Davidge, 1989; Moore, Bryant, & Furrow, 1989; Ziatas, Durkin, & Pratt, 1998). A third perspective claims that language is important in theory of mind because both develop in the context of social interaction and conversations with others, especially in the home with family members (Garfield, Peterson, & Perry, 2001; Peterson & Siegal, 2000; see also chapters by Dunn & Brophy, and Nelson, this volume, chapters 3 and 2). On this view, because of their primary deficits in social reciprocity, children with autism have less access to these kinds of communicative interactions and therefore fail to develop a rich understanding of mental states.

In this chapter, we argue for a different hypothesis regarding the relationship between language and theory of mind in autism. We propose that the acquisition of sentential complements is the key to understanding why some children with autism are able to pass false-belief tasks (Tager-Flusberg, 1997, 2000a). Children with autism are especially dependent on language, particularly knowledge of sentential complements, to bootstrap their meta-representational capacity. This hypothesis draws on the important theoretical and empirical work conducted by Jill de Villiers and Peter de Villiers and their colleagues with normally developing preschoolers and deaf children (de Villiers, 2000; de Villiers & de Villiers, 2000; see J. de Villiers, this volume, chapter 10; P. de Villiers, this volume, chapter 13).

Sentential Complements and Theory of Mind in Autism

Two classes of verbs take sentential or tensed complements: verbs of cognition (e.g., *think, know*) and verbs of communication (e.g., *say, ask*):

(1) Lauren <u>asked</u> where the book was hidden.
(2) Kelly <u>said</u> the book was in the closet.
(3) Eva <u>thought</u> the book was in the bedroom.
(4) Susan <u>knew</u> the book was on the desk.

Both kinds of verbs convey the attitude or belief of the person who is communicating or holding a mental state. The syntactic and semantic properties of these kinds of complements, which have obligatory tensed clauses embedded under the main verb of communication or cognition, allow the embedded clause to have a different truth-value than the main clause. They are thus uniquely suited for representing propositional attitudes, especially for the explicit representation of a falsely embedded proposition, as in examples (2) and (3). As de Villiers and de Villiers explain: "Thus, complementation provides a means of representing someone's mental world, and that mental world could be distinct from our mental world" (de Villiers & de Villiers, 2000, p. 194).

There is growing evidence from studies of normally developing preschoolers on the important role that sentential complements play in the development of a representational understanding of mind. Cross-sectional studies have found that performance on false-belief tasks is correlated with knowledge of sentential complements (e.g., Tager-Flusberg, 1997), and a longitudinal study conducted over the course of one year in a group of 3-year-olds by de Villiers and Pyers (2002) found that sentential complements predicted later theory-of-mind ability independent of more general language growth. Using a training study methodology, Hale and Tager-Flusberg (2003) found that training young children on sentential complements led to significant increases in performance on a set of false-belief and related tasks (see also Lohmann, Tomasello, & Meyer, this volume, chapter 12). These latter studies found that the acquisition of sentential complements led to changes in performance on theory-of-mind tasks, but not vice versa.

Thus far, research on the role of sentential complements in the development of theory of mind in autism has been limited to cross-sectional studies. We conducted a set of three experiments with a group of 20 adolescents with autism and a comparison group of 20 adolescents with mental retardation of unknown etiology (MR), who were matched on age, IQ, and language (Tager-Flusberg, 2000a). The adolescents in these experiments were given two trials of a location-change false-belief task and classified as either passing (35% of the autism group and 45% of the MR group) or failing, using standard criteria.

The experiments assessed the participants' knowledge of the syntactic and semantic properties of complement constructions. One experiment tested the participants' knowledge of the embedding structure of sentential complements, following the methodology introduced by de Villiers and her colleagues (de Villiers, Roeper, & Vainikka, 1990). We told brief stories accompanied by photographs, followed by a complex wh-question that contained either a communication or cognition verb. Following de Villiers et al. (1990), we took the participants' ability to answer these test questions as evidence of their knowledge of complement constructions. In one story, a girl was riding home when her radio fell off her bike. On arriving home, she found out that the radio was broken after plugging it in a wall socket and finding that it no longer worked. The story provided temporal information about when the radio broke (when it fell off the bike) and when the girl was convinced that it was broken (when she plugged it in at home). Thus, both these pieces of information were available as potential answers to the test question: *When did the girl **think/know** that she broke the radio?* A second experiment tested the ability to extract the content of a clause embedded under a communication verb (*say*) in different contexts: mistakes, lies, and true statements. For each context, there were two stories, presented in random order. At the end of each story, the participant was asked: *What did X say?* The third experiment investigated participants' knowledge of a semantic property of cognition and communication verbs: referential opacity, based on a task used by de Villiers, Pyers, and Broderick (1997). We presented four stories, each of which included two main characters (e.g., Sarah, her mother), a container (e.g., a box), its contents (e.g., candy), and function (e.g., a gift). In each story, only one character (mother) knows the contents and function of the container. Under these conditions, statements such as "*Mother knew/said the gift/candy was on the table*" are acceptable, but "*Sarah knew/said the gift/candy was on the table*" is not acceptable, because for Sarah, the contents and function of the box are opaque. For each story, we asked a series of yes/no questions, including verbs of communication or cognition, that would be true for one character (mother) but false for the other (Sarah). Additional control questions were also included.

Across all three experiments, performance by participants in both groups on the complementation tasks was significantly related to whether they passed or failed false belief. Although general language ability was correlated with false-belief performance, in regression analyses complement knowledge was the single best predictor of performance on the false-belief task. However, for the autism group, false belief was significantly related only to performance on the complementation stimuli that involved communication verbs; in contrast to the MR group, the adolescents with autism showed little sensitivity to the conceptual or linguistic properties of the cognition verbs used in these studies.

These findings provide support for the view that the key factor predicting which individuals with autism (and MR) will pass false-belief tasks is knowledge of sentential complements. Furthermore, the studies revealed that in autism, only a restricted class of sentential complements was significantly related to theory-of-mind performance: complements for verbs of communication. The findings suggest a unique route to theory of mind in autism, one that is heavily dependent on language but has little regard for the language of mental states. From the experiments conducted thus far, it is difficult to make strong claims regarding the relationship between sentential complements and theory of mind in autism because they were limited to correlational analyses with relatively small numbers of adolescents with autism. Thus, there is no strong evidence that language determines theory of mind and not the reverse. Only longitudinal designs are able to provide stronger evidence regarding the direction of the relationship between language and theory of mind (Astington & Jenkins, 1999; de Villiers & Pyers, 2002).

A Longitudinal Study of Language and Theory of Mind in Autism

Over the past five years, we have been conducting a relatively large-scale study of language and theory-of-mind development in children with autism. This study is part of a broader longitudinal investigation of cognition, behavior, brain structure, and function in autism; however, in this chapter we focus our presentation on the developmental relationships between the acquisition of a representational theory of mind and language in children with autism. We were specifically interested in exploring several questions that have dominated studies on normally-developing preschoolers and which emerged from our earlier studies on theory of mind in adolescents with autism:

1. Does knowledge of sentential complements predict performance on false-belief and related tasks, beyond developments in general language ability? If so, are the syntactic or semantic properties of sentential complements more specifically linked to theory of mind?
2. For children with autism, do verbs of communication provide more significant predictive relations to theory-of-mind performance than verbs of cognition?
3. Does knowledge of sentential complements predict developmental changes in theory of mind or do changes in theory of mind predict the acquisition of sentential complements?

To address these questions, we report here on the data collected from the children at two time points spaced about one year apart. At both time points, the children were given a battery of theory-of-mind tasks, tapping knowledge and false-belief understanding, and a set of complementation tasks that included verbs of cognition and communication.

Participants

The study included 51 children with autism who were between the ages of 5 years 4 months and 14 years 2 months at the start of the study. Diagnosis of autism was made on the basis of the Autism Diagnostic Interview-Revised (ADI-R; Lord, Rutter, & Le Couteur, 1994) or the Autism Diagnostic Observation Schedule (ADOS; Lord, Risi, Lambrecht, et al., 2000) and was confirmed by an expert clinician using DSM-IV criteria (American Psychiatric Association, 1994). Children whose autism could be attributed to another medical or genetic condition (e.g., Rett syndrome, fragile X syndrome, tuberous sclerosis) were excluded from the study.

Descriptive Measures

The children's IQ scores were obtained using the Differential Ability Scales (DAS; Elliot, 1990), which provide full-scale, verbal, and nonverbal standard scores. We also administered two standardized language tests: the Peabody Picture Vocabulary Test (PPVT-III; Dunn & Dunn, 1997) and the Expressive

Vocabulary Test (EVT; Williams, 1997), which measure single-word vocabulary. Because these tests were normed on the same sample and the scores obtained on them were highly correlated in our group of children with autism, r (51) = .82, p< .001, we combined the standard scores from the PPVT and EVT to yield an aggregate measure of vocabulary.

Table 14.1 presents the descriptive characteristics of the 51 children enrolled in the study at the first time point. At the second time point, there were 34 children who returned and who had not reached ceiling on our test measures.[1]

Experimental Measures

General Language

Following de Villiers and Pyers (2002), the general language measure that we used for this study was the Index of Productive Syntax (IPSyn; Scarborough, 1990), which is a measure of the emergence and use of syntactic and morphological structures. A natural-language sample was obtained from a half-hour interaction between each child and his or her mother as they played with a standard set of age-appropriate toys. This interaction took place in the laboratory and was audiotaped and videotaped for later transcription. The language samples were transcribed using the SALT transcription format (Miller & Chapman, 2000) by a team of research assistants trained in transcription procedures. Transcripts were prepared by one person and checked by a second trained transcriber using both the audio- and video recordings. All transcription disagreements were resolved through consensus. After omitting the first 10 child utterances from the transcript, a corpus of 100 consecutive, complete, and intelligible child utterances was selected and coded using the IPSyn. The IPSyn provides an index of language development by scoring the use of specific examples of morphological and syntactic structures. There are 59 items on the IPSyn, each worth a maximum of 2 points, resulting in a maximum total IPSyn score of 118.

Table 14.1 Descriptive Characteristics of the Children with Autism

	Mean	Standard Deviation	Range
Age	8;3	2;4	5;4–14;2
Full-Scale IQ	81	19	51–141
Nonverbal IQ	87	21	49–153
Vocabulary score	80	18	40–124

Sentential Complements

Our measures of sentential complements were based on a task developed by J. de Villiers and her colleagues (de Villiers, 2000; de Villiers & Pyers, 2002). Children were presented with brief stories, accompanied by a picture, and then asked a wh-question, which tested their ability to extract complements from sentences. We included both true and false complements so that we could separate out the syntactic and semantic properties of sentential complements. True complements tap the ability to extract embedded clauses, thus requiring syntactic knowledge of embeddings. False complements also tap knowledge of the conflict between reality and the content of the embedded clause and thus tap both syntactic and semantic knowledge. There were two stories for each of the main measures: communication or cognition verb with true embedded clauses and communication or cognition verb with false embedded clauses. Here is one example (cognition/false):

> This is a story about Mary and her friend. One day Mary thought, "The stores are closed today." The stores were really open. Then they went to movies.
>
> Test question: *What did Mary think?*

All the stories followed this same general format. We used the direct quotation version, rather than sentences with a "that" complementizer (e.g., *Mary thought that the stores were closed*) because we wanted to avoid the more complex past tense verb forms that might have challenged the children's linguistic limitations (cf. Roberts, Rice, & Tager-Flusberg, 2000). Research by J. de Villiers (personal communication, March 2002) has found that young normally developing children find both forms, that-complementizer and direct quotation, equally hard. The order of the key sentences containing the embedded clause and describing reality was counterbalanced across examples. We included this control on the order of the key sentences to ensure that children would not simply repeat the last thing they had heard. Each story was about a different main character. The stories were presented in random order, and children were scored one point for each correct answer (verbatim quote, indirect quote, or gloss). Thus, they received four complement scores each ranging from 0 to 2: communication/true, communication/false, cognition/true, and cognition/false.

Theory of Mind

Children received three tasks that tapped their understanding of knowledge and belief.

1. *Perception/Knowledge.* Based on Pillow (1989) and Pratt and Bryant (1990), this task tested the ability to infer knowledge from perceptual access. On each of two test trials, children observed one doll

who looked in a box and another doll who simply touched the box and were then asked a knowledge question (*Does X know what's in the box?*). Scores on this task ranged from 0 to 2.

2. *Location-Change False Belief.* Based on Wimmer and Perner (1983) and Baron-Cohen et al. (1985), this task included 2 stories in which an object was moved while the main character was absent. The stories were told using props, and participants were asked a knowledge (*Does X know where Y is?*), prediction (*Where will X look first for Y?*), and justification question (*Why?*). Scores on this task ranged from 0 to 6.

3. *Unexpected-Contents False Belief.* Based on Perner, Leekam, & Wimmer (1987), this task called for participants to be shown two different familiar containers that had unexpected objects inside. Test questions included representational change (*When you first saw this container, what did you think was inside?*), knowledge (*If I show this container to X, will X know what is inside?*), and false belief (*What will X think is inside?*). Scores on this task ranged from 0 to 6.

We examined children's performance on each of the test questions on the different theory-of-mind tasks. They were all significantly correlated with one another, at least at the .01 level, with correlations ranging from .36 to .72. We therefore combined all the scores on the test questions to yield a more robust composite theory-of-mind score that had a maximum of 14.

Different versions of the theory of mind and complementation tasks were developed, and children were randomly assigned to one of the versions in the first year of testing. In the second year, they were given a different version to avoid repeated-testing effects.

Results

Table 14.2 presents the correlations between age and the main language variables from the first year with the theory-of-mind score from both the first and second years. Because nonverbal IQ scores were not significantly correlated with either the language measures or theory of mind, we did not include this variable in the analyses presented here. The correlations in table 14.2 are all high and statistically significant, with the exception that age at the start of the study did not correlate with theory of mind in the second year.

Our first set of analyses looked at the concurrent predictors in the Year 1 data. We investigated which of our complement measures were the best predictors of theory-of-mind data, using a stepwise multiple regression analysis. On the first step, we entered the control variables, age and IPSyn score, which together accounted for 43% of the variance, $F(2, 33) = 12.5$, $p < .001$. On the

Table 14.2 Correlations with Year 1 and Year 2 Theory of Mind Scores

	Year 1 Theory of Mind	Year 2 Theory of Mind
Year 1 Measures		
Age	.419*	.114
IPSyn	.576**	.611**
Communication/true complements	.589**	.413*
Communication/false complements	.741**	.577**
Cognition/true complements	.630**	.557**
Cognition/false complements	.631**	.410*
Theory of Mind Year 1		.835**

* p. < .05
** p < .001

second step, the only complement score to enter the regression model was communication/false, explaining an additional 25.3% of variance to theory of mind, F_{inc} (1, 32) = 25.7, $p < .001$. In a second stepwise regression model, we entered the communication/true score and then communication/false, after the initial control variables were entered. In this model, communication/true accounted for 18% of the variance beyond the control variables, F_{inc} (1, 32) = 14.5, $p < .001$. Communication/false then accounted for an additional 9% of the variance, which was also statistically significant, F_{inc} (1, 31) = 9.0, $p < .01$.

These findings indicate that knowledge of sentential complements is a significant concurrent predictor of theory-of-mind performance in children with autism. As we found in our earlier studies, communication verbs are the only significant predictors in this group. Because we found in the final analysis that the true and false complements each explained variance, this suggests that both syntactic and semantic aspects of complements are important factors in performance on theory-of-mind tasks.

In the second set of analyses, we investigated longitudinal predictors of theory of mind, using the Year 1 measures as predictor variables and Year 2 theory-of-mind score as the dependent measure in a second series of stepwise multiple regression analyses. On the first step, we entered control variables, which included IPSyn score and theory of mind from Year 1. Together, these accounted for 74% of the variance in theory of mind in Year 2, F (2, 22) = 30.8, $p < .001$. As before, the only complement measure to enter the model on the second step was communication/false, which contributed an additional 5.8% variance, F_{inc} (1, 21) = 5.9, $p < .05$. In a follow-up analysis, when we forced communication/true complements in the equation at the second step, it did not explain significant additional variance; however, when communication/false complements was subsequently forced in the equation, it accounted for 8.4% additional variance, F_{inc} (1, 20) = 9.3, $p < .01$. In a final series of analyses, we investigated whether theory of mind at Year 1 predicted complement scores in Year 2. None of these analyses were significant.

Discussion of Longitudinal Findings

The data from our longitudinal study confirm many previous studies that demonstrated that language is the single most significant factor to influence performance on false-belief tasks in children with autism. Our data suggest that both general and specific linguistic abilities are important in explaining how some children with autism are able to pass theory-of-mind tasks. Thus, we found that IPSyn scores, a measure of general syntactic and morphological development, explained a significant amount of the variance in the theory-of-mind score, especially in the analyses of the concurrent predictors of theory of mind. At the same time, specific knowledge of sentential complements accounted for significant additional variance in predicting both concurrent and longitudinal performance on theory-of-mind tasks. These data show that children with autism who have more advanced language skills and who have acquired sentential complements are able to use this linguistic knowledge to master tasks that tap a representational understanding of mind.

We also replicated our earlier findings, which showed that children with autism depend uniquely on knowledge of complements for communication verbs to foster their performance on tasks tapping a representational theory of mind. As noted earlier, because we included both true and false complements, we were able to examine the role of syntactic (true complements) and semantic (false complements) properties of sentential complements. Our data, especially from the longitudinal analyses, show that the ability to handle false complements with verbs of communication is the crucial predictor for theory of mind in children with autism, suggesting that they depend on these linguistic structures for an explicit representation of how there may be a conflict between reality and the content of what someone says, which helps them to solve tests that assess their understanding of knowledge and belief. Finally, our results confirm the findings from other longitudinal and training studies with normally developing preschoolers (Astington & Jenkins, 1999; de Villiers & Pyers, 2002; Hale & Tager-Flusberg, 2003) that language predicts changes in theory of mind but that theory of mind does not predict changes in either general language ability or, more specifically, sentential complements.

Why Language Matters for Theory of Mind in Autism

Autism involves profound impairments in understanding mental states. Even high-functioning people with autism or Asperger syndrome have difficulty interpreting the mental states of other people (e.g., Baron-Cohen, Wheelwright, Hill, Raste, & Plumb, 2001; Kleinman, Marciano, & Ault, 2001), and they rarely talk about the mind (e.g., Baron-Cohen et al., 1986; Tager-Flusberg, 1992). In their everyday lives, people with autism lack an intuitive understanding of other people, suggesting that for them the mind remains opaque.

We have proposed that theory of mind encompasses both social-perceptual and social-cognitive components (Tager-Flusberg, 2001; Tager-Flusberg & Sullivan, 2000). The social-perceptual component entails real-time judgments of mental states based on information available in faces, voices, or body gesture. The social-cognitive component, which includes a representational understanding of mind, involves reasoning about the content of mental states by integrating information across perceptual cues and sequences of events over time. These components, or levels of theory of mind, can be viewed within a developmental framework (see figure 14.1).

The social-perceptual component of theory of mind builds on the innate preferences of infants to attend to human social stimuli, especially faces and voices (e.g., Fernald, 1989, 1993; Johnson & Morton, 1991; Mehler & Dupoux, 1994). The developing ability to interpret mental-state information from these stimuli is based on the interaction of these innately specified mechanisms with social information in the world, obtained through interactions with other people. The social preferences of infants that promote continued interactions with people might be driven by affective motives—the intrinsic reward of social stimuli. By

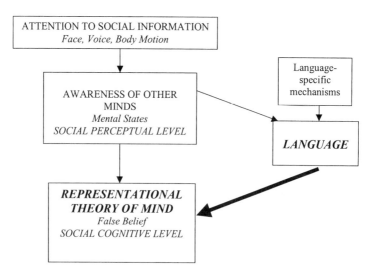

Figure 14.1. Schematic model of the acquisition of a representational Theory of Mind.

the second half of the first year of life, infants use perceptual information from faces, voices, and gestures to interpret the intentions and emotional states of other people; they may also use more subtle cues such as eye gaze to judge what another person is attending to or planning to do (cf. Baldwin, 1993; Baron-Cohen, 1994; Repacholi, 1998). Thus, the perceptual component of theory of mind emerges first in development and is available to infants for making a range of mental-state judgments about other people.

The social-cognitive component of theory of mind builds on the earlier emerging perceptual component. This component is involved in making mental-state inferences that depend on integrating information not only from perceptual cues but also from sequences of events over time. The social-cognitive component of theory of mind is more closely linked to other cognitive or information processing systems, such as working memory (needed for integrating information) and language. The development of the cognitive component of theory of mind begins during the early preschool years when children begin to talk and reason about epistemic states (Bartsch & Wellman, 1995). It is firmly in place by 4 years of age, when young children have the meta-representational capacity to pass false-belief and other related tasks. Language plays an especially significant role in the development of this component of theory of mind (de Villiers, 2000; Hale & Tager-Flusberg, 2003).

In autism, there are fundamental deficits in the ability to read and use mental-state information available from faces, voices, or body gestures, that is, in the social-perceptual component of theory of mind, which may begin very early in infancy when they fail to attend to social stimuli. Even if older, higher-functioning individuals are able to pass false-belief tasks, they continue to show deficits on tasks that tap these aspects of theory of mind (Baron-Cohen et al., 2001; Kleinman et al., 2001; Klin, 2000; Klin, Jones, Schultz, Volkmar, & Cohen, 2002). Thus, in autism the social-perceptual component of theory of mind is fundamentally impaired. Nevertheless, we argue that a small percentage of children with autism develop the ability to pass false-belief tasks *via language*, bypassing the social-perceptual foundation that underlies a representational understanding of mind in nonautistic people.

In autism, language is the single most significant prognostic factor for long-term cognitive, social, and adaptive outcomes (Howlin, Mawhood, & Rutter, 2000; Mawhood, Howlin, & Rutter, 2000; Ventner, Lord, & Schopler, 1992). Our research suggests that one way in which language plays a crucial role in these outcomes is that it helps to bootstrap an understanding of false belief and related aspects of social-cognitive components of theory of mind. Some children with autism, the minority with normal or near-normal linguistic ability, can use language to reason logically through false-belief tasks, or to interpret what others know or believe on the basis of their experience with specific events. Instead of depending on a conceptual understanding of mental states that is grounded in the social-perceptual component of theory of mind, in autism, they rely on language as the sole route to understanding propositional attitudes; there is no independent language-of-thought in the domain of theory of mind. In an analogous way, while the majority of people can find their way from one place to another using their spatial cognitive skills applied to map reading, there are some who have quite limited spatial skills and, instead, translate the information from a map into a set of verbal directions. Just as one can bypass the language-of-thought for space by replacing it with language, people with autism bypass the language-of-thought for mind-reading by transposing theory of mind into language.

More specifically, our findings suggest that children with autism are especially dependent on acquiring semantic and syntactic knowledge about verbs of communication for passing social-cognitive theory-of-mind tasks. In contrast, normally developing preschoolers appear able to use linguistic knowledge from both verbs of communication and verbs of cognition. De Villiers and Pyers (2002) and Lohmann et al. (this volume, chapter 12) found no difference between these types of verbs in their studies demonstrating the influence of sentential complements on the acquisition of theory of mind. Similarly, in our earlier cross-sectional studies comparing adolescents with autism to adolescents with MR, there was no difference between the verbs of communication and cognition for the latter group; however, the autism group was especially dependent on knowledge of complements for verbs of communication. These linguistic constructions uniquely provide the format for representing the content of mental states via analogy to the contents of speech. Statements about a person's thoughts or beliefs entail the capacity to represent mental representations, whereas statements about a person's utterance are considered to be public or overt representations (cf. Sperber, 2000). Public representations are less abstract, and, although they may convey information about a speaker's attitude or mental state, they can be interpreted at a linguistic level without any mentalistic attribution. Thus, persons with autism can process sentences that contain verbs of communication without representing a speaker's mental state; these sentences do not require conceptual understanding of mental states. Some high-functioning children with autism gain the understanding that people may say things that do not match reality and are able to express and interpret this linguistically using sentential complement constructions. Through listening and speaking about what people say, rather than what they might think, children with autism develop the capacity to represent that a person can hold a false belief. But, despite having achieved this level of understanding other minds, the minority of people with autism who pass false-belief tasks remain profoundly impaired in their ability to judge others' mental states from nonverbal social information and thus continue to suffer significant difficulties in negotiating the social world in their everyday lives.

There are still many questions that remain to be answered about theory of mind in autism. We do not know whether those children who pass false-belief tasks have any conceptual understanding about mental states or whether they understand belief and knowledge as intentional states. If they continue to lack a conceptual understanding, how do they interpret talk about the mind in conversational discourse? How could people with autism develop a conceptual understanding of the mind? Answers to these questions will be important in advancing our theoretical models of theory of mind and in finding ways to create new treatment approaches that will foster better outcomes for people with autism.

Acknowledgments Preparation of this chapter was supported by a grant from the National Institutes of Health (PO1 DC 03610), which is part of the NICHD/ NIDCD funded Collaborative Programs of Excellence in Autism. We are extremely grateful to Susan Bacalman, Laura Becker, June Chu, Karen Condouris, Courtney Hale, Margaret Kjelgaard, Echo Meyer, Jenny Roberts, Jason Smith, and Shelley Steele for their help in collecting the data reported in this chapter; to Lauren McGrath, who helped with the data analyses; and to Laura Stetser, for her editorial assistance. We offer special thanks to the children and families who participated in this study.

Note

1. It should be noted that some children did not complete all the testing described in the discussion; this is reflected in the sample size for certain data analyses.

References

American Psychiatric Association. (1994). *DSM-IV: Diagnostic and statistical manual of mental disorders* (4th ed.). Washington, DC: American Psychiatric Association.

Astington, J., & Jenkins, J. (1999). A longitudinal study of the relation between language and theory of mind development. *Developmental Psychology, 35,* 1311–1320.

Baldwin, D. A. (1993). Infants' ability to consult the speaker for clues to word reference. *Journal of Child Language, 20,* 395–418.

Baron-Cohen, S. (1988). Social and pragmatic deficits in autism: Cognitive or affective? *Journal of Autism and Developmental Disorders, 18,* 379–402.

Baron-Cohen, S. (1994). How to build a baby that can read minds: Cognitive mechanisms in mind reading. *Cahiers de Psychologie Cognitive/Current Psychology of Cognition, 13,* 513–552.

Baron-Cohen, S. (2000). Theory of mind and autism: A fifteen-year review. In S. Baron-Cohen, H. Tager-Flusberg, & D. J. Cohen (Eds.), *Understanding other minds: Perspectives from developmental cognitive neuroscience* (pp. 3–20). Oxford: Oxford University Press.

Baron-Cohen, S., Leslie, A. M., & Frith, U. (1985). Does the autistic child have a "theory of mind?" *Cognition, 21,* 37–46.

Baron-Cohen, S., Leslie, A. M., & Frith, U. (1986). Mechanical, behavioral and intentional understanding of picture stories in autistic children. *British Journal of Developmental Psychology, 4,* 113–125.

Baron-Cohen, S., Tager-Flusberg, H., & Cohen, D. J. (Eds.). (1993). *Understanding other minds: Perspectives from autism.* Oxford: Oxford University Press.

Baron-Cohen, S., Tager-Flusberg, H., & Cohen, D. J. (Eds.). (2000). *Understanding other minds: Perspectives from developmental cognitive neuroscience.* Oxford: Oxford University Press.

Baron-Cohen, S., Wheelwright, S., Hill, J., Raste, Y., & Plumb, I. (2001). The "Reading the Mind in the Eyes" test-revised version: A study with normal adults, and adults with Asperger syndrome or high-functioning autism. *Journal of Child Psychology and Psychiatry, 42,* 241–251.

Bartsch, K., & Wellman, H. M. (1995). *Children talk about the mind.* New York: Oxford University Press.

Benson, G., Abbeduto, L., Short, K., Bibler-Nuccio, J., & Maas, F. (1993). Development of theory of mind in individuals with MR. *American Journal on Mental Retardation, 98,* 427–433.

Bishop, D. V. M. (1983). *The Test for Reception of Grammar (TROG).* Manchester, UK: University of Manchester.

Cassidy, K., & Ballaraman, G. R. (1997, April). Theory of mind ability in language delayed children. Paper presented at the biennial meeting of the Society for Research in Child Development, Washington, DC.

Cutting, A. L., & Dunn, J. (1999). Theory of mind, emotion understanding, language, and family background: Individual differences and interrelations. *Child Development, 70,* 853–865.

Dahlgren, S., & Trillingsgaard, A. (1996). Theory of mind in non-retarded children with autism and Asperger's syndrome. A research note. *Journal of Child Psychology and Psychiatry, 37,* 759–763.

de Villiers, J. (2000). Language and theory of mind: What are the developmental relationships? In S. Baron-Cohen, H. Tager-Flusberg, & D. Cohen (Eds.), *Understanding other minds: Perspectives from developmental cognitive neuroscience,* 2nd ed. (pp. 83–123). Oxford: Oxford University Press.

de Villiers, J. G., & de Villiers, P. A. (2000). Linguistic determinism and the understanding of false beliefs. In P. Mitchell and K. Riggs. (Eds.), *Children's reasoning and the mind* (pp. 189–226). Hove, UK: Psychology Press.

de Villiers, J., & Pyers, J. (2002). Complements to cognition: A longitudinal study of the relationship between complex syntax and false-belief understanding. *Cognitive Development, 17,* 1037–1060.

de Villiers, J., Pyers, J., & Broderick, K. (1997, November). A longitudinal study of the emergence of referential opacity. Paper presented at the 22nd annual Boston University Conference on Language Development, Boston, MA.

de Villiers, J., Roeper, T., & Vainikka, A. (1990). The acquisition of long-distance rules. In L. Frazier & J. de Villiers (Eds.), *Language processing and acquisition.* Dordrecht, Netherlands: Kluwer.

Dunn, L. M., & Dunn, L. M. (1981). *Peabody Picture Vocabulary Test.* Circle Pines, MN: American Guidance Service.

Dunn, L. M, & Dunn, L. M. (1997). *Peabody Picture Vocabulary Test* (3rd ed.). Circle Pines, MN: American Guidance Service.

Dunn, L. M., Dunn, L. M., Whetton, C., & Pintilie, D. (1982). *British Picture Vocabulary Scale.* Windsor, UK: NFER-Nelson.

Eisenmajer, R. & Prior, M. (1991). Cognitive linguistic correlates of "theory of mind" ability in autistic children. *British Journal of Developmental Psychology, 9,* 351–364.

Elliot, C. D. (1990). *Differential Ability Scales.* San Antonio, TX: Psychological Corporation/Harcourt Brace.

Fernald, A. (1989). Intonation and communicative intent in mothers' speech to infants: Is the melody the message? *Child Development, 60,* 1497–1510.

Fernald, A. (1993). Approval and disapproval: Infant responsiveness to vocal affect in familiar and unfamiliar languages. *Child Development, 64,* 657–674.

Fisher, N. (2002, April). Language and theory of mind in children with autism and learning difficulties. Poster presented at the International Conference "Why Language Matters for Theory of Mind," Toronto, Canada.

Frith, C. & Frith, U. (2000). The physiological basis of theory of mind: Functional neuroimaging studies. In S. Baron-Cohen, H. Tager-Flusberg, & D. J. Cohen (Eds.), *Understanding other minds: Perspectives from developmental cognitive neuroscience* (pp. 334–356). Oxford: Oxford University Press.

Garfield, J., Peterson, C., & Perry, T. (2001). Social cognition, language acquisition and the development of the theory of mind. *Mind and Language, 16,* 494–541.

Hale, C. M., & Tager-Flusberg, H. (2003). The influence of language on theory of mind: A training study. *Developmental Science, 6,* 346–359.

Happé, F. (1993). Communicative competence and theory of mind in autism: A test of relevance theory. *Cognition, 48,* 101–119.

Happé, F. (1994). *Autism: An introduction to psychological theory.* London: University College London Press.

Happé, F. (1995). The role of age and verbal ability in the theory of mind task performance of subjects with autism. *Child Development, 66,* 843–855.

Howlin, P., Baron-Cohen, S., & Hadwin, J. (1999). *Teaching children with autism to mind-read: A practical guide.* New York: John Wiley.

Howlin, P., Mawhood, L., & Rutter, M. (2000). Autism and developmental receptive language disorder—a comparative follow-up in early adult life: I. Social, behavioral and psychiatric outcomes. *Journal of Child Psychology and Psychiatry, 41,* 561–578.

Jenkins, J., & Astington, J. (1996). Cognitive factors and family structure associated with theory of mind development in young children. *Developmental Psychology, 32,* 70–78.

Johnson, M. H., & Morton, J. (1991). *Biology and cognitive development: The case of face recognition.* Oxford: Blackwell.

Kjelgaard, M., & Tager-Flusberg, H. (2001). An investigation of language impairment in autism: Implications for genetic subgroups. *Language and Cognitive Processes, 16,* 287–308.

Kleinman, J., Marciano, P., & Ault, R. (2001). Advanced theory of mind in high-functioning adults with autism. *Journal of Autism and Developmental Disorders, 31,* 29–36.

Klin, A. (2000). Attributing social meaning to ambiguous visual stimuli in higher-functioning autism and Asperger syndrome: The Social Attribution Task. *Journal of Child Psychology and Psychiatry, 41,* 831–846.

Klin, A., Jones, W., Schultz, R., Volkmar, F., & Cohen, D. J. (2002). Defining and quantifying the social phenotype in autism. *American Journal of Psychiatry, 159,* 895–908.

Leslie, A. M., & Roth, D. (1993). What autism teaches us about metarepresentation. In S. Baron-Cohen, H. Tager-Flusberg, & D. J. Cohen (Eds.), *Understanding other minds: Perspectives from autism* (pp. 83–111). Oxford: Oxford University Press.

Lord, C., Risi, S., Lambrecht, L., Cook, E. H., Lenventhal, B. L., DiLavore, P. S., Pickles, A., & Rutter, M. (2000). The Autism Diagnostic Observation Schedule-Generic: A standard measure of social and communication deficits associated with the spectrum of autism. *Journal of Autism and Developmental Disorders, 30,* 205–223.

Lord, C., Rutter, M., & LeCouteur, A. (1994). Autism Diagnostic Interview-Revised: A revised version of a diagnostic interview for caregivers of individuals with possible pervasive developmental disorders. *Journal of Autism and Developmental Disorders, 24,* 659–685.

Mawhood, L., Howlin, P., & Rutter, M. (2000). Autism and developmental receptive language disorder—a comparative follow-up in early adult life: I. Cognitive and language outcomes. *Journal of Child Psychology and Psychiatry, 41,* 547–559.

Mehler, J., & Dupoux, E. (1994). *What infants know: The new cognitive science of early development.* Oxford: Blackwell.

Miller, C. (2001). False-belief understanding in children with specific language impairment. *Journal of Communication Disorders, 34,* 73–86.

Miller, J., & Chapman, R. (2000). Systematic analysis of language transcripts (SALT) (Version 6.1) [Computer software]. Madison: University of Wisconsin, Language Analysis Lab.

Moore, C., Bryant, D., & Furrow, D. (1989). Mental terms and the development of certainty. *Child Development, 60,* 167–171.

Moore, C., & Davidge, J. (1989). The development of mental terms: Pragmatics or semantics? *Journal of Child Language, 16,* 633–641.

Ozonoff, S., & Miller, J. (1995). Teaching theory of mind: A new approach to social skills training for individuals with autism. *Journal of Autism and Developmental Disorders, 25,* 415–433.

Perner, J., Frith, U., Leslie, A., & Leekam, S. (1989). Exploration of the autistic child's theory of mind: Knowledge, belief and communication. *Child Development, 60,* 689–700.

Perner, J., Leekam, S., & Wimmer, H. (1987). Three-year-olds' difficulty with false belief: The case for a conceptual deficit. *British Journal of Developmental Psychology, 5,* 125–137.

Peterson, C., & Siegal, M. (2000). Insights into theory of mind from deafness and autism. *Mind and Language, 15,* 123–145.

Pillow, B. (1989). Early understanding of perception as a source of knowledge. *Journal of Experimental Child Psychology, 47,* 116–129.

Pratt, C., & Bryant, P. (1990). Young children understand that looking leads to knowing (so long as they are looking into a single barrel). *Child Development, 61,* 973–982.

Repacholi, B. M. (1998). Infants' use of attentional cues to identify the referent of another person's emotional expression. *Developmental Psychology, 34,* 1017–1025.

Roberts, J., Rice, M., & Tager-Flusberg, H. (2000, June). Tense marking in children with autism: Further evidence for overlap between autism and SLI. Paper presented at the Symposium on Research in Child Language Disorders, Madison, WI.

Scarborough, H. S. (1990). Index of Productive Syntax. *Applied Psycholinguistics, 11*, 1–22.

Semel, E., Wiig, E. H., & Secord, W. (1987). *Clinical Evaluation of Language Fundamentals-revised* (*CELF*). San Antonio, TX: Psychological Corporation.

Sparrevohn, R., & Howie, P. (1995). Theory of mind in children with autistic disorder: Evidence of developmental progression and the role of verbal ability. *Journal of Child Psychology and Psychiatry, 36*, 249–263.

Sperber, D. (2000). Metarepresentations in an evolutionary perspective. In D. Sperber (Ed.), *Metarepresentations: A multidisciplinary perspective* (pp. 117–137). Oxford: Oxford University Press.

Swettenham, J. (1996). Can children be taught to understand false belief using computers? *Journal of Child Psychology and Psychiatry, 37*, 157–165.

Tager-Flusberg, H. (1992). Autistic children talk about psychological states: Deficits in the early acquisition of a theory of mind. *Child Development, 63*, 161–172.

Tager-Flusberg, H. (1993). What language reveals about the understanding of minds in children with autism. In S. Baron-Cohen, H. Tager-Flusberg, & D. J. Cohen (Eds.), *Understanding other minds: Perspectives from autism* (pp. 138–157). Oxford: Oxford University Press.

Tager-Flusberg, H. (1997). The role of theory of mind in language acquisition: Contributions from the study of autism. In L. Adamson & M. A. Romski (Eds.), *Communication and language acquisition: Discoveries from atypical development* (pp. 133–158). Baltimore, MD: Paul Brookes.

Tager-Flusberg, H. (1999). A psychological approach to understanding the social and language impairments in autism. *International Review of Psychiatry, 11*, 325–334.

Tager-Flusberg, H. (2000a). Language and understanding minds: Connections in autism. In S. Baron-Cohen, H. Tager-Flusberg, & D. J. Cohen (Eds), *Understanding other minds: Perspectives from developmental cognitive neuroscience*, 2nd ed. (pp. 124–149). Oxford: Oxford University Press.

Tager-Flusberg, H. (2000b). Understanding the language and communicative impairments in autism. L. M. Glidden (Ed.), *International Review of Research on Mental Retardation*, Vol. 20 (pp. 185–205). San Diego, CA: Academic Press.

Tager-Flusberg, H. (2001). A re-examination of the theory of mind hypothesis of autism. In J. Burack, T. Charman, N. Yirmiya, & P. Zelazo (Eds.), *The development of autism: Perspectives from theory and research* (pp. 173–193). Mahwah, NJ: Erlbaum.

Tager-Flusberg, H. & Sullivan, K. (1994). Predicting and explaining behavior: A comparison of autistic, mentally retarded and normal children. *Journal of Child Psychology and Psychiatry, 35*, 1059–1075.

Tager-Flusberg, H., & Sullivan, K. (2000). A componential view of theory of mind: Evidence from Williams syndrome. *Cognition, 76*, 59–89.

Ventner, A., Lord, C., & Schopler, E. (1992). A follow-up study of high-functioning autistic children. *Journal of Child Psychology and Psychiatry, 33*, 489–507.

Williams, K. T. (1997). *Expressive Vocabulary Test*. Circle Pines, MN: American Guidance Service.

Wimmer, H., & Perner, J. (1983). Beliefs about beliefs: Representation and constraining function of wrong beliefs in young children's understanding of deception. *Cognition, 13,* 103–128.

Yirmiya, N., Erel, O., Shaked, M., & Solomonica-Levi, D. (1998). Meta-analyses comparing theory of mind abilities of individuals with autism, individuals with mental retardation, and normally developing individuals. *Psychological Bulletin, 124,* 283–307.

Zelazo, P., Burack, J., Benedetto, E., & Frye, D. (1996). Theory of mind and rule use in individuals with Down's Syndrome: A test of the uniqueness and specificity claims. *Journal of Child Psychology and Psychiatry, 37,* 479–484.

Ziatas, K., Durkin, K., & Pratt, C. (1998). Belief term development in children with autism, Asperger syndrome, specific language impairment, and normal development: Links to theory of mind development. *Journal of Child Psychology and Psychiatry, 39,* 755–763.

15 Genetic and Environmental Influences on Individual Differences in Language and Theory of Mind: Common or Distinct?

Claire Hughes

> It was six men of Indostan
> To learning much inclined,
> Who went to see the Elephant
> (Though all of them were blind),
> That each by observation
> Might satisfy his mind . . .
> —John Godfrey Saxe (1816–1887)

Like the elephant of Indostan, the relationship between language and theory of mind can be described in many ways, as the variety of chapters in this book illustrate. For example, progress has been made in elucidating *structural* features of language (e.g., the syntax of complementation) that may facilitate the acquisition of a theory of mind (J. de Villiers, this volume, chapter 10; Tager-Flusberg & Joseph, this volume, chapter 14). Similarly, advances have been made in exploring various *functional* relations between language and theory of mind (Nelson, this volume, chapter 2; Baldwin & Saylor, this volume, chapter 7). The goal of this chapter is to expand this range of answers still further by arguing that links between theory of mind and language exist at several levels (social, psychological, biological) and so include the common influence of both *genetic* and *environmental* factors. Furthermore, as we shall see, different factors may have particular salience at different developmental periods.

The chapter begins with some general comments about why the relation between language and theory of mind is likely to be very complex. Two related points concern definitions for theory of mind and developmental shifts in the nature of relations between theory of mind and language. A third point concerns the distinction between the factors that underlie associations between individual differences in theory of mind and language, and those that underpin developmental links between these two domains. Taken together, these points highlight the need for a greater range and sophistication of methodological designs within theory-of-mind research. In response to this gap, in the second part of this chapter I consider the merits of the twin-study design as a novel methodological perspective from which to investigate individual differences in theory of mind. This section begins with an outline of some of the terms used in behavioral genetic research, and of the rationale for twin studies. Next, findings from the only published theory-of-mind twin study to date (Hughes & Cutting, 1999) and from a more recent and much larger twin study (Hughes, Jaffee, Happé, et al., in press) are briefly presented. The chapter ends with a discussion of how the contrasting findings from these two studies may suggest developmental change in the relations between individual differences in theory of mind and language.

Conceptual Complexities

The Impact of Different Definitions

Although the term "theory of mind" was originally coined to refer broadly to the attribution of mental states to the self and others (Premack & Woodruff, 1978), it quickly became synonymous with success on a set of tasks designed to test children's understanding of mistaken (i.e., false) belief (Baron-Cohen, Leslie, & Frith, 1985; Wimmer & Perner, 1983). Two consequences of this operational but narrow definition were (1) a heavy research focus upon 3- to 4-year olds, since it is in this age period that most children begin to succeed on standard false-belief tasks; and (2) an emphasis upon belief and knowledge states (rather than intentions, perceptions, emotions, and desires).

A clear indication that equating theory of mind with success on false-belief tasks is inadequate comes from the paradoxical contrast between 3-year-olds' failure on false-belief tasks and their evident success in negotiating everyday social interactions. In other words, under this narrow definition, "theory of mind" appears to have no fundamental significance for children's social competencies (and is therefore in danger of becoming theoretically empty). That said, as indicated later in this chapter, individual differences in false-belief performance are associated with diverse socially relevant domains (although the factors underlying this association remain poorly understood).

Partly in reaction to the widespread failure of socially competent 3-year-olds to succeed on false-belief tasks, many researchers (e.g., Astington, 2001; Dunn, 1999a; Moses, 2001) now subscribe to much broader definitions of theory of mind that encompass a wide range of mental states (from perception to intention, cognition, and emotion). Within this broader framework, two contrasting kinds of definition for theory of mind can be offered (Davies & Stone, 2003; Tager-Flusberg, 2001). These emphasize either formal propositional knowledge (of a set of interconnected principles that state how the mental world works) or socioperceptual skills that provide an implicit social know-how that allows us to negotiate the mental domain. Since we need language to make our ideas explicit, it seems obvious that language matters much more for theory of mind when the latter is defined as an explicit and formal conceptual domain rather than a set of implicit socioperceptual skills. However, it may be that the contrast is more qualitative than quantitative: the formal definition for theory of mind highlights the importance of structural features within language (e.g., embedded clauses), whereas theory of mind as defined as social intuition is more likely to depend upon the functional properties of language as a vehicle for communication and social exchange with others.

Developmental Shifts

The two kinds of definition for theory of mind outlined in the preceding section clearly lead to contrasting accounts of how theory of mind develops. This point is pertinent to the current debate surrounding precursor or fledgling theory-of-mind skills in late infancy (e.g., joint visual attention, social referencing, imitation, communicative vocalizations and gestures), which are interpreted generously by some (e.g., Baldwin & Moses, 1994; Dunn, 1999b; Meltzoff, Gopnik, & Repacholi, 1999; Tomasello, 1999) and cautiously by others (e.g., Butterworth & Jarrett, 1991; Moore, 1999). As a result, these two definitions (explicit vs. implicit knowledge of mental states), again lead to contrasting interpretations of the relationship between theory of mind and children's emerging linguistic competencies.

One such contrast concerns the direction of influence. Specifically, viewing theory of mind as an implicit understanding of mental states opens up the possibility of bidirectional transactional influences between theory of mind and language (under its formal definition, theory of mind emerges much later in development and so is unlikely to have much influence upon early language acquisition). However, the widely reported correlation between language and theory of mind does not demonstrate that the relationship between these two domains is *causal*, as it could equally reflect the common influence of one or more external factors. A further contrast that emerges from the different developmental windows highlighted by the two alternative definitions for theory of mind therefore concerns the type of shared factor that might underpin the association between language and theory of mind. For example, as is discussed later in this chapter, common effects of genetic and environmental influences may show contrasting salience in accounting for the phenotypic correlation between language and theory of mind for different age groups.

Individual Differences versus Age-Related Change

Another reason for the relatively slow progress in disentangling the nature of the relationship between language and theory of mind is that researchers often fall into the trap of relating findings of correlations between individual differences in these two domains to theoretical models that posit *developmental* dependencies between language and theory of mind. Indeed, researchers commonly refer to "3-year-olds" and "4-year-olds" as if each of these labels described a homogeneous sample, so that within each age group both individual differences and age-related effects are assumed to be negligible. These assumptions can be challenged by studies that involve larger and more representative samples of children from more tightly specified age groups.

Such studies have shown that, although only a single index of a capacity that develops across the life span (Happé, Winner, & Brownell, 1998), false-belief performance is correlated with diverse socially relevant domains, including shared pretense (Hughes & Dunn, 1997; Youngblade & Dunn, 1995), communication (Slomkowski & Dunn, 1996) and sensitivity to criticism (Cutting & Dunn, 2002). Although language skills also correlate with each of these social skills, the correlations with false-belief performance hold up even when individual differences in verbal ability are taken into account.

Indeed, it is now clear that the apparent universality of age-related developments in theory of mind was an artifact of the relatively homogeneous, middle-class samples recruited in early research; when samples from families with diverse socioeconomic status (SES) are employed, individual differences are striking (e.g., Cole & Mitchell, 2000; Cutting & Dunn, 1999; Holmes, Black, & Miller, 1996). Note that SES contrasts in language use are widely recognized (e.g., Burt, Holm, & Dodd, 1999; Dammann, Walther, Allers, et al., 1996). Part of the answer to the question of why language matters for theory of mind may therefore hinge on these SES contrasts in children's linguistic environments.

Support for the importance of children's communicative environments in their development of false-belief comprehension comes from studies of hearing-impaired children (P. de Villiers, this volume, chapter 13). In particular, major delays in false-belief success have been reported for hearing-impaired children whose parents are not fluent users of sign language but not for hearing-impaired children whose parents are fluent signers. One particularly fascinating finding to emerge from this work is that hearing-impaired children show no deficit in deception, suggesting that different aspects of theory of mind may have contrasting origins.

Novel research designs that capture the transactional nature of the relationship between theory of mind and verbal competencies are therefore needed. These might include longitudinal studies and intervention studies. The few intervention studies conducted so far have aimed to explore the relative importance of functional and. structural aspects of linguistic environments (e.g., discourse vs. syntax) on theory-of-mind development (Lohmann, Tomasello, & Meyer, this volume, chapter 12). Here, the findings, while interesting, suggest relatively small effect sizes for the impact of intervention programs.

However, intriguing findings from recent longitudinal work suggest that such interventions may be very much more successful if placed within the context of the child's existing close relationships. For example, Meins and colleagues have reported that mothers who showed high sensitivity to their infants' intentional states had children who performed particularly well on theory-of-mind tasks at early school age, and this predictive effect was independent of the positive effects of a secure attachment relationship (Meins, Fernyhough, Fradley, & Tuckey, 2001). More striking still are Dunn, Cutting, and Fisher's (2002) longitudinal findings from a study of young friends, followed up across the transition to school. In particular, hierarchical regression analyses showed that social insight (rated from a semistructured interview with each child about his or her new best friend) was predicted by the earlier sociocognitive competencies of both the children themselves *and* their original friends. Together with the significant positive effect of siblings (Jenkins & Astington, 1996; Ruffman, Perner, Naito, Parkin, & Clements, 1998) and other family members (Lewis, Freeman, Kyriakidou, Maridaki-Kassotaki, & Berridge, 1996), the findings from each of these studies indicate that individual differences in the "mind-mindedness" of the people with whom children share a close relationship have a significant influence on children's developing understanding of others (see also Dunn & Brophy, this volume, chapter 3). Future intervention studies might therefore build on these longitudinal findings by involving familiar others as well as unknown research workers in intervention programs.

More generally, these findings have sparked a growing interest in the nature and extent of social environmental influences on individual differences in theory of mind. This new generation of studies (e.g., Astington, 2003; Cutting & Dunn, 1999; Vinden, 1999) stands in contrast to earlier work in which individual differences in theory of mind were regarded as minimal and development was viewed as essentially maturational, with children's social environments having no more than a triggering role (Leslie, 1994). However, it remains possible that these individual differences are heavily influenced by genetic factors. In the next section, we therefore turn to the puzzle of how to distinguish environmental from genetic effects.

Disentangling Environmental from Genetic Effects

Distinguishing genetic from environmental effects requires genetically sensitive research designs (e.g., studies of twins, adopted children, or children in step-families). Such investigations provide unique insights into the causes of individual differences in young children's understanding of mind, for three reasons. First, existing evidence for genetic influence rests heavily on findings from atypical populations, such as individuals with autism (see Bailey, Palferman, Heavey, & Le Couteur, 1998, for a recent review) or Turner's syndrome (Skuse, James, Bishop, et al., 1997). Extrapolating from pathology to normal individual variation may well be unwarranted, and direct assessment of genetic influences in a sample of normally developing children is therefore needed. Second, phenotype-based accounts of environmental effects may be misleading, since environmental influences on child characteristics typically covary with genetic effects. In particular, research findings in psychiatric genetics over the past 20 years have led to a growing recognition of the extent and importance of gene-environment correlations and interactions (Eaves, Last, Martin, & Jinks, 1977). Third, genetically sensitive designs enable an important refinement in the concept of environmental influences, since they provide a means of distinguishing between shared and nonshared environmental influences. These concepts of gene-environment correlation and interaction and shared/nonshared environmental influences may be novel for some readers, and so a brief explanation is provided, before we move on to the rationale (and potential weaknesses) of twin studies.

Gene-Environment Correlation (GrE)

There are two types of GrE: passive and active. Passive GrE refers to the fact that most parents who provide children with their home environments also pass on their genes. Passive GrE has been researched in relation to the effects of parental depression (Murray & Cooper, 1997) and parental antisocial behavior (Rutter, Maughan, Meyer, et al., 1997), but much less is known about passive GrE in relation to the effects of parental cognitive ability. One research avenue mentioned earlier in this chapter is the exploration of parental cognitive attributes such as maternal mind-mindedness (Meins, Fernyhough, Russell, & Clarke-Carter, 1998) that are likely to be salient for children's acquisition of a theory of mind (and may well be mediated by parental discourse style). In the literature on this topic so far, the possible influence of passive GrE has largely been overlooked. In particular, it is not clear whether maternal mind-mindedness is a feature of a specific attachment relationship, as proposed by Meins et al. (2001), or rather reflects individual differences in the mother's general propensity to attribute intentionality to infants, as described by Reznick (1999). The effects of passive GrE are more likely to be significant within the latter of these two accounts.

Active GrE refers to the role children play in selecting certain environments or eliciting certain responses from others. In other words, individual children shape and select their environments, and their behavior influences how other people behave toward them (Rutter, Maughan, et al., 1997). In contrast to passive GrE, the key issue raised by active GrE is that of differentiating parental effects on children from children's effects on parents. More specific research questions concern which aspect of the child's character, cognitive functioning, or behavior affects either other peoples' responses or their own shaping and selecting of environments (Rutter, Dunn, et al., 1997). With regard to the role of language for theory of mind, individual differences in communication skills have a salient influence on how effective children are at shaping and selecting environments (e.g., initiating and maintaining interactions with peers, articulating their own needs and feelings) and on how others respond to them (e.g., evoked amusement, sympathy, avoidance of misunderstandings or conflict). However, longitudinal data are needed, both to distinguish the direction of effects and to ascertain the ages at which such child effects are maximal.

Gene-Environment Interactions (GxE)

Gene-environment interactions refer to the indirect effects of genes that arise through influences on the susceptibility or resilience to specific environments. For example, we now know that there are striking individual differences in how children react to adverse environments (e.g., conflict between parents, risky neighborhoods). Understanding the nature and role of genetic influences upon these individual differences in environmental risk exposure is vital if we are to create effective policies of intervention and support. With regard to the relation between language and theory of mind for example, it may be that genetic contributions to individual differences in early language development amplify the effects of between-child contrasts in the social environments that might support (or hinder) developments in children's understanding of mind.

Shared and Nonshared Environment

Shared environmental factors are defined as those that serve to increase sibling similarity, whilst nonshared environmental factors are defined as those that serve to decrease sibling similarity. That is, the distinction between shared and nonshared environmental influences is entirely based on *outcome*. This is an important point, since factors that appear to be familywide may actually have a differential impact upon individual members of the family. For example, when a family changes address, one child in a family may miss former friends, while another may quickly find lots of new friends and so settle very well; similarly marital conflict or maternal depression or other seemingly shared experiences may have a differential impact upon siblings. Indeed, one of the most robust findings to emerge from behavioral genetic studies is that, for a wide variety of traits, the strongest environmental influences are typically child-specific, or nonshared (Plomin & Daniels, 1987). This finding has clear implications for investigations into relations between theory of mind and language. At a methodological level, the importance of nonshared environmental influences highlights the importance of collecting data from more than one child in any single family. Conceptually, child-specific effects support theoretical models that highlight the active role played by the child in processing and interpreting information (e.g., following the metaphor of the pint glass that is half-empty or half-full).

However, estimates for nonshared effects can be inflated by measurement error, leading to exaggerated contrasts between shared and nonshared effects. In addition, for a few outcomes (e.g., antisocial behavior), there is evidence for substantial shared environmental influences. Note that some of these shared environmental effects may actually have their origins outside the home. For instance, siblings who are close in age often share the same peer group. This point brings us nicely to the subject of twin studies, since twins are often in the same class at school and so especially likely to interact with the same network of peers.

The Twin Study Rationale

The most widely used genetically sensitive design is the twin study, which hinges on comparisons between genetically identical monozygotic (MZ) twin pairs and fraternal, dizygotic (DZ) twin pairs who on average share only half their genes. This contrast provides what has been described as "the perfect natural experiment" (Martin, Boomsma, & Machin, 1997) through which to assess the bottom line of transmissible genetic effects on behavior, regardless of the number of genes involved, the complexity of their interactions, or the influence of nongenetic factors. Early twin studies relied on very simple comparisons of the co-twin intraclass correlations for MZ and DZ pairs. For example, doubling the difference between these two correlations provides a rough estimate of the heritability for a given trait, which if subtracted from the MZ co-twin correlation gives an estimate of shared environmental influence; similarly, 1 minus the correlation for MZ twins provides an estimate of nonshared environmental influence (though measurement error also needs to be taken into account, especially in univariate analyses). At this point, it should be said that twin comparisons do have limitations. These arise chiefly from the nature of twin samples and from the assumptions made by twin models.

Twin Samples

Two types of concern have been voiced in relation to twin samples. The first stems from the low participation rates and the volunteer recruitment methods found in many twin studies. In particular, volunteer samples often show greater numbers of MZ or concordant pairs and so may lead to skewed heritability estimates. Researchers today therefore attach considerable importance to recruitment methods, and epidemiological samples with high participation rates are recognized as especially valuable.

The second, more general concern about twin samples is that twins are special in many ways, and so caution is needed in extrapolating findings to the general population. With regard to theory of mind, for instance, the experience of being a twin may give children an unusual advantage in developing awareness of false belief as they become accustomed to other people making mistakes about the identity of each twin. This possibility is relatively easy to put to the test, since it leads directly to the prediction that, ceteris paribus, identical (MZ) twins should outperform fraternal (DZ) twins on standard false-belief tasks, as MZ twins are physically much more similar (and more likely to be dressed in matching outfits) than DZ twins.

When language is also considered in relation to theory of mind, another contrast between families with twins and those with singleton children becomes important, namely the typical patterns of communicative interactions within each type of family. Communication between twins is broadly similar to that between closely aged siblings; however, there is evidence for an elevated incidence of "secret language." This can take two forms: generally directed speech that is intelligible only within the twin/sibling pair, and private language directed exclusively to the other twin/sibling. However, in most cases this "secret language" appears to be a transient developmental phenomenon that declines rapidly between 20 and 36 months (Thorpe, Greenwood, Eivers, & Rutter, 2001) and so is unlikely to influence developments in children's understanding of mind across the subsequent preschool years. In contrast, there are persistent differences in mother-child interactions in families with twins and those with closely aged singletons. In particular, mothers with twins show significantly less frequent and less elaborate talk with each child and spend less time in reading and booksharing, with group mean differences of 0.5 to 1 SD (Rutter, personal communication, August 2000). Several observational studies have highlighted the potential importance of these kinds of parent-child interaction for children's acquisition of a theory of mind (Dunn, 1996a, 1996b, 1996c). However, the form of this relationship (e.g., linear relation or threshold function) is not yet known, and this should be kept in mind when considering how far the results from twin studies can be applied to the general population.

Assumptions of the Twin Study Design

The two most important assumptions made in twin studies are that (1) MZ and DZ twins share equally similar environments, and (2) DZ twins share, on average, 50% of their genes. In relation to the first of these, MZ twins do in fact often share more similar postnatal environments than DZ twins, and this can inflate heritability estimates. However, it appears that the greater similarity in environments is usually not a cause of MZ twins' greater phenotypic similarity but rather a consequence of their genetic identity (Reznick, Corley, & Robinson, 1997). In addition, violations of the second assumption generally serve to reduce heritability estimates. For example, assortative mating has been well documented for a number of traits, including cognitive ability. As a result, DZ twins often share more than 50% of their genes (Vandenberg, 1972), and this leads to rather conservative estimates of heritability. Taken together, the problems for these two assumptions of twin studies have opposite influences and so may minimize each other. Certainly, it is reassuring to note that, perhaps because of these opposite effects, findings from twin studies are very similar to those from adoption studies, which involve quite different assumptions (Plomin, DeFries, McClearn, & Rutter, 1997).

Structural Equation Model Fitting (SEM)

One of the most important advances in twin studies has been the development of sophisticated statistical modeling techniques. The use of SEM enables researchers to go beyond simply partitioning variance into genetic and environmental effects to test specific hypotheses on questions such as whether different traits or outcomes share common genetic influence and hypotheses about possible mechanisms involved in sex differences.

The standard SEM model used in twin studies is the ACE model, in which A = additive genetic effects, C = shared environment, and E = nonshared environment. How do these models compare with the simple rule-of-thumb estimates provided by direct comparisons of co-twin correlations for MZ and DZ twins? For simple univariate analyses, ACE models give very similar results but have the advantage of including statistics[1] that provide an index of the *significance* of genetic, shared environmental and nonshared environmental influences. Moreover, SEM also enables *multivariate* analyses that allow one to explore the relationship between particular traits. For example, in a bivariate analysis, the correlation between two traits/abilities can be partitioned into effects of common genes and common environment. The SEM approach is especially useful for considering relationships among factors, since measurement error is estimated and removed, leaving only common variance. In addition, since SEM is a confirmatory technique, its key strength lies in its ability to test the predictions from competing theoretical accounts. These can be very simple or complex. The goal of SEM is to find the simplest model with a good fit to the data.

The First Theory-of-Mind Twin Study

Recently, Hughes and colleagues reported findings from the first twin study of individual differences in theory of mind (Hughes & Cutting, 1999; Hughes & Plomin, 2000). In this study, 119 pairs of 3;6-year-old twins (61 MZ pairs and 58 DZ pairs; mean age = 42 months, SD = 1 month) were tested in two sessions, in a lab and at home, and given (1) a battery of nine theory-of-mind tasks (including tests of deception, prediction and explanation of false belief) and (2) vocabulary and verbal comprehension subtests from the Stanford-Binet Intelligence Scales. As expected, theory-of-mind performance was significantly correlated (r (236) = .42) with verbal ability. Bivariate model-fitting analyses were then conducted to explore whether this correlation reflected common genetic influence or common environmental influence.

Hughes and Cutting (1999) reported that maximum-likelihood model-fitting analyses provided an estimated heritability of 67% (i.e., genetic factors accounted for 67% of the sample variance), supporting predictions from nativist accounts of theory of mind (e.g., Baron-Cohen, 1995; Leslie, 1994). The best-fitting model attributed environmental influences on theory of mind primarily to child-specific factors (nonshared environment accounted for 33% of the variance, while just 7% was attributed to shared environment). Moreover, although only one-third of the genetic influence on theory of mind overlapped with genetic influence on verbal ability (supporting modularist accounts of theory of mind), this common genetic influence accounted for about half of the phenotypic correlation between theory of mind and verbal ability.

These findings provide a fresh perspective upon the results of phenotypic studies, confirming, for example, that sibling effects are unlikely to be symmetrical (Ruffman et al., 1998) and highlighting the active role played by children in shaping their own social environments (Dunn & Plomin, 1990). Studies of this kind help us to focus on the processes by which child-environment interactions come to have specific effects. However, as the authors themselves acknowledge, this twin study is limited by the relatively small sample size—detecting effects of shared environment can require very large samples (n >1000; Martin, Eaves, Kearsey, & Davies, 1978)—and the volunteer recruitment method (which may oversample both middle-class families and families in which MZ twins appear identical). In addition, focusing on a single age group provides only a snapshot view of the factors that underlie individual differences, and so comparable findings from different age groups are needed.

A New and Larger Twin Study

As noted, the findings from Hughes and Cutting's (1999) twin study of individual differences in theory of mind are thought provoking but require replication in a much larger sample. Here I provide a brief summary of findings from a recent study involving 1,116 pairs of same-sex 5-year-old twins. The full account of this large study and its results is yet to be published (Hughes et al., in press).

The overall focus of this new research program is the origins of antisocial behavior. Families were therefore selected (from a British epidemiological cohort, the "Twins Early Development Study," or TEDS; Plomin & Dale, 2000), using an "enriched" sampling design to ensure sufficient base-rates of problem behaviors. Two-thirds of the sample represent English and Welsh families with children born in the mid-1990s (maternal age 15 to 48); the remaining third constitutes an oversample of mothers under 20 at the birth of their first child. Early first childbearing was chosen as being a simple and known risk factor for childhood problem behaviors. The twin pairs were 56% MZ, 44% DZ; 49% of the sample were male. The study participation rate was 93%, which is very impressive given the relatively high proportion of children from disadvantaged families (e.g., 18% from single-parent families).

In many ways, then (e.g., size, diversity), the sample for this study is unique, especially when compared with the small and unrepresentative samples that are typically recruited in studies of childhood theory of mind. Note also that this study involved ten times as many children as took part in Hughes and Cutting's (1999) study. This tenfold increase provides much greater sensitivity to environmental effects and also allows for investigation of any gender differences in theory-of-mind skills (Charman, Ruffman, & Clements, 2002). In addition, because the children in this study were slightly older than those tested by Hughes and Cutting (1999), a broader range of tasks could be administered. Specifically, all the children were visited at home within a few weeks of their fifth birthday and given a diverse set of theory-of-mind tasks (including first- and second-order false-belief tasks and nice/nasty surprise emotion-inference tasks); this test battery had previously been demonstrated to show good internal consistency and test-retest reliability (Hughes et al., 2000).

Note also that the scale of the present study required a language measure that was simple and quick to administer, and so the vocabulary subtest from the WPPSI (Wechsler Preschool and Primary Scales of Intelligence; Wechsler, 1974) was chosen as being widely used and well validated against more comprehensive language assessments. In addition, vocabulary has been used as the chief language index in many of the studies that report a strong association between language and theory of mind (e.g., Happé, 1995).

As predicted, individual differences in total theory-of-mind scores were significantly correlated with individual differences in WPPSI vocabulary scores. In the full sample of 2,208 five-year-old children, the correlation between theory of mind and verbal ability was r = .40 (p < .001). Structural equation modeling (SEM) techniques were used to examine the key factors underlying this correlation, as well as to investigate the relative salience of genetic and environmental influences upon individual differences in both theory of mind and verbal ability.

As mentioned earlier, the findings from this study have yet to be published. However, they can be summarized very broadly as follows. There was no difference in mean theory-of-mind scores between MZ and DZ twins, indicating that regular exposure to mistaken beliefs (about their identity) is not enough to give MZ twins any advantage in acquiring a theory of mind. More important, twin-twin correlations in theory-of-mind scores showed the same value (r = .53) for both MZ and DZ twins, indicating negligible genetic influence but substantial environmental influence. Individual differences in children's theory of mind were accounted for predominantly by environmental factors (shared and nonshared) that were *specific* to theory of mind, as well as by genetic and shared environmental factors that were *common* to both theory of mind and verbal ability. Individual differences in verbal ability were accounted for by genetic and nonshared environmental factors that were *specific* to verbal ability, as well as by genetic and shared environmental factors that were *common* to both theory of mind and verbal ability. Overall, environmental factors accounted for 63% of the variance in theory of mind, and only genetic factors that were shared with verbal ability contributed to individual differences in theory of mind. The association between theory of mind and verbal ability was accounted for by common effects of shared genes, shared environment, and socioeconomic status.

In other words, as far as individual differences are concerned, the question "Why does language matter?" may be a red herring, since the association between language and theory of mind can be explained by common effects of shared genes and shared environmental influences. However, the findings from this second twin study also highlight the importance of identifying shared environmental factors that are common to both verbal ability and theory of mind.

Shared Environment, Language, and Theory of Mind

Which shared environmental factors might have a common impact upon both language and theory of mind? One set of factors includes the frequency, style, and content of various forms of family discourse. For example, salient discourse between parent and child might include joint narratives about the motives and causes of people's actions (with regard to either real events within the family or imagined events in children's play or storybooks). In contrast, salient discourse between siblings probably occurs in rather different contexts, such as that of cooperative play or of shared jokes. Future research should include investigations into which aspects of family discourse appear critical. For instance, is it simply the overall frequency of family talk that matters, or is the substantive content important? Similar questions can be asked regarding the relative importance of the style and pragmatic context of such discourse (cf. Dunn & Brophy, this volume, chapter 3). Indeed, it may be that the collective impact of family discourse is greater than the sum of its parts—for example, learning across a variety of contexts may be what matters (cf., the "general apprenticeship" model put forward by Lewis, Freeman, Kyriakidou, & Maridaki-Kassotaki, 1995).

Complementing research on family talk might be new work that focuses on the cognitive-affective components of family relationships (Bugenthal & Johnston, 2000). That is, understanding how family members (especially parents, but also siblings) view the child is important for explaining and, if necessary, changing their behavior toward the child. For example, new directions for research on maternal mind-mindedness might include investigations of the extent to which individual differences in mind-mindedness among other family members (e.g., fathers and older siblings) also predict variation in children's theory of mind and verbal ability and the extent to which the impact on these two domains is indeed common rather than distinct.

Finally, given Reznick's (1999) report of a significant correlation between parental perceptions of intentionality (mind-mindedness by another name?) and family SES, future research on this topic may also shed light on the nature of SES-related contrasts in children's understanding of mind and verbal ability. Here it is worth noting that economic adversity is one of the most studied risks in the larger social environment, and considered a "main effect" with a risk that is mediated by impoverished parenting. Improving parent-child relations may therefore bring about positive changes in children's adjustment and social understanding, even if the family continues to experience significant financial strain.

Speculative Conclusions

The outline of findings presented in this chapter is sufficient to demonstrate that the results from the large twin study did not replicate Hughes and Cutting's (1999) results regarding either the importance of genetic factors or the modularity of theory of mind. In this section, I therefore tackle the interesting question of why the results from these two twin studies of theory of mind should be so different.

The simplest answer to this question might be "size matters." In other words, Hughes and Cutting's (1999) study may have lacked the power required to detect the shared environmental influences that appeared dominant in the subsequent, much larger study. Certainly, shared environmental effects are generally regarded as difficult to detect, primarily because their confidence limits are typically very wide (Rutter, Silberg, O'Connor, & Simonoff, 1999).

A second possible answer hinges on the aforementioned multifaceted nature of theory of mind. Recall, for example, that hearing-impaired children of nonsigning parents show major delays in false-belief comprehension but are not delayed in their ability to deceive. Could it be that the differing results from the two twin studies reflects the contrasting complexity of the tasks used? Given the findings from hearing-impaired groups, it is perhaps significant that deception tasks were used in Hughes and Cutting's (1999) study but not in this larger study. However, within the larger study, effects of task complexity ("standard first-order false-belief vs. "advanced" second-order false-belief and emotion-inference tasks) were nonsignificant, suggesting that task differences are unlikely to explain this between-study contrast. Here it is worth noting that meta-analytic findings also show minimal effects of task format (Wellman, Cross, & Watson, 2001).

We turn now to the third and perhaps most interesting account of the between-study contrast, namely that there may be *developmental change* in the relative salience of genetic and environmental influences upon individual differences in theory of mind. Specifically, genetic factors may play a limiting role in the early stages of theory-of-mind acquisition, with environmental factors becoming increasingly important in subsequent years. Of course, the results from two studies of individual differences in children of different ages provide very indirect evidence on which to base this kind of developmental story (the best test would be to follow up the children from the first study, but as they are already 8 years old, this would also require a new battery of advanced theory-of-mind tasks). Nevertheless, it is interesting to note that this speculative proposal does echo recent hybrid accounts of theory-of-mind development. For example, one account that straddles competing theoretical perspectives (e.g., nativist vs. theory-theory vs. simulation theory) is the proposal made by Meltzoff et al. (1999) that certain innate structures (e.g., neonatal capacities for facial imitation) jump-start infants' developing understanding of mind but that social environments are crucial for later developments in young children's understanding of mind.

So why might one expect a shift from genetic to environmental influences upon individual differences in theory of mind from ages 3 to 5? Perhaps the most significant contrast between the children who participated in the two twin studies discussed in this chapter is that the children in the second study had all made the transition to school. Although many young children attend private nurseries or day-care centres well before the transition to school, our experience suggests that this is less common among families with twins, for whom private child-care is often prohibitively expensive. Starting school has a significant impact on children's social worlds for at least two reasons. First, the transition to school is accompanied by a significant widening of children's social horizons beyond the family to include teachers and peers. Note that this broader social environment is relatively independent of genetic factors (unlike families, in which genetic and environmental influences come hand-in-hand), and this might also contribute to the increasing salience of environmental influences on individual differences in theory of mind. Second, the transition to school brings with it a dramatic realignment in the importance of specific kinds of relationship; in particular, children's relationships with friends, siblings, and peers increasingly eclipse the parent-child relationship (Donelan-McCall & Dunn, 1997; Kochenderfer & Ladd, 1996; Ladd, 1990). This is important, as numerous studies have indicated that it is children's social exchanges with other children (e.g., in pretend play, in joking and teasing, in shared cooperative activities) that provide particularly fertile arenas for developments in their understanding of mind (Dunn, 1999a; Dunn et al., 2002).

Although longitudinal twin data on individual differences in theory of mind are not yet available, it is worth noting that for other traits, twin studies have demonstrated a difference between effects as they apply at any one point in time and effects as they apply over the course of development. For instance, Cherney and colleagues (Cherney, Fulker, Emde, et al., 1994; Cherney, Fulker, & Hewitt, 1997) found a very weak nonshared environmental effect on cognitive functioning as assessed over a five-year time span, despite stronger effects at any one time-point. By contrast, shared environmental effects played a greater role in continuities over time. As noted by Rutter and colleagues (Rutter et al., 1999), this probably occurred because shared effects tend to derive from influences that are relatively persistent, whereas many child-specific influences are much more time-limited and show much weaker correlations over time. As a result, there is greater opportunity for shared effects to accumulate, because even though nonshared effects may be influential at any one time-point, they may pull in different directions at different times.

Finally, a few caveats about the conclusions from these twin studies of theory of mind. First, it is worth reiterating that while the current findings are relevant to accounts of why there are such striking individual differences in the performance of 5-year-olds on theory-of-mind tasks, they do not necessarily cast any light upon the mechanisms that underlie either age-related improvements in theory of mind or disorders, such as autism, in which theory-of-mind skills are seriously impaired. Second, it is perhaps misleading to consider the relations between language and theory of mind in isolation from other important factors, such as individual differences in emotion expression and understanding and executive control of thought and action. Future work should attempt to bring together these distinct perspectives upon individual differences in children's understanding of mind, so that, like the learned men of Indostan, we can form a picture of the whole elephant!

Acknowledgments The Medical Research Council funded the second twin study. I would also like to extend warm thanks to all parents, children, and teachers who participated in this study.

Note

1. The χ^2 goodness-of-fit statistic, the comparative-fit index (CFI), and the root mean square error of approximation (RMSEA) all indicate the relative fit of different models to the observed data. In this way, simpler models that show an equally good fit can be chosen in preference to more complex models.

References

Astington, J. (2001). The paradox of intention: Assessing children's metarepresentational understanding. In B. Malle, L. Moses, & D. Baldwin (Eds.), *Intentions and intentionality: Foundations of social cognition* (pp. 85–104). Cambridge, MA: MIT Press.

Astington, J. W. (2003). Sometimes necessary, never sufficient: False belief understanding and social competence. In B. Repacholi & V. Slaughter (Eds.), *Individual differences in theory of mind: Implications for typical and atypical development* (pp. 13–38). New York: Psychology Press.

Bailey, A., Palferman, S., Heavey, L., & Le Couteur, A. (1998). Autism: The phenotype in relatives. *Journal of Autism and Developmental Disorders, 28,* 381–404.

Baldwin, D., & Moses, L. J. (1994). Early understanding of referential intent and attentional focus: Evidence from language and emotion. In C. Lewis & P. Mitchell (Eds.), *Children's early understanding of mind: Origins and development* (pp. 133–156). Hove, UK: Erlbaum.

Baron-Cohen, S. (1995). *Mindblindness: An essay on autism and theory of mind.* Cambridge, MA: MIT Press.

Baron-Cohen, S., Leslie, A., & Frith, U. (1985). Does the autistic child have a "theory of mind"? *Cognition, 21,* 37–46.

Bugenthal, D., & Johnston, C. (2000). Parental and child cognitions in the context of the family. *Annual Review of Psychology, 51,* 315–344.

Burt, L., Holm, A., & Dodd, B. (1999). Phonological awareness skills of 4-year-old British children: An assessment and developmental data. *International Journal of Language and Communication Disorders, 34,* 311–335.

Butterworth, G., & Jarrett, N. (1991). What minds have in common is space: Spatial mechanisms serving joint visual attention in infancy. *British Journal of Developmental Psychology, 9,* 66–72.

Charman, T., Ruffman, T., & Clements, W. (2002). Is there a gender difference in false belief development? *Social Development, 11*, 1–10.

Cherney, S., Fulker, D., Emde, R., Robinson, J., Corley, R., Reznick, J., et al. (1994). A developmental-genetic analysis of continuity and change in the Bayley mental development index from 14 to 24 months. *Psychological Science, 5*, 610–614.

Cherney, S., Fulker, D., & Hewitt, J. (1997). Cognitive development from infancy to middle childhood. In R. Sternberg & E. Grigorenko (Eds.), *Intelligence, heredity and environment* (pp. 463–482). Cambridge: Cambridge University Press.

Cole, K., & Mitchell, P. (2000). Siblings in the development of executive control and a theory of mind. *British Journal of Developmental Psychology, 18*, 279–295.

Cutting, A., & Dunn, J. (1999). Theory of mind, emotion understanding, language and family background: Individual differences and inter-relations. *Child Development, 70*, 853–865.

Cutting, A., & Dunn, J. (2002). The cost of understanding other people: Social cognition predicts young children's sensitivity to criticism. *Journal of Child Psychology and Psychiatry, 43*, 849–860.

Dammann, O., Walther, H., Allers, B., Schroeder, M., et al. (1996). Development of a regional cohort of very-low-birthweight children at six years: Cognitive abilities are associated with neurological disability and social background. *Developmental Medicine and Child Neurology, 38*, 97–108.

Davies, M., & Stone, T. (2003). Psychological understanding and social skills. In B. Repacholi & V. Slaughter (Eds.), *Individual differences in theory of mind: Implications for typical and atypical development* (pp. 305–352). New York: Psychology Press.

Donelan-McCall, N., & Dunn, J. (1997). School work, teachers, and peers: The world of first grade. *International Journal of Behavioral Development, 21*, 155–178.

Dunn, J. (1996a). Arguing with siblings, friends, and mothers: Developments in relationships and understanding. In D. I. Slobin, J. Gerhardt, A. Kyratzis, & J. Guo (Eds.), *Social interaction, social context, and language: Essays in honor of Susan Ervin-Tripp* (pp. 191–204). Mahwah, NJ: Erlbaum.

Dunn, J. (1996b). The Emanuel Miller Memorial Lecture 1995: Children's relationships: Bridging the divide between cognitive and social development. *Journal of Child Psychology and Psychiatry, 37*, 507–518.

Dunn, J. (1996c). Family conversations and the development of social understanding. In B. Bernstein & J. Brannen (Eds.), *Children, research and policy* (pp. 81–95). London: Taylor and Francis.

Dunn, J. (1999a). Making sense of the social world: Mindreading, emotion and relationships. In P. D. Zelazo, J. W. Astington, & D. R. Olson (Eds.), *Developing theories of intention: Social understanding and self control* (pp. 229–242). Mahwah, NJ: Erlbaum.

Dunn, J. (1999b). New directions in research on children's relationships and understanding. *Social Development, 8*, 137–142.

Dunn, J., Cutting, A., & Fisher, N. (2002). Old friends, new friends: Predictors of children's perspectives on their friends at school. *Child Development, 73*, 621–635.

Dunn, J., & Plomin, R. (1990). *Separate lives: Why siblings are so different*. New York: Basic Books.

Eaves, L., Last, K., Martin, N., & Jinks, J. (1977). A progressive approach to nonadditivity and genotype-environmental covariance in the analysis of human differences. *British Journal of Mathematical and Statistical Psychology, 30*, 1–42.

Happé, F. (1995). The role of age and verbal ability in the theory of mind task performance of subjects with autism. *Child Development, 66*, 843–855.

Happé, F., Winner, E., & Brownell, H. (1998). The getting of wisdom: Theory of mind in old age. *Developmental Psychology, 34*, 358–362.

Holmes, H. A., Black, C., & Miller, S. A. (1996). A cross-task comparison of false belief understanding in a Head-Start population. *Journal of Experimental Child Psychology, 63*, 263–285.

Hughes, C., Adlam, A., Happé, F., Jackson, J., Taylor, A., & Caspi, A. (2000). Good test-retest reliability for standard and advanced false-belief tasks across a wide range of abilities. *Journal of Child Psychology and Psychiatry, 41*, 483–490.

Hughes, C., & Cutting, A. (1999). Nature, nurture, and individual differences in early understanding of mind. *Psychological Science, 10*, 429–432.

Hughes, C., & Dunn, J. (1997). "Pretend you didn't know": Preschoolers' talk about mental states in pretend play. *Cognitive Development, 12*, 477–499.

Hughes, C., Jaffee, S., Happé, F., Taylor, A., Caspi, A. & Moffitt, T. E. (in press). Origins of individual differences in theory of mind: From nature to nurture?

Hughes, C., & Plomin, R. (2000). Individual differences in early understanding of mind: Genes, nonshared environment and modularity. In P. Carruthers & A. Chamberlain (Eds.), *Evolution and the human mind: Language, modularity and social cognition* (pp. 47–61): Cambridge: Cambridge University Press.

Jenkins, J. M., & Astington, J. W. (1996). Cognitive factors and family structure associated with theory of mind development in young children. *Developmental Psychology, 32*, 70–78.

Kochenderfer, B., & Ladd, G. (1996). Peer victimization: Cause or consequence or school maladjustment? *Child Development, 67*, 1305–1317.

Ladd, G. (1990). Having friends, keeping friends, making friends, and being liked by peers in the classroom: Predictors of children's early school adjustment? *Child Development, 61*, 1081–1100.

Leslie, A. (1994). ToMM, ToBY and Agency: Core architecture and domain specificity. In L. Hirschfeld & S. Gelman (Eds.), *Mapping the mind: Domain specificity in cognition and culture* (pp. 119–148). Cambridge: Cambridge University Press.

Lewis, C., Freeman, N., Kyriakidou, C., & Maridaki-Kassotaki, K. (1995, March). Social influences on false-belief access: Specific contagion or general apprenticeship? Poster presented at the biennial meeting of the Society for Research in Child Development, Indianapolis, IN.

Lewis, C., Freeman, N. H., Kyriakidou, C., Maridaki-Kassotaki, K., & Berridge, D. M. (1996). Social influences on false belief access: Specific sibling influences or general apprenticeship? *Child Development, 67*, 2930–2947.

Martin, N., Boomsma, D., & Machin, G. (1997). A twin-pronged attack on complex trait. *Nature Genetics, 17*, 387–392.

Martin, N., Eaves, L., Kearsey, M., & Davies, P. (1978). The power of the classical twin study. *Heredity, 40*, 97–116.

Meins, E., Fernyhough, C., Fradley, E., & Tuckey, M. (2001). Rethinking maternal sensitivity: Mothers' comments on infants' mental processes predict security of attachment at 12 months. *Journal of Child Psychology and Psychiatry, 42*, 637–648.

Meins, E., Fernyhough, C., Russell, J. T., & Clarke-Carter, D. (1998). Security of attachment as a predictor of symbolic and mentalising abilities: A longitudinal study. *Social Development, 7*, 1–24.

Meltzoff, A., Gopnik, A., & Repacholi, B. (1999). Toddlers' understanding of intentions, desires and emotions: Explorations of the dark ages. In P. D. Zelazo, J. W. Astington & D. R. Olson (Eds.), *Developing theories of intention: Social understanding and self-control* (pp. 17–41). Mahwah, NJ: Erlbaum.

Moore, C. (1999). Intentional relations and triadic interactions. In P. D. Zelazo, J. W. Astington, & D. R. Olson (Eds.), *Developing theories of intention: Social understanding and self-control* (pp. 43–61). Mahwah, NJ: Erlbaum.

Moses, L. (2001). Some thoughts on ascribing complex intentional concepts to young children. In B. Malle, L. Moses, & D. Baldwin (Eds.), *Intentions and intentionality: Foundations of social cognition* (pp. 69–84). Cambridge, MA: MIT Press.

Murray, L., & Cooper, P. (1997). Postpartum depression and child development. *Psychological Medicine, 27,* 253–260.

Plomin, R., & Dale, P. (2000). Genetics and early language development: A U.K. study of twins. In D. Bishop & L. Leonard (Eds.), *Speech and language impairments in children: Causes, characteristics, intervention and outcome* (pp. 35–51). Philadelphia: Psychology Press/Taylor & Francis.

Plomin, R., & Daniels, D. (1987). Why are children in the same family so different from one another? *Behavioral and Brain Sciences, 10,* 1–60.

Plomin, R., DeFries, J. C., McClearn, G. E., & Rutter, M. (1997). *Behavioral Genetics.* New York: W. H. Freeman.

Premack, D., & Woodruff, G. (1978). Does the chimpanzee have a theory of mind? *Behavioral and Brain Sciences, 1,* 515–526.

Reznick, J. (1999). Influences on maternal attribution of infant intentionality. In P. D. Zelazo, J. W. Astington, & D. R. Olson (Eds.), *Developing theories of intention: Social understanding and self control* (pp. 243–268). Mahwah, NJ: Erlbaum.

Reznick, J., Corley, R., & Robinson, J. (1997). A longitudinal twin study of intelligence in the second year. *Monographs of the Society for Research in Child Development, 62(1, Serial No. 249).*

Ruffman, T., Perner, J., Naito, M., Parkin, L., & Clements, W. (1998). Older but not younger siblings facilitate false belief understanding. *Developmental Psychology, 34,* 161–174.

Rutter, M., Dunn, J., Plomin, R., Simonoff, E., Pickles, A., Maughan, B., et al. (1997). Integrating nature and nurture: Implications of person-environment correlations and interactions for developmental psychopathology. *Development and Psychopathology, 9,* 335–364.

Rutter, M., Maughan, B., Meyer, J., Pickles, A., Silberg, J., Simonoff, E., et al. (1997). Heterogeneity of antisocial behavior: Causes, continuities and consequences. In R. Dienstbier & D. Osgood (Eds.), *Nebraska symposium on motivation: Motivation and delinquency* (Vol. 44, pp. 44–118). Lincoln: University of Nebraska Press.

Rutter, M., Silberg, J., O'Connor, T., & Simonoff, E. (1999). Genetics and child psychiatry: I. Advances in quantitative and molecular genetics. *Journal of Child Psychology and Psychiatry, 40,* 3–18.

Skuse, D. H., James, R. S., Bishop, D. V. M., Coppins, B., Dalton, P., Aamodt-Leeper, G., et al. (1997). Evidence from Turner's syndrome of an imprinted X–linked locus affecting cognitive function. *Nature, 387,* 705–708.

Slomkowski, C., & Dunn, J. (1996). Young children's understanding of other people's beliefs and feelings and their connected communication with friends. *Developmental Psychology, 32,* 442–447.

Tager-Flusberg, H. (2001). A re-examination of the Theory of Mind hypothesis of autism. In J. Burack, T. Charman, N. Yirmiya, & P. Zelazo (Eds.), *The development of autism: Perspectives from theory and research* (pp. 173–194). Mahwah, NJ: Erlbaum.

Thorpe, K., Greenwood, R., Eivers, A., & Rutter, M. (2001). Prevalence and developmental course of "secret language." *International Journal of Language and Communication Disorders, 36,* 43–62.

Tomasello, M. (1999). Having intentions, understanding intentions, and understanding communicative intentions. In P. D. Zelazo, J. W. Astington, & D. R. Olson (Eds.), *Developing theories of intention: Social understanding and self-control* (pp. 63–75). Mahwah, NJ: Erlbaum.

Vandenberg, S. G. (1972). Assortative mating, or who marries whom? *Behavior Genetics, 2,* 127–157.

Vinden, P. (1999). Children's understanding of mind and emotion: A multi-culture study. *Cognition and Emotion, 13,* 19–48.

Wechsler, D. (1974). *Wechsler Preschool and Primary Scale of Intelligence.* London: Psychological Corporation.

Wellman, H., Cross, D., & Watson, J. (2001). Meta-analysis of theory of mind development: The truth about false belief. *Child Development, 72,* 655–684.

Wimmer, H., & Perner, J. (1983). Beliefs about beliefs: representation and constraining function of wrong beliefs in young children's understanding of deception. *Cognition, 13,* 103–128.

Youngblade, L. M., & Dunn, J. (1995). Individual differences in young children's pretend play with mother and sibling: Links to relationships and understanding of other people's feelings and beliefs. *Child Development, 66,* 1472–1492.

Author Index

Subject Index

absent reference, 133–38
abstraction, 125, 126–32
active gene-environment correlation, 325
adjective terms, 93–95
agency, 110
age-related changes, 152, 153, 322–23
alignment, 123–40
analogy, 107–8, 125–31, 139
analytic fallacy, 35
argument from analogy, 107–8
Asperger syndrome, 309
attachment theory, 72
attitudes, 224–26
attributed intentionality, 35
autism, 20, 90, 92, 146, 220, 298–313
autobiographical memory, 41–42

background implication, 98
Backward Color Span, 283–84, 286, 287
behavior, 124
behavioral reference, 117–18
belief, 131
  ascription, 163
  complements, 227–28
  concept of, 147
  content of, 30
  as first-order state, 108
  as mental state, 251
  as mental term, 106, 125
  specific, 124
  understanding, 221
  use of *that* in German to express, 229–31

verbs of, 187, 188
  See also false-belief tasks
bootstrapping approach, 191, 199
BPVS. *See* British Picture Vocabulary Scale
British Picture Vocabulary Scale (BPVS),
  300

Cantonese language, 65, 198, 229
categories, 109, 149
CELF. *See* Clinical Evaluation of Language
  Fundamentals
change-in-location tasks, 165–66, 273, 307
Chaplin, Charlie, 186
children
  characteristics of interlocutor, 60–62
  conversation and theory of mind, 70–81
  development of theory of mind, 84–102
  discourse and quality of relationships
    with partners, 57–59
  expression of internal experiences
    without theory of mind, 113
  family interaction, 54
  individual differences in understanding
    of mind, 50–67, 100
  language acquisition and point of view,
    186–214
  language and cognitive flexibility, 144–
    58
  language pathways into Community of
    Minds, 26–46
  linguistic communication, 245–63
  and maternal input, 71–77

pragmatics
  of communicating new information, 84–102
  conversational, 9, 75
  definition of, 98
  of discourse, 59, 75
  and language, 98–101
predictability, 96
pretend (verb), 203–6, 211
pretense, 56–58, 62, 70, 77–81, 223
primate cognition, 4
principle of informativeness, 89
prior intentions, 138–39
private language argument, 110–12
propositional attitudes, 224
propositions, 224, 225–26
psychological reference, 118

realis forms, 195, 202, 205–8, 222–24, 231–32, 267
reality bias, 120
reasoning
  on cognitive states of another person, 273–74
  false belief, 188, 189, 269, 273, 282–89
  general, 26
  mental-state, 17–21
receptive language, 41–44
recoverability, 96
referential opacity, 211
relationships
  and children's understanding of mind, 50–67
  close, 50–51
  with friends, 57, 62, 63
  parent-child, 113
  quality of, 57–58
  with siblings, 57, 62
relevance, 97
relevance theory, 97–98
representation, 6, 7, 164, 180–81
representational development, 163–82
Rhode Island Test of Language Structure (RITLS), 285–86, 287
RITLS. *See* Rhode Island Test of Language Structure
role taking, 79–80, 81

saliency, 96
say (verb), 10, 75, 197, 201, 204, 208–10, 224, 230, 239
second-order knowledge, 108
self, 34
self-directed movement, 110

self-expression, 119
self-reflection, 148
self-regulation, 149
SEM. *See* structural equation model
semantic development
  and language games, 112–18
  and mental-state concepts, 13–16, 118
  of mental terms, 111
semantics
  as complex language, 28, 36
  lexical, 9–10
  of mental-state verbs, 187
  and syntax, 6–7, 195, 196, 209
sensory information, 93–95
sentential complement. *See* complement(s)
shared attention, 26, 35, 247
shared environment, 325–26, 331–32
shared knowledge, 96
shared play, 57, 58, 62
siblings, 54, 57, 62
sign language, 37, 189, 190, 268, 271–82
"Simon Says," 147
social experiences, 27
social knowledge, 120
social-pragmatic theory of language, 247
social understanding, 51, 61, 62–66, 245–63
source domain, 126
spatial-mapping task, 150
spontaneous narratives, 41
sticker-finding hide-and-seek game, 273–74
storybook characters, 72
story recall, 41, 42
story understanding, 42
structural alignment, 123–40
structural equation model (SEM), 328–29
structure mapping, 125–27
subjective preferences, 238–39
subordinate clause, 7, 10, 301–3, 306, 308
surprise face game, 274
symbols, 148–49, 246–47
synergy, 10–11
syntactic bootstrapping, 191, 199
syntax
  complement, 10, 188, 191–97, 250, 267, 319
  as complex language, 28
  comprehension, 285–86
  development, 17–21, 145, 267
  of embedded false-complement clauses, 267
  of mental-state verbs, 188